The Heart of Central New York

The Heart of Central New York

Stories of Historic Homer, NY

Martin A. Sweeney

HAMILTON BOOKS
an imprint of
ROWMAN & LITTLEFIELD
Lanham • Boulder • New York • London

Published by Hamilton Books
An imprint of The Rowman & Littlefield Publishing Group, Inc.
4501 Forbes Boulevard, Suite 200, Lanham, Maryland 20706
www.rowman.com

86-90 Paul Street, London EC2A 4NE, United Kingdom

Copyright © 2022 by The Rowman & Littlefield Publishing Group, Inc.

All rights reserved. No part of this book may be reproduced in any form or by any electronic or mechanical means, including information storage and retrieval systems, without written permission from the publisher, except by a reviewer who may quote passages in a review.

British Library Cataloguing in Publication Information Available

Library of Congress Cataloging-in-Publication Data Available

Names: Sweeney, Martin A., 1946- author.
Title: The heart of central New York : stories of historic Homer, NY / Martin A. Sweeney.
Other titles: Homer news.
Description: Lanham : Hamilton Books, an imprint of Rowman & Littlefield, [2022] | Includes bibliographical references and index. | Summary: "The Heart of Central New York is a collection of newspaper articles on the history of the town and village of Homer, New York. It offers inspiration for any public historian seeking a way to engage his or her community in acknowledging that their past peoples, events, and architectures shaped their collective identity"—Provided by publisher.
Identifiers: LCCN 2022020643 (print) | LCCN 2022020644 (ebook) | ISBN 9780761873327 (paperback) | ISBN 9780761873334 (epub)
Subjects: LCSH: Homer (N.Y.)—History.
Classification: LCC F129.H717 S94 2022 (print) | LCC F129.H717 (ebook) | DDC 974.4/72—dc23/eng/20220510
LC record available at https://lccn.loc.gov/2022020643
LC ebook record available at https://lccn.loc.gov/2022020644

"Societies continuously try to recreate themselves—shared holidays, shared news, shared traditions, shared language, shared music, shared myths, shared victories, and shared griefs. Shared origins . . . So by telling each other stories, we recreate ourselves over and over again. Where do we come from? Where are we going? Who are our heroes? Who are the villains? These stories pass our values as a society from one generation to the next.

It's how we understand each other."

—Olga Werby, *Twin Time*

"The only thing new in the world is the history you do not know."

—Harry S Truman

Cited by Merle Miller in *Plain Speaking: An Oral Biography of Harry S. Truman,* 1974, p. 26.

Contents

Map of Central New York State		ix
Preface		xi
Acknowledgments		xvii
1	Articles of 2010 and 2011	1
2	Articles of 2012	7
3	Articles of 2013	23
4	Articles of 2014	47
5	Articles of 2015	69
6	Articles of 2016	105
7	Articles of 2017	155
8	Articles of 2018	197
9	Articles of 2019	223
10	Articles of 2020	283
11	Article at the start of 2021	385
Bibliography		389
Index		395
About the Author		405

Map of Central New York State

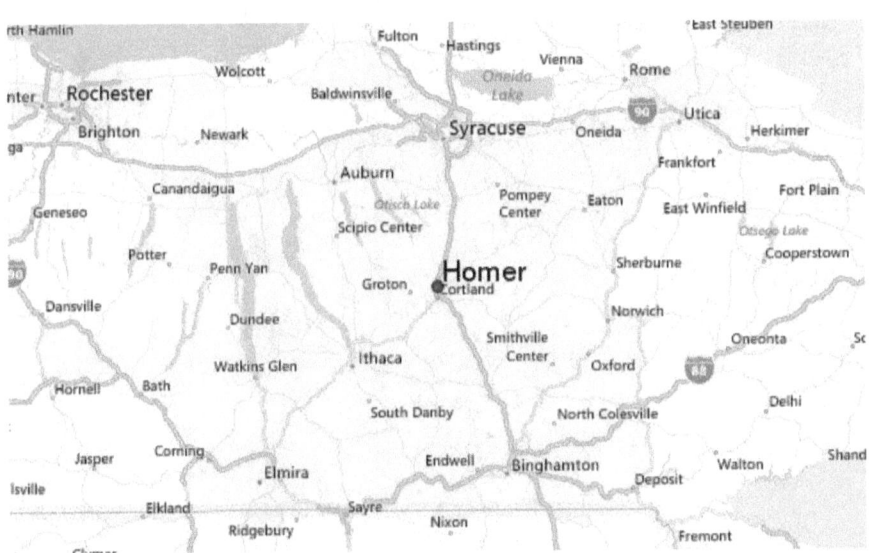

Figure 0.1 Central New York State.

Preface

Homer is a Town and a Village. Each is a municipality. Each has a Board of Trustees. The Town has a Supervisor, and the Village has a Mayor. Because they share the name of the blind Greek poet of Antiquity, even the locals have trouble understanding the difference between the two. Both are located halfway between Syracuse and Binghamton on Interstate Highway 81. Combined, they exude a sense of "community" and a uniqueness of "place."

The Town of Homer, one of fifteen townships in the county of Cortland, was established in 1794 and is approximately thirty minutes from the City of Syracuse by car. It is the third largest municipality in Cortland County with respect to inhabitants (2010 U.S. Census population: 6405). The Town, rectangular in shape on a map, features gently rolling hills and valleys which are still primarily used for agriculture. The Town also contains the hamlets of East Homer, which is mostly residential, and Little York which, located along Little York Lake, has a few small shops featuring arts and crafts, a year-round farm market and bakery, and a large greenhouse and garden store. Although many dairy and crop farms remain, the Town is a prime residential area for people working in the cities of Cortland and Ithaca to the south, and Syracuse to the north.

The Town of Homer contains the Village of Homer, which is a quaint, historic community of 3291 residents that was incorporated in 1835 but settled earlier along the banks of the Tioughnioga River. One block west of the river is Main Street in the village, along which remains a relatively unspoiled nineteenth century "downtown" with a New England-style Green surrounded by churches, houses, and the elementary school. Its geographic location made it a vibrant hub of commercial, agricultural, academic, and religious activity in nineteenth century Central New York. Today, the village of Homer considers itself to be the heart of Central New York and the southeast gateway to the scenic Finger Lakes and "wine country." It is the closest community with a mayor to the southern tip of Skaneateles Lake.

The village of Homer boasts of its Historic District and two Historic Sites listed in the State and National Registers of Historic Places. Foremost, there is Old Homer Village with over 200 architectural gems. Then, there are three rare lenticular truss bridges erected in 1881 over the Tioughnioga River, of which one is the only one of its kind in the nation. The second Historic Site is Glenwood Cemetery, a well-maintained, textbook example of the Rural Cemetery Movement with persons of national prominence buried there.

Except for two years spent residing and teaching in Poplar Ridge, NY (Southern Cayuga Central School), I have been a life-long resident of the village of Homer. After 38 years in the classroom, mostly at Homer Junior High School as a teacher of U. S. history, I retired in 2009. The year before, I had been appointed to the position of Town Historian and was provided office space at the historic Town Hall. Previous historians operated out of their homes.

2009 was the year that Homer spent an exciting week in May celebrating the bicentennial of the birth of Abraham Lincoln. Called "A Celebration of Lincoln in Paint and Print," the event paid tribute to three native-sons of Homer with significant ties to President Lincoln. They are the detective Eli DeVoe, the portrait artist Francis Bicknell Carpenter, and Lincoln's assistant personal secretary William Osborn Stoddard. Through paintings and books the latter two have contributed to what we know of "The Great Emancipator." The national Abraham Lincoln Bicentennial Commission recognized this celebration, and one of the co-chairpersons, the esteemed Lincoln scholar Harold Holzer, came to Homer and gave two lectures. Other Lincoln scholars who have lectured in Homer since 2009 include retired Rhode Island Supreme Court Justice Frank Williams, Senator and Presidential candidate George McGovern, and Professor Michael Burlingame from Springfield, Illinois, author of the definitive biography of Lincoln.

The Homer News was created just in time in late 2009. It became the perfect vehicle for a public historian to accomplish three goals regarding local history and architecture: to educate, to promote, and to celebrate his historic community. The newspaper and The Landmark Society of Cortland County (founded in the early 1970s) have been the two major means by which the community and others have been informed about what makes Homer historically unique and worthy of pride. The Society is headquartered at the History Center at Key Bank on Main Street in the village. There, it operates a small museum with plenty of artifacts and photos of an earlier Homer. Included is a portrait of Watts Barber by Francis Carpenter, the earliest Bible in the county, the 1896 guest book of the Hotel Windsor, and much more. The Society's Board of Directors is knowledgeable about local history and architecture. Its members give walking tours and annual presentations on the topics and are more than willing to consult with private owners of buildings in the Historic District on the best ways to preserve their past architectural glory.

The Homer News is a small, twelve-page community newspaper published every other Thursday. The paper is free. It is available at various places in the village and even delivered to Homer people's mailboxes. It sustains itself through paid advertisements. At one time, the circulation reached 3000. In seven years it increased to 4200.

The paper was founded by Village trustee Ed Finkbeiner and his daughter Laura. According to Ed (June 29, 2020),

> Plans for the paper started in August or September of 2009. Laura graduated from Alfred University with a liberal arts degree and a minor in fine arts that year and needed a job. I had always appreciated my local paper in Vermont, *The Charlotte News*. You can see the similarities in the folding style and only local news and good news reported. We got a template from *The Charlotte News* and used it for *The Homer News*. I know the *"The"* is not correct but I/we liked it. We were hoping people would write in about their kids' accomplishments, marriages, etc., but I think the Central New York mentality is that they like to keep personal stuff closely held. That was not the case with *The Charlotte News,* as gossip was encouraged and dialog about public events were sometimes hotly discussed in battling editorials. Everyone eagerly awaited the next issue to see what was being said about some project or other.
>
> Our philosophy was to print only good news and local activities and not stuff about whom got arrested, etc. We had some issues discussed like that but mostly, I believe, it focused on the [temporary and controversial] Town Hall move out [by the Village officials]. Not much since. The paper is a great avenue to get the citizens engaged. I am especially happy to see the Mayor of Homer, Darren "Hal" McCabe, putting a page in the paper discussing meetings, trash issues and the like. I think the paper has really helped the pubic to be informed and sometimes entertained.
>
> Laura was the editor and reporter, and I was the cub reporter, and we asked others to write for the paper. We couldn't pay anything, but it has lasted so far. After a year and a half or so, Laura needed to earn more money as the paper only broke even month to month and Laura was not liking asking for money for ads. She did it though, and it is a great testament to cold calling from a 22-year-old woman just out of college. I am so proud of her for sticking to it for as long as she did. We gave the paper to Don Ferris who always loved the newspaper business. He said he even has his old change machine that he wore on his belt when he was a paper boy. Don has grown the paper and has done an excellent job.

Don Ferris has been a Homer resident since 1976. He has owned a printing business since 1972, and he served eight years as a village trustee and ten years as a town councilman. In Don's first issue of *The Homer News* on March 15, 2012, he included this message:

> I have always been interested in newspapers and publications since I was a kid. My grandfather used to read the *Post Standard* and the *Cortland Standard* with me, and I still read newspapers and magazines extensively. When Laura and Ed Finkbeiner approached me about taking over *The Homer News*, I didn't have to give it much thought. They've done a great job getting the paper going, and I am prepared do whatever I can to continue their good work and provide a source of local "good news" and information for the residents of the Village and Town of Homer. In addition to print news, the entire contents of the paper will be available on the website www.thehomernews.com.
>
> So far there has been strong support from several advertisers, and I expect that advertising support to grow. It's my hope that this newspaper can benefit our local community in a number of ways; by sharing good news and events about our community members and by supporting our local businesses who advertise in *The Homer News*, which will help stimulate our local economy. Supporting our local advertisers will be important to the success of our newspaper.

Don, also, expressed his wish that all of the contributing writers would continue to write for *The Homer News*, since "readers have indicated they enjoy the paper's current content." And as one of those writers, I was pleased to still have a platform for the "local historian."

As the Town of Homer Historian since April 2008 (and in April of 2017 the appointed Village Historian), I did research and analysis on local history, maintained the archives, acted as a consultant, gave public presentations, and secured funding for several historic markers. As the municipal historian, I was among those invited by the Finkbeiners to contribute a column on local history to the fledgling Homer newspaper. I jumped at the opportunity. As a soon-to-retire teacher of grade 8 U. S. History and Government in the Homer Junior High School, the paper gave me a way to continue teaching history. You might say I could tell the stories of the past and skip the headaches—the disciplinary and administrative matters. It was an ideal retirement job. As the saying goes, and it is true, "You can take the teacher out of the classroom, but you cannot take the classroom out of the teacher."

Through the years, in my column I strived to put flesh on the bones of the past by applying details and a touch of humor. I wanted the past to come alive for my readers and to be interesting and fun as I had tried to do for my junior high students. I encouraged readers to share their recollections of past places and events in Homer and to make learning about local history an interactive experience. I especially wanted residents, those with deep roots and those with new roots in the community, to develop a lively interest and a shared pride in the community's identity as "Historic Homer, NY." This included a sense of obligation to be stewards of past architecture and past stories. As members of a community, they need to realize that their individual and collective actions are contributing to that heritage which will be chronicled and interpreted by the public historians of tomorrow.

Hopefully, the articles have provided Homer guidance in where the Village and Town want to go in the future. Perhaps, the community will seek to capitalize on the opportunities to engage more in heritage tourism. You cannot make that determination until you know where you have been. You have to know the stories of past generations in your community and its environs first. You need to grasp the community's contribution to the rich, historical tapestry that is the county, the region, the state, and the nation. Once you have a sense of the past then you truly have a sense of place.

The stories of Homer's past collected here are presented in the chronological order in which they were published in the newspaper. Note that some historical topics were selected to resonate with what readers were experiencing at the time in their own lives, such as the COVID-19 pandemic. I left it to my discretion as to which articles merited inclusion. As I did so, I recalled being greeted a few years ago, before his untimely passing, by Donald Barber, Homer's retired funeral home director. It was after a Sunday Mass when "Donny" said, "I enjoy your articles in the Homer paper." I thanked him and said, "But some are not as good as others." He smiled, and with a wry humor so typical of him, responded, "I know, but I discipline myself to read them all." We shared a guffaw together, and I departed with a memory to be cherished.

Then, too, there were the many installments that were chapters in two published books, *Lincoln's Gift from Homer, New York: A Painter, an Editor and a Detective* and *Murder in the Winter Solstice: A Narrative of a True Murder Mystery in Homer.* They are not included. Twelve installments on the life of Homer's Andrew D. White, who co-founded Cornell University and served as its first president, are not included, but reference is made to White in other articles collected here. Starting in mid-June of 2018, a series of twenty-one installments appeared in the paper on "A Brief History of Education in Homer: 1819–2019." These were omitted from this book because, as part of Homer's observance of 200 years of a state-approved school on the Green, they were published by The Landmark Society as a bicentennial souvenir booklet. Though I am grateful for them, only a few articles submitted by invited "guest columnists" have been included in this book.

Articles culled out for inclusion were definitely those by me that had surprised readers. It was fun to learn of their reactions to these facts:

Homer had a recipient of the Congressional Medal of Honor for valor during the Civil War.

Homer had a general hospital and a training school for nurses.

Homer manufactured jinrikisha wheels for export to Hong Kong and China.

Eleanor Roosevelt visited Homer in 1924.

A Homer restauranteur was responsible for feeding the Combined Chiefs of Staff in Washington, D.C., during World War II.

The painted mural in the Post Office was originally going to be of a semi-nude female.

Homer once had "houses of ill repute."

The COVID-19 pandemic of 2020 presented an ideal time for this public historian to hunker down at home, to cull out the "best" of a decade of articles for this collection centered on the theme of "community," and to craft some new articles. Some editing of the writing and content was required, especially in keeping with findings made since their original publications. My overarching goal in preparing this book was to demonstrate for public historians and others how the press can be used successfully as a tool for providing a community with a sense of its identity. Like a volume of poems, this volume of stories is more than the sum of its parts. In this case, a vibrant, often overlooked heritage comes into view with greater clarity for both the community and others interested in regional history.

Finally, we are a story-telling species, and what has been assembled here represents the stories of those who once called the town and village of Homer "home." And as you read these vignettes, listen. You will hear voices. These are the voices of the past and present reminding us of the values that gave/give direction and meaning to people's lives and that for them

"HomeR is where the Heart is."

Acknowledgments

This project has been a lifetime's adventure. Undertaking the research, writing, and publication of this compilation of over 100 newspaper articles would not have been possible without the inspiration and assistance provided by several individuals over many years:

*Mrs. Helen Carty, my Homer Central grade 8 English teacher, made her students diagram sentences and grasp how words make sentences, sentences make paragraphs, and paragraphs make all the essays and term papers I would write in high school, college, and two graduate schools—the State University College at Cortland and the Maxwell School of Citizenship and Public Affairs at Syracuse University. Appropriately, one article in this book is about an early Homer grammarian who invented a way to diagram sentences. Thank you, Mrs. Carty.

*The late C. Robert Clark was my Cortland College undergraduate advisor and New York State history professor. He lived in the old temperance tavern in the village of Homer. He encouraged my research into the Sweeney immigrants to Central New York and their story. I appreciated the good-humored academic mentoring, Dr. Clark.

*The late Josephine Richardson Brown was a World War II bride from Australia who took up residence in Homer with her American soldier husband Don Brown. Josephine developed a reputation for being a witty, opinionated, and excellent reporter of the Homer section of the *Cortland Standard*. In addition, she was the historian for the Town of Homer for 13 years and often wrote historical pieces on the Village of Homer. It was these articles, filled with human interest and humor, that led me to think I might enjoy being the municipal historian someday. My first article written as Homer's Town Historian in 2008 was for the *Cortland Standard*, and it was a brief biography of Josephine Brown. She did not know she was being my role model.

* Ed Finkbeiner and daughter Laura are the co-founders of *The Homer News*. Without them, the vehicle for my articles would never have existed. And there would be no book.

* Don Ferris is the editor and owner of *The Homer News* today. I am grateful for his support, especially when my articles grew longer and longer and required more page space and ever smaller font size. Many times, he found visual images to go with my printed words when I could not. I am indebted to him for gathering the impressive images selected for this book.

*I would be sorely remiss if I failed to single out for gratitude Edmund Raus, Jr., of Homer. A retired historian who served at Manassas National Battlefield Park, Gettysburg, and Fredericksburg-Spotsylvania, Ed has authored books and articles on the Civil War and, in particular, the role of Cortland County in the conflict. In his research, he has found "nuggets of gold" that he has shared with me. I am most appreciative and so pleased he took up his abode in Historic Homer.

*Much gratitude must go to Brooke Bures, Associate Editor at Rowman & Littlefield, and to the editorial review board and production staff of Hamilton Books for finding merit in publishing this volume of "microhistory."

*My loving wife, Carla Chrzan Sweeney, has been my confidant for over forty-six years. She came to appreciate history more when she discovered she had a relative at the Battle of Bunker Hill and another relative forced by the British to put a torch to Buffalo in the War of 1812 before he was made to run the gauntlet (and survived).

*I offer my thanks to those readers in the community and beyond who responded over the past decade by bringing in photographs, artifacts, researched material, and personal recollections of the past or by sending in notes and emails of support. Others consented to submit articles as a "guest columnist." This book is a gift of love and gratitude for my supporters, especially the elected and appointed officials of the Town and Village of Homer, Russ Darr and the Board of The Landmark Society, my friends Dave and Sue Quinlan, and my children Charlotte and Martin, Jr., all who firmly believe history matters.

                Martin A. Sweeney * Homer * New York

Chapter 1

Articles of 2010 and 2011

July 15, 2010

First Issue

A HISTORY OF A HOMER NEWSPAPER

History is being made in more than one way with this maiden issue of *The Homer News*. It has been 48 years since Homer has had its own weekly [or bi-weekly] newspaper. *The Homer Independent* stopped publishing in 1962, after a three-year run. The earliest weekly was the *Cortland Courier* published in Homer in 1811 and 1812, followed by the *Western Courier* between 1820 and 1823 and the *Cortland Observer* from 1825 to 1835. Then, readers received news via the *Homer Eagle* and the *Protestant Sentinel* in the 1830s, the *Path Finder* in the 1860s, and the *Homer Times* in the early 1890s. Between 1877 and 1919, *The Homer Republican* was a well-read weekly. Originally it was circulated as the *Cortland County Republican* from 1855 to 1877, and its office was in Mechanics Hall, a large wooden building located where the Homer Center for the Arts is situated today. In all, some fourteen weeklies were printed in Homer in different times between 1811 and 1962, including *The Homer Post* during the Great Depression.

This column will seek to inform and entertain on matters of local historical interest. Homer is rich in stories of past people and events and architectural structures. Homer has 220 buildings listed on the National Register of Historic Places, and more may be added. If only their walls could talk! What tales would we hear? To pass on the accounts of a locale's people, events, and places requires the historian to research primary source materials such as weeklies and other newspapers of the time being examined.

Additional sources historians turn to are diaries, letters, and other materials in print. But there is a problem here for future historians. Few people keep diaries anymore. In the computer age, who mails handwritten letters? E-mail, IM, and Tweets are today's means of social networking. Writing is fast becoming a lost art, as any teacher can tell you. Technology permits fast and easy "paperless" communication, and primary source material is lost in cyberspace. The Civil War may have turned out differently if the War Department had had text messaging instead of telegraph to connect with generals in the field. Imagine Lincoln prodding General McClellan into instantaneous military action with "r u gonna move?" and receiving back "lol, Sir." The exchange would disappear unless Lincoln's assistant personal secretary, Homer native-son William O. Stoddard, hit the "Print" button.

Historians need a "paper trail." The recent discovery of printed material, photographs, and artifacts from two Homer Central School time capsules–one from the 1890s and one from the 1950s–revived interest in local history. It also points up the need for the present generation to document and store vital information about us and leave it to the next generations. Write down stories and descriptions of who you are and what you do and what you value. Store it where family members will find it or give it to your municipal historian. What better gift for grandparents to leave grandchildren than a record of their lives and times. There is more to a legacy than money and property.

So, while this paper is adding its name to the list of newspapers once published in Homer, it is also "making history" in a second way by contributing to that "paper trail." Today's *Homer News* will be tomorrow's primary source for some historian. It will document the names, businesses, activities, interests, challenges, and values of people who called Homer "home" in the early twenty-first century. It will add to that rich chronicle from which this column will seek to share "snippets" with you in each issue of *The Homer News*.

In the same issue

SLAVERY IN THE HISTORY OF HOMER

[2020 Note: *I wanted my first contribution to The Homer News to be drawn on an account I used in the classroom to disabuse students of the notion that the antebellum North was the section of the nation always opposed to slavery. Not so. More importantly, it shows how a community's values can change over time. The Homer community's perspective on slavery in the 1830s changed by the 1860s.*]

Reverend John Keep was born into an agrarian and Christian household in Longmeadow, Massachusetts, on April 20, 1781. At the age of fourteen he committed himself to God and to His service. He graduated Yale College in 1802 with a class of sixty members, all of whom he outlived. He studied theology for a year under the Reverend Asahel Hooker of Goshen, Connecticut. Ordained as a minister in 1805, Keep settled the next year in Blandford, Massachusetts, and married Lydia Hale, daughter of Judge Hale of Goshen.

After sixteen successful years in Blandford, Keep received two calls, one from Brunswick, Maine, and one from Homer, New York. If he accepted the former, he would be the preacher to Bowdoin College and an instructor in moral philosophy. If he accepted the latter, he would be the pastor for four hundred Congregationalists in the wilderness of Central New York. After visiting both places, he chose Homer, a little hamlet nestled in a valley between forested glacial moraines. His parish was about ten miles square, and his congregation was scattered through a population of six thousand. Besides an abundance of farming folk, there were teachers, merchants, millers, tanners, carpenters, masons, innkeepers, four physicians, and a lawyer, Horatio Ballard, who had arrived in 1803. These were hard-working people with a great respect for the past and an abiding faith in their future.

Keep earnestly set about in 1821 to familiarize himself with the circumstances of all and to keep a paternal eye upon his flock. This earned the thirty-three-year-old the affectionate name of "Father Keep." Not only did he conduct services of worship every Sabbath in a wooden edifice on the "Common" within the hamlet, but three evenings each week he journeyed to the outlying "district schools" to preach the Gospel. These meetings were well attended and resulted in many conversions.

At this time, he was becoming quite ardent in expressing his view that Christianity required more than talk of moral principles. Action was required. He managed to secure the placement of the temperance pledge into the church covenant. Two years before he arrived, an academy was built next to the church on the Common, and in 1822, he successfully gained the admittance there of female students. He saw himself as an instrument of God's will and a vocal proponent of reform and rights for all of God's children. Keep had always considered slavery to be a sinful abomination before God. At first, he believed slaves in America should be liberated and sent to Africa, where the American Colonization Society supposed they belonged. As the abolitionist William Lloyd Garrison began to argue for immediate emancipation on the soil, Keep pondered the matter and came out in full support of the unconditional abolitionists.

Slavery in New York State was legally abolished in 1827, but six years later there was no agreement in Homer that human bondage should be terminated in the southern states. Keep spoke his mind from the pulpit but was met with some dissension. Farmers who raised hogs in the area did not wish to risk losing the slave state of Maryland as a profitable market for pork shipped by flatboats down the Tioughnioga River. Economic conservatism in Homer trumped political liberalism, and a consensus was reached in 1833 that it was time for a change in minsters. After rowdies sheared his horse, John Keep left Homer in 1833 with his wife Lydia and went west.

In Ohio, Keep gathered with other abolitionists to found Oberlin College, the first college in America to accept blacks and women. From its inception, there was no doubt that Oberlin would be co-educational, but the vote on admitting blacks was close. It fell to "Father Keep" to break the tie and to cast the deciding vote. As of 1835, students were to be regularly admitted "irrespective of color." Keep served faithfully as a college trustee until his death in 1870. A hotbed of abolitionism, Oberlin became known as "the town that started the Civil War."

The present brick Congregational edifice on the Green was built during the Civil War–a decisive event in which Homer boys fought and died to save a Republic and free a Race. Five days after the decisive battle at Gettysburg, Keep returned to Homer for the dedication of the church. Apparently still feared as the old firebrand dismissed in 1833, he was not invited to give the sermon but was kept safely "confined to the prayer of dedication."

In 1901, when the Homer Congregationalists celebrated the centennial anniversary of their faith community on the Green, Rev. Theodore T. Munger returned and spoke of Keep's role in Homer: "I do not hesitate to pronounce him not only the greatest of your pastors, but the most effective citizen the town has known . . ." Munger addressed Keep's "ability to measure the questions that were coming to the front in both church and state, his clear insight into their meaning and drift, and his courage and wisdom in maintaining them alone and under an opposition which led to ostracism." Munger concluded, "As I look back upon him, I think he was at least half a century ahead of his day."

"Father Keep" made an impact on Homer. After he had departed from Homer in 1833, a few Congregationalists, like Simeon S. Bradford, defiantly picked up the anti-slavery banner and held anti-slavery meetings, such as the one once "held in the schoolhouse near Factory Hill on Monday evening at early candle-light." Young Francis B. Carpenter, born in Homer in 1830, heard his parents talk of the angry clamor generated by such meetings and their belief in the righteousness of abolitionism, as preached by "Father Keep." Later, when Carpenter's brother, Private William Wallace Carpenter, sacrificed his life on the altar of freedom at Gettysburg, not granting freedom to those in bondage would have meant to Carpenter that his brother's death had been in vain. The struggle for emancipation was felt personally by Carpenter, and when President Lincoln promulgated the *Emancipation*

Proclamation, Carpenter the artist felt in 1864 an obligation to document in paint on canvas the "moment of moral grandeur" when the groundbreaking policy was first read to Lincoln's Cabinet.

After Lincoln's assassination, Carpenter's image of the Great Emancipator immediately became a revered artifact of the nation's abolitionist movement. On May 7, 1865, at the ripe, old age of eighty-four, "Father Keep" sent the thirty-five-year-old Carpenter a piece of heartfelt praise from Oberlin. Addressed to "my dear boy," the letter contained these complimentary and prophetic words: "I have been much gratified by the sight and study of your splendid and very popular painting of President Lincoln and his Cabinet. Now it is sure that your name as an artist will hold a high position in all future history of your country."

Indeed, the former pastor of the Homer Congregational Church influenced both the abolition movement in America and a Homer native son. The latter captured in paint the iconic image of Lincoln, an early martyr in the "civil rights movement."

SOURCES

Bacon, Benjamin Wisner, *Theodore Thornton Munger: New England Minister* (New Haven: Yale University Press, 1913, 17, 18).

Best, Frank E. *John Keep of Longmeadow, Massachusetts and his Descendants* (Chicago, Illinois: Frank E. Best, 1899). Copy in Homer Town archives, 61–65.

Brandt, Nat, *The Town That Started the Civil War* (Syracuse, NY: Syracuse University Press, 1990).

Howe, Herbert Barber, *Jedediah Barber* (Columbia University Press, 1939) and *Paris Lived in Homer* (Cortland, NY: Cortland County Historical Society, 1968). Also, Howe's bound, typewritten documents on Keep (Homer, NY: Archives in the Homer Town Hall).

Johnson, Curtis D., *Islands of Holiness: Rural Religion in Upstate New York, 1790–1860* (Ithaca and London: Cornell University Press, 1989), 81–82, 11, 120–123.

Keep, John. Letter to Carpenter, cited in Mary Bartlett Cowdrey's extensive research notes on Carpenter and transcriptions of selected entries in his diary (Cortland County Historical Society).

August 12–October 7, 2010

Articles were published on Homer's three "Lincoln men": Stoddard, DeVoe and Carpenter. The material researched from countless primary and secondary sources and reported in the newspaper found its way into the chapters of *Lincoln's Gift from Homer, New York* in 2011 and into future articles in *The Homer News*.

Chapter 1

October 21, 2010–March 15, 2012

Scattered through the issues of *The Homer News* were sixteen installments titled *A Narrative of a True Murder Mystery in Homer*. The material was garnered from newspaper accounts of 1894–1895 and federal census records of 1880. Readers were encouraged to be sleuths and see if they could determine "who done it?" The last installment appeared in the first issue of the newspaper under new management with Don Ferris as Editor. Readers who had followed the series learned that no one was ever convicted for the murder of Patrick Quinlan four days before Christmas in 1894. Nevertheless, the installments were published in book form by year's end by the Cortland County Historical Society as *Death in the Winter Solstice: A Narrative of a True Murder Mystery in Homer*. Retired SUNY Cortland history professor Len Ralston edited the manuscript and complained that the story "doesn't go anywhere." Indeed, it did not; such is life. The reader was left hanging at the end along with the author when it should have been a convicted murderer (or two). And who wants to be known for being from a place where one can get away with murder? The lack of justice was frustrating and still is.

I recognized that if flesh was applied to the bones of this "cold case," an intriguing piece of historical fiction could be crafted. Thus, *The Suffragette's Saga: A Murder Mystery* came into being. It was published in 2019, the centennial year of women gaining the legal right to vote in America. In this fictionalized account of the murder of 1894, justice prevailed, and, hopefully, readers felt as satisfied with the outcome as the author. Some social and political history was sneaked in along the way. You cannot help it when you have been a teacher for almost forty years.

However, there is more to the Town and Village of Homer than its three unique "Lincoln men" and an unresolved case of murder, as the following "snippets" from the community's past reveal.

Chapter 2

Articles of 2012

April 19, 2012

HOMER'S INVENTOR OF GRAMMAR

Those who spent their junior high school years in Homer Central may recall being asked to go to the blackboard to diagram simple and compound sentences for Mrs. Helen Carty. Whether you found the experience intimidating or fun in her English class, you came away knowing the parts of speech and sentence structure—all of which, in pedagogical theory, prepared you to write effectively. What you may be surprised to learn is that the concept of diagramming sentences did not originate with Mrs. Carty, but it was promulgated by a far earlier Homer educator named Stephen Watkins Clark.

Clark was born in Naples, NY, on April 24, 1810 and received his early education at Franklin Academy in Prattsburg, NY (Steuben County). Upon graduating from Amherst College in 1837, he began a 33-year career as an educator in New York State by first teaching English at the Academy in nearby Groton. From 1840 to 1845, he was the Principal for Monroe Collegiate Institute in Elbridge. For its Department of Teacher Education, Clark prepared a manuscript on the principles of grammar and how to present it. The manuscript unexpectedly became a book, *A Practical Grammar*, with a long sub-title: *In which Words, Phrases, and Sentences Are Classified According to Their Offices and Their Various Relations to One Another: Illustrated By A Complete Set Of Diagrams*.

Clark's book of some 300 pages was quite revolutionary. It presented an ingenious way of analyzing sentence structure. Instead of parsing sentences in the classical tradition, students were asked to make diagrams. The parsing method, derived from the instruction of Latin, required students to memorize rules and definitions and to recite them by rote. Then they were called upon to stand beside their wooden desks and apply them to sentences by accurately classifying each word by its "part of speech," tense, and number and function in the sentence. This was difficult and tedious work—challenging for teacher and student alike. Clark set about to have students arrange parts of a sentence into diagrams, and, as noted in his preface, this would be analogous to using maps in geography and graphs in geometry as representative models.

Actually, Clark's diagrams were words placed in "balloons" on paper or a student's slate, which gave the appearance of being a string of sausages. The "subject (noun)" of a sentence was attached to the "predicate (verb)" which was attached to the "object"—as in the simple sentence "Dogs carry fleas." The sentences Clark asked students to diagram were usually taken from flowery verse, such as "There youth and beauty tread the choral ring, And shout their raptures to the cloudless skies." Clark advised English teachers: "It is believed that this practice, repeated every day, will be an agreeable and profitable exercise." Apparently, teachers concurred, for *A Practical Grammar* found its way into classrooms and bookshops across the nation—and in every school where Clark was employed after leaving Elbridge in 1845. Multiple editions and revisions of the book ensued, and Clark's career path can practically be charted by his books.

The 1847 revised edition indicates the author was "Principal at East Bloomfield Academy." This school was south of Rochester in Ontario County. Clark was there from 1845 to 1852. In 1852, he was widowed for a second time and married for a third. From 1852 to 1864 Clark was the Principal and English instructor at the Cortland Academy on the Homer Green. Interestingly, the "fortieth edition, revised" of his book (now digitized and online) was published in 1866 and lists him as "Principal of Cortland Academy" and "Author of *First Lessons in English Grammar* and *Analysis of the English Language*." The copyright date for these books, 1860 and 1864, reveal they were written by Clark during his tenure in Homer.

The Homer schoolmaster went on to be proprietor and superintendent of the Parma (N. Y.) Institute from 1864 to 1869 and principal of the Rochester (N. Y.) Military Academy from 1869–1870. He retired in 1870 and lived in Parma for eleven years and then in Spencerport until his death on March 13, 1901.

In time, Clark's use of "balloons" for diagramming sentences gave way to the use of lines and angles that many can recall from their childhood. Today, when grammar is taught at all, "tree diagrams" are frequently employed as a means of modeling sentence structure. Whatever the mode of diagramming, it can be traced back to Homer's grammarian, S. W. Clark, who sought to give some elegant logic to written English, though some of us who try to write today cannot tell you what is meant by a "dangling participle."

OK, now up to the board, please, and let's see you diagram that last sentence.

[*Note: In 2008, the Homer Town Hall turned 100 years old, and the Town asked for a researched history of the building. Drawing from material in the municipal archives, the following installments in the Homer newspaper resulted and now appear on the Town's website.*]

July 5, 2012

HOMER, N.Y.: A TOWN AND ITS HALL

When Cortland County marked its bicentennial in 2008, the Town Hall for the Town of Homer observed its centennial celebration and commenced renovations to keep it in use for another hundred years. Of course, there would have been no Hall to preserve without the Town, and the origins of the Town of Homer predate the origins of the County of Cortland by fourteen years. And what an interesting story it is of the Town of Homer, of some of its citizens who went on to state and national fame, and of its historic Hall at 31 North Main Street in the village of the same name as the Town's. It is an account of men and women striving to offer their skills and talents to do their best to bring themselves and their neighbors the municipal services needed in their lifetimes; it is an account of a building that has had to be many things to many people. It is, above all, a story of adaptability through the past 221 years. This is the first of a series of monthly installments on our local history as taken from the Town of Homer Minutes of 1795 to the present, along with nineteen other sources.

EARLY RESIDENTS AND THE ORGANIZATION
OF THE TOWN OF HOMER

The first residents of the valleys and hills carved by the glaciers in Central New York were the Onundagaono members of the Haudenosaunee, or "people of the long house." They were not unfamiliar with the densely forested hunting land here, where deer, wolves, bears, and panthers were among the denizens of the woods. The first settlers of European descent to arrive in what would become the Township of Homer and the County of Cortland were Joseph and Rhoda Todd Beebe and her brother, Amos Todd. Originally from New Haven, Connecticut, they journeyed up the Tioughnioga (pronounced tie-off-ni-o-ga) River to take possession of Lot No. 42 in New York State's Military Tract. This Tract of 1.75 million acres of wilderness was parceled out into lots as payment for soldiers who fought successfully in the Continental Army for independence from Britain. Because Robert Harpur, a clerk in the office of the State Surveyor General, was enamored of the Greek and Roman names he came across in his classical education, names like Virgil, Tully, Solon, Cincinnatus, and Homer were assigned to locales in the area. Occasionally a few names from British literature, such as Dryden, Locke, and Milton were scattered in as well.

Arriving in the autumn of 1791, it is believed that the first three intrepid pioneers built a temporary shelter near the spot now marked by a large boulder and plaque erected in 1924 at the intersection of Hooker Avenue and Route 11 at the north end of the village of Homer. Like the Native Americans before them, these pioneers were able to demonstrate an ability to adapt to the harsh wilderness of central New York. Twice, according to lore, Rhoda Beebe was required to fend for herself. When the men went off to fetch runaway horses, a wolf had poked its nose into the rude shelter, but fortunately it merely sniffed and chose to leave her unscathed. Another time, in winter, when the men went down to Windsor, NY, for provisions, Rhoda's food ran out before they returned, and she was forced to subsist on roots and tree bark. Eventually, these settlers made their way to their Lot at the top of West Hill, cleared it, and started farming on what is now part of the Sweeney farm on Route 90. Agriculture has remained a significant occupational pursuit within the town, though many now commute to jobs nearby in light industry and higher education.

Back in 1793, when George Washington had started his second term as President of the young Republic, there were six families in the area, all from New England. The Beebes and Todd were joined by John Miller and his sons, Silas and Daniel; John House; James Mather; and James Moore. Darius Kinne came late in 1793, and others soon followed.

Like any fledgling culture trying to survive, the citizens of the newly independent Republic knew the importance of organization and government at the grassroots level. In 1794, Onondaga County broke off from Herkimer County. On March 5th of that year, Homer, derived from the name of the Greek poet, was organized as a huge township of Onondaga County and included what is now Cortlandville, Solon, Cincinnatus, Virgil, Harford, Lapeer, Taylor, and the southern halves of Truxton and Cuyler. The few residents of this 300 square mile township were to be served by town officers appointed by three Onondaga County judges.

On April 5, 1795, these town officers met at the home of "Squire" John Miller. The next year, the first election of a Homer Town Board was held. Only white males who owned property were legally eligible to vote, and the property qualification would remain until the new state Constitution of 1822. The "Squire" was elected the first supervisor of the Town of Homer. John Keep was "judge;" Amos Todd was the first "collector;" and Peter Ingersoll was the first town clerk. The clerk position continued to be an elected post until 1963 when it became an appointed position and has remained so. Today, the Town Clerk is responsible for maintaining town records, maintaining a record of local laws, issuing licenses and permits (such as marriage licenses, dog licenses, and conservation licenses), collecting town and county taxes, and taking the minutes at all Board meetings.

The early Town Minutes were handwritten (some more legibly than others), and writing continued until typing was used in 1943. The Minutes for the 1790s reveal some interesting job titles. There was a "constable," or law enforcement officer, and a "fence viewer" whose paid responsibility was to see that all fences constraining livestock were kept in good repair by their owners. The "poormaster" took the indigent into his home and was allocated public funds for their needs (early welfare program). The "pound keeper" maintained an enclosure to keep stray animals—cattle, sheep, and swine—until they were claimed by the owner and compensation made for any damages sustained. The "sealer of weights and measures" was paid to attest to the accuracy of all scales and weighing devices used in commercial transactions.

By 1795, there were 29 families in the town. Four years later, there were fifty-two families. The first male child to be born in the town was born to the Moores, and, appropriately, they named him Homer. The first female child was Betsey House. The first wheeled vehicle in town was an ox cart brought in by John Hubbard in the spring of 1795, and the first frame building was a barn put up by Col. Moses Hopkins in 1798.

Annual town board meetings were held at board members' homes until Tuesday, April 7, 1801. That meeting was held "at the meeting house in Homer" which was also "the school house on Lot No.45." Lot No. 45 included the "Common," or what would become the "Green." The same edifice was used for both worship and schooling. Buildings were multi-functional even then. Later the structure was moved and now serves as the rear portion of the private residence at No.87 South Main Street.

Some of the resolutions drafted by the Town Board in the 1790s included: "no inhabitant of this Town shall bring in or take the care & charge of any cattle belonging to any inhabitants of any other Town (bulls excepted) upon the penalty of one Dollar per head . . .;" "that the inhabitants of the Town build a bridge across the river at the mill;" and "all four footed beasts shall run at large . . . horses excepted." This last resolution was replaced in 1812 by this one: "That horses, cattle, sheep & hogs be not suffered to run at large within half a mile of any meeting house, mill stone or tavern." In 1801, the board voted to "give 4 Dollars for every wolf shot" and one dollar for bears killed during the months of May through August. Later, panthers were added to the list. In 1802, one Elijah Hayden, for the offense of swearing in public, was fined a sum of thirty shillings to be handed over to the poormaster. Look at the money the Town could bring in today by reinstating that ordinance!

August 2, 2012

HOMER GROWS RAPIDLY IN THE 1800S

In its early years, the Town held special meetings for the purpose of laying out the roads in the town. The early Minutes show the Board to be almost entirely focused on dividing the Town into Road Districts and establishing the boundaries of "Publick Roads." Trails through the forests and swamps would become designated roads duly noted in the records. A marking point for delineating one such road in 1797 was simply "a yellow birch tree." The designated direction of a road could be appealed. A panel of three judges made the final decision. The town's "commissioners of highways" laid out the roads, directed repairs, and constructed bridges. Each road district had a "pathmaster" who supervised road maintenance and had the power to annually assess each male resident several days of labor on the road. The records list their names and the number of days assessed. Clearing the woodlands and maintaining the dirt roads, especially after the damages of storms, was crucial to this growing agrarian community in the center of the state.

In 1798, Solon broke off from the township, and Virgil did so in 1804, but the population of the town of Homer grew rapidly. The 1810 census shows the number to be 3000, scattered over an area of gently rolling hills and valleys. Besides farmers, there were teachers, preachers, merchants, millers, tanners, carpenters, masons, innkeepers, four physicians, and at least one lawyer, Horatio Ballard, who had arrived in 1803.

In 1808, Cortland County, of which the Town of Homer was a part, separated from Onondaga County. By act of the State Legislature, Cortland County was officially born on April 8, 1808. Soon after this event, a farmer and silversmith, John Osborn, arrived and set up a residence and a shop. It was in his house on the Albany Post Road (now No. 5 Albany Street)—the first made of brick—that a grandson named William Osborn Stoddard was born in 1835. Stoddard would later go on to serve as an assistant personal secretary to President and Mrs. Lincoln at the Executive Mansion (now called the White House) during the bloody American Civil War.

In 1813, during the War of 1812 with England, in which several citizens of the town participated, the Town was divided up by three "school commissioners" into some 27 school districts. The Minutes for 1815 show that

$300 was to be raised for the support of the schools and $200 raised for the support of the poor. Also, it was mandated that "every pathmaster be a fence viewer." Consolidation of governmental functions was apparently of concern back then, too. Among the votes taken in 1822 was one calling for Rufus Chafee to "clean the meeting house this week for $2.75." Among those in 1823 was one calling for the prosecution of Ira Hammond in a case of child support. Apparently, "derelict dads" is not just a modern phenomenon.

In 1818, Amelia Jenks Bloomer was born in the village and spent her childhood here (43 N. Main). Later, she moved to Seneca Falls, attended the Woman's Rights Convention there in 1848, and became an advocate for women's rights. She popularized a style of women's clothing called "bloomers."

As one peruses the Minutes of the 1820s, one begins to spot the names of Rufus Boies, Townsend Ross, John Keep, and Noah Smith. These were prominent men of the day who secured a charter in 1819 for an academy on the Common. Among the first trustees of the Academy was Jedediah Barber, the owner of the Great Western, a mercantile emporium on Main Street that was the Walmart of nineteenth century Central New York. Farmers of the region brought agrarian products, like pork and wool, for "Uncle Jed" to send down the waterways to Baltimore and bought from him manufactured goods they could not make for themselves, like nails, tumblers, and wallpaper. Portraits of Barber and the other academy trustees would later be captured forever in oil on canvas by a young Homer native, Francis Bicknell Carpenter. Later, Carpenter would come into national prominence by painting the likenesses of five U. S. Presidents.

In 1829, the southern portion of the township separated from Homer, and the Town of Cortlandville was created. A former local historian, the late R. Curtis Harris, once pointed out that a vote taken in 1829 to poll the feelings of the residents of the town about the proposed division had the following outcome: 616 against, 120 in favor, and 38 blank ballots. Harris concluded that the division was made and that "the passage of that law in the face of such an overwhelming local expression against the division suggests the perpetration of dastardly political skullduggery."

The Minutes for April 16, 1833, show that the location of Town Meetings changed. They would be held in "the Basement Story of the Episcopal Meeting House." That church with white clapboards had just been built the year before and still stands to this day on the Homer Green. The church would be referred to as the "Town Hall" in 1849. In 1835, Andrew Dickson White, born at the intersection of the Albany Post Road and Main Street in Homer, was baptized in this church, unaware, of course, that he was destined to become the first President of Cornell University in nearby Ithaca and a U. S. ambassador to Germany.

By 1835, a community within the township, also named after the Greek poet, was expanding around a "Common" lined with churches and the Academy. In that year, the Village of Homer was incorporated. Today, with a population of 3,291, it is the largest community in the Township. The hamlets of East Homer and Little York are also included in the Town.

Former town historian, Josephine Brown, once noted that during the 1830s "it appeared that the town supervisor changed about every year—as the tax levy increased a supervisor was out of a job." Such has been the nature of the relationship between the elected official and the electorate.

In 1831, the amount of bills allowed against the Town by the Board of Supervisors was $539.33. In 1849, under Supervisor Fred Ives, the town had an end of the year balance of $2.09. Samuel Sherman took over the post the next year, and the amount raised by tax was $3,125.89 for county expenses, $250 for highway expenses, $394.15 for the school district, and $250.58 for town expenses. In 1860, Giles Chittendon was town supervisor, and the tax levy was $7,919.56. In one decade, taxes had nearly doubled. Now, the town tax levy is six figures, or $501,902, and total appropriations for 2012 amounted to $1,670,893.

August 30, 2012

HOMER DURING THE CIVIL WAR AND THE NATION'S CENTENNIAL

In 1845, the United States annexed Texas, and a war for territorial expansion ensued with Mexico. The result was the taking of the northern half of Mexico, which included California, where gold was discovered in 1849. Americans from North and South moved westward in search of gold and fertile farmland. This opened debate over the Southern desire to take slaves as "property" protected by the Constitution into the West. When the ability to compromise failed, a War Between the States—then called "the Rebellion"—broke out in April of 1861. President Lincoln put forth an order for 75,000 volunteers to come forward to quash the rebellion. Later, Homer called for a special town meeting for August 19, 1862. By a vote of 360 to 3, a resolution was carried calling for "fifty dollars to be paid to each person who should volunteer from the town of Homer from July 2nd 1862 until the whole number of the quota should be raised . . . under the two last calls of the President of these United States." The bounty was raised to higher amounts over the next three years. Three months short of the war's end in 1865, the amount was $400 per volunteer who enlisted for one year, $500 for two years, and $600 for three years. Three men were to receive bounties for having secured substitutes to enlist in their places.

To preserve the Union and end slavery, men from Homer served in such regiments as the 76th and the 157th, and men from Homer made the ultimate sacrifice. Among them, Private William Carpenter, Francis B. Carpenter's 28-year old brother, died from wounds received at Gettysburg, and Asa Moore, a 17-year old bugler, starved to death in July of 1864 at the infamous prison camp at Andersonville, Georgia.

The Spanish-American War of 1898 and the international military conflagrations of the twentieth century would exact their price, as well. Homer names would appear on casualty lists well into the twenty-first century, right up to the name of Private Shawn Falter, who died in Iraq on January 20, 2007.

It was in Washington, D.C., in 1862, that Homer's William Osborn Stoddard was asked to make copies of an order President Lincoln had drafted. It was the Emancipation Proclamation calling for the freeing of slaves in the rebel states and beginning the process that would lead to the Thirteenth Amendment, which ended slavery forever in the United States. In 1866, Francis B. Carpenter returned to his hometown with the painting he did in 1864 of Lincoln that would make this native son famous. *The First Reading of the Emancipation Proclamation before the Cabinet* was exhibited on October 8. To see it, people filed up the stairs to what was later called the Keator Opera House on the third floor of the Barber Block on Main Street. Eventually, with the help of his good friend Stoddard, Carpenter would see the painting come to hang, as it does today, in the Capitol building in Washington, D.C. In 2007, Harold Holzer, acclaimed Lincoln scholar and Senior Vice President for External Affairs at the Metropolitan Museum of Art in New York, credited Homer's Carpenter with being "the most important artist ever to portray Abraham Lincoln." Both Stoddard and Carpenter wrote books about Lincoln and life at the White House in the 1860s. These are primary sources used by Lincoln scholars to this very day. Stoddard even described how he had the pleasure of introducing Homer's Jacob M. Schermerhorn and his daughter Anna to President and Mrs. Lincoln during the wealthy businessman's visit to the Executive Mansion.

Of course, Lincoln would never have been President were it not for the fine detective work of a man born in a log cabin on the Scott Road in 1809, the same year Lincoln was born in a log cabin in Kentucky. Eli DeVoe was his name. He was one of the men involved with thwarting a plot to assassinate the President-elect on February 23, 1861, when his train was scheduled to stop in Baltimore while on route to the nation's capital. Ironically, in 1865, DeVoe would participate in arresting two of the conspirators in the successful plot to assassinate Lincoln and the unsuccessful attempt made on the life of Secretary of State William H. Seward (from Auburn, New York). Thus, three lads who grew up in Homer played pivotal roles in the life and iconic imagery of Abraham Lincoln.

Yet another local hero of the era was Sgt. Llewellyn P. Norton of Company L, 10th New York Cavalry. For having charged, on horseback, a Confederate artillery position and for capturing two men and a fieldpiece, he was awarded the Congressional Medal of Honor. The actual presentation, however, was not made until 1888. Upon returning from the war, he may have lived in or worked from the house at the northeast corner of the Green and sold insurance. He did reside on Grove Street in the village in his final years.

William Osborn Stoddard made a visit to the Village of Homer in 1863, just after the battle of Gettysburg had been fought. He found the place changed. The Common was now a park-like Green with a newly built edifice of brick for the Congregationalists. These projects, along with a new cemetery west of the village, the Glenwood, were all spearheaded by the civic-minded Paris Barber. Paris was one of the sons of the merchant Jedediah Barber. "Uncle Jed," in 1863, was rebuilding his Great Western store after the first one was destroyed in a fire in 1856.

In 1867, "Uncle Jed" was in his 31st year (out of 33) as president of the academy's trustees, and the original school needed to be replaced. On April 2, 1867, at a special town meeting, consideration was given to a resolution calling for the raising of $20,000 in taxes "for the erection of a new Academy building in the Village of Homer" to replace the edifice constructed in 1819. 466 were in favor of the tax, and 140 were opposed. A new school was built. Others would go up on the same site through the ensuing years.

In 1876, the United States was one hundred years old. For the Centennial Exposition in Philadelphia, Paris Barber planned to construct a colossal human figure made entirely of the stalks, husks, and tassels of corn. For the design of "King Corn," he consulted Francis Carpenter, the portraitist he had befriended and abetted in the 1840s. Finding his lifelong friend and benefactor too ill to make the trip to Ithaca to seek financial support for the project from Cornell University, Carpenter went in his place. No financial support was forthcoming, and the project terminated in the spring of 1876 with the death of Paris, just two weeks after the death of his father, Jedediah.

To celebrate the nation's centennial locally, the Reverend William A. Robinson prepared a "Sketch of the History of Homer N.Y." and read it on the Fourth of July. The oration began with these words: "To compress a hundred years into twenty minutes is a feat rivaling the achievements of the railroad and the telegraph in annihilating space." If only this "unofficial" town historian could see what the technology of 136 additional years has done in "annihilating space."

September 13, 2012

HOMER IN A TIME OF NATIONAL TRANSITION

Post-Civil War America was in transition. A different way of life was emerging in the 1870s. It was the so called "Gilded Age," an age in which the rich got richer and the poor got poorer. It was an age giving rise to big business, new services, and the belief in technology's superiority over Nature. That belief culminated in an avoidable disaster in 1912 involving an "unsinkable ocean liner" called *Titanic*.

In 1878, a special town meeting was called in Homer to elect a supervisor to fill the vacancy caused by the resignation of S. McClellan Barber, son of Paris Barber. The result was 276 votes for A. Judson Kneeland and 127 for David H. Hannum. While Hannum, a clever horse trader, landowner, and banker, would be the inspiration for the colorful, folksy protagonist in Edward Noyes Westcott's bestselling novel *David Harum* (published in 1898), he apparently was not all that popular with the voters of Homer in 1878. Could it have been his unfortunate conviction for fraud in 1868 and his attempt to gain money from the Cardiff Giant Hoax the next year (more fraud) that stuck in the public's mind? His reputation would posthumously improve over time, as he was linked with the fictional Harum—proving the increasing power of the printed word in the "Gilded Age."

Also, in 1878, the Town Board approached the Officers of the Episcopal Society about the possibility of purchasing the Episcopal meeting house (in the basement of which the Board had been holding meetings for 43 years) for the Town's purposes. The Minutes for February 20, 1883, show that protracted negotiations had been abandoned. The next year, the Board held a public vote and moved to relinquish all claims to the basement of the church as soon as the Town, with or without participation of the Village, could secure a site and construct a building to serve as a firehouse and with "a large room to be situated on the first floor, fronting the street, to be used jointly by Town and Village, for town caucuses, Town meetings, corporation meetings or other public meetings...." In the 1890s, Board meetings were held at the First National Bank on Main Street, and annual town meetings were conducted at different locations: the Murray Building, the Porter Block, the "vacant store" in the First National Bank building, and the Hakes Block. Clearly, one permanent location to conduct the town's business and from which to provide new services was needed.

At "the turn of the century," the following businesses were headquartered in the nearby city of Cortland, and the Town of Homer exacted of them a "special franchise tax": Homer & Cortland Gas Light Co., Cortland Home

Telephone Co., Cortland & Homer Electric Co., and Cortland County Traction Co. This last business provided a new and popular service: electric trolley service, and it was taxed $7,500. It carried passengers between Cortland and the park in Little York.

History was made in Homer on February 17, 1903, when mechanical "U. S. Standard voting machines were used for the first time," instead of paper ballots. The records show that "the taking off the returns from the machines was accomplished in 17 minutes." The Town Board decided that three machines were to be purchased for $500 each. Consider the time-saving progress being made! Of course, this was to be trumped in 2009 when the town first used electronic voting machines.

Indeed, the first two decades of the new twentieth century witnessed the "progressive movement." Americans were eager to correct economic, social, and political ills, and that desire for progress was keen in Homer, too. At the biennial town meeting of February 19, 1907, Fire Chief E. C. Darby and the Fire Council of the Homer Fire Department offered a resolution "in regard to a joint Village and Town Building" to be erected "upon the plot of ground formerly occupied by the National Hotel in North Main Street. . . ." These reasons were cited for such a building: office space for Town and Village officials; safe repository of town and village documents; storage of "voting pharphanalia [*sic*]"; a jail "with better facilities for handling criminals;" "a suitable auditorium where public meetings can be held without the expense of paying rent, the lack of such a hall being felt most keenly in both village and town life"; "more capacious and easily accessible quarters for the companies of the local Fire Department;" and "a place for holding political caucuses, party meetings, and elections." The eighth reason clearly shows the spirit of the times: "Homer should have such a building to maintain its reputation as a progressive community, and to hold its own with other towns of similar size in this and neighboring counties. . . ." A motion was made and carried "that the Town Board appoint a Committee of Five to look into the matter of a joint building." M. J. Pratt, the Town Supervisor, along with George Klock, W. H. Foster, George A. Brockway, and Harry Hull comprised the Building Committee appointed on February 23, 1907. They thought it best to combine an engine house (fire station) with the Hall and to build it south of the Union Building (the lot where the David Perfetti residence is as of this writing). They secured an option to buy for $3000.

The site the Fire Department wanted was selected, but plans would not include an engine house. For ninety years this site had been occupied by a hotel built by Enos Stimson. As of 1894, the bustling village had three hotels to accommodate travelers passing through Central New York State.

Through the years, under changing management, each hotel had changed names and had experienced fires at different times, causing great confusion decades later for those trying to correctly identify photos and postcards of the fires. A "lower hotel" (only one balcony across the front) stood where the present fire station stands; it was destroyed by fire in 1934. The "upper hotel" (with a balcony along two sides) was known as the National at the time of its fire in November 1904. On the northeast corner of Main Street and Water Street and at the eastern end of Clinton Street, the National had boasted of 52 rooms, a stable to accommodate 100 horses, and one flush toilet. According to the late Anna Hilton of The Landmark Society, during the 1904 fire, "the crockery was thrown from the windows" while the feather beds were "carried down the ladders." At an estimated loss of $12,000, it is this hotel fire that opened a space in which the Town Hall could be constructed.

The owner of this piece of property was Burdette H. Griffin, who had served the town as a justice of the peace from 1901 until his resignation was accepted on May 1, 1906. The Fire Council's petition, also, stated that Griffin "has publicly announced his deep interest in this proposition and is willing to give the sum of $500.00 toward purchasing the site," the value to be determined by a representative of the town, a representative of the village, and a third to be named by the other two.

Image 2.1   Electric Streetcar No. 16 was built by Jackson & Sharp in late 1895. *From* In Cortland County Traction: The Story of Cortland's Trolley System *by Richard F. Palmer and Shelden S. King, 1992, copy in archives, Town Hall, Homer, NY.*

November 8, 2012

THE TOWN OF HOMER BUILDS A HALL

On June 11, 1907, a special village election was held to decide the question of purchasing the site at the corner of Main and Water Street, constructing an edifice there for joint Town and Village use, and furnishing it, with the Town picking up 35 percent of the cost and the Village 65 percent. On January 28, 1908, at a special town meeting held in the Porter Block on Main Street, eligible voters got to determine if the Board should be authorized to issue bonds not to exceed $22,000 and to add to the assessment roll for the year 1908 $1,000, making a total of $23,000 for the purpose of purchasing the Griffin property, erecting a Town Hall, and furnishing it. 376 ballots were cast. 291 were "Yes," 77 were "No," and 8 were "Spoiled and Mutilated Ballots." Two weeks later, five individuals were appointed to supervise the construction project: F. M. Briggs, W. H. Foster, W. A. Coon, S. F. Andrews, and D. N. Hitchcock.

At the same meeting, a resolution was carried calling for the appropriation of $100 "to assist said town in celebrating the One Hundredth anniversary of the formation of Cortland County." Cortland County had reached the centennial mark, and Homer was to build a Town Hall.

Sixty-year-old Charles F. Colton of Syracuse was the architect selected, beating out the plans submitted by four other architects from Elmira, Binghamton, New York, and Syracuse. He was a prominent designer whose buildings in Syracuse still stand, including City Hall.

According to the Homer *Republican*, the contract for the construction was awarded on April 25 to William L. Hoag of Tully, who trumped eight others with the low bid of $20,983. Separate contracts were awarded for excavation, masonry, carpentry, heating and plumbing, electrical, and interior finishing.

Ground for the foundation was broken on May 20, 1908. The basement walls were of concrete. The basement story above grade was to be ten feet and constructed of rock-faced "Miracle" cement blocks. The story above the basement was to be seventeen feet to the cornice and made of smooth-faced "Miracle" cement blocks. The blocks were cast in Syracuse by the "Miracle" Cement Block Manufacturing Company. The company's business manager, E. C. Ide, had come to Homer to tout the block's many points of superiority over other makes of cement work and to explain that the firm had been casting cement for about eleven years and this particular patent process block for four years. The blocks were to be two feet long by eight inches high and ventilated, having 30 percent air space. The blocks were to be stained brown in color with a soft, light gray block for trimming, which, supposedly, was to provide the effect of brown stone and granite. The same "Miracle" blocks were used in the foundation of the school building in nearby Preble, New York.

The architectural plans called for a 57 x 52-foot assembly hall in the basement, and an auditorium and stage on the upper floor. No doubt, this was to compensate for the recently closed Keator Opera House on Main Street. Located on the third floor of the Barber Block, this had been the main gathering place in the village until it was deemed too costly to install the fire escapes that had been mandated by the State. The Town's 60 x 53-foot auditorium was to have removable chairs and a seating capacity of 504. A balcony with a capacity of 194 more seats made a total capacity of 698 seats. The vestibule at the west end was to have a short flight of stairs leading to the auditorium, with a ticket office at the lower level. Two office spaces, one in the north corner and one in the south corner, were to be at the upper level. The stage at the east end was to have an opening of 30 feet and a depth of 27 feet, with a dressing room in the basement and a stairway leading to the northeast corner of the stage above. At the rear of the basement and beneath the stage would be the lock-up with three cells, an office for police court, the heating plant, and coal bins. The lock-up was to be fireproof and noise proof. A kitchen, pantry, storage room, offices, closets, and two toilet rooms with flush closets and lavatories were to be at the front end of the basement.

By October 1908, the roofing was nearly completed, but it was determined that the dome planned for the new Town Hall "be covered with copper instead of tin" for an extra $100. In addition, 752 chairs were to be purchased from Briggs Bros. Furniture store on James Street, Homer. The old jail cell was to be sold to Contractor Hoag for $75, and three jail cells were to be purchased from Pauly Jail Building Company for $645. The Village put in a six-foot cement walk in front of the Hall. By mid-November, the Lane Plumbing & Heating Company of Cortland was installing the steam heating plant. Plastering was completed and most of the wainscoting was done. The anticipated completion date was December 15th. As Anita Jebbett, the current Town Clerk, has observed, to build with the date "1908" carved in stone over the entrance reveals a contractor constructing "with confidence." The actual completion was only off by ten days but still within the calendar year still visible over the front entrance.

On Christmas Eve day, 1908, the building committee made a final inspection, and the Town Board accepted the building "with the exception of the plumbing, which will be accepted when certain necessary changes are made." The Homer *Republican* proclaimed the building to be "beautiful" and "a credit to the architect . . . the contractor, the building and town committees, and to the town which caused it to be constructed." The paper also cited the absence of the kind of criticism and fault-finding one frequently found engendered by such building projects. [*Note: See the article in the issue of November 7, 2019 for more discovered on the matter.*]

It boggles the modern mind that the Town Hall was up and running in seven months' time, but as Fred Forbes, the current Town Supervisor, has stated, "One must keep in mind that there were no state mandates and 'red tape' to slow things down, like today." Someone had the presence of mind and a Conley folding plate camera to photographically document the phases of construction. The seven glass negatives, owned by Patricia Gray Jackson, were conveyed to the town's historian by Frances Armstrong, and they were developed for the Town into seven remarkable 8×10 prints by Industrial Color Labs of Syracuse. These images now grace a wall of the Board Room in the Town Hall. The scaffolding shown in the prints would never have passed inspection by today's O.S.H.A.!

Chapter 3

Articles of 2013

January 10, 2013

HOMER TOWN HALL DEDICATION

On Wednesday, January 13, 1909, the scenery for the stage in the new Town Hall, from the Chicago firm of Sosman & Landis Co., was delivered. Thomas Knobel of Homer, who had the contract for stage settings in the auditorium, was busily installing the fittings for the various curtains and expressing his pleasure with the scenery of woodlands, a grand parlor, a kitchen, and a prison. Knobel himself had hand-painted the scene of the Village Green on the drop curtain, the same curtain that had originally been used for Dr. G. A. Tompkins' drama, "The Village Green," that had been performed at the Keator Opera House. Now, it is clear how retired Homer teacher, Rona Knobel, comes by her interest in art and drama. It is genetic!

According to the Homer *Republican* of January 28, 1909, the Town Hall had been officially opened to the public two days earlier for a grand dedication. All afternoon on the 26th, it was reported, throngs of visitors were greeted and escorted through the building by Town Supervisor Melvin J. Pratt, Town Clerk Lewis M. Austin, and President of the Village [mayor] Dr. L. W. Potter, along with members of the village board, the town board, the building committee, and their wives. Mrs. W. H. Foster played the piano that had been purchased from R. J. McElheny for $290, and C. D. Dillenbeck, the electrical contractor, operated the stage lighting switchboard to show off the possible lighting effects.

A reception was held that evening, during which musical selections were provided by Alvord's eight-piece orchestra. At 7:30 PM the curtain was raised, and the town and village officers took their seats upon the stage presided over by Dr. Potter, President of the Village. He spoke of his pleasure "to be called upon to preside at the first formal meeting to be held in the town hall and that the people had deemed it fitting that something in the nature of a dedicatory exercise should be held." He complimented the efforts of the building committee and praised them for "having erected the building without exceeding the appropriation." He then introduced Attorney E. W. Hyatt as Homer's "City Judge." Hyatt spoke at some length about the past record of the town and of the noble example left by the past generations. Next, a rendition of "Annie Laurie" was performed by a glee club consisting of Rev. Albert Broadhurst, Fred T. Newcomb, R. J. McElheny, Carl E. Bates, Charles F. Fisher, Ralph S. Bennett, and Fred J. Nixon. The audience responded by clamorously calling for more. The club responded twice to encores by "singing popular college airs with fine effect." County Judge J. E. Eggleston of Cortland then offered his recollection of the many leading citizens of Homer who had made a name for themselves and congratulated the present citizens for showing pride in their town. The orchestra then played while Thomas Knobel exhibited the stage curtains, scenery, stage settings, and stage equipment. The general satisfaction expressed by all that day with the building was "most gratifying, and especially so to . . . the building committee and town board." Today, a door near the Board room leads to a short flight of stairs that takes one up onto the old stage and into the past. Sadly, the curtains and equipment of that first day are either tattered or gone.

The price for entertainments in the new Hall was set in 1909. Local parties would be charged $20 per night and outside entertainments would be charged $25 per night. Rehearsals would cost a dollar an hour. The first public entertainment ever given there was a benefit concert on the evening after the official opening. Proceeds were to go toward buying furnishings for the hall. The program consisted of local talent presenting recitations, orchestral selections, and several solos by voice, violin, piano, and cello. The newspaper claimed that the most pleasing were the soprano solos by Miss Marsh of the Cortland Conservatory of Music. The acoustic properties of the hall were deemed to be "excellent."

Local talent again took the stage as Triumph Hose [Firefighting] Company presented the comic opera, "The Sleeping Princess," on February 9th and the farcical comedy, "Charley's Aunt," on February 10th. Both fundraising performances played to a packed house.

The municipal offices were first occupied in December, 1908, and in January of 1909 a motion was made and carried "that the assembly room of Town Hall be designated as polling place of Town Meeting to be held Feb. 16th 1909." The Hospital Aid Society was given use of the Hall's basement. The upper room on the southwest corner of the Hall was to be outfitted for use for Town Board meetings and as the office of the Town Clerk, and the northwest corner room would be used for Village Board meetings. In more recent years, one room was suitable for both groups to conduct their separate meetings. In 1912, in response to a growing population and additional paperwork, the position of Deputy Town Clerk was created, and it has been filled by appointment ever since.

In 1914, the Dillon Brothers, managers of The New Cortland Theater, site of "picture shows" and live vaudeville entertainment in Cortland, requested use of the Town Hall for a "picture show"—a foreshadowing of the adaptability of the edifice that would come in twenty-four years. Movies in the "silent film" era were shown on weekends in the Union Building (now the branch office of First Niagara Bank) on Main Street, Homer. The price of admission was ten cents. The films came with sheet music for the young pianist, Florence Foster Durkee, to provide the only background sound. Printed dialogue appeared on the silver screen, alternating with scenes from cliffhanger serials filmed in Ithaca's gorges before the film industry [Wharton Brothers] at Stewart Park moved to Hollywood, California. By force, Homer was truly "a community of readers" back then.

That same year, 1914, bids were accepted for the painting of the Town Hall, and a flag was purchased to go on the Hall. In 1916, the Board had to contend with a community health issue. It determined that any child of age 16 or younger who entered and remained in the Village of Homer from an area infected with infantile paralysis was to be quarantined for at least three weeks. That meant the child was to be confined to his/her home with visitors forbidden under penalty of a $25 fine. That was a stiff penalty for the times. Consider the amount of entertainment that could buy!

March 7, 2013

THE POST-WORLD WAR I TOWN OF HOMER

Town records make no mention that the United States was involved in the Great War in Europe from 1917 to 1918, other than permitting the Red Cross to use the Hall free of charge and noting that it was "impossible to buy stone on account of the war." The Academy prepared a long list of names of the faculty and students who went off to serve in the war. Some never got to graduate because they dropped out to serve their country and "to make the world safe for democracy." On February 11, 1919, the board was authorized to purchase a "Soldiers Honor Roll Register" and "to register all returning soldiers and sailors as requested by the War Dept. at Washington."

This mandated list was to be compiled by a newly mandated position. Every city, town, and village in the state was required to appoint a municipal historian. Mabel B. Hyatt was the first to hold the appointed post of Homer Town Historian. There was a long period of time when no one filled the post at all. Interest renewed in 1974. Since then, the post has been held by Miss Ella Perry, Mrs. Josephine Brown, and this writer.

In the 1920s, Frank Kinney was contracted to build a vault with a steel door and frame in the northwest room in the basement of the Hall "to store the Town Research at a cost of $285." The Town archives are stored there today, and the Village has a separate vault in the same room. Town historians operated out of their own homes until 2007 when space was provided in the Town Hall.

"Doughboys" returning from "Over There" may have thought the Town Hall would be a fine post-war site of entertainment. After all, the Homer Academy's Centennial Ball was held there on the evening of June 27, 1919. In December of 1919 the Homer Band was permitted to rent the assembly room for roller skating and dancing. However, the next month the skating was terminated because "the skates were splintering the floor."

Once women in New York State finally got the right to vote in 1917 and across the nation in 1920 upon the ratification of the 19th Amendment, women in Homer started holding such positions as poll inspector, tax collector, and overseer of the poor. However, no woman sat at the Board table as "councilman" until the year 2000. Mrs. Frances K. Armstrong holds that distinction. She was appointed January 5, 2000, to fill the post vacated by Donald Ferris upon his election as County Treasurer, and then she became the first woman to be elected to the Town Board. She is still active in civic-minded organizations today. Amelia Jenks Bloomer would be pleased.

The 1926 Senior Class of Homer Academy left its mark on the Town Hall—literally. A three-act play, "The Mummy and the Mumps," was performed there on April 22 and 23. The cast left their names on the stage walls where they still remain, along with the graffiti of other townsfolk of a bygone era, making a rather interesting archaeological artifact.

The "Roaring Twenties" saw an increasing demand for the "horseless carriage." That meant Henry Ford's Model T and Model A automobiles. It is no surprise, therefore, to find the Town Board focused in the 1920s on road repair and bridge building. For example, in 1922, the Board authorized the expenditure of $2,000 for construction on Clinton Street of a bridge 30 feet in length to handle traffic over Factory Creek (just west of the present Homer Intermediate-Junior High School). In addition, a resident of Spafford submitted a wish to start a bus line between Homer and Skaneateles, using the Scott Road.

Other matters taken up in the 1920s included repair of the ceiling of the Town Hall. The interior was to be re-varnished and redecorated and the exterior repainted. Two 2 and one-half gallon fire extinguishers were bought, and the exits were marked with red lights. The allowed capacity was set at 336 persons, a number determined by the width of the existing exits. A Brockway truck, manufactured in Cortland by a company that had first begun in Homer, was to be leased for $1775. The Cortland County Traction Company and the New York Power and Light Corporation were contracted to supply electrical lines for "light, heat, and power" along the town's highways. W. J. Stafford provided coal to heat the Hall for the budgeted amount of $40.12, and on June 17, 1929, William E. Burdick was appointed the first "Enumerator" to make a list of dogs in the town. Truant officers were to be paid $3 per call to round up students "playing hooky" (skipping classes for no legal reason). In 1930, the title was changed to "attendance officer." Do we need to bring that job back? As today, during the next decade unemployment was a major concern.

May 30, 2013

THE TOWN OF HOMER IN THE GREAT DEPRESSION

Signs of the Great Depression of the 1930s can be clearly detected in certain money-saving adaptations deemed necessary by the Homer Town Board.

- The salaries of Board members and election inspectors were reduced.
- The seven voting districts were reduced to five.
- The post of town attorney was cut, with the understanding that the county attorney could provide legal advice.
- The inadequate "Village Lockup" was closed, and persons arrested were henceforth to be detained at the County Jail in Cortland.
- The "Gospel Fund" that had existed since 1808 "for the support of the Gospel & Schools," was appropriated in 1931, and the entire amount of principal and interest, $2060.96, was distributed among the thirteen school districts of the town.
- Road work was to be done under "work relief projects."
- A new, more efficient heating system was to be installed at the Hall, and insurance on the Hall was cut by $8,000.
- Redecorating and repairing the building would be done by "unemployed labor and to be paid for by the Federal C. W. A." The Civil Works Administration was a New Deal program providing the unemployed with five months of work constructing and improving buildings and bridges.
- The "poor account" was renamed "welfare" (until 1947).
- The fees for renting out the Hall were cut in half, which was probably a good thing, considering all the folks who found enjoyment dancing on the stage or attending "amateur shows" during the '30s.

- In 1933, the basement of the Hall was rented out for $50 a month for use by the *Homer Post* to print its newspaper. Three years later, during the persistent hard times, the *Post* was evicted for inability to pay the rent.

Of all the names recorded in the history of the Town of Homer, there are five from this Depression era that are worthy of singular attention for their longevity of service. They are Harold L. "Cap" Creal, J. Henry Knobel, Earl Gutches, Elma Mineah, and George Vernum.

Harold "Cap" Creal, born and raised in western New York State, graduated from Cornell University in 1921 and came to the Homer area to take up farming, at which he was extremely successful for 65 years. In 1931, friends asked him to run for town supervisor, but he declined. The next evening, four friends came by to say they were not asking but telling him to run. They were certain his many contacts in the farming community would help. So, "Cap" was elected town supervisor and served for seven years during the Depression. As town supervisor, he set up a Cortland County work program. This paid 30 cents an hour for a 44-hour week. Later, the federal government set up a similar program. Creal's energetic leadership later came into play when he served as a New York State Assemblyman from Cortland County for twelve years and Director of the State Fair for over a decade. Known as "Mr. New York State Agriculture," he lived into his nineties. When asked how one could attain such longevity, he wryly replied, "Pick your ancestors."

J. Henry Knobel became Town Clerk in 1934, when Creal was Supervisor. Knobel, son of an earlier Town Clerk, Thomas Knobel, would have the distinction of the longest tenure of office of all the Clerks. He would serve for 31 years, until he died in office, in the Town Hall, on February 2, 1965. Fittingly, the current Town Clerk, Mrs. Anita Jebbett, is a descendent of the Knobels. J. Henry was her grandfather, and Thomas was her great- grandfather. Civil service must be in the Knobel Family's blood.

Earl Gutches of East Homer was another who rendered long and faithful service to the town. He was a town justice for 54 years. Upon his death in 1959, he was the oldest justice in the state in point of continuous service. Gerald Young took his place, serving many years as a justice and later as the supervisor and a councilman.

Mrs. Elma Mineah was the first female deputy clerk, serving from 1934 until she became the first female town clerk on February 4, 1965. She gave up the job in the fall of 1969 because of mandatory retirement.

On June 13, 1932, George Vernum, a former mounted New York State trooper with a down-state accent, was appointed town constable, thus beginning a long career in the environs of Homer as "George the Cop." At the next Board meeting, Harry and Ethel Davis were granted a license to operate a dance hall in the Buckingham Place north of the village, with the stipulation that it close at midnight on Saturdays. Enforcement, no doubt, fell to Constable Vernum. In 1937, additional tasks of "Dog Warden" fell to Vernum (remember the post of "pound keeper" in the early 1800s?). In 1939, he became school attendance officer, too. Thus, Vernum was charged with bringing in pets that strayed from home and students who strayed from school. In this era, the Town handed law enforcement over to the County Sheriff's Department, and Vernum was hired by the Village of Homer to be Chief of Police, a post he held until retirement in 1956. Today, a village park bears his name. Do you know where it is located?

June 13, 2013

THE TOWN HALL AS THE CAPITOL THEATER

A Special Meeting of the Homer Town Board was called on April 26, 1938. This was for the purpose of hearing a lengthy presentation by William M. Priven of Staten Island. He proposed to rent the Town Hall for a motion picture theatre. At a meeting on May 10th, the Board unanimously rejected Mr. Priven's proposal. Present at the same meeting, however, was a Mr. Shay of the Corona Theater of Groton who made his pitch for using the Town Hall for a motion picture theater. On May 16th, the Board traveled to Groton to meet with the proprietors of the Corona Theater. They looked over the theater arrangement, discussed the possibilities of changing the Town Hall into a movie theater, and returned to Homer—but not until after they had taken in the show, of course.

Next, the Board decided it would be best to bring the matter before Homer's Chamber of Commerce, in hopes of ascertaining public opinion as to the desirability of a theater. On July 14th, the Chamber presented a petition signed by 103 persons, "including nearly 100 percent of the businessmen of the village," calling for the leasing of the Hall for use as a movie theater. It needs to be recalled that the motion picture industry fared quite well economically during the 1930s, because for 25 cents and through the cinematic magic of Hollywood one could escape from the travails of the Great Depression. Thus, on August 18, 1938, the Board entered into "an agreement with the Townhall Homer Theatre Corporation" to lease the auditorium, the stage, and the main entrance for a theater. Thus, the Capitol Theater came into being. No doubt, the dome on the Hall was reminiscent of the one on the nation's Capitol Building, and so the theater derived its name. With a marquee over the front entrance, the Town Hall was also a movie theater for eighteen years.

Another change to the Hall came in the fall of 1939. The old Board Room on the ground floor in the rear of the Town Hall was rented to Leonard

Denison as a radio service shop for $10 per month or $100 if rented by the year. The shop remained there until January 1948.

On the snowy afternoon of March 8, 1940, the Board spent the afternoon observing different vehicles up for consideration for snow plowing operations. What did they see? The seven-ton Brockway plow slid off in a ditch. A county plow came to render aid and was also ditched. The Caterpillar grader pulled them both out. The Board bought the Caterpillar.

On December 8, 1941, after the Japanese attacked Pearl Harbor, the United States entered the Second World War. The next month, the Board made the Hall's basement available to the Post Office Department "in event the local office was burned or destroyed by enemy action during the present emergency." In the rear, the jail cell block was removed, and in the front, Murray Briskin, theater manager, had new front doors installed. That Christmas season, the Newton Line Company and its president, Ed O'Connell, hosted a party in the theater for its employees and their children. There were party hats for the children and a visit from Santa upon the festively decorated stage.

During the war years, the Capitol (telephone no. 255), with its concession stand offering popcorn and candies, had two complete shows nightly—at 7 and 9 PM—with a newsreel first. There was a Saturday matinee at 2 PM and continuous shows Sundays and holidays from 2 to 11 PM. Some senior citizens today can recall going to the "very nice" Capitol as youngsters. They can tell you that Jane Fellows was either a ticket-taker or a ticket seller. They can even name the projectionists: Carlton Niederhofer, Jim Hawley, Leonard Denison, Harold "Jack" LeRoy, and Floyd Hamilton. In 1942, the price of admission was 25 cents for adults in the balcony and 30 cents for adults in orchestra seats. Children were "always 11 cents." Tax was included. On October 14 through 16, 1942, the featured film, appropriately enough, was "To the Shores of Tripoli," starring John Payne, Randolph Scott, and Maureen O'Hara. The Capitol was, as well, "the official issuing agents for war bonds."

By 1946, admission for adults had increased to 40 cents and to 12 cents for children. A movie calendar for March and April had advertisements for A. B. Brown & Son on the Cortland-Homer Road (Tel.222) and Jackson's Meats & Groceries at 42 James Street, with "free delivery every day" (Tel.77). Sunday and Monday had a double feature, "all in Technicolor": Comedians Abbott and Costello starred in "In Hollywood," and James Craig and Ava Gardner could be seen in "She Went to the Races." On Wednesday and Thursday, "The Princess and the Pirate" was featured, with the legendary Bob Hope, Bing Crosby, and Virginia Mayo. April started off with Judy Garland and Ray Bolger in "The Harvey Girls."

Saturday matinees found the youth of the village coming to see the latest Hopalong Cassidy or Roy Rogers western. Before the main feature, there would be cartoons and a Flash Gordon or Rin Tin Tin serial. The space adventurer or the clever canine would get into some thrilling "cliffhanger" situation, but the moviegoer would have to return the next Saturday to see how it all played out, just as you will have to read the next installment to learn about . . . The Town in the Post-World War II Era.

June 27, 2013

THE TOWN IN THE POST-WORLD WAR II ERA

While Europe was in conflagration in the last year of World War II, a destructive fire befell the village of Homer. On the evening of January 26, 1945, Supervising Principal Louis J. Wolner calmly asked everyone attending a basketball game in the school gym to depart in an orderly fashion. Fire was ravaging the elementary section of the Homer Academy on the Green (School District No. 1). Classes had to be housed at various places around the village—the Episcopal Church, upstairs in the fire station, Phillips Free Library—until a new addition was ready in 1951. The basement of the Town Hall was used, too, for grade three classes. The auditorium/theater had frequently been used through the years for school plays and even commencement exercises.

In January of 1948, it was the Hall's turn to experience a fire. Insurance of $7,363.41 covered the repairs, and fire insurance was increased from $16,400 to $51,400. The recently centralized school districts, known as Homer Central School, gave up occupancy of the Hall in 1951. In lieu of rent, the Town accepted all permanent modifications the school had made to the building, and the school would paint the interior as desired by the Board.

The 1950s saw the advent of television, and the new technology in American homes was starting to adversely affect movie theaters by offering competition. The Capitol was no exception. In early 1952, Murray Briskin closed one night a week because of "the drop in attendance," and the Town reduced his monthly rent from $85 to $75. A public complaint was lodged concerning a smoke nuisance from the chimney of the Hall, and the matter was referred to Mr. Briskin, since he owned and operated the heating system. The theater lease came up for renewal in 1953, but only "after several months of bickering between lawyers" was an acceptable agreement reached, and the next year the rent was reduced to $60 and then to $50.

On June 7, 1955, Mr. Briskin informed the Board that he was terminating the lease and closing the Capitol Theater. As of July 3, 1956, the Capitol Theater officially ceased to be. The marquee on the front of the Hall was removed in 1959, but remnants inside are visible today. There is the ticket booth, the original carpeting and seats in the balcony, the projection booth, the original four carbon rods needed to project images, and the graffiti upon the walls of the stage. [*The seats in the balcony and the projection booth have since been removed during the latest interior renovations to the Hall.*] There, one finds, scrawled among the names of townsfolk, the title of one film, "The Talk of the Town," a 1942 release starring Cary Grant as an unlawfully imprisoned activist.

Upon entering the Hall today, visitors are greeted by two movie posters from the 1930s, and for a moment one is transported back to an earlier era. One can almost smell the buttered popcorn again and hear the dashing Rhett Butler tell the headstrong and beautiful Scarlett O'Hara, "Frankly, my dear, I don't give a damn." People of that era were shocked by such language being used in movie dialogue. What would they think today? [*The posters were removed during the latest interior renovation work.*]

Another recreation issue of the mid- to late 1950s involved complaints from the residents of the hamlet of Little York. It seems that boisterous swim parties were not uncommon after 10 PM on summer evenings at the site of the dam at the lower end of Little York Lake. The neighbors were seeking help from the highway patrol. Later, residents requested the area be fenced off and swimming prohibited.

In 1955, the Town Hall was only three years shy of being fifty years old. The decision was made to replace the old flat roof of the Town Hall with "a Flintcote specification, 20-year smooth surface built-up roof including flashings." The $499 bid was granted to Burden Roofing Company of Homer. The next year, the dome structure and roof were repainted with paint specifically to come "from local dealers." The local Lions Club requested permission to use the Hall for motion pictures, and it was granted "at $10.00 per night."

The post-World War II era experienced a "baby boom," an explosive increase in the nation's population. A birth occurred every seven seconds in the U.S. An expanding population in the township of Homer required more municipal services, and the Town tried to accommodate. Two sites were selected and purchased for town dumps in the mid-'50s: one on Brake Hill and another on the O'Shea Road. Littering along the roads leading to these dumps became an environmental problem. In 1957, a Zoning Commission, chaired by "Cap" Creal, was to prepare a much-needed Zoning Ordinance. Such a document was adopted April 8, 1958. In June, a vote determined that a new town highway garage was to be constructed on Prospect Street at a cost of $56,000. In August, the Hayes Ambulance Service was contracted to provide ambulance service for the residents of the Town and Village of Homer. A Town Planning Board was appointed in February of 1959, with John Gustafson as chairman, "to provide for the sound growth and development of the Town." That mission has been pursued by that Board to the present day. A

Youth Recreation Program was initiated and a gravel quarry just north of the village became a municipal swimming pool operated by both the Town and the Village. Today, it is known as Albert J. Durkee Memorial Park, but swimming is no longer permitted there. Mr. Durkee was co-founder of Durkee's Bakery, which operated in Homer and Cortland from 1931 to 1972.

1958 was the Sesquicentennial, or 150th anniversary, of the County of Cortland. To celebrate its past, Homer had a long parade down Main Street, complete with floats and horses and bewhiskered members of the "Brothers of the Brush." Being hirsute was "in." Actually, it was required of male citizens, or you paid a two dollar "fine." The Sixties were just around the corner. Facial hair, long locks, bell-bottom jeans, tie-dyed T-shirts, and sandals would be the fashion standard for young males after the "British invasion" by the Beatles.

July 11, 2013

THE TOWN OF HOMER IN THE SECOND HALF OF THE TWENTIETH CENTURY

With the movie theater gone, the 1960s began with a discussion of possible uses of the Homer Town Hall. Alterations were suggested, and alterations were made. Office space for the Town Supervisor, Town Clerk, Tax Collector, and Assessors was provided. The possibility of selling the Town Hall to the Cortland County Extension Service for its County headquarters was considered. Local dentist, Dr. Lloyd Haverly, representing the Homer Recreation Commission, pursued the possible use of the basement for a Youth Recreational Center. Then, the Onondaga-Cortland-Madison Board of Cooperative Educational Services (BOCES) expressed interest in renting office space in the Hall, and ground floor office space was provided. A small, renovated room at the back of the Hall was provided the Village for a police office for $300 annual rent, and Virgil Moffitt could use the auditorium for "Sunday Night Musical Entertainments on a trial basis, for $20.00 per night." Apparently, the trial run was not satisfactory; a later request by Mr. Moffitt for the Sertoma Club to rent the auditorium on a Sunday night for a Western Jamboree fundraiser was denied.

In 1967, a New Building Construction Code for the Town went into effect, and Charles W. Jermy, Sr. was the first to be appointed Building Inspector to enforce the ordinance. New housing developments were springing up in the town, which created additional roads for the Town Highway Department to maintain under Highway Superintendent John Vaber. He served with dedication from 1950 to 1973.

The matter of renting the auditorium became a moot point in 1969. The auditorium space was renovated for BOCES to use. Carpeted office space with two toilets was installed and used until the McEvoy Center in Cortlandville was completed in 1971. The transformation work was done by students enrolled in BOCES' building trades program to give them a real life, on-the-job construction experience. Today, standing in the balcony, one can see the handiwork, including heating and ventilation ducts, nestled into a space once filled with rows of chairs—a veritable symbol of adaptability. When BOCES vacated the Hall, the Village offices moved from James Street to the office spaces in the Hall. In 1971, facing a space crunch, the Homer Central School rented administrative office space in the basement of the Hall. Renting continued until a new Junior High School was annexed to the Intermediate School in 1974, thus allowing the administration to return to the south wing of the High School, where it is today. [Administrative offices moved to the north side of the high school gymnasium as part of the most recent capital project.]

In the early 1970s, town assessors were reduced in number from three to one. This appointed post was filled by Lawrence E. Fitts, who held that position continuously until September 30, 2007, possibly making him the longest serving assessor in the state. Also, a Code of Ethics Ordinance and a Code of Ethics Board was established. A Snowmobile Ordinance determined where snowmobiles could and could not be operated. The two town dumps were closed, and a county-wide sanitary landfill was created that still exists today but not in the Town of Homer.

The feasibility of consolidating town and village governments was discussed in the 1970s, as it would be again in 2007 when the state offered grant money as incentive. A proposed consolidation of the towns of Homer and Scott simply generated heated debate when the topic of merger was brought to the public again in 2009 and 2010.

By the summer of 1975, the United States had experienced two "wounds": a protracted war in Vietnam that had just ended and the resignation of a President after a scandal called "Watergate." "Healing" for the nation came in the form of preparations for its bicentennial and a chance to celebrate what was good about our past. The appearance of the Town Hall needed sprucing up in time for the occasion. Paint applied to the blocks had peeled off after only two years. A bicentennial parade made its way down Main Street on July 3, 1976, and members of the Board participated.

It was about this time, too, that the Cortland County Nutrition Program took up residence in the basement of the Town Hall to provide nutritious meals for senior citizens. To many residents of Homer, the basement of the Town Hall is known today as the David Harum Senior Citizens Center.

An active group gathers there, and they sure know interesting stories about Homer's past.

A town ordinance was passed in 1976 prohibiting dogs from being allowed to run at large. Compare that with the year 1796 when horses were the only creatures to be so prohibited. The fine for the twentieth century dog owner was $10.

In 1978, the Board voted unanimously to oppose the establishment by the state of nuclear waste depository sites in the County "because no one has had a satisfactory knowledge of what can happen over the years to the storage of such waste materials." The proposed sites generated much controversy, and protests from citizen activists succeeded in keeping the radioactive waste out.

In 1983, there was another protest. Some twenty residents attended a Town Board meeting. They were there to protest the colors being used in the painting of the Town Hall. The dome was to be a copper color, but when the paint was applied, a pink tone appeared, which, Josephine Brown recalled, prompted some rather colorful descriptions of what the dome looked like that "could not be printed in a family newspaper."

On October 19, 1991, the bicentennial of the first settlement of the Town was celebrated. A program of speakers and a skit on David Harum was held at the high school auditorium. The event was captured for posterity on something called "video" and placed in the Town's archives. At this time of celebration, the much-respected William Wright was into his sixth term as Town Supervisor, and Town Attorney Robert Jones had been offering legal counsel for three decades. 1994 saw the issue of consolidation of town and village services again raised as a cost-saving measure, but neither the town nor the village indicated too much excitement about the prospects. The real issue of controversy in 1996 was the proposed construction of a Pennfield Corporation feed mill in Little York, where residents felt it threatened the quality of their life.

In 1998, the Village Recreation office in the Hall became the Assessor's office, and the Recreation department moved to the present site south of the fire station on Main Street and was joined by the other Village officials on October 26, 2010. [Today, the Assessor's Office and the Recreation Office are both housed in a renovated Town Hall.] The decade of the '90s concluded by seeing the town budget surpass the million-dollar mark for the first time. Remember, in 1831 the amount was all of $539.33, but, of course, back then the roads were not maintained by sanders, plows, pay-loaders, and asphalt compactors, nor did workers receive health care insurance or state retirement funds, and million dollar property and liability insurance policies were unheard of.

July 25, 2013

TOWN HALL RENOVATIONS AND TOMORROW

It was liability concerns, aesthetics, and an appreciation of history that prompted the Town Board to start renovating the Town Hall, from the top down. As the building entered into the twenty-first century, its interior had offices with all the technology of the age—computers, faxes, printers, calculators, and copiers—but its exterior showed signs of deterioration. The removal and repair of the cupola atop the dome began in November of 2003. After 95 years of exposure to pigeons and the elements, the wooden structure was crumbling and hanging precariously from its post. Woodford Brothers Inc. of Tully used a cherry picker and a crane to bring it safely to the ground. They took it to Tully for restoration. Eight months later, a refurbished cupola with a new gleaming copper top was reattached.

The Woodford Brothers used, in 2002, two orange and white steel supports, drilled into the sidewalk, to hold up a roof over the front entrance. This was required because the weight of the four Roman-style columns (originally built in Syracuse) to support the roof was starting to wear on the block foundation. The dome, front steps, and the windows were sorely in need of repair, and handicap accessibility needed to be addressed to comply with the federal Americans with Disabilities Act. An application for a $350,000 state grant to fix the building was denied. Surplus funds were then dedicated to the task of restoring the front portico, completely redoing the town court, and installing a wheelchair-accessible elevator. A Syracuse architectural firm, Crawford and Stearns, was hired for the project of bringing the landmark back to life.

In June of 2006 the Board approved a resolution to purchase a vacant house immediately north of the Town Hall (No. 33 North Main Street). The house was bought from the county for $34,220 in back taxes. The site was eyed by the Board for a possible parking lot for the restored Hall. A public hearing on the subject showed division. Half the speakers supported razing the house and creating 20 to 30 parking spaces. The other half deplored the loss of property tax money for the town. Discussion also focused on which of four locations to use for the installation of the elevator. In the end, the Board voted to put in a parking lot and to install the elevator at the northeast corner of the Hall after renovations were made to the courtroom. This was all according to designs by preservation architect, Randy Crawford. The cost was close to $700,000.

Paul Yaman Construction started work on the front portico in the summer of 2006, with December 8, 2006, as the deadline date. After months of costly delays, partly due to winter and to poor casting work by Steps Plus of Syracuse, the front entrance did not open to the public again until August 1,

2007. Putting in the front sidewalks and moving the flagpole to the north side of the entrance was done by Homer contractor Tom Kile.

As the century-old landmark situated in the Homer Historic District celebrated its centennial in 2008, renovations continued. Further exterior and window work have been done [and a complete interior update], even after the Town received the Tender Loving Care Award in 2011 from the Central New York Preservation Association. The Homer Town Hall is still adapting. It is a symbol of the 6,405 townspeople it serves in a 50.37 square mile area—a people mindful of the past and yet trying to adapt to the requirements of the future. In May of 2009, the Town and Village supported "Homer's Celebration of Lincoln in Paint and Print"—a weeklong salute to Homer's connection to "The Great Emancipator" through Carpenter, Stoddard, and DeVoe. While being acclaimed as "a new Lincoln mecca," the Town has been ever conscious of the challenges posed by the Great Recession and by the proposed use of windmills, hydrofracking, and solar panels to resolve America's energy problems. Countless numbers of individuals have served the Town during the past 222 challenging years. To mention them all and the problems they confronted would require a book.

Through the years, the names of the public officials working in the Town Hall have changed, and so, too, have the functions of the Hall. Like a versatile actor, the building has taken on many roles: center for municipal services, jail, courthouse, movie theater, dance hall, roller-skating rink, newspaper office, radio repair shop, classroom, school business office, senior citizens center, and, yes, even home to a colorfully painted cigar store Indian princess who will greet you in the front foyer. Stop in! If she could talk, what would she say? She might bid you to consider how far the Town has come since the days when the indigenous Americans traveled along the Tioughnioga River. She might ask you how much you appreciate this town with its unique history that at times has intersected in significant ways with the nation's history. She might inquire if you value the collection we possess of 220 well-preserved architectural structures in the Historic District of the Village. She might urge you to imagine the possible roles the Homer Town Hall will be asked to play in future years. And she may ask all of us to realize the great opportunities that await us for heritage tourism here in Homer. Remember, economically and educationally history is "the gift that keeps on giving."

October 17, 2013

LITTLE YORK: A HAMLET NOT TO BE OVERLOOKED

The next three articles cover the early history of the hamlet of Little York in the Town of Homer. They are liberally drawn upon materials meticulously researched by Mary Dexter of Cortland over a period of several years and compiled in unpublished form by her in 2002. Much gratitude is due to Mary and to Larry and Sylvia Nye for bringing this trove of information to the municipal historian's attention and for placement in the Town's archives.

Too many people traveling on Interstate 81 or north on Route 281 zoom by the kettle lake carved by the glaciers at the foot of Mount Toppin and bearing the name of Little York. They are aware of seasonal cottages and year-round homes lining the lake. They know of an old pavilion at the northern end of the lake in the Town of Preble that is the summer home of Cortland Repertory Theater in Dwyer Memorial Park. Little thought is given to the cluster of homes and shops at the southern end of the lake that comprise the small hamlet of Little York that is within the Town of Homer. The old advice about needing to "slow down and smell the roses" applies here. It's time to slow down to appreciate a community that can trace its origins back to the beginning of the nineteenth century and currently plays host to a variety of businesses.

Today, in keeping with the area's agrarian past, Bill Anderson's Farm Market is the first to welcome northbound folks to Little York. Located on the west side of Route 281, it offers a delicious and nutritious selection of fresh fruits and vegetables at affordable prices. The Crawl Space, located in the renovated Little York Grange Hall, is not what its name might imply and is worth an exploration. Owned by Larry and Sylvia Nye, it offers an array of Central New York artists' works, from oil paintings and photography to handcrafted fashion accessories tastefully intermixed with antiques and collectibles. Across the busy state highway is the former Anderson Farm that has been transformed over the past forty years into the magical shop and studio of the talented wood and metal sculptor, Tino Ferro. A stroll through the barn and its grounds, known as Frog Pond Farm, reveals an extensive collection of delightful creations by the Ferro family, both realistic and phantasmagorical, that are simply not to be missed. A Taste of Country offers the passing motorist refreshing ice cream delights, while Dandy's Mart provides gasoline and sundry staples. Another former farm on 281 is now the home of Little York Plantation, where for forty years Dick and Jackie Crane have been operating Central New York's premier garden center, gift shop, and landscaping company. Back on the Crossroads, where a train depot once stood, is K & H Motorsports, owned by the Niswender Family. At the intersection of the Crossroads and Route 11 can be found the agri-business operation known as New Hope View Farm LLC. Four miles up the Cold Brook Road, artisans Dave and Lee Seward operate the always intriguing Two Hawks Gallery, while Linda Pearson's Kaleidoscope of Quilts on the west side of the lake is a quilter's dream come true. And word has it that joining these businesses and helping to create an enclave of artisans in Little York will be Suzanne L. DuVall, a certified goldsmith, at 5691 Route 281, bringing thirty years of experience in creating distinctive jewelry in gold, silver, and platinum.

This thriving little hamlet with its impressive assortment of businesses can trace its roots back to the end of the American Revolutionary War. In 1782, the State of New York set aside 1.75 million acres of wilderness in the center of the state to be parceled out as lots to compensate soldiers who had fought in the Continental Army. In 1790, the lots were randomly assigned to eligible soldiers or their heirs. The first to claim a lot in what would become Cortland County were Joseph and Rhoda Beebe and Rhoda's brother, Amos Todd. It is believed that they purchased Lot 42 from a Revolutionary soldier who preferred cash to a pig in a poke. These intrepid settlers arrived from Connecticut in 1791 and began clearing Lot 42 (at the top of West Hill on Route 90 in Homer) the next year.

Military Lot 6 in the Town of Homer, 600 square acres, was drawn by Thomas Hunt. Soon thereafter, he sold the lot to land speculators in New York City, who, in turn, began selling off parcels. John Clark made the first purchase from Lot 6 in 1802 for $200. The Clark Family's fifty acres were in the southwest corner of Lot 6, or what is now the west side of U.S. Route 11, a short distance south of the Crossing Road. In 1807, 550 acres of Lot 6 were sold to Jabez Newland Cushman.

Cushman was born in 1766 in Plympton Township, Plymouth County, Massachusetts. He and his wife Polly Cooper later moved to Pomfret, Connecticut, and then to the Town of Homer about the same time that Noah Carpenter migrated from Pomfret and settled on land now on Route 11 between the Village of Homer and the Little York Crossing Road. Carpenter's grandson, Francis B. Carpenter, would become famous for painting portraits of five U.S. Presidents, including Abraham Lincoln. In 1807, Cushman subdivided the bulk of his land and sold off parcels for smaller farms. He kept for himself forty acres south of the crossroad and adjacent to the stream that flowed southward out of Lower Lake, the small pond anchoring the chain of seven glacial ponds stretching north in the valley. By 1810, those who had purchased parcels of Lot 6 included Philip Arnold, Levi Bowen, James Chandler, Abel and Allen Kinne, David Merrick, Samuel Northway, Jacob Pratt, and Mathias Spencer.

It was Jabez Cushman who built before 1810 the crossroad, dam, bridge, and first sawmill for the seminal community of Little York. His brother, Oliver, a blacksmith, and his son, Elisha, were involved in the construction of the mill and dam. The sawmill provided the lumber needed for additional mills, shops, and residences. Prior to 1813, Cushman had a woolen factory built, and in the summer of that year he constructed a "grist mill with two runs of stones." A machine shop soon followed to house a recently patented triphammer. It was built east of the mill pond that was created by the placement of the dam across the south flowing stream. The grist mill and the woolen factory were south of the crossroad and faced each other across a canal or flume.

In 1814, Cushman ran an ad in the *Cortland Observer* announcing that he was the "Agent" for the "Homer Woolen Manufacturing Company." Seeking to do business with the area farmers who made their living primarily by raising sheep, Cushman stated that his company would produce "country Cloth" as well as "Superfine Broad Cloths in the best manner . . . and . . . in a stile [sic] far superior to any in this county." The ad went on to point out that purchases of cloth could be made via the barter system, if produce was "delivered by the first of January next." The looms used for making these textiles are believed to have been housed in a structure across the way on the north side of the crossroad.

John and Alvin Sampson, also transplants from Plymouth County, Massachusetts, purchased or leased the factory in May of 1813 for $1,000. In November they defaulted on their mortgage, and Lizer B. Canfield bought the property at public auction for $1100. In February of 1818, the Sampsons brought suit against Cushman in the amount of $1,791.81 and won. The court instructed the Sheriff to seize all the property belonging to Jabez Cushman and to sell it at public auction. For the price of $16.50, the property and assets were purchased by Manly Miles, Cushman's neighbor and son-in-law. Around this time, Cushman must have decided because of his business reversals to leave Little York and head out West. It was reported that he died in August 1819 "four hundred miles up the Missouri River." Though the men in Little York who followed Jabez Cushman are credited with the growth of the community, Cushman deserves praise for the vision to open to settlement the area near the kettle lake. It was he who harnessed the waterpower and built and operated four different industrial enterprises in the northern wilderness of the Town of Homer. Cushman certainly was the founder of Little York.

November 7, 2013

HOW LITTLE YORK GOT ITS NAME

People often ask, "How did the hamlet of Little York come by its name?" The definitive answer is unknown, but the earliest reference is in a deed from 1830 in which Jabez Cushman's grist mill is cited as "Little York Mill." The building, 36' by 40', stood three stories high and operated for over 130 years. Initially, Little York residents bought shares in the grist mill and it functioned as a partnership. Powers Mudge became the sole proprietor in 1873, and Grover Allen was believed to be the final owner. The structure was razed in 1946.

Cushman's woolen factory, about the size of a one-car garage raised up one story over the canal east of the dam, involved partnerships with many of Little York's residents through the 1830s. The operation ceased around 1840. The building was used as a machine shop in 1843 and later to produce shingles, wooden shoe pegs, churns, and chopping knives.

The sawmill on the east side of the mill pond at the south end of the lake was, for a brief period of time, owned by Elisha Grow. Grow migrated from Connecticut early in the settlement's development and cleared a farm north of the crossroad and east of the mill pond. It was Grow who set aside land for the community's cemetery, where he buried at least one child in 1827. And it is on the west side of the cemetery that he donated land for a school. Both sites are now in the shadow of the Interstate 81 overpass spanning the crossroad. Grow was known for providing horse-drawn wagons every Sabbath for those needing transportation to attend church services in the village of Homer.

A second sawmill erected by Jabez Cushman on the west side of the dam was purchased in 1813 by Jacob Pratt. By 1817, one of the sawyers operating the sawmill in partnership with Pratt was Asa Maxwell. Sometime before 1821, the sawmill was destroyed, most likely by a fire. Maxwell was the sole proprietor at the time, and he took in Adam Van Allen of DeRuyter, New York, as a partner and with most unusual contractual terms. Van Allen was to invest $1,000 in the cost of rebuilding the mill, while Maxwell was obligated to complete the rebuilding before March 1, 1822. In addition, Van Allen was to agree to another responsibility—"to keep and maintain and support" Maxwell's wife, Abigail "for her natural life." It seems that Asa and Abigail Maxwell had separated and agreed to live apart, but since Asa was bound by law to provide for his wife, he saw fit to include her in the sawmill transaction. Interestingly, succeeding partners in the sawmill entered into similar agreements with Maxwell. This continued until 1843, when Maxwell, then residing in Ohio, ceased to hold half interest in the property. No further mention is made in the historical record of Abigail Maxwell, and the mill was transformed into a tannery by Lyman Wilcox.

The next name in the development of Little York is Gideon Curtiss, known to the locals as "Uncle Gid." Curtiss, of Norwalk, Connecticut, arrived in 1813, and for the next thirty-three years participated in the ownership and operation of the grist mill, woolen factory, and sawmill. Sometime in the 1830s "Uncle Gid" took possession of the General Store, which was located on the West Road (now Route 281) just south of the crossroad. In addition, he owned a large farm, served as a legislator in the State Assembly, and was a Quaker and abolitionist.

Another name prominent in the annals of Little York is James Elbridge Cushing. Also a migrant from Plymouth, Massachusetts, Cushing acquired property on Lot 6 in the fall of 1818 from Abel Kinne. This land was south of Little York and west of the Tioughnioga River. Below what is known as the Lower Lake, he operated a sawmill on Cold Brook where the stream feeds into the river. After a brief residency in Pennsylvania, Cushing returned by 1840 to become a partner in the General Store with Gideon Curtiss. In 1846 he bought out Curtiss and became the community's first postmaster. He held this position until his death forty years later. He, his parents, his wife, sons and daughters, and grandchildren are all buried in the small Little York Cemetery.

Theodore and Hannah Doud and their early pioneer family also chose the Little York Cemetery as their final resting place. A veteran of the War of 1812, sometimes called "America's second war for independence," Doud arrived in 1818 from Norwalk, Connecticut. He purchased a fifty-acre farm north of the crossroad and west of the lake. Unfortunately, Doud's life was one of tribulation and tragedy.

One of his sons, Hiram Doud, a blacksmith, died at the age of 34, just after setting up his shop in the hamlet (possibly where the Murphy family now resides). Then, two other sons, Samuel B. and Eli Lent Doud, were either mentally or emotionally unstable and could not be cared for at home. For many years, Samuel and Eli lived at the County Home. In 1845, Doud drew up his Will. A clause therein reveals the man's values and social conscience: "Sensible of the expense which the County of Cortland has sustained in the care of my two sons. . . ," he deemed that a sum of $200 be set aside with instructions for his daughter, Betsey Doud, " . . . to appropriate, at her discretion, for the benefit of the poor of said county or, not to . . . at all if her case should require it to secure her from becoming a public charge." Dowd's wife and two sons, Samuel and Eli, all died the same year—1850—and Dowd died the next year. Betsey sold the farm and supported herself as a dressmaker.

Every community of any size in the early 1800s had at least one tavern. Little York's was constructed sometime before 1830 by John L. Wilcox. It was located on the west side of West Road at the intersection with the crossroad. The edifice burned and was replaced by another tavern on the same site. Owned by Wesley Slawson, the "pub" served as a stagecoach stop, the site of public land auctions, and the site of court hearings. This structure, too, was destroyed by fire and replaced in 1873 by yet a third building erected by Charles Foster. Known as the Little York Hotel, it stood for more than a century until it, too, burned in 1977.

In the 1850s, probably because of the tannery, shoemaking seems to have been a lucrative part of Little York's economy. David Corey lived in Little York for twenty-seven years, making shoes. Ira and Phillip Hill bought the

Gideon Curtiss property and were shoemakers. Others who practiced the trade in mid-century were Hiram Burt and Elisha and William Burnham. One who was a shoemaker for horses was Stephen D. Perkins. He was a blacksmith in the hamlet, who stood out in one very pronounced way. In an area that was politically a bastion of Republicanism, like the rest of the county, Perkins was a staunch Democrat and extremely vocal. Following the defeat in 1860 of his candidate for president, Stephen Douglas, by Abraham Lincoln, Perkins expressed the courage of his convictions in a most unusual manner. He vowed that he would not shave again until a Democrat was elected to the White House. He had a long wait. Not until Grover Cleveland's election in 1884 did Perkins take shears and razor to his beard. One can only imagine the length of his facial hair after twenty-four years. This alone would have been worth a tourist's trip to Little York!

November 21, 2013

LAST OF THREE ARTICLES ABOUT THE EARLY HISTORY OF THE HAMLET OF LITTLE YORK

When the call to arms came in the 1860s to save the Union and free the slaves, sons of Little York responded, and some made the ultimate sacrifice. Wilbur Cogswell was the son of the miller Linus Cogswell, and he was the mill's mechanic. Young Cogswell marched off with the Third Engineers to put down the Rebellion of the Southern States. Avery Colony, Zenas Blashfield, and Washington Dayton enlisted with the 157th N. Y. Volunteers. J. J. Salisbury was first part of the 16th Artillery and later with a Mounted Rifle Brigade. Franklin Pratt of the 76th N. Y. Volunteers was wounded and came home disabled. Franklin's brother did not survive the war; he died at Gettysburg, as did Clark Stickney. Ralph Dyke had only two sons. Both answered the call to duty. William, age 20, lost an arm at Gettysburg, and Albert, age 19, died in a prison in Florence, South Carolina.

Two sons of Little York perished at the infamous prison camp in Andersonville, Georgia. William H. Gillet, the 18-year-old son of Little York's wagon maker, was last known to be in this camp where 13,000 of the 45,000 Union soldiers confined there died. The second to succumb at Andersonville was Asa Moore, oldest son of the local blacksmith, John Moore. John had a farm at the summit of Mt. Toppin when Asa was a little boy. John married a second time, and the Moores moved away. Then, Asa found himself sent back to Mt. Toppin to live with grandparents. Married a third time, John returned to Little York and took up residence on the crossroad near his blacksmith shop with his third wife and the four youngest children.

Isolated as he was on the mountaintop with his grandparents, one can conjecture that Asa may have felt a sense of rejection or estrangement from his father. He may have perceived little to dissuade him from enlisting in late 1863 with Company E of the 22nd N. Y. Cavalry. He was assigned to be a bugler. In the spring of 1864, he traveled by train from central New York to the nation's capital and was shortly sent with his unit into battle in Virginia. Taken prisoner by the Confederates, he soon found himself crammed into Camp Sumter, an 18-acre, stockaded hell-hole in Andersonville, Georgia. There, according to local records, at the age of 17, on a day in July, 1864, the bugle boy from Mt. Toppin "died of starvation."

In April of 1867, two years after the Civil War ended, Joint School District No. 5 of Homer and Preble purchased sixty square rods of land in the north portion of Burdette Salisbury's apple orchard on West Road in the hamlet. This was to be the site of a new and larger one room schoolhouse to meet the educational needs of the area's children. The building was multi-functional; it provided a place for lecturers to speak, for music recitals, for itinerant clergy to preach, and for the residents of Little York to gather and engage in discussions on the educational, social, and political issues of the day.

In the mid-1850s, the railroad connecting Syracuse and Binghamton was built through the farmlands east of the hamlet. Many employed on the work gangs laying track were Irish immigrants. The Irish arrived in America, made their way into the valley, and assimilated very quickly into the agrarian culture. Since the railroad company initially balked at designating a rail stop at Little York, the residents of the area banded together in 1875 and took matters into their own hands. Providing all the materials and labor needed, they erected a depot. In exchange for his family being permitted to take up residence at the depot, Irishman Frank Donegan served as Little York's first station master. Tragedy struck two years later, in 1877. Mrs. Donegan was away from the building milking a cow and Frank was off on an errand when the small wooden depot caught fire. It burned to the ground in a matter of minutes, and all five of the Donegan children perished. In another collaborative, community effort, another station was built almost immediately.

The following year, a gigantic undertaking was scheduled by the Syracuse and Binghamton Railroad—narrowing the gauge of eighty miles of track. The entire length was divided into sections, and the work was to be done simultaneously in the shortest time possible to not disrupt any scheduled rail service. Competition ran high among the section bosses. A burly Irish roustabout, Michael Murphy, was put in charge of the section through Little York. Amazingly, with the precision of a fine-tuned military unit working in the pre-dawn hours of June 1, 1878, Murphy's crew completed the gauge reduction of five and a half miles of track in five hours and forty-two minutes.

Another type of railroad also passed through Little York—the Underground Railroad. This secret organization for aiding slaves in escaping bondage in the South found ready support in Oren Cravath. His farm at the intersection of West Road and Cold Brook Road served during turbulent and dangerous times as a "station" on the "railroad" that moved slaves through the valley to Syracuse and ultimately to freedom in Canada.

By the "Gilded Age," the last quarter of the nineteenth century, privately owned cottages were springing up along the lake shore and Little York came to enjoy a reputation as a resort community. From late spring into summer, some of the larger homes became boarding houses and competed with the Little York Hotel for guests. The visitors availed themselves of several recreational activities. Picnic tables dotted the shore, and boat liveries (rentals) did a brisk business. Fishing was extremely popular. A small steamer offered a leisurely circumnavigation of the lake, while those seeking more physical entertainment took hikes to the top of Mt. Toppin. The climb afforded a spectacular view of the valley and the opportunity to pick berries, wild fruit, or nuts. Even the famed New York City portraitist Francis B. Carpenter was said to have hiked to the summit to enjoy some solitude and communion with Nature during summer visits to the Carpenter homestead across the valley. For more intellectual stimulation, the hotel hosted meetings of The Literary Club, The Debating Society, and card clubs. In the 1890s, the Cortland Traction Company operated streetcars with rattan covered benches between Cortland and Preble. These cars transported folks to the company-built pavilion (still standing) at the north end of the lake to enjoy scrumptious boxed lunches of sandwiches, fried chicken, boiled eggs, and cake.

It is interesting that while a school was built and then a larger one, no religious organization ever formed a congregation or built a house of worship in Little York. Instead, the citizens of the hamlet elected to be members of faith communities in Preble and Homer, and the bulk of them also chose their final resting places to be in these two neighboring communities.

By 1900, Little York had reached the peak of its economic growth. After several generations, the names of Clark, Cushing, Hobart, Pratt, and Salisbury continued. The grist mill, general store, blacksmith shops, and hotel were still flourishing, and several small enterprises were succeeding in buildings that had formerly been sawmills, machine shops, and a woolen factory. Shingles, cutlery, and gang rotary churns went out to the world bearing the stamp "Little York, Cort. Co. N.Y."

In addition, two other large businesses were prospering. Starting in 1889, the Little York Ice Company harvested tons of blocks of crystal-clear ice from the lake and stored it for future delivery to homes needing refrigeration for foods kept in the "ice box" in the kitchen. Milk, butter, and cheese, among such perishable foods, were processed at the Little York Creamery and in enough quantities for shipment via rail to large urban markets. It is interesting to note that when ice harvesting first commenced on the lake, there was litigation over the company's right to take the ice. According to the grist mill owners, ice was frozen water and they owned the water rights to the lake. The mill owners lost in court.

These enterprises of yesteryear are gone in Little York, as is the summertime swimming at the dam that was so hugely popular in the 1940s and '50s (as evidenced by the large black and white photo ensconced in Tony Ferro's art studio). And, yet, after two centuries, there are residents and enterprising businesses still adapting and continuing to cling tenaciously to that once remote land surrounding the spot in Homer Township where Jabez Cushman first harnessed the waters of the kettle lake for energy.

Image 3.1 Little York Ice Co. Horse & Wagon. *Courtesy of Bill Anderson Farm Market, Little York, NY.*

Chapter 4

Articles of 2014

January 2, 2014

THE ALBANY POST ROAD—NYS ROUTE 90

[Note: This article appeared in nine installments in the Homer newspaper. Only the first four installments that pertain to Homer are included in this collection. At the time, it was proposed that Route 90 be designated a "Heritage Byway." It was to meander from the Historic District of the Village of Homer in the Town of Homer to the Historic District in the Village of Aurora on Cayuga Lake, one of the scenic Finger Lakes of Central New York that is surrounded by reputable wineries. The goal was to develop a self-guided tour of this "Heritage Byway" and to reveal what the community of Homer was like in 1876. The nine installments could have been the basis for such a tour. The byway project never came to fruition. This scenic and historic stretch of highway from Homer to Aurora and on to Montezuma has become famous among collectors and bargain hunters for the fifty-mile Route 90 Yard Sale held the last weekend of every July.]

Let us now consider what we would have seen and experienced in late June 1876 when commencing our travel on a stagecoach pulled by four strong horses from East to West along what is now Route 90. We will be traveling through Cortland and Cayuga County, when the route was part of the rough and pot-holed Stage Road or Post Road from Albany to Buffalo—no modern, hard-surfaced highway to be sure.

Welcome, ladies and gentlemen! Please observe the rules of travel. Abstinence from liquor is requested, but if you must drink, share the bottle. To do otherwise makes you appear selfish and un-neighborly. Gentlemen are urged to forego smoking cigars and pipes if ladies are present. The odor of same is repugnant to the gentler sex. Chewing tobacco is permitted, but spit with the wind, not against it. No fare is charged; the proprietors of the scheduled stops along the way pay a monthly rate to the coach lines. Note that the suspension of the coach consists not of steel springs. Rather, the coach rests upon strong leather slings. Be prepared for some swaying motion and some teeth-rattling moments. The horses are high-spirited, but they are so admirably broke that they regulate their pace instantly to the coachman's command. Each driver drives a 12 to 15 mile "stage" and stops every five miles to water the steeds. Because of delays in changing horses and drivers and stops for dining, we will be fortunate to average four miles an hour. Plan on a twelve-hour journey from Homer to Aurora because of the hilly terrain to be traversed.

Our coach comes up over Lighthouse Hill from the west, in Cortland County. Nine of us are seated within. Three are on a front seat, three on a back seat, and three on a bench hung in the middle. The coachman, outside, sits on a bench lower than the top of the coach and enjoys his chaw of tobacco. Through the summer morning's haze, we travelers note a valley below carved by the retreating glaciers of the Ice Age and once the hunting grounds of the Haudenosaunee, or People of the Longhouse—the Iroquois. In the flats below, Farmer Kingsbury and his sons in broad-brimmed straw hats are forking the first cutting of timothy and clover up onto a hay wagon pulled by two old mares. [Interstate Route 81 cuts through the valley and hillside today.] Since 1863, the spire of the Congregational Church in the distance has poked its way up through the treetops which hide from view the little village of Homer in the Town of Homer. The first settlers of European descent arrived here in 1791: Joseph and Rhoda Beebe and her brother Amos Todd. They journeyed from Connecticut, seeking Lot No. 42 in the Military Tract of New York State, which was land set aside by the State as payment to soldiers who fought for freedom from Britain in the Revolutionary War. This Tract included the counties of Cortland and Cayuga with names from classical antiquity affixed to it by the State's Surveyor General's office. A clerk in the Office was enamored of the Greek and Roman names he came across in his classical education. Thus, the places in Central New York bear such names as Cincinnatus, Marathon, Virgil, Cato, Cicero, Romulus . . . and Homer, the Greek poet who wrote *The Iliad* and *The Odyssey*.

The first election of a Homer Town Board was held in 1796 when 29 New England families resided in the town. Only white males who owned property were legally eligible to vote, and the property qualification would remain until the new state Constitution of 1822. By 1799, there were fifty-two families. The first male child to be born in the town was born to the Moores, and, appropriately, they named him Homer. The first female child was Betsey House. The first wheeled vehicle in town was an ox cart brought in by John

Hubbard in the spring of 1795, and the first frame building was a barn put up by Col. Moses Hopkins in 1798.

Annual town board meetings were held at board members' homes until Tuesday, April 7, 1801. That meeting was held "at the meeting house in Homer" which was also "the school house on Lot No.45." Lot No. 45 was the "Common," or what would become the "Green." The edifice was moved in the early 1800s and became the back portion of a private residence [at 87 South Main Street], just yards away from the Albany Post Road.

In 1801, the board voted to "give 4 Dollars for every wolf shot" and one dollar for bears killed during the months of May through August. Later, panthers were added to the list. In 1802, one Elijah Hayden, for the offense of swearing in public, was fined a sum of thirty shillings to be handed over to the poor master. Since April 16, 1833 [and until 1908], Town Meetings have been held in "the Basement Story of the Episcopal Meeting House." That church had just been built the year before [and still stands to this day] on the Homer Green. In 1835, the Village of Homer was incorporated. The coach will make a stop in this village.

January 16, 2014

THE STAGECOACH BRINGS US TO HOMER VILLAGE

Now, in this centennial year of the nation, 1876, the coach makes its way toward the village, once it carefully descends the steep hillside and crosses a bridge, near Tower's Blacksmith Shop, spanning the Tioughnioga River—the river that the Beebes and Amos Todd followed to make their way into the wilderness.

On April 8, 1808, Cortland County, of which the Town of Homer was a part, separated from Onondaga County. The 1810 census shows the number of town residents to be 3000, scattered over an area of gently rolling hills and valleys. Besides farmers, there were teachers, preachers, merchants, millers, tanners, carpenters, masons, innkeepers, four physicians, and at least one lawyer, Horatio Ballard, who had arrived in 1803. A farmer and silversmith, John Osborn, arrived in 1808 and set up both residence and a shop on the Albany Post Road.

Once crossing the bridge, the coach comes up on the Osborn farmhouse [now No. 5 Albany Street], the first made of brick in the county. It is here that a grandson named William Osborn Stoddard was born in 1835, just eight years after slavery was prohibited in New York State. It is here, at the age of ten, that young Stoddard discovered a runaway slave in the cellar and learned that his grandfather was participating in the Underground Railroad that transported slaves out of the South and to freedom in Canada. William Stoddard went on to serve as an assistant personal secretary to Mr. and Mrs. Lincoln at the Executive Mansion [now called the White House] during the bloody American Civil War.

John Osborn, Rufus Boies, Townsend Ross, John Keep, Noah Smith and Samuel Buell Woolworth were some of the prominent men of the day who secured a charter in 1819 for an academy on the Green. Among the first trustees of the Academy, their portraits would later be captured forever in oil on canvas by a young Homerite born in 1830, Francis Bicknell Carpenter. [The eleven "Trustee Paintings," including the image of Reverend John Keep, co-founder of Oberlin College in Ohio, are now part of a collection of paintings owned by the Homer Central School District.] Later, [five U. S. Presidents would have their portraits painted by Carpenter, and] the portraitist would be best remembered for the 9 foot by 15-foot oil painting of "The First Reading of the Emancipation Proclamation before the Cabinet." This was done at the Executive Mansion during six months in 1864.

It was two years earlier that Homer's William Osborn Stoddard was asked to make copies of Lincoln's Emancipation Proclamation. This military order called for the freeing of slaves in the rebel states and began the process that would lead to the Thirteenth Amendment to the Constitution, which ended slavery forever in the United States. In 1866, Francis B. Carpenter returned to his hometown with the painting of President Lincoln and his assembled Cabinet. It was exhibited on October 8. To see it, people filed up the stairs to the Keator Opera House on the third floor of the Barber Block on Main Street [which still stands]. Eventually, with the help of his good friend Stoddard, the painting would come to hang on the Senate side of the Capitol building in Washington, D.C. [In 2007, Harold Holzer, acclaimed Lincoln scholar and then the Senior Vice President for External Affairs at the Metropolitan Museum of Art in New York, credited Homer's Carpenter with being "the most important artist ever to portray Abraham Lincoln." In 2009, Holzer delivered lectures in Homer on Carpenter and Stoddard. Both Stoddard and Carpenter wrote books about Lincoln and life at the White House in the 1860s, which would become primary sources used by Lincoln scholars.]

Of course, Lincoln would never have been President were it not for the fine detective work of a man born in a log cabin in the Town of Homer in 1809, the same year Lincoln was born in a log cabin in Kentucky. Eli DeVoe was his name. He was one of the men involved with thwarting a plot to assassinate the President-elect on February 23, 1861, when his train was scheduled to stop in Baltimore while on route to the nation's capital. Ironically, in April of 1865, Detective DeVoe would participate in arresting Mary Surratt and Lewis Payne, two of the conspirators in the successful plot to assassinate Lincoln and the unsuccessful attempt made on the life of Secretary of State William H. Seward [from Auburn, New York]. [For a detailed account of the lives of Carpenter, Stoddard, and DeVoe, read *Lincoln's Gift from Homer, New York* (2011) by this writer.]

Just west of the Osborn House and at the spot where the Post Road becomes the Main Street of Homer, a tavern greets the arrival of our coach, one of four coaches that makes this trip daily. This is "Wisdom's Gate," built in 1816 by Joshua Ballard in the Federal Style, with Palladian windows. Its portly proprietor jovially welcomes everyone. He urges the driver to water his horses and the coach passengers to partake of lodging or the fresh ham and biscuits placed upon the table in the large dining room. The most colorful innkeeper here was a Quaker named George Washington Samson. In the 1830s, any traveler hoping to quench his thirst with a glass of whiskey or rum was soon in for disappointment. Samson was a "temperance man," and his establishment was a "temperance tavern." An empty decanter, without a cork, suspended from the ceiling in the barroom, signified to all the tee-totaling character of the premises. Samson entertained his guests with a pet rooster trained to crow on command.

Across the Post Road from the tavern, on the other corner, is a structure built in 1819, also in the Federal Style. [The steep Mansard roof, the projecting dormer windows on the third floor, and the brackets supporting the eaves reveals a remodeling done in the French Second Empire Style in the 1880s.] This is the birthplace of Andrew Dickson White. White was the first president of Cornell University over in nearby Ithaca, NY, sited on farmland provided by the wealthy Ezra Cornell. This was soon after President Lincoln signed the Morrill Act of 1862 which established the university as a land-grant college. White and Stoddard, born only three years apart, were childhood chums in this neighborhood and explored the banks of the nearby river together. When their fathers, Horace White and Samuel Stoddard, quit as clerks in the local store, The Great Western, both families relocated to Syracuse, and the boys continued to be friends [for the rest of their lives].

Directly across Main Street from the tavern, we cannot help but notice a lavish estate. Known as "The Hedges," [now 90 S. Main St.], the property was purchased in 1841 by Jacob Maus Schermerhorn. The stately brick Italianate house and beautiful formal gardens in a riot of colors are worthy of a man successful in banking, building, and farming. Schermerhorn made a name for himself in the national affairs of the Republican Party and was acquainted with President Lincoln. By 1865, his income was reported to be in excess of $43,000, making him the wealthiest man in Cortland County and able to afford the fanciest carriage in the Village.

The residence due north of "The Hedges" [86 S. Main] is in the formal symmetrical style of the Federal Period. It was once the home of the Williams Family, the owners of a woolen factory in the upper part of the village. Mr. Williams purchased wool from the local sheep farmers and made fine woolen cloth, at least until cotton became too competitive for Cortland County farmers to raise sheep.

Chapter 4

Image 4.1 **Birthplace of William Osborn Stoddard.** *Courtesy of Don Ferris.*

Image 4.2 **Wisdom's Gate, a temperance tavern.** *Courtesy of Don Ferris.*

Image 4.3 Birthplace of Andrew D. White. *Courtesy of Don Ferris.*

Image 4.4 "The Hedges" at 90 South Main Street. *Courtesy of Don Ferris.*

January 30, 2014

A GLIMPSE OF THE GREEN

As the stagecoach resumes its journey and heads north up Homer's Main Street, passing John Osborn's silversmith shop and the Unitarian Church on the right [neither exists today], one may fail to catch a glimpse on the left of another impressive Italianate structure built in 1868, three years after the end of the Civil War. A cupola adorns the flat roof [and the porch was added a century later].

North of this residence is that of David Hannum. Hannum came to Homer in 1838 and became known as an enterprising landowner, a slick salesman, a shrewd horse trader, and a partner in a moneymaking scheme known as the "Cardiff Giant Hoax." The perpetrators of the hoax tried to convince people in 1869 that a large figure carved from stone was really a prehistoric, petrified man unearthed on a farm in Cardiff, near Lafayette, NY. The showman P. T. Barnum offered $50,000 for the giant. When he was turned down, he put his own replica on display in New York, claiming that his was the real giant and the Cardiff Giant was a fake. Though attributed to Barnum, it was Hannum who coined the expression "There's a sucker born every minute" in reference to spectators paying to see Barnum's fake of the real fake giant. [Hannum became famous in 1899 with the publication of a novel by Edward Noyes Westcott titled *David Harum*. Hannum is believed to be the model for Harum, and the story's setting, Homeville, is said to be Homer. The book was a bestseller at the beginning of the last century. A movie contributed to the folklore. It was made in the 1930s starring Will Rogers as a folksy, philosophizing David Harum, but the racism in it is offensive to today's sensibilities.]

Soon, the coach driver barks out commands and uses the four reins to have the team of horses make a sharp left [onto what is now called Cayuga Street] to head toward Cayuga County. A full day of travel lies ahead, but fortunately the coach is not tightly packed with unwashed, corpulent passengers during this summer humidity. On the corner to the left is a large wooden structure called Mechanics Hall. Here are shops, the office of the *Homer Republican* newspaper, six apartments, and the first studio of an aspiring, fifteen-year-old portraitist named Frank Carpenter. This is the commercial hub of the Village in the nineteenth century, and west of the Hall is the First Baptist Church.

[Mechanics Hall was destroyed by a fire. In its place, in 1893, the Baptists built a house of worship from local bricks in the Richardson Romanesque Style popular in that era. In the twenty-first century, the Baptists built a larger, more modern church on Route 281, and this became the Homer Center for the Arts, which showcases ever-changing artwork in a gallery and performances by internationally acclaimed vocalists and musicians in the former sanctuary. Arlo Guthrie and Judy Collins have entertained here. The attached building on Main Street is "The Fountain House," once the parsonage of a much-respected Baptist minister. At this writing, the Director for the Center for the Arts, Dan Hayes, has office space here, and a "visitor's center" is proposed to be created here with local artifacts and information about Historic Homer, walking tours, and the "Heritage Byway" that proceeds West.]

If the coach and its occupants are in no great hurry, it would be a good idea for us to take in the nearby Green. The Homer Green is part of Lot No. 45 of the Military Tract. Originally, it was a New England-style "Common," a place for the early inhabitants—six families by 1793, mostly from Massachusetts—to graze their livestock. Then, a village ordinance was passed in the 1830s banning cattle, sheep, horses, geese, and swine from running at large on the Common. The fine was set at one dollar.

The first settlers held church services down by the river in Asa White's gristmill [behind the present Town Hall, where ruins of Darby's Mill are still visible]. In 1799, they formed The First Religious Society of the Town of Homer, and in 1805 they were deeded the Common for purposes of worship and education, which has been the norm along the periphery ever since. The first school, built in 1801, was located on the north side of the Green and was also used for worship until it was moved to a spot back on South Main Street across from "The Hedges." [The First Religious Society still exists, and it still owns the Green. Therefore, there is a Christmas Nativity Scene on this very public spot every year.] During the Civil War, the civic-minded Paris Barber of Homer headed up efforts to replant trees on the Common to make it more like a park, though the farmers complained about how difficult it had been to clear the trees for grazing in the first place.

A large hotel [where the fire station is now] with a tavern is a busy establishment on Main Street, as is the National Hotel at the other end of Main Street [where the Town Hall is now]. Main Street [now Route 11] is part of the turnpike that runs north to Syracuse. The village has about four taverns, kept busy by travelers, the local farmers, and the hard-working men employed at the Brockway Carriage Factory that was just incorporated last year [1875].

The Green has been the site of gatherings of the G.A.R., or Grand Army of the Republic. A local Civil War hero, Sgt. Llewellyn P. Norton of Company L, 10th New York Cavalry, charged, on horseback, a Confederate artillery position and captured two Rebels and a fieldpiece. For this action he is to be awarded the Congressional Medal of Honor. [The actual presentation, however, was not made until 1888. Norton returned to Homer, sold insurance, and lived in a house on Grove Street.]

At the far northwest corner is the oldest structure on the Green, the Episcopal Church [now it is "The Little White Community Center" and is owned by the Village for use by The Landmark Society and The Homer Center for the Arts]. The white clapboard structure was built in 1832, at a cost of $3,300. The co-founder and first president of Cornell University, Andrew Dickson White, was baptized here in November of 1835. His grandfather, Asa White, owner of the local gristmill, built the oldest house in Homer, a saltbox style house, in 1799. It was moved in 1822 to Clinton Street [and is still there but clad in modern siding and with an annex].

South of the church is the Homer Academy. Built in 1819, it was first called the Cortland Academy. This is a very progressive, co-educational school, having admitted females as early as 1822. Students from far and near attend. The boarding of students by local families is a significant part of the local economy. Homer's native-son, Francis Bicknell Carpenter, born in 1830, attended for one semester in the 1840s, and Stoddard attended, as well.

[There has been a state-approved school located on the Green since the charter of 1819. The school has gone by different names through history, and reconstruction has occurred after each of three fires. The most recent was in 1945. Miraculously, each time, the eleven portraits of the early Academy Trustees done by Carpenter managed to survive. Today, the Homer Central School District owns the eleven paintings—one of the largest collections of work by Carpenter in the world. And there are over twenty other portraits by Carpenter at other institutions surrounding this Green. The current school is the Homer Elementary building for grades K–2. The Academy school bell of 1893 over the front entrance is electronically rung every school day at 8:30 am and on the Fourth of July.]

South of the school is the church, with a tall spire, that is affiliated with The First Religious Society. This is the Congregational Church. The first Congregational Church was a wooden structure built here in 1805, using the architectural plans of Asher Benjamin. It was used for school commencements because it could accommodate a big gathering. The students somewhat irreverently nicknamed it "God's Old Barn." This brick edifice was built during the Civil War and dedicated just five days after the Battle at Gettysburg. Five days after that the funeral was held here for its Superintendent of the Sabbath School, Private William Walllace Carpenter, brother of Francis Carpenter, the painter. William was mortally wounded at Gettysburg. His last written words from a hospital in New York were: "Tell the children of the Sabbath School to meet me in Heaven." [Later, Carpenter painted his brother's portrait, which graces a wall of the church parlor.]

In 1821, an influential pastor came to the church. The Reverend John Keep, affectionately known as "Father Keep," was a social reformer. The congregation accepted all his views at first. [They supported the idea of education for girls and temperance and public censure of those who failed to attend church on the Sabbath, but he ran into trouble when he joined the abolition movement in 1832 and called for the emancipation of slaves in the Southern states. The local farmers and merchants feared that taking an anti-slavery position would jeopardize their lucrative trade relationship with folks in the slave-owning state of Maryland. Barrels of pork and firkins of butter were sent by flatboats down the Tioughnioga River and ultimately ended up at Baltimore, Maryland. In 1833, economic conservatism trumped political liberalism, and a change in pastors was deemed appropriate . . . and Father Keep concurred. Joining other abolitionists in Ohio, he helped to found the co-educational Oberlin College, and in 1835 he cast the vote that determined that admission should be regularly open to all "irrespective of color." He was invited back to Homer for the dedication of this church. He attended but did not give the sermon. The dedication committee thought it was safer to confine the old radical firebrand to the prayer of dedication. [In 1901, when the church celebrated its centennial, the Homer Academy graduate and Yale theologian, Reverend Theodore Munger, spoke of Keep as "the most effective citizen the town has known" and as a man who was "at least half a century ahead of his day." One of Carpenter's Trustee Paintings is that of Father Keep. The church was gutted by fire in 1970 but restored at great expense.]

The Methodist Church at the southwest corner of the Green was built in 1841. Before that, the faithful used a one-room schoolhouse on this site. One of Homer's earliest teachers, Adin Webb of Connecticut, offered instruction here. [The present church of gray stone was constructed in 1912, as the congregation increased in size and wealth.]

February 13, 2014

THE COACH HEADS WESTWARD ON THE TURNPIKE

Now, the coach lurches forward and proceeds smartly west [on Cayuga Street] past some homes but mostly through farmland owned by the late Jedediah Barber. Barber died a couple months ago [in 1876] and was best known locally as "Uncle Jed" and as the proprietor of The Great Western, a three-story emporium of brick built in 1863 on Main Street to replace the wooden store that burned in 1856. [The Walmart of nineteenth century Central New York still stands with shops on the ground floor and newly constructed, modern apartments on the second floor and on the third floor's former Keator Opera House.]

The coach passes over the tracks of the railroad from Syracuse to Binghamton. Bringing the train through Homer was one of Jedediah Barber's business ventures, along with a bank on Main Street [the building still stands north of the Barber Block].

When the coach reaches the foot of West Hill and the intersection of West Road [now Route 281], we passengers can see Glenwood Cemetery on the left. This is a park-like cemetery designed by Paris Barber during the recent Civil War. [The Barbers, David Hannum, Carpenters, and other Homer notables are buried here.] If we took the country lane that is West Road to the north, it would take us past an Underground Railroad "station" from the pre-Civil War era located at the corner of West Road and Cold Brook Road. Soon after, we would arrive at the little hamlet of Little York, near the kettle lake of the same name on the northern edge of the township. What a great spot for swimming, fishing, and boating on a day like today, but our destination is to Cayuga Lake today.

Our coach begins the arduous climb up the hill past O. B. Andrews' Rock Springs Cheese Factory on the right where 366 cheeses sell for six cents per pound [gone now; the house up the hill from the gas station/car wash is the site]. As we slowly ascend, we might do well to recall that in the early years of the Towns of Central New York, special meetings occurred for the purpose of laying out the roads in the town. The Board was almost entirely focused on dividing the Town into Road Districts and establishing the boundaries of "Publick Roads." Trails through the forests and swamps would become designated roads noted in the Minutes. A marking point for delineating one such road in 1797 was simply "a yellow birch tree." The designated direction of a road could be appealed. A panel of three judges made the final decision. The town's "commissioners of highways" laid out the roads, directed repairs, and constructed bridges. Each road district had a "pathmaster" who supervised road maintenance and had the power to annually assess each male resident several days of labor on the road. The records list their names and the number of days assessed. Clearing the woodlands and maintaining the dirt roads, especially after the damages of storms, was crucial to this growing agrarian region in the center of the state.

The next portion of road between Homer and Genoa was originally just a blazed trail called the Homer Road until it was chartered [it is believed] as a turnpike on April 12, 1816. When this turnpike was extended to King Ferry, the whole stretch from Homer to King Ferry became part of the State's turnpike system. It was incorporated in 1817 as the Fifth Great Western Turnpike, and merchant Barber named his emporium "The Great Western" after the innovative artery. Though we refer to the road in this centennial year of our nation as "the turnpike," it ceased to be a roadway with toll gates in the late 1820s. At that time the fees charged were deemed to be insufficient to keep the roads in repair.

As the coach finally arrives at the summit of West Hill in the town of Homer, the weary and slightly lathered horses need to rest. It is hard to imagine what Amos Todd and the Beebes thought when they first arrived at this elevated site in 1792. This was Lot No. 42 which they purchased from a Revolutionary War veteran, cleared, and farmed [as indicated by a NYS historical marker today on the south side of the road].

Taverns along the way provide respite for weary travelers like us and for the strong-hearted steeds that pull the stagecoaches over hilly terrain and rutty, dirt roads. One such tavern is Wright's on West Hill, up past the Todd and Beebe Farm, on the right. Ideally situated after an exhausting climb, James Wright's tavern was the first tavern in the county. Initially a log house, the establishment is now a frame house. The place does a thriving business but has limited accommodations for overnight guests. [It is now part of the home of Dean St. John.] Wright was one of the original stockholders in the Fifth Great Western Turnpike Corporation. [Appropriately, Homer Hops brewery and tasting room is nearby today to slack the thirst of those traveling along the old turnpike.] From here it is onward and westward. Shortly, we pass the small Homer West Hill Cemetery and then cross the line into the southeast corner of Cayuga County, which detached from Onondaga County in 1799.

May 8, 2014

GRANDDAUGHTER OF WILLIAM O. STODDARD DIED IN JANUARY

Eleanor H. Stoddard, descendant of Homer native-son William Osborn Stoddard, passed in early January. She visited Homer at least twice. The last occasion was in May of 2009 when she and other descendants of William O. Stoddard came for "Homer's Celebration of Lincoln in Paint and Print," which she enjoyed enormously. She appreciated the recognition given to her late grandfather and the invitation extended to her by the community to participate. She was a remarkable woman, as evidenced by her obituary below.

ELEANOR H. STODDARD, EDITOR

In *Washington Post* of January 30, 2014

Eleanor H. Stoddard, an editor for the National Science Foundation for nearly 30 years, died Jan. 7 at Chevy Chase House, an assisted living community in the District. She was 92.

The cause was complications from a stroke, said her goddaughter, Nardi Hobler.

Miss Stoddard, who was a longtime Chevy Chase resident, joined the National Science Foundation as an editor in 1955. During her tenure, she helped prepare "The Funding of Social Knowledge Production and Application: A Survey of Federal Agencies," a study published by the National Research Council.

Earlier in her career, she was a writer at *Time* magazine and an advertising copywriter for *U.S. News and World Report*. She also worked in the promotions department of the American Chemical Society.

After her retirement in 1983, she produced an oral history interview project focused on women who had served in or with the military during World War II. The tapes and transcripts of her interviews are archived at California State University at Long Beach.

She also wrote the 2006 book "Fearless Presence: The Story of Lt. Col. Nola Forrest, Who Led the Army Nurses Through Heat, Rain, Mud, and Enemy Fire in World War II."

Eleanor Holden Stoddard was born in Summit, N.J., and grew up in Madison, N.J. Her grandfather was William O. Stoddard [born at 5 Albany Street, Homer], one of Abraham Lincoln's White House secretaries. She was a 1942 economics graduate of Vassar College in Poughkeepsie, N.Y., where she was senior class president.

Miss Stoddard was a member of the Potomac Appalachian Trail Club and tutored D.C. inner-city youth and adults. She moved to Chevy Chase House in 2012.

She had no immediate survivors.

—Megan McDonough

Those in Homer who were fortunate to have met Eleanor may have been cognizant that shaking her hand meant that you were shaking the hand that shook the hand that shook *the hand* of President Abraham Lincoln. One was not far removed at all from the Great Emancipator.

May 22, 2014

HARRY CLARKE OSTRANDER: THE ADVENTUROUS TRAVELER BEHIND THE MAGIC LANTERN SHOWS

In section 15 of Glenwood Cemetery there is an unpretentious stone engraved with the name of Harry Clarke Ostrander, along with the year of his birth and the year of his death. In his late 80s, Harry had come to live out his last days with his niece, Florence Armitage Bundy, in the village of Homer. His niece's children loved the stories he would tell and the odd hand-tinted slides he would project onto a white bed sheet via a device he called his "magic lantern." They were enthralled. And why not? Uncle Harry was very much an adventure-loving citizen of the world, having in his lifetime traveled to five continents, having made three around-the-world trips, and having visited China five times. And now, of all places, he was in their living room in Homer in 1957 showing images of exotic places.

Harry Ostrander's adventurous life had commenced in 1869 in Clyde, NY. He was the oldest of six children born to Henry and Alla Waterbury Ostrander. The Ostranders moved to Waterloo, NY, where Harry was schooled and showed an interest in oratory and art. After high school, he briefly studied art at the prestigious Cooper Institute in New York City.

In August of 1893, Harry went to Chicago for three weeks to take in the World's Fair. There, he came down with the "travel bug," which he indulged by traveling around the United States. His sister Jesse (pronounced Jess-ee) developed the photographs he took. In 1901 he took an 8-month trip outside the US. His itinerary included England, France, Spain, Holland, Germany, Italy, Greece, Algeria, Morocco, Palestine, and a visit to Egypt to see friends he had made at the Chicago World's Fair. With a camera in tow, he took extensive photographs of his journey.

By 1908, Yonkers, NY, was his home base from which he wrote articles for magazines and newspapers in California about his travels through the States, Mexico, and Cuba. In 1911, he sailed out of New York for a five-month trip around the world by tramp steamers. This trip took in Gibraltar, Algeria, Tunis, Morocco, Sicily, Egypt, Turkey, Arabia, India, Ceylon, Java, Burma, Singapore, the Malay States, Thailand, Vietnam, China (arriving two months before the Chinese Revolution), Japan, Honolulu, San Francisco, and back to New York.

Upon his return to the States, he gave his first lecture to a women's club in Trenton, NJ. The young, dashing, charming, and gifted storyteller was an immediate sensation. For the rest of his life, he traveled in the summer and lectured through the winter. While lecturing he projected his hand-tinted glass slides with "the magic lantern," or stereopticon. His most popular lectures had these titles: "Around the World in Ninety Minutes," "Mexico, the Egypt of the New World," and "Religions of the Orient." A person who attended his "China and Japan" show in 1914 wrote this: "Harry C. Ostrander's travel talks are growing rapidly in public favor. . . . Few lecturers who have come to Washington have had so artistic a series of photographs." In the 1920s, Harry earned passage on ocean liners by giving shipboard lectures with illustrations of the places to be visited. He now had over 70 lecture topics with slides to use at colleges and museums.

In 1929 he took six months to make 21 different voyages on 20 different ships. He returned with 2,500 photographs taken in 20 different countries. The years of the Great Depression were hard on Harry. Bookings for his travelogues declined and he lost many of his negatives to a fire. He began selling photos to magazines such as Travel and National Geographic. Still, he managed to travel every summer. In 1935, the Dutch government paid him to photograph throughout the Dutch East Indies.

While Harry had steady clients well into the 1940s, his hand-painted glass slides had trouble competing with new technology. In an age of film travelogues, audiences found his slides to be "quaint." In 1945, at the age of 76, he made an eight-country tour of South America. Then, in 1950, at the age of 81, he made one more trip to China. The trip would be his last.

He eventually came to Homer to live out his remaining days with his niece, Florence Armitage Bundy, the youngest daughter of his sister Jesse. The adult Bundy children today have vivid memories of an elderly man who delighted them as children by taking out his "magic lantern" and showing them intriguing, colorful images of faraway places—a different country every evening.

Harry Ostrander died in 1957 at the age of 88, not knowing that in 2009 his images would delight Chinese audiences who eagerly came to see an exhibition of his photographic legacy in Kunming, China, courtesy of the Schenectady Museum to whom the Bundy Family had donated crates of Uncle Harry's glass slides.

Harry's story is one of several recalled during a walking tour of "Glenwood: The Cemetery Paris Built." Contact Kathy Beardsley to arrange for your family or group to enjoy this informative tour.

Appreciation is extended to Gail Bundy for making the material about her great-uncle available for this article.

June 5, 2014

[*Note: In lieu of my column, the following piece was run on the front page.*]

MARTIN SWEENEY ADDRESSES GROUP AT MEMORIAL DAY CEREMONIES

Editor's Note: Due to technical problems, some of the participants at the May 26 Memorial Day ceremonies in Glenwood Cemetery could not hear Mr. Sweeney's comments. We feel that the comments are of enough significance to be printed here.

Thank you, Mike [McDermott], and thank you for the invitation to participate in this longstanding tradition we call Memorial Day.

Folks, we are now well into the nation's observance of the Sesquicentennial of the American Civil War. From 2011 through 2015, we note what happened 150 years ago. It was 150 years ago this past May 13th when Pvt. William Christman of Pennsylvania was the first to be laid to rest at what was to be designated as Arlington Military Cemetery. And would you believe that after 150 years, the government is still paying for that conflict? Each month, 84-year-old Irene Triplett of Wilkesboro, North Carolina, collects $73.13 from the Department of Veterans Affairs. It is a pension payment for her father's military service in, yes, the Civil War. Private Mose Triplett married so late in life to a woman so young that their daughter is alive today—the last child of any Civil War veteran on the VA benefits rolls.

It was 150 years ago today—May 26, 1864—that Union forces were preparing for the next day's battle at Pickett's Mill, northwest of Atlanta, Georgia. Casualties would be in the extreme. In Washington, DC, the Commander-in-Chief and President, Abraham Lincoln, signed a document creating the territory of Montana out West. And in the state dining room of the White House, Homer—born Francis B. Carpenter was four months into a six-month project. The 34-year-old artist was painting on canvas the scene of President Lincoln announcing to his Cabinet in 1862 that the War to preserve the Union was to have an additional reason to be waged: freedom—freedom for the slaves. Two days later, on May 28th, 1864, four men from this community came by to see firsthand how the 9 foot by 14-foot painting was progressing. One of the four men was Carpenter's 64-year-old father, Asaph Carpenter. Asaph had always opposed slavery, and now he reveled in his son's painting of the scene of moral victory over slavery. But it would require eleven more months of military struggle to make that victory a reality, and the Commander-in-Chief would pay a fearful price himself.

Young men from Homer fought and died in that war. They are buried here in this park-like cemetery which Homer's Paris Barber designed in 1863 while the war was being fought.

150 years ago, Homer's Asaph Carpenter had already lost a son to the war. Twenty-seven-year-old Private William Wallace Carpenter, Superintendent of the Sabbath School for the Congregationalists, died in 1863 in a New York City hospital from wounds sustained at Gettysburg. On a day in July, while he was buried in the upper southwest corner, the funerals of Capt. George A. Adams and Private Morris I. Shattuck were held in Homer. They were members of William Carpenter's regiment. Francis Carpenter recorded only this in his diary that day: "a solemn time for Homer."

Then, there are the three Babcock brothers of Homer. Two of them died in Civil War battles and are buried here. The third has a monument here, but he is not buried here. He was interred where he died—in the infamous prison camp at Andersonville, Georgia—making three empty chairs at the family table. What a price for one Homer family to pay!

These local fallen heroes are not forgotten and should not be forgotten. Their graves and those of countless others from our community who served in the many wars fought abroad since the Civil War are decorated with American flags. Our Mike McDermott personally sees that flags are placed in Scott, East Homer, Little York, Cold Brook, West Hill, Atwater, and some at St. Mary's. Flags are placed here each May by Boy Scouts and Cub Scouts sponsored by the local American Legion post. That's 1,100 flags! Why? Why do we bother? Why do we encourage our youngsters to place spring flowers upon these graves? Why do we continue to honor those who fought and died in uniform years and years ago? That was then; we live in the now.

The fact that we have set aside a day annually to memorialize our fallen soldiers speaks volumes about us, the living, and what we value. We value our fallen soldiers and remember them for what they valued. In many cases, but not all, they valued freedom. They fought and died in the Civil War so that we might continue to be free to have "a government of the people, by the people, and for the people." They fought that there might be "a new birth of freedom" for all—regardless of the color of that four millimeters of superficial surface tissue we call "skin."

Is that so much different from the reason U. S. doughboys entered World War I 100 years ago this July 28th—to allow Europe to be free to practice democracy? Is that so much different from the reason G.I.s fought in WWII, Korea, and Vietnam—to free others from the murderous grip of totalitarianism? Is that so much different from the reason we have waged an ongoing war against international terrorism since September 11, 2001? To guarantee Freedom? Freedom for ourselves and freedom for others?

Freedom. Freedom is not something you can hold in your hand, like a credit card. It is like the wind; you cannot see it, but you can see its effects. It is not tangible like land or water or precious stones. But it is precious. It does exact a cost. It has a price. History reveals that freedom does give direction and meaning to the lives of Americans. History shows that freedom has been something worth living for and worth dying for. In November, we observe Veterans Day. We honor all men and women, living and dead, who wore the uniform. But it is in late May when communities across the land parade down their streets to their cemeteries to remember those in uniform who were sacrificed upon the altar of freedom.

Sadly, the observance of Memorial Day has diminished over recent years. It seems many Americans nowadays have forgotten the meaning and traditions of Memorial Day. At many cemeteries, the graves of the fallen are increasingly ignored, neglected. People don't bother to display the flag. Some communities have not held a parade in decades, but that is not the case here in Homer. Many feel that when Congress made the day into a three-day weekend with the National Holiday Act of 1971, it made it all the easier for people to be distracted from the real spirit and meaning of the day. It has tended to be merely seen as the start of summer. No doubt, this has contributed greatly to the general public's nonchalant observance of Memorial Day.

But therein we find the wonderful irony. We have no government forcing us to observe Memorial Day. We have a choice. We have freedom. We celebrate that freedom—a freedom that was purchased at a supreme cost over the past 150 years and earlier. Let us continue to teach our children; let us choose to never forget.

June 19, 2014

HOW DID THE HEALTH CAMP ROAD RECEIVE ITS NAME?

The Health Camp Road connects Routes 13 and 11along the hills in the Town of Homer. It has an interesting name. In late February, John W. Talbot, a member of the Homer Central School Class of 1962 who now resides in Waterloo, NY, contacted me about the origins of the road's name. He knew that a classmate of his, Donna Greenwood-Balfe, lived in what was called "the Health Camp" on Health Camp Road with her parents Lloyd and Eunice Greenwood, but he was curious about the camp's purpose. He wanted to know if it had been a clinic, orphanage, detention home, or something else. Drawing a blank and finding nothing in the Town's archives, I directed John to contact the always reliable Cortland County Historical Society. In short order, John and the Society's capable Director, Mindy Leisenring, produced the needed information.

According to an article published in the October 25, 1945, issue of *The Syracuse Herald Journal*, the camp was known as the Far View Camp. It was established in the 1920s under the auspices of what was then the State Committee on Tuberculosis and Public Health, and it was supervised by the New York State Department of Social Welfare. It was completely funded by money derived from the Christmas Seal Campaign, which today is a major fundraiser of The American Lung Association.

The Far View Camp, overlooking Homer Valley, operated every summer, providing "an eight-week health building program for 50 underprivileged children between the ages of six and 12" from Cortland County. Selection of the campers was made by the county health department and the nurses of the public schools in the county. The camp's staff consisted of a superintendent, a trained nurse, four camp counselors, and a cook. In the early years that staff may have been provided by the Cortland Normal School, the genesis of today's S.U.N.Y. College at Cortland.

Following an inspection of the camp in August of 1945, Margaret F. Williams, the State's senior social worker and advocate for child welfare, reported that the camp was "a worthwhile and needed service to a group of children of this county." That group was apparently those children deemed in need of gaining weight. This is quite the opposite of some camps today that are focused on curbing obesity in children.

In the fall of 1945, the camp was added to the list of agencies that was to draw funds from the County Community Chest, the forerunner of today's United Way. Between November 5 and 15, 1945, the Community Chest of Cortland County hoped to reach its goal of collecting $117,150 from local businesses and workers.

In 1953, Far View Camp ceased its operation and the property was auctioned off to Clifford Kimberly of McGraw and has served as a private residence since. And that is how the road running near the former "health camp" derived its name.

December 4, 2014

MEMORIES OF MOROTAI, MALARIA, AND MATSUDA

A while back, I was provided a two-page, undated document that had been typewritten by the man who had been my barber in my youth, the affable, ever smiling "Bill" Dillon. I found it to be an interesting description of his experience in the military during World War II, of which I had never heard him talk. It seems to be a letter to another veteran. With his permission, it is shared here. This is the first of two installments.

Schuyler (Bill) Dillon, 32737897, 14 Warren St., Homer, N.Y.
Vol. for draft January 22, 1943
Active duty January 29, 1943
Basic training at Kearns, Utah
Kearns, Utah to Hammer Field, Calif.
Fort Logan back to Hammer Field
Hammer Field to Camp Pinedale, Calif.

I was assigned to the 515th Hdqtrs. Unit at Pinedale as a Baseball player for the Post team. I signed up as a replacement for the 7th Radio Sq. with a friend of mine, Ed Schlechter, who also worked in Hdqtrs. We came home for a 30 day furlough and on our return I was assigned to Hdqtrs. Supply under Sgt. Perkins and Ed went to Hdqtrs. Office as a clerk. I think at the time the Det. Teams were out on maneuvers but shortly after were alerted to leave. We didn't have much time to get acquainted so not too many knew us. I remember hearing that most of the members of the teams had been together for quite some time, radio schools, training, etc.

The POE, boat ride, submarine alert, two meals a day, the poor guys seasick, and the chow are treasured memories today, but at the time something else. After our short stop at Finschhafen [a town and port in eastern Papua New

Guinea, in southwestern Pacific Ocean] then on to Hollandia [a town on the northern coast of New Guinea] I settled in with Hdqtrs. Supply. I don't remember but I'm sure your different teams had been already sent out to the islands. Not too long after our arrival at Hollandia Sgt. Perkins told me to pack up as I was being sent to Det. #3 to replace your supply Sgt., a guy by the name of Purcell. Maybe you remember him. Since this was my first plane ride, it is one I'll always remember: a C-46 cargo plane loaded with equipment, metal landing strip, just clearing the jungle on takeoff, no parachutes (I wouldn't jump anyway), and a landing at Morotai [one of Indonesia's northernmost islands]. I couldn't seem to recognize anyone I really knew in your outfit but soon met Suetsuki Toyofuku, Oscar our cook, and also some of the body-builders. I remember at one time Lt. Webb decided the men needed more exercise and wanted everybody to play volleyball. About six of us who refused had to take machetes and cut back the jungle around our area. I have a few pictures of this. I picked up Malaria for the first time at Morotai and was sent to the hospital with a Matsuda I think. I remember how bad he looked. I guess I was the same; it knocked the hell out of me. I lost quite a lot of weight and weaker than a wet cat but was glad when they let me come back to camp. I had a couple more relapses while there but didn't go to the hospital again. When we were in Leyte [an island in the Visayas group of the Philippines] waiting to come home I got it real bad but stayed in the tent and knocked it out myself. Bad stuff

December 18, 2014

THIS IS THE SECOND OF TWO INSTALLMENTS ON BILL DILLON'S YEARS IN THE SERVICE.

I came home on an aircraft carrier—a nice trip and quite a change from the one we went over on. I was at Camp Stoneman [a United States Army military facility located in Pittsburg, California, which served as a major staging area for the Army in World War II and the Korean War] I think for a day or two. Then my name came up for a train ride to Fort Monmouth, N.J. After we received our discharges about four or five of us went out on the town for one last fling. The next morning we all split up to go our separate ways, all agreeing to write, etc. I do hear from Schlechter and also Suey Toyofuku about once a year at Christmas time but nobody else. I was glad to see the old home town but still wouldn't give up those three years of experience for anything.

There were quite a few of my friends home already from the service. They would meet in my Dad's Restaurant every day and welcome the newest one out, usually starting with coffee in the morning and changing later on. Lots of parties.

I tried bartending for my Dad again. I found out I still would rather do something else. So I went to work for the Highway Dept. That lasted until the fall of 1946 when my barber friend talked me into being a barber with him. In the spring of 1947 I bought the shop, he left for Florida, and I also got married. I had a very good business for 26 years, finally selling out in 1972 and taking a job at Cortland State University as a Maintenance Supervisor where I'm at today [as of the time of Bill's writing]. In this past period of time we have had 4 children—three boys and one girl—and now two grandchildren—both boys. My wife and all the children have been very fortunate health wise. The two older boys are married, my daughter is in college, and one boy is in high school. I have also been lucky—no health problems except for a little grey hair and the weight is about the same as when I was in the service but it must be softer.

I personally think the service is a great experience. I know there are many things I will always remember—good times and bad. You may do whatever you wish with this. I would be glad to pay my share of any expenses and would appreciate any information on a reunion if one is planned.

Glad to hear from you. Good luck.

Bill

Chapter 5

Articles of 2015

January 1, 2015

WHEN A CIRCUS CAME TO TOWN IN 1935

At the time of the passing of Charlie R. "Jug" Crosley of Carroway Hill Road, Homer, in 2012, the following news articles were brought to my attention. The articles reported an event involving a twelve-year-old Crosley and some other Homer lads. There is something about these news clippings from the summer of 1935 that makes one nostalgic and leaves one wondering if youngsters in the age of the Internet and videogames still play outdoors, explore Nature, and creatively enjoy the realm of the imagination.

The first is a one-paragraph announcement:

Boys Preparing Circus
For Friday, Saturday

Arthur Blanden, Donald Huttleston and Charles Crosley are having a circus at the Huttleston home, 6 South William Street, on Friday and Saturday of this week and great preparations were being made for the event which is attracting attention of boys and girls throughout the village. The performances start promptly at 2.

The event took place on August 2 and was found to be as worthy of coverage by the local newspaper the following day as one of Homer's old traveling circus shows managed by Sig Sautelle:

Boys Put 'Big Top' to Shame
With Rare Circus Stunts
Three Homer Youths Show Freaks in Back
Yard Exhibition—Crowd Attends

Homer, Aug.3: A circus was given yesterday afternoon by three Homer boys before a series of audiences which totaled 60 persons, many of them adults. Donald Huttleston, in whose back yard the circus was given, Arthur Blanden and Charles Crosley, were barkers, side-show men and performers. They were so pleased with yesterday's turnout that they repeated the show today.

Persons who went into the side show to see the freaks shouted "fake" when the exhibit of a "horse flying through glass" developed to be a horse fly in a glass tumbler. Crosley worked this Barnum act on the unsuspecting neighborhood.

On exhibition were collections of moths, shells, birds' eggs from 20 species, fossils, nests, insects, and in the live collection, a goat, Guinea pig, rabbits, bantam chickens, a 36-inch milk snake, salamanders, deer mice, native fish, water bugs and frogs.

The acts by the trio included a snake charming exhibition by Blanden, a clown act, and as a finale, a hula hula dance, in which the youths were togged out in skirts made of cat tail reeds and necklaces of maple leaves.

The boys had borrowed rugs to make side walls for their tent and had also borrowed benches used on the village green for the comfort of the spectators. It was certainly worth the price asked, all declared. The boys collected two cents for the main show and one cent for the side shows.

February 26, 2015

WHEN IZZY AND MOE CAME TO HOMER

On February 14, 1922, a man walked into the David Harum Hotel on Main Street in Homer [where the fire station is now] and presented himself to the man behind the bar, Harry Cortright. He introduced himself to Cortright as a traveling tobacco salesman. He said he had some fine cigars for sale at a reasonable price. Being of an affable nature and genial in conversation, the salesman was able to convince Cortright to agree to purchase an allotment of cigars that would be delivered at a later date. To seal the deal, the salesman offered to buy drinks, and Cortright produced the requested libation.

What Cortright did not know was that this was no salesman. This was Prohibition Agent No. 1, Isidore Einstein, a federal agent sworn to enforce the 18th Amendment that deemed the manufacture, transportation, and sale of alcohol to be illegal effective January 17, 1920. By selling liquor to Einstein, Cortright had committed a crime.

The next day, Einstein reappeared at the David Harum Hotel. With him was his partner and fellow agent, Moe Smith. The pair had obtained a search and seizures warrant from U.S. Commissioner Wickham of Binghamton, and they had local law enforcement personnel with them. Stepping behind the bar, all they could find was a solitary pint of liquor. They then proceeded to conduct a thorough search of the premises, which included the upstairs. There the pair came upon a room with a placard on the door. The placard read "Quarantine for Influenza." Unfazed, the pair ordered Cortright to open the door. He refused. So, the pair broke it down. "Inside was enough 'evidence' to convict a few hundred," Einstein later told reporters.

Before the day was over, based upon a lead they were provided, the pair visited the Central Tire store on Port Watson Street in the city of Cortland. Behind a pile of tires and inside some of them, they found a large quantity of liquor. The pair claimed the store had been a distribution center for booze for some time. As a result of the two raids in Cortland County, three men were arrested and set to appear before United States Commissioner Wickham in Binghamton on Thursday, Feb. 23, 1922.

District Attorney Albert Haskell, Jr. (whose scrapbook contains news clippings about this event) was enthusiastic about the success of these raids and complimented Einstein and Smith for their accomplishment. They, in turn, spoke highly of Haskell's efforts in the operation. Soon after Haskell's recent election to the position of DA, the press had reported: "The district attorney is determined to stop the sale of intoxicants both in public places and in private houses and says he will spare neither time, pains nor money to accomplish that end. He feels that a good start has been made." Haskell had conducted a few successful raids earlier in the south and east ends of the City of Cortland, and the newspaper went on to report that "All beverages seized are stored in the basement at the court house, which smells like a brewery, and are under lock and key." Apparently, Haskell's efforts at law enforcement had come to require the use of two of history's most famous enforcers of Prohibition.

Working under the direction of Chief Field Agent John S. Parsons of Oswego and in conjunction with DA Haskell, Einstein and Smith arrived in Syracuse by train and then swept down upon Cortland. Without prior announcement of their arrival in the county, even to other local law enforcement officers, Einstein and Smith were able to use the element of surprise to their advantage. By the time of these two raids, Einstein and Smith, known in the popular press as "Izzy and Moe," had become household names. Mere mention of their names put fear and a healthy respect for the eighteenth amendment in the hearts of men and women engaged in bootlegging. On a train ride from Monticello to Port Jervis, the pair were recognized, and upon arrival at Port Jervis, the engineer, in true Paul Revere fashion, hopped off and ran from gin mill to gin mill yelling, "They're coming. Izzy and Moe is [sic] coming!"

By early 1922 the agents were well on their way to becoming famous for using guile and jovial geniality to best the bootleggers in sensational operations. With well over 1,800 arrests and convictions to their credit, Izzy and Moe kept coming across new challenges. Even they had to smile about the novel way Homer and Cortland proprietors had tried to conceal their booze.

"Few bootleggers have shown the brains evidenced by the proprietors of 'David Harum's' place in hiding the stuff," declared Izzy to a reporter. "It was the first time we've been faced with a quarantine sign, duly authorized by the board of health. I've never seen liquor quarantined before," he added, smiling. "Well, Izzy, bootleggers seldom put the stuff in automobile tires, notwithstanding the movies," Moe interrupted, "and that's what we found at Cortland."

The ratification in 1919 of the amendment to establish Prohibition required federal and local police forces to recruit new members rapidly in order to enforce the law. With no background in law enforcement, but speaking several languages (Yiddish, Hungarian, German, Polish, with a little Russian, French, Spanish and Italian) in addition to English, Izzy Einstein, a 1901 immigrant from Galicia, signed up as Prohibition Agent No. 1. In a short time, he invited his friend Moe Smith to join him as a partner. Though both were personally indifferent to temperance, they felt the law must be upheld, no matter how hard it was to enforce. Besides, it was good employment, and they were good at it. According to the February 28, 1938 issue of *Time,* in their joint career they made 4,932 arrests, of which 95 percent (around 4,680) gained convictions. They confiscated 5 million gallons of liquor, worth an estimated $15 million, and thousands of bartenders, bootleggers and speakeasy owners were sentenced to jail.

In late 1925, Izzy and Moe were "laid off" in a reorganization of the bureau of enforcement. A report in *Time* magazine suggested they had attracted more publicity than wanted by the new, resentful political appointee heading the bureau, although the press and public loved the duo. By 1930, both men had moved on and were working as successful insurance salesmen.

Izzy died in 1938 after a leg amputation for diabetes, and Moe died on Dec. 16, 1960. The New York *Herald Tribune* called them "the only prohibition agents whom the public liked." "Their exploits and disguises touched America's funny bone," stated the paper. To root out bootleggers, they posed as vegetable vendors, conductors, churchgoers, and grave diggers. They raided stills in cemeteries, basements, garages, and once in the backroom of a church.

Izzy, wearing a fake goatee and posing as a delegate from Kentucky, and Moe, wearing a cowboy hat and posing as a delegate from Montana, even infiltrated the 1924 Democratic National Convention in the old Madison Square Garden in search of illegal alcohol. They came up short. Only soda pop was available. One sting operation involved the pair crawling up onto the beach at Coney Island, shivering with cold and demanding of a suspect enough stimulant to save their lives. Another sting had the two coming forth from a car barn and informing a suspected bootlegger that they had nearly frozen to death in the line of duty during the long, cold night and pathetically inquiring if a little alcohol might not be had to revive them. When the liquor was provided, the pair provided another arrest to record.

Moe claimed that the accounts of their disguises were overdone by the press. In a 1933 interview, he said, "We didn't disguise none. If we went to a golf club to make a pinch, and put on golf knickers, the papers said we were disguised." The real agents looked nothing like the G-men in the movies. Moe looked more like an affable, prosperous automobile salesman. Izzy, in need of a shave, tended to be scruffier in his sartorial appearance, with buttons missing on his vest. Both were a bit overweight and gave no outward sign of being physically fit federal agents. And neither ever carried a firearm, not even during arrests.

Nevertheless, the successes of Izzy and Moe became legendary. The two who passed through Homer but once were described in a 1925 *Time* article as having experienced thrilling adventures comparable to those experienced by Robin Hood "—adventures as thrilling as those of Sir Launcelot, as those of Richard Cœur de Lion, as those of Don Quixote de la Mancha."

March 12, 2015

THE HOMER OF AMELIA JENKS BLOOMER

The great nineteenth century social reformer Amelia Jenks Bloomer, whose married name became associated with the controversial pantaloons outfit sported by women advocating for equal rights, spent her childhood in the village of Homer. Born here on May 27, 1818, Amelia Jenks was a Homer resident until the Jenks Family moved to Seneca Falls, NY, when she was seven years old. She was present at the Seneca Falls Convention of July 1848 when the Declaration of Rights and Sentiments was drawn up calling for political rights for women. The next year, she created *The Lily*, a newspaper for women. Her efforts have been remembered in numerous ways, including becoming the namesake of an annual feminist booklist: The Amelia Bloomer Project. This honors the top feminist books for young readers.

What was Homer like when Amelia was growing up here? To understand, here is a brief self-guided tour you can take at your leisure. It will familiarize you with the neighborhood around the Town Hall on North Main Street as Amelia would have known it.

First, it is important to understand the attraction people felt to Homer, a little settlement in the heart of early nineteenth century Central New York. Homer was a growing commercial center on the banks of the Tioughnioga River and only some thirty miles from the Erie Canal to the north in 1832 and with a railroad line passing through in the 1850s. Add to that economic appeal, the presence of a progressive co-educational academy on the Green that was intertwined in that day with religion, namely the Congregational Church next door. People came here for agrarian and mercantile work and to raise their families along religious principles. Social reform in the early 1800s was debated in the classroom, preached from the pulpit, and discussed at the family dinner table. In the 1820s, the academy's Supervising Principal Samuel Buell Woolworth and the Congregational minister John Keep advocated for social reforms like temperance, abolition of slavery, and women's rights—about fifty years before such causes gained heavy popular support.

In this kind of intellectual climate, the young Amelia Jenks found herself as she began her life at the home at 43 North Main Street. We begin our walk here at her childhood home. Stand at the side and notice how the residence was built incrementally over the years. As families increased in size and wealth, additions were added on, usually toward the road.

As we walk south from here along Main Street, notice when other houses were built. (Hint: the oval plaques on the front indicate the year the building was constructed.) Which ones were here when Amelia was a child, and which were not?

We come now to the Town Hall at 31 North Main. When Amelia was a child, on this site stood a hotel built by Enos Stimson. Later, it was known as the National Hotel. It boasted of 52 rooms, a stable to accommodate 100 horses, and one flush toilet (for the guests, not the horses). In 1904 the hotel was consumed by fire. It was reported that "the crockery was thrown from the windows" while the feather beds were "carried down the ladders." As the late Anna Hilton of Homer once explained, "Have you ever smelled burned goose down?" At an estimated loss of $12,000, it is this hotel fire that opened a space in which the Town Hall could be constructed in 1908. Some nearby homes are said to have been built using lumber retrieved from the ruins of the old hotel.

It is at a spot behind the Hall that Homer had its beginnings. Walk to the bridge spanning the river. The first settlers from New England arrived in 1791. It is here on the west bank of the Tioughnioga River that Asa White built a water-powered grist mill in 1798—the first in Cortland County. Here the growing number of farm families could get corn ground into meal and wheat into flour. Here is where they gathered for Sabbath meetings (church) and for a general meeting place—even on nights when wolves were howling up on the nearby hillside and panthers were on their nocturnal prowls. There are some ruins and a millstone of the last mill—the Darby Mill—along the riverbank. The mill pond was behind a dam, approximately where some beavers have had the good sense to build theirs. It was a fine spot for swimming in the summer and for ice-skating in the winter. The Jenks property was adjacent to the river.

We will now walk back up Water Street (formerly Mill Street). Some shops were located along this Street and a tannery near the river. At the end of the Street you see a stately home at 18 North Main. On this spot, in 1799, Asa White built his home, a salt-box style frame house. Around 1826, the house was moved to its present location at 20 Clinton Street. It is the oldest of the 220 structures in the Historic District today. Asa was the grandfather of Homer-born Andrew Dickson White. Andrew, with Ezra Cornell, founded Cornell University and was its first president. According to Andrew D. White, the success of the Academy in Homer as a co-educational institution of learning influenced the decision to make Cornell University coeducational.

With the house removed two years after the Jenks Family departed from their home, in its place, this Greek Revival home was built by Connecticut-born Jedediah Barber. Jedediah and Matilda Barber moved to Homer from Tully in 1811 and raised two more generations of Barbers here. In 1812, they built The Great Western, a three-story mercantile emporium of wood on Main Street which was the Walmart of Central New York in the nineteenth century. Without a doubt, the Jenks family patronized this store. Everyone did. Evidence of Barber's commercial success is this brick structure with magnificent fluted Ionic columns from an Asher Benjamin sketchbook and fine iron grilles in the frieze below the roofline.

Jedediah was one of the founders of the academy on the Green chartered by the state in 1819, one year after Amelia Jenks was born. For 50 years he served on the Board of Education, very much aware that children should not be lacking as he had been in receiving an education. He and his son, Paris Barber, befriended a teenaged boy named Frank Carpenter who showed an aptitude and skill for portrait-painting. It was Paris who brought furniture across the street to the earliest section of the Sherman Exchange building on the corner of Water and Main [was razed in 2020]. And it was Paris Barber who paid the rent for the future famous painter of Lincoln as "The Great Emancipator" to have his studio on the second floor.

The building and the next two attached sections were owned by William Sherman. Sherman constructed a building here in 1827, three years after the Jenks Family left Homer. The other additions date to 1853 and 1860. Here, Sherman made a fortune and a name for himself manufacturing the first machine-made iron nails made in New York State. These were the famous "S" nails, with the letter "S" for Sherman on the nail head. Today, these nails are used to date the age of a structure. See how important Homer was as an early commercial center in the heart of the state? Local contractor Tom Neiderhofer purchased this historic Sherman Block and restored it to its nineteenth century appearance as the Homer Exchange, where farmers from miles around arrived to exchange agricultural products for items they could not make for themselves, such as nails.

Evidence of Sherman's prosperity is the next structure, his home, also owned and beautifully restored by Tom Neiderhofer. This is the Federal style home built by Sherman in the 1820s of local grey stone. It was covered in stucco in 1918. Note how well the color now matches the color of the brick house across the street—a federal style house owned by a doctor in the 1840s. Inside the Sherman Mansion, at this time, will soon be a full service restaurant, where one can find three rooms, one each dedicated to Francis Carpenter, William Stoddard, and Eli DeVoe, three native-sons of Homer with significant connections to President Abraham Lincoln.

The next two large brick buildings down the east side of the street are important. The first building was originally built by Jedediah Barber as a bank. Once the railroad came through with his support, he entered the banking business, giving out loans. Two disasters hit the Barbers in the 1850s. The railroad venture busted, and the Barbers lost money, and The Great Western burned. The Barbers rebuilt on the site, which is the tall three-story building of brick housing Bev & Co and the Olde Homer Shoppe. This was the Great Western built in 1863, with an opera house on the third floor. In 1866, Homer's Frank Carpenter brought to the opera house his famous painting done at the White House in 1864. This is the one showing Lincoln reading the Emancipation Proclamation before the Cabinet members for the first time. Up two flights of stairs paraded folks to see the painting on exhibit in 1866 before it was taken to be shown at the Cortland Agricultural Fair, an annual event started by Homer's Paris Barber.

There is a story that a barrel of molasses broke open in the cellar of The Great Western, leaving the floor covered with two inches of the sweet liquid. Word spread quickly, and soon all the boys in the village were trying to get into the cellar to dip their fingers into the tasty molasses and convey it to their mouths.

"All roads lead to Homer" was the expression in the days of young Amelia Bloomer. Why even a farmer in Virgil would nose his horse toward "Uncle Jed's store" in Homer and bypass Cortland completely. Then, Cortland became the county seat and a larger commercial center than Homer. Looking back on it, we are sure glad they did! It allowed us to remain small and quaint, like a Norman Rockwell painting.

The National Hotel was called the "upper hotel" and a "lower hotel" was where the fire station is now. In the time of Amelia Jenks' childhood in Homer, four stagecoaches passed through Homer daily, and hotels and taverns did a brisk business in the community, bringing folks from far away and news of a society that would slowly address the lack of equal rights for women and blacks. The history books would describe how those rights came thanks to efforts made by the likes of Homer's Amelia Jenks Bloomer.

In 1850, Amelia returned to Homer to visit friends. It was reported in the newspaper that as she made her way down Main Street in her "bloomers," it was not without giggles from a troop of local boys following her. We do not giggle anymore at the sight of trousered women, nor do we find it appropriate to ask the question "Who wears the pants in the family?" Let us remember Amelia Jenks Bloomer's contribution to significant social and political changes and take pride in Homer's part in her early development.

April 9, 2015

THE ASSASSINATION AND THE ICONIC IMAGE OF LINCOLN

April 14th marks the 150th anniversary of the assassination of President Abraham Lincoln. The following are excerpts from *Lincoln's Gift from Homer, New York* (McFarland and Company, Inc., 2011) which describes the reactions of three sons of Homer—William Stoddard, Francis Carpenter, Paris Barber—and the response of Secretary of State William Seward of Auburn, New York.

On April 18, 1865, William and [his brother] Harry were in the Statehouse in Little Rock. They had heard frightful news from Washington that an attempt had been made upon the life of Secretary of State Seward, but the next news, brought by an agitated Army captain, struck like a bolt of lightning: "Marshall Stoddard, President Lincoln is assassinated!" The President had been shot on April 14th and had succumbed the next morning at 7:22 A.M. William was shocked. He stumbled out the door. He was further shocked to find men crying openly in the formerly rebel street—men who grasped "that in the murder of Abraham Lincoln the really best friend and protector of the future interests of the defeated South had been taken away." William Stoddard had personally lost a friend and a statesman he was proud to have served. Writing four days later to [the President's personal secretary] John Hay, Stoddard reflected upon their mutual loss: "Men who had never seen him wept when the news came. How shall we say our sorrow—who knew him as he really was?"

Frank Carpenter was in New York City when news came to him of Lincoln's assassination. In his diary he wrote "God have mercy upon the nation." Two days later he wrote "Got out the original study of Mr. Lincoln and had a good cry over it." The funeral train bearing the coffin of the assassinated President back to Springfield stopped in New York, and Carpenter went to City Hall to pass by the open casket and pay his respects. Near the casket, Carpenter's original study of Lincoln was displayed. The next day, he witnessed "The great funeral procession in honor of the universally lamented President," and wrote in his diary: "New York never saw such a day." Sixteen horses pulled a wagon bearing the presidential casket up Broadway to 14th Street. At Union Square, it went west to Fifth Avenue and then north on the great boulevard to 34th Street, and from there to the Hudson River Railway Depot, at the corner of 30th Street and 10th Avenue. Thousands of mourners lined the streets and all along the tracks to Springfield.

The next month, Carpenter wrote to Mrs. Owen Lovejoy: "The death of our beloved President overwhelmed me, as it did all those who were permitted to come so near him, with sorrow, such as was never before experienced upon the death of anyone not of the family circle. It seemed too awful to be true!" Carpenter's Emancipation Proclamation painting was on exhibit in Pittsburgh when word arrived of the conspiracy against the government, including the failed attempt on Seward's life and the murder of Lincoln just a few days after General Lee had surrendered. The public's interest in seeing the painting intensified. At one point, the doors to the exhibit had to be closed, because the crowd pressing forward was becoming unmanageable.

In Washington, D. C., Secretary of State Seward was confined to his bed, suffering from the multiple knife wounds murderously inflicted upon him by Lewis Thornton Powell. News of Lincoln's death was withheld from the Secretary. In his critical state, his doctor felt telling him about the assassination would cause a shock too great for him to bear. Nevertheless, Seward arrived at the tragic truth. On the day after Lincoln died at the Peterson boardinghouse across the street from Ford's Theater, Seward asked that his bed be moved around so he might have a view out his bedroom window. As he surveyed the spring foliage emerging upon the tops of the trees in the park across the street, he noticed the American flag on the roof of the War Department building. It was at half-mast. He studied it briefly and then blurted out to an attendant: "The President is dead!" No amount of denial could convince him otherwise. "If he had been alive," the Secretary reasoned, "he would have been the first to call on me; but he has not been here, nor has he sent to know how I am; and there is the flag at half-mast." The man who had entered Lincoln's administration in 1861 as the President's political rival had, in time, come to see Lincoln as a dear friend and respected statesman. He felt the loss deeply. Later, Carpenter would write that Seward's "inductive reason had discerned the truth, and in silence the great tears coursed down his gashed cheeks, as it sank into his heart."

In Homer, New York, Paris Barber was just leaving the office of the Homer *Republican* newspaper in Mechanics Hall when a boy came rushing in, shouting "Lincoln's dead, telegraph says so." Paris was shaken to his very core. How could this be? Lincoln, with a stroke of his pen, had resolved the moral issue of slavery. To this act Paris had given his full endorsement, and now its author had been martyred, one of the last casualties of the cruel war that had just ended. Paris was not alone in asking: How could God permit this? With his faith rattled and tears streaming down his face, Paris drove home to share the nightmarish news with his family. Neighbors soon came by. For the better part of an hour they sat with the Barbers in their living room [on Clinton Street], grieving in silence. Indeed, the entire nation was thrown into an unprecedented period of mourning. By his assassination Lincoln was immediately elevated from the position of a mere mortal to that of a secular saint, and interest in having a print of the martyred president increased immediately.

Before Lincoln's assassination, Carpenter had hoped the United States Government would show a willingness to purchase the Emancipation Proclamation painting, but that willingness had not materialized. Fortuitously, Carpenter had been shrewd enough to make plans for another way to make money from the painting. Soon after completing the painting, he arranged with New York publisher Derby & Miller to produce a print of the painting for public sale. Alexander Hay Ritchie, a well-known engraver in New York, was contracted to reproduce the painting as a steel engraving for $6,000.

Carpenter started working on a smaller version of the painting—twenty-one by thirty-three inches—for Ritchie's use. He brought the painting with him during a vacation visit to Homer. On Saturday, August 19, 1865, needing "material assistance," he "went to the village and got a group of men together like [in his] Emancipation picture" and had the photographer Luther Barker make him an ambrotype. Homer's very tall butcher, Burdett Newton, was asked to sit at a table as Lincoln. Lewis Henry posed for Stanton; "old Mr. Gardner" for Welles; Ki Munger for Seward; Mr. Hicok for Blair; Mr. Wardell for Smith; and Judge Reed for Bates. A visitor from New York named Mr. Gillett was commandeered to stand in as Chase.

From this small painting, Ritchie produced a high-quality print. Though a fire on Broadway in New York consumed Carpenter's small painting, the steel plate was spared, and [journalist] Noah Brooks predicted that the engraving would be "prized in every liberty-loving household as a work of art . . . a perpetual remembrance of the noblest event in American history." Carpenter gave copies to each Cabinet member depicted in the painting. An autographed copy was given to his parents [in Homer] as a Christmas present.

Around May 7, 1865, at the ripe, old age of eighty-four, "Father [John] Keep" [former pastor of the Congregational Church in Homer] felt compelled to send Carpenter a piece of heartfelt praise from Oberlin. Addressed to "my dear boy," the letter contained these complimentary and prophetic words: "I have been much gratified by the sight and study of your splendid and very popular painting of President Lincoln and his Cabinet. Now it is sure that your name as an artist will hold a high position in all future history of your country."

Besides artist's proofs for fifty dollars, india proofs were available for twenty-five dollars and plain prints for ten dollars. A thousand orders were placed within two months, representing $40,000. By the 1880s, Derby & Miller boasted to have made 30,000 prints from the original steel plate before it wore out. When Mrs. Lincoln, the President's widow, received a print, she acknowledged it on June 3, 1866, and included this endorsement: "I have always regarded the original painting, as very perfect, and the engraving, appears to me quite equal to it."

April 23, 2015

AN OLD-FASHIONED WINTER

Some meteorologists have reported that this past winter was one of the worst on record in the state for snow and the number of days of below freezing temperatures. It makes one wonder how people dealt with the challenges of the winter season in earlier eras. I came across a book by Lincoln's assistant personal secretary and native son of Homer, William Osborn Stoddard, which provides a glimpse into the answer. After his stint in the White House, Stoddard enjoyed a long career through the late 1800s and into the next century as an author. He wrote some seventy-six books, mostly highly popular, fictional adventure stories for young boys. One such book, published in 1885 by Charles Scribner's Sons, has the title **Winter Fun**. *The title does not seem fitting for the chapter titled "An Old-Fashioned Snow." I find little in it that I would characterize as "fun" and much to make me appreciate the Village and Town work crews that strive to keep our streets and highways open in this century. Here are excerpts that very well may have been inspired by Februarys Stoddard recalled as a youth in Syracuse or during visits to his grandfather's farmhouse at No. 5 Albany Street in the village. Sometimes, art imitates life:*

There have been several light and fleecy falls of snow since the arrival of the "city cousins" at the farmhouse, but they had been only about enough to keep the sleighing in good order. The weather was bracingly cold; but, for all that, Aunt Judith more than once felt called upon to remark—

"The winters nowadays ain't nothin' at all to what they used to be."

"We'll have more snow yet," said the deacon, "Don't you be afraid. . . . Boys, it's going to be a big one this time, real old-fashioned sort. We must get out the shovels, and keep the paths open . . ."

More and more of it; and the men and boys came in from the barns after supper as white as so many polar bears, to stamp and laugh and be brushed till the color of their clothes could be seen.

Then the wind began to rise, and the whole family felt like gathering closely around the fireplace; and the flames poured up the wide chimney as if they were ready to fight that storm.

The boys cracked nuts, and popped corn, and played checkers. The deacon read his newspaper. Mrs. Farnham and Aunt Judith plied their knitting. Susie showed Pen how to crochet a tidy. It was very cozy and comfortable; but all the while they could hear blast after blast, as they came howling around the house, and hurled snow fiercely against the windows.

"If this keeps up all night, there won't be any going to meeting to-morrow, let alone school on Monday."

It did keep up all night; and the blinding drifts were whirling before the wind with a gustier sweep than ever, when the farmhouse people peered out at them next morning.

Every shovel they could furnish a pair of hands for had to be at work good and early, and the task before them had a kind of impossible look about it . . .

There was a drift nearly ten feet high between the house and the pigpen, and a worse one was piled up over the gate leading into the barnyard. . . . [The children] dug away manfully at that drift, or, rather, at the hole they meant to make through it, while the grown-up shovellers toiled in the direction of the barnyard-gate . . .

It sounded a great deal as if the hungry quadrupeds in the pen were explaining their condition to all the outside world, or trying to, and cared very little how much work it might cost to bring them their breakfast. . . . Before the great drift at the gate could be conquered, it was breakfast-time for human beings, and there was never a morning when coffee and hot cakes seemed more perfectly appropriate . . . but the barn was reached, and all the quadrupeds and bipeds were found, safe and hungry, and were carefully attended to . . .

They were all tired enough to go to bed early, but the first rays of daylight next morning saw them all rushing out again. Port felt a little stiff and sore, but he determined to do his part at road-breaking.

The snow lay pretty level in the roads, for the greater part; and you could see the top rails of the fences here and there, enough to go by.

Chapter 5

A little after breakfast the wide gate was swung open, and then the deacon's hired man came down the lane, driving the black team at a sharp trot, with the wood-sleigh behind them.

Faster, faster, through the gate, and out into the snow, with a chorus of shouts to urge them on.

The spirited, powerful fellows reared and plunged and snorted; but before long they seemed almost disposed to call it fun, and enjoy it.

"Up the road first!" shouted the deacon. "We'll break that way till we get beyond Stebbins's."

There was work for men and boys, as well as horses; and the snow-shovels were plied rapidly behind the plunging team. Porter Hudson quickly understood that a great deal of road could be opened in such a way as that, if all the farmers turned out to do it. They were likely to; for none of them could afford to be blocked in, and public opinion would have gone pretty sharply against any man who dodged his share of such important work as that.

It was hardest on the horses, willingly as they went at it; and at the end of an hour or so the deacon brought out his second team, a pair of strong brown plough-horses. When they were tired, out came the best yoke of oxen; and it was fun enough to see the great, clumsy creatures, all but buried in a deep drift, slowly but strongly shouldering their way forward, and every now and then trying to turn around and get out of the scrape.

"A skittish yoke wouldn't do," said Corry. "They wouldn't move any way but backwards."

Long before that, the road had been opened "beyond Stebbins's, . . ."

They were now pushing their work towards the village, and could already catch glimpses of other "gangs," as Vosh called them, here and there down the road. In some places, where the snow was not so deep, they made "turn-outs" wide enough for loaded sleighs to pass each other.

"If we didn't," said Vosh, "one team'd have to lie down and let the other drive over it."

He could not tell Port that he had ever seen that done, but he added, "I've had to burrow through a drift, team and all, when there wasn't any turnout made."

That was very much like what they had been doing all day, and they kept it up through all the next; but, when Tuesday night came, it was pretty clear that "the roads were open." A sleigh came up from Benton with a man in it who had business with the deacon, and who had some remarkable yarns to tell about the depth of the drifts on the other side of the valley.

"Deacon Paulding's house was just drifted clean under, barns and all. He had to make a kind of a tunnel to his stable, before he could fodder his critters."

"You don't say!" exclaimed Aunt Judith. "Snowed under! I've known that to happen any number of times when I was a girl. Good big houses too; not little hencoops of things. . . . I must say, though, this 'ere's a right good old-fashioned snow, to come in these days."

May 7, 2015

WHEN THE KLAN WAS DRIVEN OUT OF CORTLAND COUNTY

The infamous white supremacist organization called the Ku Klux Klan originated in Tennessee after the Civil War. Over time, its membership and activities spread West and North, and its "hate list" expanded to include more than blacks. By the 1920s, the Klan was active in Cortland County, and there is reason to believe that a meeting of the K.K.K. was held in the Homer Town Hall. District Attorney Albert Haskell, Jr., was the father of an aunt of this writer.

The following story was reconstructed from these sources: Seven issues of the *Cortland Standard* from April 10, 1924 through May 15, 1924; "The Night the KKK Struck at Marathon," in *Syracuse Herald-American*, Sunday, May 2, 1965, 3; Chester L. Quarles, *The Ku Klux Klan and Other Racialist and Anti-Semitic Organizations: A History and Analysis*. Jefferson, NC: McFarland & Company, 1999, 62; Wyn Craig Wade, *The Fiery Cross: The Ku Klux Klan in America*. New York: Oxford University Press, 1998, 165; *1924 Directory*, Cortland County Historical Society; and *The 7 Valley Villager*, Vol.11, No. 12, April 25, 1963, pp. 3–4, 12.

The purpose of this account is to present interesting historical facts from ninety-one years ago, to not cast aspersions on anyone or any locality, and to leave it to the reader to derive some lessons about human nature and how it has manifested itself in past human behavior. What follows is the first of five installments.

The place was the little village of Marathon, New York, on the banks of the Tioughnioga River. The time was sometime after nine o'clock in the evening of Thursday, April 10, 1924, ten days before Easter. Five black automobiles pulled up in front of the Central Hotel owned by Thomas Walsh. Twenty men, dressed in sheets and white hoods, disembarked. Some took up positions in front of the establishment while the others rushed inside. Lyman Cronk, the hotel's night clerk, was confronted by the white-garbed band.

"Where's Tommy?" demanded the tall one who appeared to be in charge.

"He's out of town," responded the startled clerk.

"Then who's in charge?" shouted the leader.

"Well, I'm staying here tonight," replied Cronk, who decided to ask a pointed question of his own. "What authority do you have to come into this hotel like this?"

His question was met with a saber blow to his upper torso delivered by the ringleader. The blow was enough to make the clerk lose his footing, but neither his clothing nor his skin was cut. A couple other hooded men seized him, shouting "Where's your stuff?" "Stuff" meant bottles of alcohol prohibited by the Eighteenth Amendment. A struggling Cronk denied that there was any there. Then the leader began calling off numbers in his hoarse, husky voice. Different men responded to these coded orders of a premeditated plan by running through the rooms of the hotel, tipping over beds, and taking the night staff quite by surprise.

Out in the street, pedestrians and traffic were being halted and detained by the hooded sentries as the ransacking occurred within. A small crowd was forming.

Meanwhile, west of the bridge, members of the Osco Robinson Post of the American Legion were hosting a gathering attended by nine members of the Legion posts of Cortland and Homer. The business portion of the meeting was conducted by Commander M. S. Birdlebough of the Marathon post. County Commander Harold M. Clements of Cortland spoke briefly of the importance of membership for all posts and of the responsibilities entrusted to veterans. Claude McKinney, commander of Cortland City Post, No. 489, urged members to support the work being done at a camp for disabled veterans near the Raybrook Sanitarium outside of Saranac Lake. Henry C. Walrad, a member of the Cortland City Post, spoke highly of the treatment he had received as a patient of the sanitarium and asked those present to "assist their buddies in times of peace as they did so faithfully in the days of 1917–1918." A social hour was to follow including a light repast of sandwiches.

When the time came to eat, a member of the Marathon post was sent out to go over the bridge to a lunchroom to fetch the coffee. A few minutes later, he returned without the coffee and breathlessly explained, "I was stopped from crossing the bridge. There's a masked man, and he wouldn't let me cross." Not to be deprived of their refreshments, the veterans responded by marching out of the clubrooms, as if they were again part of the American Expeditionary Force of 1917. They proceeded to the bridge led by county commander Clements.

At the bridge, one of two robed individuals ordered the group to halt and to advance no further. "Are you a sheriff?" questioned Clements. When informed to the negative, Clements countered, "Nobody but the sheriff can tell me to stop when I decide to go anywhere." One of the guards then thrust his hand menacingly into his pocket and gave the appearance of having a concealed weapon upon his person. Unfazed by this move and at Clements order, "Come on, fellows," the group continued their advance across the bridge. They came upon bottles smashed at the curb in front of the hotel and a group of citizens standing spellbound as a party of hooded men boarded automobiles. One of the Legionnaires, A. N. Robinson, unable to dodge one of the exiting vehicles, found himself stepping up on the car's fender and hood and being carried several feet before he was able to jump off unhurt. The vehicles sped out of town, with cut-outs open, engines racing, and running boards loaded with ghostly figures brandishing sabers overhead. According to a news reporter, "It was a dramatic exit." However, it was not an exit made without the license plate numbers of two of the cars being noted by the Legionnaires. The next morning the numbers were turned over to Sheriff Frank W. Chrisman and the District Attorney.

The District Attorney was thirty-three-year-old Albert J. Haskell, Jr., of 30 Charles Street, Cortland. Haskell was a lawyer trained at Cornell University (Class of '15), an active Republican, a communicant of St. Mary's Roman Catholic Church in Cortland, and a charter member of the Cortland Rotary Club founded in 1919. Running unopposed in the election for the District Attorney post in 1921, DA Haskell now found himself thrust into the public limelight by this nighttime raid in Marathon by the Ku Klux Klan.

May 21, 2015

The Ku Klux Klan had been founded in Pulaski, Tennessee, in 1866, by ex-Confederate leaders who sought a return of white supremacy in the post-Civil War South. Initially, their goal was to don ghostly attire and scare superstitious freedmen from voting. When that approach failed over time to yield results, more physically violent methods, including murder, came into play to "keep the black man in his place." With the end of World War I, lynching of blacks by Klansmen was not uncommon in America, and Klan membership grew exponentially. The Invisible Empire had spread out West and well above the Mason-Dixon Line. The Klan's "hate list" had also grown. By 1920, not only blacks, but Jews, Catholics, immigrants, and foreigners were viewed as un-American and unacceptable elements by the Klan, and Klan members had infiltrated American politics.

According to Wyn Craig Wade in *The Fiery Cross: The Ku Klux Klan in America,* even President Warren G. Harding was sworn in as a member of the Klan in the Green Room of the White House. To express his appreciation, Harding presented the five-man induction team with War Department license tags granting them the right to run red lights anywhere in America. As the Klan grew in political strength, it would feel emboldened to conduct a march down Pennsylvania Avenue in the nation's capital on August 8, 1925. Carrying American flags, 35,000 Klansmen displayed their brand of patriotism and bigotry as they paraded past the White House with their hoods removed. The Invisible Empire was brazenly visible.

The Klan was certainly no longer a mere right-wing Southern organization by 1924. As reported by *The Cortland Standard* published on the Thursday of the raid upon Marathon, twenty-five men, said to be Klansmen, were arrested and ordered to be held without bail in Ebensburg, Pennsylvania. The Pennsylvanian Klansmen were charged with murder and riot in connection with a confrontation that occurred the previous Saturday in Lilly between townspeople and visiting Klansmen. After hearing conflicting testimony about the riot and the ensuing three deaths and multiple injuries, Judge John A. Evans declared that in the opinion of the court "it was unlawful in Pennsylvania for a body of men to assemble when dressed in gowns and masks." "Such demonstrations," he said, "tend to put people in fear and it is unlawful in this state to stage any demonstrations having that effect." The judge defined the law pertaining to rioting and declared that "any person who participated was liable for actions by anyone in the crowd."

In the 1920s, the Klan was active in Cortland County. There was an active solicitation of new members. Prospective candidates were handed a three by five card which stated:

> Mr. _____ of _____
> Your friends say you are a
> native born, white, gentile American Citizen (100 per
> American). Therefore, as you believe in America First and
> white supremacy at all times, you will not fail to be in the
> town hall, Homer, Monday, Oct. 1, at 8 p.m.
> Knights of the Ku Klux Klan will speak upon the most powerful
> secret, non-political and thoroughly American organization
> in existence. If you hear the rumblings in the distance, you can
> not afford to miss this opportunity. Don't judge this great law-
> abiding order by hearsay. Come and hear the truth.

Klan activities in Cortland County, including cross burnings on the hill east of Homer, had gone unimpeded because they had remained within the law. There was no disposition to arrest them. If anything, such meetings as those held at the Homer Town Hall, were protected under the First Amendment of the Constitution. They had a right to peaceably assemble and they had a guaranteed freedom of speech. But this event in Marathon seemed to the law enforcement officials to be particularly egregious and merited action. Speaking to reporters the next morning, DA Haskell bristled with indignation: "Heretofore the Klan in this section has been treated as any other fraternal organization. Last night's occurrence prompts action!" Officials pointed out that this raid, the first public demonstration or overt act by the Klan in Cortland County, was in violation of the law. An investigation was to be launched immediately, and the guilty, if any, prosecuted. Affidavits had been obtained from members of the American Legion party, and evidence would be collected in Marathon. Haskell vowed, "Any of the Klan members identified will be arrested and prosecuted."

That afternoon, Colonel Robert L. Rice of Cortland was arrested. DA Haskell informed the press that Rice was the "king kleagle" of the Ku Klux Klan in Cortland and that two charges were being preferred against him—inciting to riot, following the raid by Klansmen in Marathon the night before, and being at the scene in mask in violation of the penal law. In addition, Paul Allen and Marvin Kinney had been "detained on indication of having been members of the raiding party." To these charges, Rice responded by denying knowledge of or any participation in the raid. He maintained that he had not authorized the raid and that it was "without his sanction or consent."

This was Rice's stated position when he was arraigned in Marathon that evening before Justice A. Carley Adams. A big crowd gathered for this event, and the newspaper pointed out that one man in the assembly caused a stir "when he removed his rubber boots and stood attentively in his stocking feet." Rice pleaded not guilty to the charges and demanded an examination, which Adams set for the next Wednesday at two in the afternoon. Bail was set at $500 and was promptly supplied by George F. Dann and Arthur L. Stevens. Not being represented by counsel, Rice asked the court for an adjournment to obtain a lawyer.

Four others were also arraigned at the time: Marvin C. Kinney, Paul A. Allen (but the paper incorrectly used the last name of Stevens), Irving L. Strauf, and Hartsell O. Adams. They were charged with disorderly conduct and pleaded guilty. Each was fined ten dollars. Since some of the men did not have enough money with them to pay the fine, Rice paid their fines. In connection with the raid, DA Haskell managed to secure affidavits, some of which were sworn to by some of the men arraigned on disorderly conduct charges. Irving L. Strauf admitted to being stationed on the bridge as one of the guards, and the affidavit sworn to by Marvin C. Kinney read as follows:

> At 7:30 I started from the office of the Ku Klux Klan in Samson block [corner of Groton Avenue and Main Street, Cortland], alone, with instructions from Rice to join a party of eighteen men. All the members of the party had hoods and masks when they started out, which they put on about one mile from Marathon. Robert L. Rice, Kleagle of the Cortland branch of the K. K. K., was in charge of the party. Rice was the organizer of the expedition to go to the Walsh hotel in Marathon to look for booze. We went to the Walsh

hotel, and when we reached there had our hoods and masks on.
The members of our party searched the Walsh hotel
for liquor. I was stationed outside to stop pedestrians as they
came along the street. I probably stopped twelve to fifteen
pedestrians. Captain Rice stationed me in an open space just
below the hotel. Captain Rice was the leader and instigator
of this trip to the Walsh hotel, and was in mask and hood.
(cited in *The Cortland Standard* of Saturday, April 12, 1924, 2)

June 4, 2015

On the afternoon of his arrest, Rice granted the *Cortland Standard* an interview. It was reported in the April 12, 1924, issue of the newspaper. He emphatically stated,

The Knights of the Ku Klux Klan did not sanction the raid
made in Marathon on Thursday evening. The conviction of
the four men for disturbing the peace interests me because
they are none of them members of the Klan. Further, we will
gladly pay $50 in cash to anyone who can prove they are
members of the Klan. Our organization is solely for the
protection of the laws of the land, and not for breaking them.

The law needing protection in Rice's view was most likely Prohibition, or the Eighteenth Amendment, which in his estimation was being flagrantly violated by that Irishman, Tommy Walsh of Marathon. At the conclusion of the interview, Rice handed a letter to the reporter which he claimed to have received that morning. The letter was sent from nearby Truxton, New York, warning Rice that reliable sources had informed him that "enemies of the Klan are but waiting their chance to shoot you," and he felt obligated to forewarn Rice to be on his guard. This was reported by the paper.

Boldly, Rice proceeded to offer a thousand-dollar reward for anyone who could prove that he had led or was implicated in the raid on the Central Hotel. He went further. He called for a mass meeting of Klansmen in Marathon, which was said to be attended by one hundred hooded Klansmen. At this meeting, Rice, the King Kleagle, called for the impeachment of District Attorney Albert Haskell. The crowd cheered.

Rice went on: "The Klan is after the gumshoe politicians. . . . We'll tar and feather every one of them. We have one or two to get in Cortland County. In Cortland there are 103 bootleggers, 67 in the Italian section alone." Rice announced that Cortland's city officials were "heavily bribed" and that "we are trying to find the bootleggers and then we are going to expose them." Then, his vitriol was directed back on Haskell: "He has failed to enforce the law!" "We declare war," he proclaimed, "on any officer who does not live up to his obligations." A large portion of his speech then became an attack on Catholics, Jews, and blacks, and the extolling of the virtues, aims, and objectives valued by the Klan: "There are no Catholics, Jews or Negroes in the Klan; they have their own organizations. We are the only Protestant, militant organization in the country and we have a right to organize!"

It was clear to any rational person in attendance, if there were any, that the Klan was using the most broken and unenforceable federal law in American history, the Prohibition law, as a pretext for going after Catholics in Cortland County. What did the booze-selling Irishman, Tommy Walsh, the bootlegging Italian immigrants in the East Side of the city of Cortland, and the young DA of Cortland have in common? They were all Catholics—perceived as having allegiance to a Pope headquartered in a foreign land and a liturgical ritual that involved the consumption of wine. To nativist Americans, Catholicism equaled an intolerable foreign practice and an affront to pure Americans, who, by their definition, were W.A.S.P.—White, Anglo-Saxon (meaning English in origin), and Protestant. Though, with the passage of time and generations of marriages, it was increasingly doubtful that many under the white robes of intolerance could really claim to have 100 percent W.A.S.P. blood.

Not done yet with his rant, Rice then produced the letter from Truxton, which he claimed to be penned by a minister of that community, and read it to the hooded assembly:

> I have been informed from reliable sources that enemies of
> the Klan in Truxton [a reference to the Irish Catholic population
> known to reside there] are but waiting their chance to shoot you.
> I feel that it is my duty as a Protestant American and especially
> as a minister of the Gospel to inform you so that you may be on
> your guard. Yours for America, First, last and all the time . . .

Then the Kleagle, the representative of bigoted threat and intimidation, concluded his diatribe by publicly challenging Haskell. He announced that he had been informed that very afternoon that a petition was being circulated by friends of the Klan in Cortland calling for the impeachment of lawyer Haskell if he persisted in pressing charges against the Klan leader. The assembly was enthralled and convinced that the battle lines were now drawn, and that right was on the side of the vigilante enforcers of moral control.

June 18, 2015

By 2 P.M. on Wednesday, April 16, 1924, the Firemen's Hall in Marathon was packed to the doors with humanity, many from the city of Cortland. The crowd was said to number 300, including "a score of women." Even the stairs were filled by those eager to attend the examination of Robert L. Rice, Kleagle of the Ku Klux Klan, on a charge of inciting to riot at Marathon on the night of Thursday, April 10th. Justice A. Carley Adams presided. The defendant was represented by Attorney Floyd W. Hoag of Syracuse.

As Defendant Rice and then District Attorney Haskell, representing the People, entered the room, the place burst into raucous applause. Champions of each side in this legal contest were audibly present, but Justice Adams quickly squelched any further demonstrations in his courtroom. The *Cortland Standard* (April 16 and 17) indicated that there were two or three strangers in attendance who were alleged to be Klansmen and with whom the defendant's lawyer was observed conferring.

The Prosecution took the floor first. DA Haskell called as witnesses the four men who had made sworn affidavits—Marvin Kinney, Hartsell O. Adams, Paul Allen, and Irving Strauf—but when their names were called, there was no response. Their testimony was crucial to the prosecution of the case. Where were they? Why were they not there? As reported by the *Cortland Standard* (April 17), a flummoxed Haskell explained to the court that the four witnesses called had not been subpoenaed since they had already made sworn statements but that he had expected Mr. Kinney to be present. Baring this setback, Haskell said he would like to proceed by calling three more witnesses.

First to be sworn in to testify was Harold Clements, county commander of the American Legion. Clements told of how he and other Legionnaires had been ordered to stop on the bridge that night by two men in hoods and robes. He described how one of the men had stuck his finger out inside his pocket as though he had a gun. Finding that the men were without authority, he said that his group proceeded on.

Next to be called was Legionnaire A. N. Robinson. He told of bottles being broken at the curb.

The DA asked, "Could you smell what was spilled?"
"I could," answered Robinson.
"What did it smell like?" probed Haskell.
"Shoe blacking" was the response, and chuckles broke out in the room.
Haskell asked, "Do you know the smell of liquor?" More laughter emitted from the room.
"I think I do" was Robinson's reply.
"Was this liquor?"
"Not good liquor."

This was too much. Now everyone joined in the laughter. The justice, the lawyers, the defendant, everyone was unable to contain themselves and filled the hall with guffaws. No humor was found in the rest of Robinson's testimony, as he described his harrowing experience of being struck by one of the cars as it left the scene. He said the car had come straight at him, forcing him to mount the hood and to be carried several feet before jumping off.

"Were you hurt?"
"No, I was not."
"Were you able to recognize the driver?"
"No, the driver wore a hood."

The last witness called was Claude McKinney. He affirmed that at least one of the cars had followed a zigzag course in leaving the scene. Like the two witnesses before him, McKinney told of noting two license numbers, of going to the court clerk's office to ascertain the names of those who had taken out these licenses, and then of complaints being lodged with the sheriff by Mr. Clements and Mr. Robinson.

All three witnesses were cross-examined by Attorney Hoag. He probed each one, particularly about the actions of the men who had halted them. Robinson and McKinney were asked about their positions on the crosswalk when the car allegedly swerved toward them, as they had claimed in their testimonies. The defense also questioned the two of them as to the width of the street and asked if there were ruts in the road. They said they had seen no ruts.

With the completion of the cross-examination, District Attorney Haskell stood and asked to address the court. He spoke firmly and the press covered it:

> I want to call attention to the spirit of fairness in which this
> case is being conducted. The prosecution is being conducted
> as any and all other cases arising in the course of duty.

Haskell then moved for adjournment and asked the court, "without prejudicing the defendant," to issue subpoenas for the four witnesses who had failed to appear. Attorney Hoag said he had no objections, and all agreed to adjourn until Thursday afternoon, May 2nd, when court would resume at the same location.

With that, the gavel was brought down by Justice Adams. The subpoenas were served that evening. Again, the next day's *Cortland Standard* drew attention to the presence of two strangers in the court seated with Attorney Hoag: "He consulted with them from time to time, but their identity was not revealed." Other than this rather ominous observation, the paper reported that "Yesterday's proceedings were orderly, dignified, and devoid of excitement."

Chapter 5

July 2, 2015

The case of the People vs. Robert L. Rice resumed in Marathon on the afternoon of May 1, 1924. The crowd of 300, mostly from Cortland, who had come "to see what they might see," expected the district attorney to call as witnesses the four men who had previously made affidavits implicating Rice. Instead, Haskell announced, "I am willing to stand on the affidavits of Hartsell O. Adams, Paul A. Allen, Irving Strauf, and Marvin C. Kinney, which have been put into the court record. I have no desire for a direct examination of these men, but they are in court for cross-examination if Attorney Hoag for the defense wishes to cross-examine."

Hoag replied, "If the District Attorney does not care for direct examination, I have no desire to cross examine."

The main witness of the afternoon was Lyman Cronk, whom the newspaper listed as a "rheumatic." As the caretaker of the hotel the night of the raid, Cronk was asked by Haskell to tell the court what he saw transpire.

"I saw hooded and blanketed intruders coming into the hotel."
"How did they enter?"
"Well, they filed into the room in nice shape."
"What happened when one of them asked who was in charge?"
"I said that I was staying here, and I asked him what authority he had to come into the place, and he hit me a blow with a saber. Right over the heart, too!" Cronk added.
"Was it a hard blow?"
"Well, I'd say it was. I was black and blue for two weeks."
"Were you scared?"
"Well, the saber had a sharp point, but I wasn't afraid the leader, the tall man, would stick it into me. I wasn't afraid at all; I knew they wouldn't hurt me."
"And what happened next?"
"The leader, the tall man, began calling off numbers, and as he did different men did his bidding."
"What did they do?"
"What did they do? They ransacked the place is what they did."
"Was any furniture destroyed?"
"No, no furniture was destroyed . . . but the beds were tipped over."
"Were any other weapons used?"
"Yes, one man had a revolver of blued steel."
Upon cross-examination, Cronk was asked, "Did you actually see any of the visitors tipping over the beds?"
"No, I can't say that I did."
"Did the man with the revolver make any attempt to use it?"

"No, sir, he did not."
"Did the visitors break anything at all?"
"Yes, they broke some bottles?"
"Bottles containing what?"
After a bit of a pause, Cronk gave an answer: "Embalming fluid, home cider, and colored water."

There had been frequent bursts of laughter during Cronk's examination, but this last testimony drew the biggest expression of amusement, to which the witness registered his personal pleasure.

Three other witnesses were questioned briefly, including G. M. Temple, the janitor at the hotel that night, but their testimonies added nothing of substance to the hearing. The next thing the much-entertained crowd knew the hearing was being adjourned. After a mere forty minutes, the crowd was visibly disappointed and let down.

The hearing was adjourned until May 17th, but as the press reported, it was essentially "without date," since the grand jury was to sit the next Monday and would report long before May 17th. The Rice case would obviously be one of those considered. At the close of the hearing, subpoenas for witnesses for the hearing in May were issued.

If anyone had anticipated a continuation of the battle between the vitriolic Klansman and the dedicated DA, they were in for a disappointment. A change of heart, perhaps prompted by sound legal counsel from the "two strangers" attending the hearings, brought the matter to an abrupt close. On the morning of May 15, 1924, Robert L. Rice, Klansman, pleaded guilty in Supreme Court to the charge of conspiring with Hartsell O. Adams, Marvin G. Kinney, Paul A. Allen, Irving Strauf, and some fourteen others not known to the Court in the Marathon raid of April 10th. The fine imposed was $400 or 400 days in jail. Rice produced a large roll of bills and proceeded to count out $400 in tens and twenties.

"In passing sentence," intoned Justice Rhodes from the bench, "I have proposed to be lenient as Mr. Rice has frankly admitted that he made a mistake and had no business being in Marathon under conditions and circumstances as charged and that he did not realize the seriousness of the offense. The Court is certain there will be no repetition and that the public will be protected should there be another offense." Then with a firm gaze fixed upon Rice, Justice Rhodes continued, "And should parties be brought before me for sentence, the penalty will be more severe." Duly chastised and $400 poorer, the defendant departed.

At noon, reporters asked District Attorney Haskell to comment on his recent nemesis. All Haskell would say, with a slight smile, was "I understand that Mr. Rice is leaving town." Later, the paper would report that the Klansman "has not been heard from since." Years later, *The 7 Valley Villager*

(April 25, 1963, p. 4) would report on this past event and draw this conclusion: "For the first time in the history of New York State, a Kleagle of the Ku Klux Klan was hauled into court, convicted and forced to pay the penalty for Klan outrages."

August 13, 2015

HISTORIC HOMER: GATEWAY TO HERITAGE TOURISM IN CENTRAL NEW YORK

Holidays are much more than festive occasions on a calendar. Thanksgiving, Christmas, Martin Luther King, Jr. Day, and Presidents Day provide an opportunity to set aside some time to remember persons and events of the past that have significantly shaped our values, traditions, and collective identity as a people. There are, however, some persons and events of the past that are worthy of on-going commemoration in a physical form. These persons and events often have public spaces set aside to honor them with plaques, markers, street names, preserved architecture, and statuary.

Residents of Central New York are or should be keenly aware that their region abounds with historical persons worthy of memorialization. Clinton Square in Syracuse has statuary recalling the famous public rescue in 1851 of William "Jerry" Henry from the enforcers of the Fugitive Slave Law of 1850. Another runaway slave, Harriet Tubman, has her final residence in Auburn dedicated to her participation as a "conductor" in the Underground Railroad movement. Auburn, too, is the site of a statue of William Henry Seward, the secretary of state in the Abraham Lincoln and Andrew Johnson presidencies. Nearby, Seward's residence, brimming with artifacts, has been wisely preserved and is open to public inspection.

Further down the road, at Seneca Falls, the tourist finds the Women's Rights National Historic Park. Here the first women's rights convention was held in 1848. Here the names of Susan B. Anthony, Elizabeth Cady Stanton, Frederick Douglass, Matilda Joslyn Gage, and other great figures of vision and conviction are recalled for assembling for the cause of women's suffrage and abolition. Another attendee at the convention and Seneca Falls resident was Amelia Jenks Bloomer, the advocate for temperance and for an item of radical women's apparel that bore her last name. "Bloomers" became synonymous with social reform and the movement for women's rights. Her home in Seneca Falls is listed in the National Register of Historic Places. Her birthplace, Homer, New York, now boasts of 220 structures listed in the Register.

Homer's location in the center of the state and on the I-81 corridor makes it "The Gateway to the Finger Lakes" and to Syracuse for visitors coming up from southerly directions. Those who pass through Homer's Historic District for the first time are amazed by its well-preserved architecture and by streets lined with stately trees and with American flags patriotically fluttering in the breeze. More than once the comment has been made about its Norman Rockwell appearance, and one visitor stated, "I thought I had driven onto the set of a Civil War era movie."

This observation is appropriate when one realizes that since "Homer's Celebration of Lincoln in Paint and Print" in 2009 during the national observance of the bicentennial of the Civil War president's birth, no less than five Lincoln scholars have visited and spoken in Homer. The first was Harold Holzer, the esteemed author and editor of over forty books on Lincoln and a commissioner of the national Abraham Lincoln Bicentennial Commission that enthusiastically endorsed the Homer week-long observance. He gave two lectures. This was followed by Jason Emerson, who spoke at the Phillips Free Library on his book *The Madness of Mary Lincoln.* Then, the late U. S. Senator and presidential candidate George McGovern came to promote his biography of Abraham Lincoln. Thus far, as part of Homer's observance of the Sesquicentennial of the Civil War, two other contributors to the vast knowledge of Lincoln have lectured in Homer. In September of 2011, retired Chief Justice of the Supreme Court of Rhode Island and chair of The Lincoln Forum, the Honorable Frank J. Williams, spoke at the Homer Intermediate-Junior High School on "Lincoln and the Constitutionality of the Emancipation Proclamation." Williams was followed in November by the award-winning Lincoln biographer Professor Michael Burlingame of the University of Illinois at Springfield. He spoke at Homer's Center for the Arts, addressing the question "What New Can Possibly Be Said about Abraham Lincoln?" Williams has agreed to return to Homer in June of 2015 and to lecture again as part of a traveling exhibit on Lincoln and the Constitution during the Civil War.

What is it about Homer that magnetically draws experts on Lincoln? Why is it that Harold Holzer of The Lincoln Forum, a national organization devoted to all things dealing with the sixteenth president of the United States, has dubbed the Town of Homer "a new Lincoln mecca?" The reason is because the town lays claim to three native sons with direct connections to Lincoln's life and legacy. Until the Lincoln bicentennial, not much was made of their roles by the bulk of the population of the town.

Though an historical marker stands on the birth site of Homer's Eli DeVoe, few realized that private investigator DeVoe helped to thwart a possible assassination plot against Lincoln in 1861. The more famous detective, Allan Pinkerton, uncovered a conspiracy in Baltimore to murder Lincoln and prevent him from ever arriving by train to become the President. Lincoln refused to change plans after receiving Pinkerton's report. When DeVoe infiltrated the cell of conspirators and independently corroborated Pinkerton's fears for Lincoln, the President-elect avoided harm by sneaking into Washington, DC, on a different train. Ironically, both Lincoln and DeVoe were born in log cabins in 1809. One was destined to become a great President, and one was destined to save a great President.

William Osborn Stoddard was born in the Village of Homer in 1835. The house still stands at No. 5 Albany Street, one of the earliest brick houses built in Cortland County. Not until 2009 was there a New York State marker erected curbside to announce the birth site of the assistant personal secretary to Mr. and Mrs. Lincoln. Stoddard was responsible for opening the President's mail each day and for making the introductions as the Lincolns greeted those who came to White House receptions and dinners. It was Stoddard who, at Lincoln's bidding, made handwritten copies of the President's draft of the Emancipation Proclamation. In the 1870s, it was Stoddard who testified before a Congressional committee and lobbied for the Government to accept as a gift the oil painting of "The First Reading of the Emancipation Proclamation before the Cabinet." The image of Lincoln with sad, drooping eyes has become iconic.

The painter responsible for capturing on canvas what he called the "moment of moral grandeur" was Francis Bicknell Carpenter. Born in Homer in 1830 (there is a marker), he studied portraiture under Sanford Thayer in Syracuse and made a name for himself painting the movers and shakers of nineteenth century America, including five Presidents. Prints made of his paintings of Lincoln and his book *Six Months at the White House with Abraham Lincoln: The Story of a Picture* were bestsellers after the shocking assassination in 1865 elevated the president to secular sainthood in the public's mind.

DeVoe, Stoddard, and Carpenter are Homer's "Lincoln Trifecta." Lincoln scholars appreciate the opportunity to visit the place where these three were born and raised and to ask "Why Homer? How do you explain that this dot on a map named after a blind Greek poet produced so many prominent names in the early nineteenth century? Did the stars align just so?"

Celestial bodies may not have aligned, but geographic, economic, educational, and religious forces did. Nestled in the heart of the state, Homer developed a robust, pioneer agrarian economy which benefited from its location on the Tioughnioga River and its proximity to the Erie Canal passing through Syracuse. These accessible water routes permitted a brisk trade of products in Homer—products that passed through The Great Western Store established in Homer by Jedediah Barber as the Walmart of the early 1800s. In the1850s, more wealth in the area was stimulated by the construction of the railroad through Homer. It connected Syracuse and Binghamton and provided freight and passenger service for the merchants and farming folk of Homer.

Another significant source of revenue was from boarding out rooms to students from Central New York and further afield who came to the prestigious Cortland (later Homer) Academy. Built on the west side of the Green and chartered in 1819 by the state, the school attracted the best and the brightest to its progressive, co-educational curriculum. By the 1840s, it was graduating such luminaries as Theodore Munger, the Yale theologian and abolitionist; Dr. Stephen Smith, founder of the New York City Board of Health; and Amelia Stone Quinton, co-founder of the Women's National Indian Association. Both Stoddard and Carpenter studied under Supervising Principal Samuel B. Woolworth before Woolworth moved on to become the secretary of the New York State Board of Regents.

Education and religion were intertwined agents of reform in the 1800s. Right next door to the Academy was (and still is) the Congregational Church, which experienced the Second Great Awakening in the form of its pastor from 1821 to 1833, the Reverend John Keep. "Father Keep" was a proponent of temperance, co-education, and abolition. He taught that slaves and social ideas should be unfettered. This radical thinker went on to help establish Oberlin College in Ohio as a co-educational school open to all "irrespective of color."

It is amazing how, in an age devoid of email and the social media, Keep, Carpenter, Stoddard, Munger, and another native son of Homer, Cornell University's co-founder and first president, Andrew D. White, managed to carry on communication with each other and with others. Through handwritten letters (now a dying art in the computer age) they maintained an active dialogue and collaboration on matters of art, social issues, and political affairs. For them, human freedom and dignity was a moral imperative worthy of discourse.

Today, in Homer, near the firehouse on Main Street, is a steel girder from one of the New York City towers brought down on 9/11. It is an appropriate site for a lasting memorial to the first responders of that infamous event and to American resilience in the face of attacks upon our *freedom*. At the other end of the village's Main Street commercial establishments stands the stately Town Hall constructed in 1908. Here has been proposed another memorial to *freedom*. Known as the Lincoln Monument Project, this memorial will consist of six pieces in bronze by the renowned sculptor Frank Porcu to commemorate the three native-sons of Homer—Carpenter, Stoddard, and DeVoe—who contributed to the life and iconography of "The Great Emancipator." The project calls for the installation of life-sized statues, plaques, and a bas-relief of Carpenter's famous painting of the moment when Lincoln first broached freedom of the slaves to his full Cabinet—a moment that Carpenter, in his bestseller, called "an act unparalleled for moral grandeur in the history of mankind" (pp.10–11). The municipal building is an ideal spot for using public art to inform residents and visitors to Homer that the community once played a significant role at the intersection of local, regional, and national history. What a gateway to and boost for heritage tourism and to revitalizing the regional economy of Central New York State.

This was published online by *New York History Review* in January of 2015 and will be in hard copy in December 2015.

September 24, 2015

THE OPENING OF THE 1856–1857 SCHOOL YEAR IN HOMER

Now that we are beginning another school year, let us look back to see what the opening of school at the Academy on the Green was like 159 years ago. This is a letter written by E. Belcher Fish, a new teacher at the Academy, to his cousin. Spelling and punctuation and paragraphing (or lack thereof) have been left as in the original document. Spaces indicate indecipherable writing. See what you can learn about the politics and academic workload of the times.

Homer Aug 31st 1856

Cousin Mary

Yours of the 19th _____ was duly received on my arrival at Homer to enter upon my duties as a teacher in the Academy & right to have been answered befor this, but my time has been so much occupied that I have had no time for letter writing & should not have now only as it trespasses on holy time or _____ other write after church on Sunday as I am now doing. I was very glad to hear from you & also to learn that you were well, & pleased with the country as well as that at last you had obtained a situation in school. I was at Harford about three weeks before I came here & staid there two or three hours & took teas at your father's. They were there all well as usual & had just received a visit from Julia Ann Case (formerly Brown) & Cornelia Waldo. I came here the 7th of Aug & have now been in school a little more that three weeks. The number of students in the Institution is nearly two hundred and more coming every week. I have as yet but twenty one that study in my room. I have eight recitations each day as follows at 8 AM "Teachers Class" numbering 35 members 9 AM Class in "Elementery Algebra", 25 members, 10 AM Class in "Reading & Spelling", 12 members, 11 AM Class in Prac. Arithmetic, 35 members, 1 1/4 PM Class in McNally's Geography,

19 members, 2 PM Class in Clark's Grammar 42 members, 2 3/4 PM Class in Prac Aritemetic (Advanced) 32 members, 3 1/2 PM Class in reading & Spelling 10 members. So you can see my time is pretty well occupied in school hours, and when you take into consideration the fact that the text books here used are entirely new to me you will probably conclude that the most of my time out of school is employed in preparing myself for the recitation of each day. Now then taking above Programme of exercises as the criterion by which to judge, do I now earn my $7 1/2 a week pretty well _____ taking it for granted that I do my duty? There is on thing pretty certain, they will have to raise the wages or lessen the labor if they keep me here another term. I am very glad to learn that the Boys are doing well. I hope Aaron's health may improve & his strength increase as he becomes acclimated to the country. I am also glad to hear that you are interested in the great effort which is being made throughout the entire North & West in behalf of Freedom in Kansas & Freedom of Speech & of the Press thro' the land. I also thank you for your good opinion of me in regard to this question. I trust that I shall always be found on the side of Freedom, let what will come. I need no lecture on that point, and I am heartily sorry that there are any. professionally intelligent men in our land that do, but such is the case. The Republican Movement is the one upper most in the minds of a very large majority of the people of the free states and I think there is no doubt but the Freemont will be our next President & God grant it for I feel certain if the Republicans fail this fall, the whole North West will ultimately be turned over to the power of the Slave oligarchy of the South, which may God forbid. But my sheet is full. Give my best regards to the Boys & tell George that I have looked in vain as yet for a letter from him. Please accept for yourself of the best wishes of your sincere friend & cousin.

E B Fish

October 8, 2015

A CIVIL WAR SOLDIER'S LETTER

As a follow-up to the last article in this column, the letter of teacher E. B. Fish to his cousin describing the start of a new schoolyear at the Academy on the Green, I offer his letter of June 1863. This one he writes as a Union soldier in the Civil War. You will note that this is a primary source with valuable insights as to the life and times of those in uniform 152 years ago.

In the Field before Port
Hudson June 1863

Cousin Mary

Without waiting for an opportunity to make those "apologies" which have become so necessary to fashionable letter writing at the present day, in reference to "Long delay in answering yours & c" I seat myself to improve a few leisure moments this morning in replying to your very welcome letter of April 26th which came to hand a week ago today and was perused with great interest. There, now, "school marm" is a sentence for you to analyze, put in "Diagram" & parse according to Prof. Clark. Will you do it? You will conclude I presume on looking at the date of this that I am now, at least where there is & has been some fighting done & to be done, which is most assuredly the case. You have probably seen in the northern papers that acct. of Gen'l Banks' expedition up the "Teche" through Franklin & other fronts to Opelousas, & its results. He went thence to Alexandria on Red River a distance of eighty five miles which we marched in less than three days & a half. We remained at A. a little more than a week taking a short excursion of about thirty miles up to "Pine Woods" & back in the time which occupied two days & a half of our week's rest. We then took the "back track" about fifty miles over our former route to a point near Holmesville where we struck off across the country to Summerport on the Atchafafaya (Shafalia) River which we crossed and continued on our way to "Bayou Sara" "en route" to Port Hudson. We crossed the Mississippi at "Bayou Sara" which is a small village about fifteen *miles* from Port Hudson on Monday night, & on Tuesday finished on our way to this point a distance of about thirteen miles & over the most hilly road I have ever seen in the whole southern country. The 1st hill which we had to climb from "Bayou Sara" being almost the "Fac Simile" of the "Big Hill" out of Ithaca & made me for the moment almost think I was there. We arrived here the same day about sundown. Wednesday morning May 27th our boys had their first engagement at Port Hudson with the rebels, and it was a very severe one I can assure you. It cost our Co a 1st Lieut. & two privates killed besides quite a number wounded, letting alone the loss in the rest of the regt. & Brigade. Two of the most prominent & worthy officers on our Gen'ls (Weitzel) staff were killed during this day's fight, the act. Adj Gen'l & Chief Engineer. We were victorious however and drove the enemy back into & through their 1st line of entrenchment, our boys occupying that line and compelling the enemy to fall back into their 2nd line of defenses. We have retained the position thus gained for two weeks past & our fellows at some points are so near the rebel lines that they can toss their crackers over the breast works to them. We have been lying here over two weeks and are likely to have quite a "siege" of it as we are getting "Mortars & heavy "Siege Guns" into position so as *soon* to encircle the devoted "Port" & garrison in a perfect wall of fire & pour a heavy shower of "Shot" & "Shell" upon their doomed heads for doomed they are, and Port Hudson must inevitably fall into our hands ultimately, or Gen'l Banks' military reputation will be ruined & his chances for a nomination for the next Presidency utterly destroyed. I sometimes think that if twere not for so much of this Political juggling & rivalry between our prominent military Leaders the war might have been ended before this, & I do not know but that the prophesy of a certain prominent Southern man, "That the war will not end during Lincoln's Administration" is likely to prove true from the same cause. My position is one of comparative safety, as I am acting Ordinance Sarg't for Weitzel's Div and for the most of the time have to stay in the rear in charge of the ammunition. I am occasionally sent to the Front on business connected with the Department, at which time I go fearlessly in the discharge of my duty and I should just so fearlessly were I with my company. I certainly don't think I should show the "white feather", as some of our boys have done on this occasion. I have had several pretty close calls I can tell you. The first day here in the woods a shot from the rebels passed about six feet over my head & killed one of the mules hitched to one of my ammunition wagons about two rods from where I stood & wounded another one for me and once or twice when I have been down to the front on duty the shot & shell & rifle balls have whistled over my head like so many hailstones but I have been thus far mercifully spared and I feel content to leave my self in the hands of that kind Providence, who hath preserved my life to the present moment & "who (I know) Doeth all things well". It is certain that I shall not expose myself needlessly to danger out of mere curiosity. I had not heard of cousin Cornelia's death previous to you writing and I was very much surprised and pained to learn that she was gone. Yet such is life. Friends at home die & the news of their death comes mournfully to us while in the service of our country in the army. Sons, Husbands, Fathers & Brothers in the army die or are killed in battle & the tidings come to the "Dear ones at home" with crushing weight as the thought occurs to them "away from home" no kind friend or relative to soothe the fevered brow or close the sunken eyes or catch the last fond accents of the departing one. Yet such is the record of thousands upon thousands who have laid down their lives upon the various battlefields & in the numerous hospitals of this bloody & unholy war. There is no such young man in "D" Co or in our Reg't that I can find as you speak of in your letter so that I cannot gratify your curiosity by letting you know what "kind of a fellow he is" I am well acquainted with all of the Sarg'ts of Co "D" and I know there is no Sarg't H Norton in that Co nor in any other Co in the Reg't that I can find. He must be in the 175th Reg't instead of the 75th. I will accept your kind invitation to "come down" & assist you & Maria in singing "Harwell" & a few other old & new pieces too when the war is over if spared to see that time in good health. Till then I shall have to say ____ Nay to the_____." Will You Come Too?" for duty calls another way and I have a rougher and more rugged path to climb than the "road Musicali" It is very little singing that I do now days tho I occasionally get out my song book & find myself singing over the good old Songs of former days. Viz "The Sister's Call" "Thunderstorm" "Loved Ones at Home" & (et)c. But its all alone & not much enjoyment in it, tho' I would not be deprived of the privilege for anything. I sometimes think that I would lose almost any other "Gift" with which the "Creator" has endowed me than the "Gift of Music" small tho' it be, it affords one so much company. Give my love to all and write again soon and _ oblige.

 Your Cousin E. Belcher Fish

December 3, 2015

"HOMER" BY ISAAC MARSHALL SAMSON

Historians usually learn of the past from what has been recorded in prose, but occasionally one comes across material that is in verse. Such is the case when I came across in the Town archives a little, 37-page booklet published in Homer in 1900. The title was simply POEMS and its author was Isaac Marshall Samson, one of the members of the George Washington Samson Family that occupied "Wisdom's Gate," the "temperance tavern" on the corner of Main and Albany Street in the 1830s. The second poem in the booklet is titled "Homer." In thirty-two lines it captures what the poet most appreciated about living here 115 years ago—the things that Nature and humankind had done to make the town hospitable for residents and visitors alike. The poem provokes us to ask "What words would we use today to describe our community? What do we most appreciate about the place we call home?"

HOMER

  Near a silvery stream, between two hills,
  A lovely town is seen,
  With schools, churches and mills,
  Shops and village green.
  The gentle slope of either hill
  Towards that lovely town,
  Has sparkling streamlets or rills,
  Rushing out of the ground.
  The flowery lawns and cooling shades
  Attract the passer by.

A landscape here is outlaid
For every artist's eye.
On the streets the wheelmen ride,
And make a lively run;
Ladies and gents ride side by side,
To chat and have their fun.
This is a town of health and ease,
Where cares do not abide.
You can bask as you please
In sun or fireside.
The soft breeze from the hills,
In the summer heat,
Pervades the groves and arbors fills,
And makes a cool retreat.
The hills and vales and little streams,
And songsters on the fly,
Will fill your mind with pleasant dreams
Of pleasures long past by.
The lofty trees and flowering lawns,
With streets broad and fine,
Will compare, in prose or songs,
With towns upon the Rhine.
("wheelmen" means bicyclists)

Chapter 6

Articles of 2016

January 14, 2016

THE WOMAN'S PLACE

Recently, I was discussing with a reader of my column about the daunting difficulties faced by the women who were part of the early settlement of the Town of Homer in the 1790s. The responsibilities shouldered by women in any era have been challenging, but due to modern conveniences that we take for granted we lose sight today of the rigors endured by our grandmothers and female ancestors before them. Allow me to describe what life was like for women in rural Central New York State in the 1890s.

One hundred twenty years ago, you would find girls at an early age being inculcated by their mothers in the need to act responsibly. A girl would be expected to assist her mother in domestic chores around the house, to learn the tasks required of a rural wife and mother of the day, including helping her with the care of any younger siblings. A mother was often delighted that her firstborn was a girl, since this meant she would have someone to assist with her domestic burdens.

A mother explained to her daughter that a woman was measured by the condition of her home. An untended yard and garden, a house in need of paint, and untidy interior rooms signified a failure on the part of the woman to provide an orderly environment for her family—an environment that fostered good health and virtuous standards. In addition, within the home, the girl would be taught how to bake bread, can fruit, and do the laundry.

Baking bread required twenty-four hours. First, a sponge for white bread, consisting of yeast, sugar, water, and flour, had to be set and left to rise overnight. The next day, the sponge was divided into loaves and set aside to rise again for forty-five minutes before being baked in the wood-burning stove. The intensity of the heat could affect the baking process. A young girl would discover that it took considerable practice to master the art of baking. Later in life, she might find herself increasingly relying upon the purchase of bread from the bakery in the village.

Canning fruit was equally demanding work. After picking the fruit with her mother in the family's orchard or in nearby woods, the girl assisted in the canning. It was not unusual on a particularly hot July day for the females of the family to make ten quarts of black raspberries into jam and four pounds of currant jelly. The next day, they might can five more quarts of berries. The kitchen was stifling hot, and the women would have stiff necks and aching shoulders on the following day. They had to remind themselves of how good the fruit would taste next winter. True, fruits and vegetables packed in tin cans were available in stores in the village, but these foods were more expensive and often left a "tinny" taste in the mouth. Later, a woman might experience a twinge of guilt when she purchased a canned item in town, though it helped her to escape the tyranny of the kitchen.

It must have been difficult for women to get up any enthusiasm for Mondays. Traditionally that was washing day. Doing the laundry must have been the most taxing. The young girl would be taught by her mother how to sort and wash the clothes. First to be done were the delicate and white fabrics. Ginghams and calicos were second, and the woolens last. One tub was filled with very warm, soapy water. A mother showed her daughter how to rub the soiled clothes in the soapy water but cautioned her not to use the washboard for delicate fabrics, just for the other clothes. A second tub, empty, received the scrubbed clothes. Hot water heated on the stove was then poured over the clothes. Soap was added, the tub covered, and the clothes boiled for half an hour. After being drained in a basket, the clothes were placed again in the tub to be rinsed with clean water, wrung with a wringer, and hung on a clothesline outside to dry. In winter, the clothes froze "stiff as a board" on the line. Laundry day had to be sheer drudgery, and the rural housewives could not help but envy the people in the village or in Cortland who could afford to have domestics or sent their washing and ironing out to be done.

Life for the Victorian housewife was absorbed in eating, sleeping, canning, baking, cooking, cleaning, washing, sewing, raising poultry, tending the garden, attending Sunday church services, and birthing and raising the children. Time passed in neither totally pleasant nor totally unpleasant fashion; it simply passed—as she went about her mundane chores. Resentment must have crept in over time as women came to realize the sacrifices being made. Like a goodly number of her sex of the era, the Victorian woman began to resent that those who were considered worthy enough to look after and care for the menfolk were denied the right to vote by the menfolk occupying the seats of political power. She felt she deserved a voice and merited more than just a servile role and the expectation to make herself to appear physically attractive and to behave in public in a demure manner. A woman was expected to just accept her lot in life; a woman's place was in the home while a man's place was in the fields or in business pursuits or in political life. For her to want anything else was considered "unlady-like."

For those readers interested in learning more, I suggest Harvey Green's *The Light of the Home* (2003), which was the source for this article. The volume provides what its subtitle states: *An Intimate View of the Lives of Women in Victorian America.* Within its pages, one gains a detailed understanding of the disturbing means by which "woman's place" has been defined through American history and in the nineteenth century in particular.

January 28, 2016

RALPH RURAL'S VERSE

Seeing folks have enjoyed the ice skating on the Green that has traditionally been provided by the Homer Fire Department, I am prompted to share a poem about the Green that was written in February of 1861. It was written by "Ralph Rural," a pen name believed to have been used by Homer's native-son Paris Barber (1814–1876), who surely would have enthusiastically endorsed a place for ice skating upon the nineteenth century public space he helped to design.

On March 1, 1860, the *Cortland County Republican*, a newspaper published in Homer, ran this notice: "An invitation is hereby extended to all those interested in the improvement of the Green to make a plan for such improvement. Any design handed in will be duly considered by the Committee. All plans should be handed to either of the undersigned on or before the 25th of March next." The names of three women and three men were listed. One of them was forty-six-year-old Paris Barber. This would have caused no surprise to the citizens of Homer, for Paris was well known in the county as a horticulturalist and landscape designer. He was a logical choice to serve as president of the Homer Rural Improvement Association he helped to create. He successfully spearheaded the effort to have a more park-like space of trees and flowers in front of the churches and Academy in the village.

The same newspaper in its February 15, 1861, issue reported that the Association held a party for the community. It must have been done to generate support for a redesigned Green.

"The first Annual Festival of the Homer Rural Improvement Association filled Academy Hall last Thursday evening. The evening was passed very pleasantly. The President, Mr. P. Barber, read a history of the Association. Several Tableaux and Charades were then presented. A better exhibition of this kind was never made in Homer."

The news article was then followed by Ralph Rural's poem:

> The festival, the festival!
> It well demands a song;
> For never in that classic Hall
> Had gathered such a throng.
> It seemed as if the Carnival
> Had been transferred from Rome;
> As if its scenic wonders all
> Were acted 'neath its dome.
> As when a captured city breaks
> Her bonds and rises free,
> Then in triumphant gladness makes
> One mighty jubilee,
> So rallied forth our people wise—
> Success their efforts crown!
> To institute an enterprise
> To beautify the Town.
> Joy, Love, and Hope, were there at home,
> They were the happiest three;
> They shook the Hall from base to dome
> With harmless revelry.
> No shout of brutal bacchanal
> Made discord to the ear.
> For Temperance ruled within the Hall
> As sunshine rules the year.
> Anon impressively were shown
> Beautiful Tableaux, grand
> As if just carved from Parian stone
> By some great sculptor's hand.
> The enterprise must sure succeed
> So happily begun;
> For every man laid by his creed,
> And all became as one.
> In future years when we are gone,
> Fair children in our groves

> Shall sport upon their greenest lawn
> Or tell their gentle loves.
> I see in after time these bowers.
> Sweet voices from their glades
> Do bless the names who sowed the flowers
> And set these classic shades.

February 11, 2016

A SORELY TESTED HOMER PARENT

Parenting in any time period can be a challenge. Can anyone relate to this account of a parental situation faced by a nineteenth century father? It seems that Paris and Lydia Jane Barber, prominent Homer citizens residing on Clinton Street in the village, had three children, two girls and a younger boy. It was Paris' intent to raise the children to be curious about the world around them and to always be worthy of their parents' trust, but Charlie put that intent to the test one day.

Paris was sitting at a mahogany desk, engaged in some writing, and young Charlie was playing near the fireplace. The lad decided to interrupt his father's work to ask a question he had been pondering: "Father, may I take the brass shovel from the fireplace set and use it out of doors to make mud pies?"

Paris merely smiled and replied, "No." Both father and son returned to their tasks. After several minutes, Charlie returned with a second question: "Father, if the shovel gets broken could I have it to play with?" And Paris, still smiling, replied, "Yes, of course. When the shovel is not fit for use then it will be your plaything." Charlie went off pondering this answer. More time passed.

Then there was the sound of breaking metal. Paris looked up and was astonished to see his son standing before him holding the shovel with a piece of its handle missing.

"It got broken, father. So now I can have it, can't I?"

It has been recorded that Paris "went into direct action to the acute sorrow of his son." To be sure, Paris was not smiling at that moment. It was also recorded that the mutilated shovel continued its service at the fireplace for many years to come, bearing testimony to the fact that trust in one's children has its limitations. Perhaps, too, it served as a reminder that parental responses to children's curiosity-fed questions must be carefully thought through.

March 10, 2016

AND HOW WAS SCHOOL TODAY?

History notes that some children seem to have a propensity for involving themselves in pranks at school. According to his memoirs, Homer's native-son and the assistant personal secretary to President Lincoln, William Osborn Stoddard (1835–1925), was not above some classroom mischief himself. On one occasion, which he only confessed to some thirty years after the fact, he deftly managed to capture an assortment of stinging insects—wasps, hornets, and bees—and to place them in a lidded pasteboard box. He carried the box into the Academy on the Homer Green one morning and, during recitation, carefully placed it under an unoccupied desk near his own. With a stick he knocked off the lid, and, in his words, "the new candidates for admission to the academy were free to present their credentials." As the angrily humming throng of bugs arose in the classroom, Stoddard, as planned, scrambled out the window near his desk. Hanging onto a lightning rod, the little imp managed to observe the "scene of heterogeneous and exclamatory confusion" he had caused with this Pandora's Box. During the days that followed, he derived satisfaction from the efforts of the perplexed learned men of Homer in trying to determine "how so many different kinds of stinging insects could have broken out of the same nest and how and why they had made their nest in the schoolroom."

Stoddard took delight in telling of other schoolboy antics he either observed or participated in as a pupil at the Academy. Someone (could it have been Stoddard?) climbed to the school belfry one winter and packed the bell with so much snow that it was unable to ring in the morning when it was time to summon young scholars to their desks. Could Stoddard have participated in the prank that resulted in Judge Keep's red cow making its way up the stairs of the school? Those traversing the Green beheld the sight of a bellowing horned head protruding out of an upper window.

Another student's mischief once got Stoddard into trouble, and from this experience he learned early on of the concept of injustice. He found himself being enrolled by his grandfather, Squire John Osborn, one of the founders of the Academy, in the "district school" at the south end of Main Street instead of at the Academy on the Green. Perhaps this was because the schoolteacher, Miss Hathaway, believed that if you spared the rod, you spoiled the child. Stoddard, years later, recalled, ". . . one morning I was bending over my book at my desk when down over my shoulders came several sharp cuts of a heavy switch." The blows were delivered without explanation. Afterwards, Stoddard found that the teacher thought he was the boy who had been lobbing "paper-balls" in class. Stoddard concluded: "That is the idea which lies at the bottom of most of the national declarations of war and the people who suffer are rarely the ones who were to blame." After this incident, Squire Osborn returned his grandson to his desk at the Academy. Apparently, he did not unsympathetically admonish his grandson with these words: "Well, if you didn't deserve the switching for that misdeed, you probably did for something else."

March 24, 2016

WHAT AND WHERE IS BREWERY HILL?

According to H. P. Smith's history of Cortland County published in 1885, from the establishment of the Town of Homer in 1794 until 1829 the township included the present town of Cortlandville. By Smith's account, the township of 1829 could boast of ten distilleries, six of which were located within the boundaries of the present Town of Homer. In those days, the manufacture of whiskey was the town's principal industry. In an agrarian society, distilling was, as Smith put it, "a practical and profitable method of disposing of surplus grain at home, instead of transporting it many miles to other markets." Bartering was a common means of acquiring needed goods and services one could not produce for oneself, and jugs of whiskey were comparable to currency. If one wished to purchase this good, one went to one of these distilleries and for twenty-five cents carried home a jug of the amber colored libation. Benajah Tubbs was one of these distillers, and his operation was on "Brewery Hill."

By 1839, the town of Homer had four grist mills, nine sawmills, one oil mill, one fulling mill (for cleansing and pounding/strengthening of wool), one distillery, and one brewery. The brewery was located between what was once High and Prospect Streets. This is a section of East Hill immediately above Albany Street, or what was then known as the Albany Post Road. It was right between present day River Street and Carroway Hill Road, which is the area now traversed by Interstate 81.

Historian Smith made this observation about local consumption of whiskey: "The liquor was then used with a freedom that would at the present time [1885] cause a general sentiment of horror in any community; but at the same time, the knowledge of chemistry was not so profound among the distillers as it is today, and their products consequently were of a much purer and more wholesome character than a great deal of the spirits sold at present." He added that public intoxication was, in fact, no more frequent in 1839 than in 1885.

A local historian of the 1930s, Porter K. Bennett, whose great-great-grandfather built a house in 1806 on East Hill, once spoke at a meeting of the

Cortland County Historical Society on the checkered reputation of Brewery Hill. He said that the residents of that neighborhood in its early days were known to be "independent, quarrelsome, and profane." Breaking up fights kept the local justice of the peace fairly busy. One keeper of social tranquility employed a simple, but effective method. He merely waded into a melee while swinging around his head a double-bladed axe. You might say that that cut out the nonsense.

It is possible that the reputation of the neighborhood was embellished by the local champions of temperance who put their own negative spin on Brewery Hill. More lore than fact is likely a product of this poem from 1900 by a local temperance man titled "Bad Streets in Homer":

Brewery Hill and Spring Street
    Are worse than hell in fervent heat;
    They fight, yell, get drunk and sleep,
    And drive old horse frames on the street

So, Brewery Hill developed a rather unsavory reputation. Yet, one needs to keep in mind that the Village of Homer had at least five taverns by 1900, which must have caused the constable to earn his salary. And Brewery Hill could not have been completely devoid of respectability, given the fact that a chapel and Sunday School were maintained there by clergy of the churches on the Green.

Cockfighting—a blood sport in which roosters are placed in a ring and forced to fight to the death for the "amusement" of onlookers and gamblers—is illegal throughout the United States today, but it was not uncommon on nineteenth century Brewery Hill. The sport was not confined to the Hill, however. Citizens of more genteel reputations were known to raise birds for this activity. Even William Osborn Stoddard, who was born on Albany Road within the shadow of Brewery Hill and destined to serve as President and Mrs. Lincoln's assistant personal secretary in the White House, raised game fowl when he was coming of age in Syracuse. The budding capitalist purchased a pair of Maryland birds known for their rarity of fight and beauty. From them he raised contenders for cockfights and earned the nickname of "Game Stoddard." Years later he was astonished to discover that a sporting event between Onondaga and Cortland counties had been won by "the Stoddard game fowls."

So, this simply points out that manners and morals go through changes through history. What is acceptable or unacceptable in one era may not be in another.

Yet, one activity on Brewery Hill was enjoyed through the ages: sledding in the winter months. Local boys were always coasting down the Hill's slope. A bobsled in 1900 might hit the bump at the bottom where the slope intersected an unpaved Albany Road. Then, the boys would find themselves in a snowbank while the sled continued its way over the bridge and on toward Main Street. This writer grew up on Albany Street and has fond memories of some risky sledding down the same Hill with the Kingsbury boys in the 1950s. For this writer, the muse yields a different poem:

> Brewery Hill and Albany Street
> Were heavenly fun in winter's sleet;
> We'd sled, we'd yell, we'd fall in a heap,
> Or drive our sleds out in the street.

April 7, 2016

HOMER'S REMARKABLE POSTAL SERVICE

I saw Don VanSlyke, the friendly postal carrier, trudging through snow and Arctic chill this winter to place mail in villagers' mailboxes. This got me questioning what mail delivery was like in Homer in bygone days. Thanks to the late, local historian R. Curtis Harris, the answer is available. Harris researched and compiled reams of historical material from which I have gleaned this two-installment account of the town's remarkable postal system.

The U. S. Postal Service is one of the few government agencies explicitly authorized by the United States Constitution that was ratified in 1788. It can trace its origins back to 1775 during the Second Continental Congress when Benjamin Franklin was appointed the first Postmaster General. The Town of Homer first participated in the postal system in 1808, the year that Cortland County separated from Onondaga County. At that time the Town of Homer was larger; it included what is now the Town of Cortlandville. Since the Village of Homer was the initial and largest settlement in the Town, the first post office was established here, and a local lawyer, Townsend Ross, was appointed its first Postmaster. The second post office was set up in the settlement of Port Watson, located near a mill and a dam at the head of navigation on the Tioughnioga River. A third post office in the Town of Homer was set up in Cortland Village in 1814, but mail for its patrons had to be addressed to Homer. Mail was received in the Homer Village post office and then forwarded to the outlying offices in Cortland Village and Port Watson. Offices were later opened in two hamlets in the Town of Homer: East Homer and Little York.

Through the nineteenth century, the post office in the Village of Homer was located at different sites along the east side of Main Street, ranging from Water Street south almost to Albany Street. The north end of the

Sherman Exchange block contained the post office as did the Wheadon Block (destroyed by fire and since replaced), the Brockway Block, and George Phillips' store that used to be near the Albany Street corner. The office that was located on Wall Street and Main succumbed to a fire that consumed the entire building in 1875.

In the first half of the 1800s, Homer's mail arrived by stagecoach. Coaches pulled by a team of four horses passed through the Village five times a day. Residents listened eagerly for the blast of the stage driver's horn, sounded from the crest of either East or West Hill. This signaled the arrival of the coach and any letters or parcels it carried. Folks expecting mail scurried to the post office, since no personal deliveries were made to one's residence or business. Picking up one's mail on Sunday was frowned upon and even prohibited by some of the local churches as a practice that was not keeping holy the Sabbath. According to another former local historian, Mrs. Ina Bird, prayer meetings were regularly held in the 1870s and 1880s, for which area farmers stopped their labors and also had an opportunity to pick up their mail once a week along with a copy of the weekly *Homer Republican* newspaper or the *New York Tribune*.

Postage stamps did not appear on letters until 1847. A letter was folded and sealed with sealing wax, and the price of the postage was written on the folded letter. Every letter had a separate envelope and a waybill that had to be copied. Mileage determined the cost of carrying mail. A letter traveling 50 miles cost six and a half cents. Over 100 miles and less than 200 cost twelve and a half cents, which equaled "a shillin'." Eighteen and three-fourths cents was exacted for 200 to 500 miles. Over 500 miles cost two shillings. Historian Harris noted that this last cost was comparable at that time to "the price of a gallon of whiskey, including the jug!" Every thirty days the post office was required to send a full report to Washington, DC.

For many years, the Homer post office sent mail to outlying offices. This included Scott, East Scott, Spafford, South Spafford, Dresserville, Como, Glen Haven, Tula, and Ceylon. East Scott was located approximately three miles up Cold Brook Road from present-day Route 281. About two and a half miles beyond that was Tula. Ceylon was the name designated by the U. S. Post Office for the area along the east side of the lake that was known to the locals as Fairhaven and before that as "Glenville." "Ceylon" was used to differentiate it from the long-established post office at Fairhaven on Lake Ontario. Every post office, even these country offices, was manned by salaried postmasters. Appointments as postmasters by the federal government were considered much-prized patronage plums.

Glen Haven, located at the southwest end of Skaneateles Lake, was known for over half a century for its Water Cure Sanitarium. Later it was used as a summer hotel. In 1911 the City of Syracuse bought and razed it. During its heyday, spacious buildings and numerous cottages provided accommodations for 250 people. These people, along with other summer and year-round residents nearby, received any mail from a post office in the hotel. Some mail came by boat from the village of Skaneateles, and some came by stagecoach from the Homer post office. Pulled by three horses, the Glen Haven stage met the train in Homer every afternoon and then traveled back to Glen Haven, Scott, and Ceylon. Between 1905 and 1911 the driver was George Lyon of Scott.

The method of supplying out-lying post offices from a receiving office, like Homer, by horse-pulled conveyances, was called the "Star Route System." Locally, it was started in the 1870s. The first driver of the route from Homer to Spafford's Corner via Cold Brook was C. W. Churchill. For many years, drivers like Churchill provided faithful service in all kinds of weather and road conditions. Dirt roads could be dusty in summer and muddy in spring. Ice and snowdrifts presented impediments in winter. Potholes presented challenges, as did pitch-holes. The latter were rather narrow, sharp depressions running across snow-covered roads. These were caused by sleighs and cutters regularly traveling across roadways, leaving perpendicular indentations that jostled both the mail and its deliverer. Historian Harris was told by one old-timer that it was enough to "jar your gizzard loose." The *Homer Republican* reported in 1901 that the Scott stage driver counted 460 pitch-holes between Homer and Scott.

While it was necessary for rural residents to retrieve their mail at their nearest neighborhood post office, if you were lucky enough to live along one of the Star Routes you could hand your out-going mail directly to the driver. Of course, this meant you had to be waiting for him at the roadside to hand it over as he went by. Long waits could be irksome but not as much as seeing the mailman's rig flying by as you came racing out of your home too late with important letters in hand.

In August of 1901, the *Homer Republican* announced that the federal government was to provide a new service to farmers living along the mail routes: weather forecasts. In an age without the radio, television, or computer, this source of information must have been welcomed by those whose agrarian interests were subject to the vagaries of Mother Nature. The order called for all mail carts to stick a flag out the back window. Weather predictions received the day before were provided the driver. In turn, the driver selected a flag of the appropriate color and affixed it to his rig. In this way, farmers along his route might spy the flag signifying the likely weather to expect. It was quite the innovation for its time.

April 21, 2016

THIS IS THE SECOND OF TWO INSTALLMENTS ON THE HISTORY OF THE HOMER POST OFFICE.

In September of 1903, the Homer Post Office commenced Rural Free Delivery. Mail would be brought to individual mailboxes in the countryside. The first carrier was Charles A. Fox. His route was a little more than twenty-five miles. He took present-day Route 41 out of Homer. He traveled to Scott and then down the hill to Ceylon. Turning around there, he went on around the end of the lake to Glen Haven. From there he made his way up the Grout's Mills road, through the corner at Scott Gulf, and on down the West Scott Road to the Scott Road (Route 41) near the Homer Grange Hall. He then climbed the steep hill to its crest and ran southerly along the top of Brake Hill and down to the School Road, before returning to Homer. Fox had close to five hundred postal patrons and carried locked pouches for the offices at Scott, Ceylon, and Glen Haven. For his work he received fifty dollars per month and had to furnish and maintain his own horse, wagon, and harness. There was a time where he could take a fee of ten cents for delivering messages in the village, but he was admonished to not solicit business for any merchant.

R.F.D. service from Homer was later extended to Cold Brook and Little York valleys, East Hill, and the west side of the valley below East Homer. Meanwhile, some of the outlying offices, such as Tula, East Scott, Ceylon, and Glen Haven were discontinued. Today, franked covers from these places are rare and of great value to philatelists (students and collectors of postal stamps).

Parcel post delivery service began in the U.S. in 1913. In the early years of this service, customers and postal officials were still getting used to how the service could be used. Fortunately, there is no record in Homer of the service being used to mail children, as happened elsewhere. On February 19, 1914, May Pierstorff, just short of her 6th birthday, was "mailed" from her parents' home in Grangeville, Idaho, to her grandparents' house about 73 miles away for just 53-cents worth of stamps. Actually, May was "mailed" by entrusting her to a relative who worked on the Railway Mail trains. However, the first child "mailed" in the U.S. was the son of Mr. and Mrs. Jesse Beauge of Glen Este, Ohio. In mid-January, 1913, the lad was carried by Rural Free Delivery carrier Vernon Little to his grandmother, Mrs. Louis Beague, about a mile away. The boy's parents paid 15-cents for the stamps. Oh, and by the way, they even insured their son for $50. There were other cases of "child mail" until a ban was effectively enforced in 1915.

The inhabitants of the Village of Homer continued to come to the Post Office on Main Street for their mail until 1922. In October of that year, village delivery commenced. It has been the norm ever since.

With the coming of the railroad through Homer in the mid-1850s, mail pouches arrived via the morning and afternoon trains. Later, the mail arrived without the train having to come to a stop. As a youngster growing up on the corner of Clinton Street and Maple Avenue in the Village, this writer can recall standing at the nearby train station (now the Police Department on James Street) and keeping a steady eye on the mail pouch hanging on a hook waiting to be whisked away by a fast moving train. The specially constructed catcher pouch was grabbed by the catcher mechanism in the passing railway car, and the catcher pouch would release from the holding rings on the mail crane. This technique was known as "mail on the fly." Starting in the 1870s, this technique of the Railway Mail Service was the backbone of the U.S.P.S. well into the twentieth century. When the mail clerk of the Railway Post Office car grabbed the catcher pouch on the mail crane he would at the same time kick out the outgoing mail for delivery to that village. The idea behind the catcher pouch was that there could be an exchange of mail to villages too small to justify the train stopping. As I recall, if you blinked the moment the train passed, you missed it all. One moment the pouch was hanging there, and the next second it had vanished.

Like the stage driver's horn of the early 1800s, the whistle of a locomotive in the late 1800s announced to the villagers that it was time to be "goin' for the mail." For about an hour after train time, the post office would be filled with people waiting for the sorting of the mail. This afforded a daily opportunity for the villagers of Homer to gather and to chat about business and politics, to share family news, and to gossip. This custom built a strong sense of community. "Goin' for the mail" was a task sometimes entrusted to the youngsters of a family. Besides an opportunity to prove they could handle responsibility, it gave the young ones the chance to observe the merchants and elected and appointed dignitaries of the town and village, as they waited in line for their mail. The proper way to politely interact with others was modeled for them in this public forum made available at the most grassroots level by the federal government. Later, they would note that some people entered the post office and used their own keys to open numbered brass boxes in the wall from which they retrieved letters from family and businesses that were sent from far and near.

The Homer Post Office is now on the west side of Main Street. It is a historic structure within the Old Homer Village Historic District. Built in 1937–1938, it is one of a number of post offices in New York State designed by the Office of the Supervising Architect of the Treasury Department, Louis A. Simon. It is a one story, steel frame, rectangular building clad in brick on a stucco clad foundation in the Colonial Revival style. The interior features a mural by Frank Romanelli in 1940 titled "Albany Street Bridge over Tioughnioga River."

Today, packages and enveloped mail can still be sent and retrieved at the counter of the Homer Post Office. Some of the friendliest and most good-humored people you will ever meet represent the U. S. Postal Service at that counter. Admittedly, I have yet to hear my favorite post office joke play out there: A lady bought a stamp at the post office and asked the clerk,

"Shall I stick it on myself?" The clerk replied, "It'll get there faster if you stick it on the envelope."

And the likes of a gregarious Don VanSlyke and others continually deliver mail by foot and motor vehicle to local mailboxes. They make their rounds, bearing witness to the unofficial motto of the postal system: "and these are stayed neither by snow nor rain nor heat nor darkness from accomplishing their appointed course with all speed." The words are translated from those of the Greek historian Herodotus describing the Persian system of mounted postal carriers c. 500 B.C. We may be tempted to take our local postal service for granted as it competes with modern electronic mail service, but we should not, for it strives to satisfy an ancient human need for efficient, hands-on communication and delivery of goods.

May 5, 2016

HOMER'S HOSPITAL

This is the first of a series of three installments on the history of the Homer Hospital and Training School for Nurses.

Did you know that Homer once had a general hospital? And a training school for nurses?

I know, you find it hard to believe. Most people do. But from 1888 through 1926, South Main Street in the village was the site of a medical facility serving the people of the towns of Homer and Cortlandville and those of adjoining towns and counties.

According to a thirty-one-page brochure put out in 1915, the history of the Homer Hospital commenced at a site across from the Homer Green and just south of the original building of today's Elizabeth Brewster House. The premises were purchased by Mrs. Marguerite E. Hakes. Seeing the need for a facility to treat people's infirmities, Mrs. Hakes founded a sanitarium there in April of 1888 and pioneered the hospital movement in Cortland County. Ably assisted by Dr. J. H. Robinson, she saw her dream come true after twenty-seven years of conspicuous success—the evolution of her sanitarium into a general hospital.

On October 14, 1914, several practicing physicians and surgeons from the Homer-Cortland area met at the sanitarium and made plans for a hospital to be staffed by forty doctors. Signatories to the agreement included every physician in the village of Homer. In addition, there was to be a training school for nurses. A new two-story building, attached to the sanitarium by a second floor connecting corridor and conforming to the architecture of the existing two-story building, was designed by Taber & Baxter of Syracuse to accommodate twenty-five patients. The original sanitarium was modernized and refitted. Supervision of all the activities within the hospital was assigned to Mrs. Hakes as the Matron along with an Advisory Board. The Board was comprised of five "duly licensed practicing physicians or surgeons." The Board's duties would include the selection of lecturers for the Training School for Nurses and the determination of the textbooks, the curriculum, and the teaching schedule. The Matron would also serve as the chief dietician and business manager. Reporting to the Matron would be a Superintendent of the Hospital and Training School. This person would be responsible for the operating room, the overall supervision of the nursing staff, the instruction of the nurses in training, and other tasks. The first to hold this position was Kathryn F. Hughes, R.N. Under her was Lucy Gantley, the Night Supervisor.

On December 9, 1914, ninety-six people of the Homer-Cortland area gathered at the Homer residence of Miss Hitchcock and organized the Homer Hospital Society and its Auxiliaries. Its first president was Mr. E. G. Ranney. With a membership of over 200, indicating the community's high level of interest, the sanitarium became the Homer Hospital and Training School for Nurses and would operate under the auspices of the Society. Payment of one dollar annually made one an active member of the Society. Associate members paid five dollars annually. A life member paid twenty-five dollars. Staff and auxiliary members were automatically members of the Society. The "By-Laws, Rules and Regulations" of the Hospital were unanimously adopted on January 26, 1915, at a meeting held in the Homer office of Dr. Robinson. A brochure containing the same was promptly made public.

The Society certainly knew how to market the new hospital. The brochure it issued described its location in words that would rival those of any modern-day real estate broker:

"To those in search of health and the student of the ravages of disease, the advantages of the suburban hospital are no longer a sealed book. The village of Homer, with its progressive people, broad, paved streets, electric lights, pure water, renowned academy with its perfect equipment, extensive playgrounds, churches of many denominations, colonial residences, whose beautiful porches, wide terraces, pure air, making them hospitably delightful either as permanent or summer homes; with its Lackawanna railroad and trolley transportation services affords an ideal location for a general hospital to care for the sick and injured."

The brochure added another benefit: "The Homer Hospital is easily reached by the Homer and Cortland trolley cars, which pass in front of the institution, which is sufficiently removed from the business part of the city to be free from the noises, dust and busy turmoil and yet possesses all its advantages."

As for the services that would be provided, it was pointed out that "No expense has been saved to insure the most sanitary and aseptic surroundings for the care of surgical and obstetrical patients, and the operating and sterilizing rooms will have every modern convenience. . . ." In addition, "an extensive sun parlor facing the east and overlooking the gardens and river will afford convalescents a much-desired retreat." The new hospital boasted of having an X-ray department; obstetric department; genito-urinary department; eye, ear, nose and throat department; dental surgery department; a laboratory department; an anesthetist; and three medical consultants.

Patients would be admitted and provided care irrespective of creed, nationality, or color. Cases of insanity or infectious or contagious diseases (such as the dreaded pulmonary tuberculosis, or TB) were not to be admitted. Patients could have a "cheery, well ventilated and nicely furnished" private room "with good board and competent nursing" that would not exceed $15 per week payable in advance. A few two-bed wards were available for "patients as may be unable to meet the expense of private rooms." Should any patient contract "any of the highly contagious diseases," an "isolation cottage" would be available—not large but well equipped for prompt and efficient care. Any unusual medicine, special supplies, or special nursing would entail an extra charge. Any patient bringing a nurse from outside the hospital would be responsible for an additional $3.50 per week to cover board. Indigent patients were to be "treated free, provided that at the time of application there are vacant beds in the hospital and sufficient funds in the treasury of the auxiliary to care for them." While there were no accommodations at the hospital for patients' family members or friends, there were "a number of suitable boarding houses in the vicinity." Regular visiting hours were posted as from 2 to 4 and 7 to 8 P.M., but visiting in private rooms was permitted daily between 9 A.M. and 9 P.M.

An ambulance service was available "at any hour, either day or night." Requests could be made in person or by phone at either the hospital or at the office of Briggs Brothers (local undertakers who also provided a livery service at this time in the village). The charge was "$2.00 for calls within a reasonable distance," whatever that meant.

Hospitalized patients were expected to observe five rules. First, they were to follow the rules posted in the sick room. Second, they were strictly forbidden to keep or conceal food about the sick room or bed. Third, they were to not interfere with the nurse or her duties, and they were to lower all lights and be ready to retire at 9 P.M. Fourth, any complaints against the hospital or staff member by a patient, physician, nurse, or visitor was to be made in writing to the Advisory Board, who in turn would present a copy to the accused party and provide an opportunity for defense before the Board within the next three days. And lastly, patients upon admission must leave any money or valuables with the Matron. The hospital would refuse to be held responsible for any loss which might occur through a failure of the patient to comply.

The hospital reported that between October 14, 1914 and April 12, 1915 (the first six months after its opening), 93 patients were admitted. The average cost per week per patient was $6.54. Four deaths were reported but in each case the patient was in extremis when admitted. One died from an intestinal obstruction, and three were elderly and in an unconscious condition. No deaths occurred during surgery, and the fledgling hospital was proud to note that "the mortality of the institution compares very favorably with other hospitals with their plants already fully equipped."

May 19, 2016

Now, the brochure published in 1915 provides a fascinating glimpse into the life of nurses training for certification at the Homer Hospital. Applicants were to be between 18 and 35 years of age, and it was just understood that they were females. What male would want to have a career in nursing? It was just a different mindset in the early twentieth century, with a division of labor by gender. While men and women had served as untrained nurses during the bloody Civil War, professional nursing was not yet seen after the war as an excellent career choice for both sexes, as it is today.

The Homer Training School's official application form is interesting and contains questions that would not be permissible in a later era. Besides providing one's full name, age as of last birthday, date and place of birth, signed school transcripts for *at least one completed year of high school*, and two references, one was expected to answer the following:

Are you single, married, or a widow? If married or a widow, have you children, and how many? How provided for?
Are you connected with any church? Name denomination and provide a letter from a clergyman.
Give previous and present occupation, if any.
Have you ever been connected with any training school for nurses?
Have you ever done any nursing?
Height? Weight?
Are you strong and healthy? Provide certification by a physician.

Are your sight and hearing perfect?
Are you free from domestic responsibilities which might interrupt your course in school?
Have you read and do you fully understand the regulations?

Applicants were told that "only a limited number can be admitted" and "a personal interview is desired." They were further cautioned to remember that "they are on trial" and that "the reasons for rejection are not given; the decision when given is final."

Those who passed the screening process entered an instructional program of a year and a half duration. The first two months were a probationary period. If one's teeth needed attention, the matter was to be addressed "before entering the probationary term." If one survived the probationary period, one was accepted as a "pupil nurse." One was also granted credit for the two months just completed and asked to sign a contract promising to remain for the rest of the program and "to obey the rules and regulations of the school and hospital."

The pupil nurses were expected to reside at the hospital. They received board and laundry services. The hospital prescribed a uniform—a pink dress with a white apron. The uniform and the training books were to be provided by the pupil. The pupil was to bring a good supply of other clothing and a watch with a second hand. Each item was to be indelibly marked with the owner's full name. Pupil nurses were to be paid four dollars per month for the first year and six dollars per month for the final six months. It was made clear that this money was not given as a salary; it was "given to defray any extra expense incurred while in the Training School." During any illness, a pupil would receive free care, but time lost was to "be made up at the end of the course, time not to exceed three weeks."

The pupil nurses could be called upon for duty day or night, as needed. A "day nurse" was on duty from 7 in the morning until 7 at night, and a "night nurse" was on duty from 7 at night until 7 in the morning. Every nurse was allowed one half-day off duty each week, except in emergency, "the time to be proscribed by the Superintendent of the Hospital and Training School." During the summer months, a vacation of one week was to be granted "at the discretion of the authorities, time to be deducted." Upon completion of a series of lectures given by the hospital staff and the Superintendent, pupil nurses were to sit for an examination. If they passed, they were entitled to graduation and a hospital diploma.

The nurses were expected to comply with an extensive and detailed list of the "Rules and Regulations for Nurses." It is worth presenting here in its entirety because it allows us to go back a century and imagine the culture of those who wore the pink and white uniforms at the Homer Hospital. Today's hospital nurses will find this quite interesting.

1. Nurses are required to wear the uniform and cap at all times while on duty.
2. She must see that for each new patient the orders are written on the chart by the physician or by his direction, that cards of admission are made out and endorsed by the Superintendent of the Training School and sent to the office. This card, with a record of the pulse, temperature and respiration, must be taken as soon as possible to the Superintendent of the Hospital.
3. They must wear noiseless shoes. They must not remove their cap or apron or lie down while on duty.
4. Graduate nurses and all others employed temporarily in the hospital must observe the rules and regulations of the institution in every particular.
5. Loud talking and any unnecessary noise are forbidden. Nurses must be at their meals in season and must not linger in the dining room after meals.
6. They will retire to their rooms at or before 10 P.M. All save night lights must be extinguished at 10:30 P.M. The hour of rising is 6 A.M., and before leaving room each nurse shall arrange her bed for suitable airing.
7. No nurse shall be absent from the hospital after 10 P.M. without permission from the Superintendent of the Hospital, who must require an explanation for all absences.
8. They must keep their rooms in order and always ready for inspection and every nurse shall be required to keep every part of her apartment in order.
9. They must not take visitors to their rooms or invite them to meals without permission.
10. They are not permitted to receive calls during their hours of duty without permission from the Superintendent of the Training School.
11. When relieved on account of sickness they must not leave their rooms or return to hospital duties without permission from the Superintendent of the Training School, who will call some member of the Advisory Board to attend those who need medical care. They will not consult any other physician or obtain medicine from the Hospital Pharmacy without permission.
12. They will have no relations or communications with any of the physicians, patients, or employees of the hospital, except so far as may be

necessary in the care of the patients or the regular work of the institution. Visiting in the corridors or rooms is forbidden.
13. Nurses in uniform must not go out on the street without specific permission from the Superintendent of the Training School.
14. Nurses must observe proper decorum and civility and at the entrance of an official or stranger, shall, if seated, at once arise and give the visitors prompt attention.
15. Nurses are not allowed to use the telephone while on duty except for business pertaining to the hospital.
16. The Superintendent of the Hospital and Training School is responsible to the physicians and surgeons for the medical and surgical care of the patients in the hospital, and it shall be the duty of each nurse to receive and carry out her orders.
17. They will make no comments upon the treatment of patients by the physicians.
18. Any nurse giving information to a patient or visitor—inside or outside the hospital—relative to histories, diseases or treatment of patients, will subject herself to dismissal from the school.
19. All patients must be treated with kindness and courtesy.
20. Nurses must not be absent from classes or lectures without permission.
21. The resignation of any nurse will not be accepted unless the same reason is recommended by the Superintendent of the Training School.
22. The Superintendent of the Training School, subject to the approval of the Advisory Board, may make such other rules in reference to the conduct of nurses in the hospital, as she may desire, not inconsistent with the foregoing.
23. Under no circumstances is a nurse permitted to express an opinion regarding the condition of a patient.

Anybody think they would like to sign up? To modern sensibilities, this seems like a humorless convent or a regimented, militaristic lifestyle. However, one must keep in mind that a century ago disciplined, professionally trained nurses were deemed to be the uniformed foot soldiers in combating disease and infection. The enemy to bodily health was not being confronted with the arsenal of medicines and labor-saving technology that we take for granted today. Penicillin, for example, was not discovered by Scottish scientist Alexander Fleming until thirteen years after the Homer Hospital and Training School opened its doors. Even then, it was not available for use in treating infections until 1942. Nurses of the early twentieth century waged a constant battle, with the resources at hand, to prevent the spread of disease and infection.

Image 6.1 Picture postcard of Homer's Hospital. *Courtesy of the author.*

June 16, 2016

In Homer in 1915 the curriculum for pupils at the Training School for Nurses focused on nine components:

1. The care of the sick rooms and wards, and the principles of warming and ventilating.
2. Bed-making, management of helpless patients, changing bed and body linen, giving baths, prevention and treatment of bed sores.
3. The preparation and application of fomentations, poultices, cup and minor dressings, the applications and dressing of blisters, care of burns and wounds.
4. The administering of enemata and use of catheter.
5. Antiseptic treatment of wounds, the care of patients before and after operation, the prevention or control of hemorrhage, names and uses of surgical instruments.
6. Bandaging, bandage-making and covering splints.
7. Cooking, preparing and serving delicacies to the sick.
8. Observations and records of the state of secretion, expectorations, skin, temperature, pulse, respiration, sleep, mental conditions, effects of the diet and medicine, electricity and massage.
9. A course in normal and abnormal obstetrical nursing, preparation for delivery, also care of mother and baby.
   Lectures were given by the physicians and surgeons of the Homer Hospital on subjects required by the State Education Department:

Dr. Robinson taught Ethics.
Dr. Gardner taught Medical and Surgical Nursing.
Dr. Reilly taught Anatomy and Physiology.
Doctors Atwood and Braman covered Materia Medica.
Dr. Lucid offered instruction in Surgery, Major and Minor.
Dr. Parsons had expertise in Bacteria and Pathology.
Dr. Potter covered Diseases of Children.
Dr. Chester Waterman lectured on Diseases of the Eye, Nose, Ear, and Throat.
Dr. Tarbell's subject was Nervous Diseases and Insanity.
Dr. Neary taught the intricacies of Gynecology and Obstetrics.

Because of Marguerite Hakes' years of experience operating the sanitarium, she taught the Theory and Practice of Massage and Electricity. Eight more topics were crowded into the Homer course offerings, each with a different instructor, making for a total of nineteen courses or "lectures" to be attended over a year and a half.

Today, far many more years than that are required to be a certified nurse. Professional nursing holds a unique and often underappreciated place in the American health care system, but it took years to arrive at this point. Admittedly, the early nurse education programs, like that in Homer, were little more than apprenticeship programs that used student nurses for their labor. Yet, they proved very popular with both hospitals and students and created a pattern of hospital-based nurse education that continued until the mid-twentieth century. The presence of trained nurses with their emphasis on cleanliness, orderliness and close observation of patients helped to successfully transform hospitals into today's scientific institutions of caring.

Homer's Marguerite Hakes deserves credit for her role in this movement and for mentoring nurses-in-training, though her Hospital and Training School in Homer was short-lived. Its first graduating class was in 1916, consisting of Miss Lucy Gantley, Miss Margaret Bliven, and Miss Lou Marie Angell. Ten years later it closed its doors. George Brockway purchased the property and donated the building on December 10, 1926, to what was called the "Old Ladies Home" (which evolved into today's highly esteemed Elizabeth Brewster House, an assisted living facility for men and women). Most likely, the Homer Hospital could not compete with the ever-expanding medical facility in Cortland. That facility, in the 1920s, was known as Cortland County Hospital (precursor to the Cortland Regional Medical Center on Homer Avenue). Though in existence for only a dozen years, the hospital that Marguerite envisioned satisfied a need in the Homer community and was, as one grateful patient described it ". . . a Hospital of the People, by the People and for the People."

Those who appreciated the sympathetic and practical help received within its walls spoke highly of Marguerite Hakes. They paid tribute to her in 1915 with these words:

> She has ever applied herself as a nurse who was doing real nursing and devoted little or no time to advertising. As a nurse she has objected to being in the limelight, and has been devoid of political ambitions. But she belongs in that class of nurses who quietly and devotedly stand by their tasks, administering impartially to the needs of humanity.

The work done by Mrs. Hakes and the nurses of her hospital was certainly serious and altruistic but leaves one wondering if they approached the bedpans and other chores with any sense of humor back in those days. One must wonder if they would have derived any mirth from this nursing joke:

A man came in for a routine physical at the doctor's office. "Here," said the nurse, handing the man a urine specimen container. "The bathroom is over there on your right. The doctor will be with you in a few minutes." A few minutes later the man came out of the bathroom with an empty container and a relieved look on his face. "Thanks! But they had a toilet in there, so I didn't need this after all!"

June 2, 2016

SIGNIFICANT PORTRAIT BY F. B. CARPENTER COMES TO HOMER

Friday, June 17 and Saturday, June 18 will mark the third annual celebration of Historic Homer, NY. This year's theme is "Historic Homer: The Town That Lights up the Night." It will feature the night-time exterior illumination of the historic architectural structures along the edge of the Green, which is the heart of the Historic District. Many interesting activities, along with Homer's traditional Sidewalk Sales, will draw people of all ages.

One event in particular relates to Francis Bicknell Carpenter, Homer's native son who attended the academy on the Green and went on to become famous for painting portraits of the movers and shakers of nineteenth century America, including President Lincoln. Homer can boast of being the community with the largest collection of Carpenter portraits in the world—21 to be precise. And on Friday, June 17, at 7:15 PM at the Homer Center for the Arts, another portrait will be added to the collection. This is the portrait Carpenter rendered in 1851 of his fiancée Augusta Prentiss.

In the spring of 1851, Carpenter moved from Homer to New York City to set up a studio suitable for all the commissioned work that was to come his way, including five U. S. Presidents. The next August, the twenty-one-year-old married his fifteen-year-old fiancée, the daughter of a female music teacher at the academy on the Green. The couple would have two children, and the family returned summers to Homer. Augusta and Frank are buried in the family plot in Homer's Glenwood Cemetery.

In 2015, the Town of Homer Historian and author of *Lincoln's Gift from Homer, New York,* Martin Sweeney, was contacted by Nannette Orr, the widow of Carpenter's great grandson, Henry Orr, of Katonah, NY. She wished to donate the portrait of Augusta Prentiss Carpenter in memory of Cora Carpenter Legg Orr (1908–1989), Henry's mother and granddaughter of F.B. Carpenter. It was determined that the painting would be donated to the Town of Homer and housed at the Town Hall on Main Street. Through the generosity of eight anonymous donors, the conserved and reframed portrait will be publicly unveiled and officially presented to the Town of Homer as part of the June 17–18 celebration.

On June 17 local art educator and expert on Carpenter, David Quinlan, will join Sweeney in explaining the significance of the twenty-second portrait to come to Homer. This will be followed immediately by the Homer Historic Advisory Committee's showing of a five-minute video. The video is being sent to philanthropic individuals and organizations to encourage financial support of Homer's Lincoln Monument Project. This is an effort being launched to commission bronze sculptor Frank Porcu of Long Island to create and install a lasting tribute at the Town Hall to Carpenter and the other two native sons with significant ties to the life and iconic imagery of "The Great Emancipator," President Abraham Lincoln.

There is no admission fee. You do not want to miss this historic event.

[Note: As of 2020, Carpenter's portrait of his fiancée hangs on a wall next to the old stage in the Town Hall, and the proposed Lincoln Monument has not come to fruition. It will take more than a Village to raise this monument.]

Image 6.2 **Relief woodcut print of Francis B. Carpenter in the 1850s.** *Courtesy of Phillips Free Library, Homer, New York.*

Image 6.3 **Carpenter's portrait of his fiancée Augusta Prentiss.** *Property of the Town of Homer; photographed by David P. Quinlan.*

July 14, 2016

OF CUTTERS AND RICKSHAWS

Back in mid-May I was invited to visit the historic Suggett House on Homer Avenue in Cortland. This was during a garage sale for the Cortland County Historical Society. The good folks there wanted to show me an old horse-pulled cutter with stenciling on its sides they had stored away in a garage. Complete with a buggy whip and not in all that poor a condition for its age, the light horse-drawn sleigh with room for one or two had an interesting identification tag on the back. It read "A. Stebbins, Tailor, Homer." There was a strong possibility that the cutter had been manufactured in Homer. This led me to delve into the archives and the research of past local historians to see what could be learned about the manufacturing of such conveyances in Homer's past. This is what I found:

An 1869 Directory indicates that Alex Bates owned a wagon and sleigh shop since 1859 in a brick building on James Street in the village. There was also an ad for the Empire Shop of W. T. Smith Co. It promoted "Jackson Wagons, Top and Open Buggies, Platform Spring and Lumber Wagons," but, alas, no sleighs or cutters. This shop was established sometime between 1844 and 1850 in a former pottery building on Albany Street. It seems to have been the first wagon shop in Homer to expand into a larger factory enterprise. By 1881 it was building omnibuses, and the firm moved into larger quarters in Cortland where it became known later as the Ellis Omnibus & Cab Company.

As for Homer cutters, however, the name of Charles Gage appears in 1868. An energetic, young man, Gage began making cutters in a box stall in his barn. The partition between two stalls had to be removed to permit the business to expand. Within two years he had partnered with Ossander Bishop. In June of 1871, the local newspaper reported that Gage & Bishop had 300 cutters in production for the fall trade. Gage must have possessed great organizational skills and inventive talent, because within the next decade he developed a factory two stories high that covered half a city block and rented adjacent property to store the thousands of feet of elm and basswood lumber needed for his business. In 1884 he patented a device to saw around logs, which enabled him to secure thin lumber three or four feet wide and up to 100 feet long. The *Homer Republican* newspaper of April 1882 noted that the firm expected to build 17,000 cutters during the season. By 1888, the demand for cutters must have declined. Instead, the firm commenced to manufacture wagon gear and bodies. The production of such soon reached a total of 4000 units per year.

Another Homer transportation business with an interesting history was the Fisher Manufacturing Company founded in 1880 by Willet Fisher. Fisher patented a certain "turn-under gear" for platform spring wagons. He turned out thousands of these gears in a two-storied building, 30' by 50', which was joined at the rear by a one-story blacksmith and machine shop. This was located on the north side of James Street in the first block west of the railroad tracks. Later, the firm was re-organized and went by the name Homer Wagon Co. The manager had a friend who was a missionary in the Far East. Through him orders were placed for jinrikisha wheels. Thus, wheels made in Homer, NY, appeared on conveyances traversing the streets of Hong Kong and cities of China. A fire in 1915 ended the usefulness of this site for continued manufacturing.

For the previous twenty years, Brockway had operated a cabinet-ware shop and undertaking business on the south side of James Street. The building would have been behind the present-day post-office building. In his first year as a carriage manufacturer, Brockway churned out fifty wagons and an equal number of . . . You guessed it! Cutters. Eventually, the factory moved into quarters on three acres east of the railroad tracks between James Street and Elm Street. By 1882, a July issue of the *Homer Republican* reported that Brockway Wagons would be sending forth 2500 wagons. Six years later, Brockway was the largest manufacturer of wagons in the U. S. owned by a sole proprietor, with a yearly income of over $300,000. Were cutters still being produced? Absolutely! In 1882, Brockway leased a site on Albany Street that had been vacated by the W. T. Smith Company. Its sole product was to be cutters. One thousand of them, bearing the Brockway name, were to be ready for the fall trade.

Perhaps an expert on antique cutters could tell if the cutter I saw was made by Homer's Gage and Bishop or Mr. Brockway. But what I really want to see next is an old Chinese rickshaw

August 11, 2016

THE MURAL IN THE HOMER POST OFFICE

The first of five installments

Recently, an article on the Homer Post Office in three installments appeared in this column. Because of it an interesting binder was brought to my attention. The Post Office handed me a one-and-a-half-inch thick binder labeled "Lobby Painting." Inside were copies of all the many correspondences pertaining to the commissioning and installation of the mural located on the interior north wall of the Homer Post Office above the door to the Postmaster's office. The typed and handwritten letters were arranged in reverse chronological order: from most recent (1940) to the earliest (1938). In addition, there were some documents at the very beginning and at the end that revealed the material in the binder had been ordered by Mrs. Colleen Redenback, a teacher in the Homer Intermediate School. My curiosity was piqued, and so I contacted Mrs. Redenback. She confirmed that in 2001, as a computer lab instructor, she had secured grant money and planned to engage fourth grade students and teachers in a project on local history in collaboration with Syracuse University. The goal, she said, was to create "a dynamic website where students would investigate primary source documents and create historically rich articles about local Homer history." While the ambitious website never came to fruition, Mrs. Redenback was able to purchase with District funds four files pertaining to the Homer Post Office mural. The photocopies of the files came from the National Archives & Records Administration, Still Picture Branch, NWCS, Room 5360, in College Park, Maryland. Ultimately, Mrs. Redenback handed this National Archives material in a binder to the local postmaster she had worked with on the school project. She felt it would be kept safe with him for any future history-seekers to utilize.

Good thing she did, since the files reveal the trials and tribulations of getting a mural made for the post office's lobby, the one you see today if you happen to look up to your right while waiting in line for the efficient service provided customers at the counter. The typed and handwritten communications between the artist, the Homer Postmaster, the U.S. Treasury Department's Superintendent for the Section of Fine Arts, and the Supervising Architect are fascinating. They reveal bureaucratic red tape at its entangling best. It is a wonder that decorative paint was ever applied to the wall of the Homer Post Office. This is the story behind the mural.

As part of the New Deal (but not the W.P.A. as is the common mistaken notion), murals and sculpture in post offices were produced between 1934 and 1943 under the Treasury Department's Section of Painting and Sculpture, later called the Section of Fine Arts (or "Section" for short). Besides providing employment for artists during the Great Depression, the purpose was to boost the public's morale with art that, in the words of President Franklin D. Roosevelt, was "native, human, eager and alive—all of it painted by their own kind in their own country, and painted about things they know and look at often and have touched and loved."

On May 25, 1938, Mr. Frank Romanelli (born Francesco Romanelli in Farenz, Italy, 1909) of Buffalo, NY, was informed by letter from Edward B. Rowan, Superintendent of the Section of Painting & Sculpture, that he was invited to accept the offer of a commission to render a mural for the lobby of the freshly built Homer Post Office (1937–1938). Based on the designs

Romanelli had submitted to the Bronx, NY, Post Office mural competition, a jury recommended the artist for a mural decoration "12' Wide by 4' High" over the Homer Postmaster's door. The amount to be paid was set at $800, and the work was to be completed "within a year's time."

Apparently, Romanelli did not receive this notice before he sent out a letter received on June 1, 1938, by the Section of Painting and Sculpture, Procurement Division, Treasury Department, Washington, D. C. Romanelli stated that the *New York Herald Tribune* and the *Buffalo Evening News* had reported that he was one of seventeen artists selected from the Bronx Post Office competition to do murals in other post offices. He went on to write that the news articles reported he had been selected to submit designs for a mural for the Post Office in Homer, NY, but that he had not yet received any official notification. He asked them to please advise and to send blueprints soon since he was "particularly anxious to begin work as soon as possible. . . ."

The letter of notification arrived in Buffalo, and Romanelli accepted the commission by a return letter on May 31st. He assured Superintendent Rowan that he would "be able to complete the work within a year." On June 1, an internal memo in the Treasury Department stated that a contract for the Homer decoration covering 46 square feet would be "drawn up upon the approval of the new sketches designed for this building" at an estimated cost of $17 per square foot. Two days later, Mr. Rowan sent Romanelli a letter telling him to submit his designs for the Homer Post Office for approval and that the $800 would be paid out in three installments: $250 upon approval of the preliminary sketches, $250 upon approval of the full size cartoon, and $300 upon approval of the finished product. A color sketch in the scale of 2 inches to the foot was to be submitted after submission of several pencil sketches. And a visit to the building was advised along with a conversation in person with the postmaster. The Section was to be advised of the visit first so that advance notice could be provided the postmaster. In addition, this information was included:

"It is suggested that you use subject matter which embodies some idea appropriate to the building or to the particular locale of Homer. What we most want is a simple and vital design." The letter closed by stating the Section would like the preliminary designs "at your earliest convenience" because "we would like to have the work completed in about eight months' time."

Now, you can see already the possible impediments that could arise to having the artistic project completed in a timely manner, especially in an age before speedy electronic communications.

August 25, 2016

On June 21, 1938, artist Romanelli submitted a pencil sketch that he claimed was similar to the design he submitted for the Bronx Post Office Competition and would be in keeping with the type of building housing it and with "the locality of the city of Homer." Apparently, he had no idea as to the colonial revival architecture of the building or the fact that it was located in a small, rural village and not a city, and earlier he had written that visiting Homer "would be rather difficult for me." What Romanelli submitted was a stylized depiction of a semi-nude human form popping out of some heavenly envelope during a downpour of rain or sleet or snow upon a community of blocks. This was to be in keeping with the inscription he suggested be placed over the doorway: "Neither rain nor sleet nor snow can stay these couriers etc."

There can be little surprise that Romanelli's sketch was rejected in Washington. As tactfully as possible, they informed him on June 25 that "while we are aware of the sensitive quality of your drawing and the poetic approach which you have used, we do not feel that this type of approach is convincingly related to contemporary American life." Translation: This is not going to play well on Main Street of little, conservative Homer, NY, in 1938. Instead, it was recommended that Romanelli incorporate in his design a less racy subject—the fauna of the region—as he did with his animal studies done for the Buffalo, New York, Marine Hospital and that he forget the inscription over the door.

Romanelli acknowledged receipt of the "conditions outlined" on June 13 and wrote that he would do a site visit "as soon as possible." Seventeen days later he assured Rowan that "new preliminary studies . . . will have as its theme fauna of the region." On July 14, he sent Rowan a sketch of a new proposal. The design was approved and Romanelli was informed in a letter dated July 25. Rowan stated that the "Supervising Architect was particularly pleased with your design." A contract was drawn up on August 1 and sent to Romanelli for a mural to be titled "Deer at Dawn." The artist signed it and sent it in on September 22, but earlier on August 8 he had informed Mr. Rowan that he could not answer some technical questions without doing a site visit and that he hoped to do so on a Sunday or Monday "as soon as possible." He added that he had a change of address now in Buffalo.

Now, here is where the project gets muddled. On August 23, Rowan sends Romanelli samples of canvas which are preferred by the experts in the federal office. The day before, the Supervising Architect had sent a letter to the Homer Postmaster which informed her for the first time that Frank Romanelli had been commissioned to do a mural decoration and would be arriving in Homer "in the near future." Katherine C. Newton, the Postmaster in Homer, fired off a letter on August 24 to the Supervising Architect acknowledging his letter and expressing a desire to "be allowed to offer some suggestions as to the choice of subject for such a decoration." Newton's letter is shared with Mr. Rowan, and he informs Mrs. Newton that a design has already been approved and hopefully "one which will meet with your approval."

At the end of August, Romanelli puts in a request with Rowan for an extension of time to complete the project "should eventualities require it." This was probably a sensible move since on September 8 another contract for a new design was drawn up and on September 14 the artist acknowledged receiving Mrs. Newton's request that he meet with some townspeople of Homer to discuss suitable subjects for the mural. Clearly, Romanelli is not pleased with this additional complication but does his best to politely inform Mrs. Newton that he had already been working with the federal authorities on a design that has been enthusiastically approved by them and which he hopes will be met with the same enthusiasm in Homer. Sensing Romanelli's concern, Rowan writes these words of assurance to the artist: "I do not anticipate any trouble in your having the design approved by the citizens of Homer." Little does he know . . .

On September 26, Romanelli writes to Rowan to tell him that he has not visited Homer yet and that he is afraid he will not be able to do so until he receives the first payment on the mural. So, now money is an issue, but keep in mind there is a Depression in 1938, and Romanelli frankly admits the need to "wait until I can afford the visit." Mr. Rowan shrugs this off and simply responds, ". . . it would be well for you to take the design and present it to Mrs. Newton for her consideration before proceeding with the full size cartoon." He tells him that the voucher due him will be forwarded as soon as the second contract has been cleared for approval. Approval does not come until October 17.

Meanwhile, the Section informs Romanelli to come up with a more convincing rendering of "the doe on the right and the young elm tree." Romanelli agrees to make the corrections and tells Rowan "I am happy to learn that you do not anticipate any trouble in my having the design approved by the citizens of Homer, New York." He includes a sample of the canvas to be used and the answers to requested technical questions. He intends to use thirteen colors of tube oil paints manufactured by Blockx in France and sold by Ernst Freidrichs Inc. of New York. Wall paint will be removed first. No medium is to be used except when necessary and that will be sun thickened, cold pressed linseed oil or spirits of turpentine. He describes his technique this way: "Beginning with light drawing and work in Chinese ink—working from light to dark—from lean to fat."

On October 31, Romanelli informs Rowan that he has received the first payment of $250, has sent a color sketch of the fauna design to Mrs. Newton, and will be arranging a meeting in Homer as soon as possible. Four day later, Mr. Rowan responds: "It will be appreciated if you can get in touch with the Postmaster at your earliest opportunity so that further progress of the work will not be delayed. Kindly inform me at once of the outcome of the meeting." Was this going to be a productive meeting?

September 8, 2016

The meeting scheduled for the artist in Homer did not go well. According to Romanelli's letter to Rowan, the artist visited Mrs. Newton on Monday, November 7, and presented his two-inch scale color sketch. In his words, "Although she said she liked my design her disappointment was obvious and when she called in certain of the townspeople it was not unapparent to me that she and her fellow townsmen had other ideas for the wall space. . . ." He said that he asked Mrs. Newton to write to Mr. Rowan and provide "some idea of what sort of mural would appeal to the people of Homer." Mrs. Newton had some subject in mine, and he hoped Mr. Rowan would advise him as soon as possible as to "the wisest course of action under the circumstances." He concluded by cautioning that "every little delay now will shorten the time I might spend perfecting the mural." At this point, five months have passed since Romanelli was informed he was offered the commission, and the folks of Homer now wish to weigh in on the mural's design, as well they should since they would have to live with the final product. What could go wrong next?

Further disappointment for Romanelli happened next. He receives a letter from Rowan explaining that Rowan agrees with the opinion expressed in Postmaster Newton's letter to him: ". . . I am compelled to admit that I concur that a design including cows and sheep would be much more appropriate and acceptable to the Homer, New York, Post office than an arbitrary design of deer." He goes on to state: ". . . to my way of thinking a straightforward presentation of the New York hills with their shrubs and trees would have greater meaning for me than the rather thin decorative treatment of hills presented in your former sketches. Don't you agree that such a treatment would possess greater vitality?" Romanelli, if truth could be known, would not have agreed, but unfortunately the sketch he had produced was of a landscape more apt to be found out in Idaho or Montana than Central New York State. And on November 25 Rowan asked for revisions closer to what Mrs. Newton had suggested in her letter to Rowan on November 10. She wrote:

"My dear Sir:

Mr. Frank Romanelli of Buffalo came to Homer Monday November the seventh, bringing the miniature mural which is to have a place in this office.

The painting, while pleasing in design and detail, has no local appeal. It would be most suitable in the Adirondack region, the natural habitat of the deer. We had hoped that something of local or historical interest could be used. Homer is the home of David Harum; it is in the heart of the dairy country. Our Tioughnioga River is of legendary fame. Nearby is Skaneateles Lake renowned for its picturesque beauty. Cows and sheep graze on the hills overlooking our village.

We have no fault to find with Mr. Romanelli's work, we only wish the mural could portray some local interest. I am enclosing some views of our old bridges with the graceful willows and the hills in the background. If life is needed in the picture, cows or sheep would add a local interest."

Mr. Rowan responded, "I sincerely believe that we will procure a mural which will be satisfactory in every way to you and the other citizens. Your courtesy and intelligent suggestions relative to this matter are greatly appreciated."

Romanelli was not about to lose the remaining payments of his commission because of some cows and sheep. Thus, he agreed to do new pencil sketches with "as much local flavor as possible." By the time he has new sketches to submit, it is mid-January of the new year, 1939. He makes it clear that "this sketch is not absolutely final" and that he would appreciate any criticism or suggestion.

And criticism he gets. Mr. Rowan writes to him on January 16. He approves of the subject matter but adds this: "I must be frank in telling you, however, that in our opinion the design is somewhat empty." He instructs Romanelli to get the design approved by Mrs. Newton and then by the Section, to complete another technical outline, and to expect another contract to be drawn up soon. And Romanelli follows through, this time for a design titled "Albany Street Bridge over Tioughnioga River." He agrees to add cattle (but no sheep apparently) and Mrs. Newton gives her approval on May 17, 1939. But the canvas sample he submits is not approved. He is told that pure linen canvas assures "the greatest permanency." Romanelli chooses a canvas that gains approval and informs Rowan he wants to get his oil paints from a different French firm, Lucien LeFevre-Foinet. Can the project move forward now?

Of course, not. On May 24, Rowan writes to Mrs. Newton to tell her that while she has approved the subject matter for the mural, his office finds "the quality of the painting is not up to the standard which this office is maintaining for the decoration of Federal buildings." He tells her Romanelli is being asked to further study the matter and Rowan's office will handle it.

By letter, Rowan informs the artist that his design "is not equal to your previous work and it does not meet the aesthetic standards maintained by this office . . ." The only element in the painting that is acceptable is . . . the cow! And even that should be moved to the left, advises Rowan. Furthermore, the drawing of the two cows on the right is deemed to be "pretty weak" and "the willows are definitely in need of personal observation." Rowan expresses regret for demanding Romanelli go back to the drawing board, but "the fuzzy quality of the painting as well as the drawing of the other elements in the design are not acceptable. . . ." Romanelli probably questioned if it was such a good idea for him to have taken on this commission to create public art.

September 22, 2016

Weeks passed. Not until July does Romanelli submit another pencil drawing to Rowan. He tells Rowan that this one "is superior to any sent you wherein the local scene of Homer was used" and "is in a style that appeals to me and therefore was not forced." Does the Section like this design? Not yet. Rowan informs Romanelli that it shows "improvement over any of the previous designs," but more is required. He suggests that "the hills on the left be spotted with some cattle in order to make this a little more interesting." And "the cattle on the left in your sketch seem a little too arbitrary." He urges the artist to use a color palette like the one he had used for the Marine Hospital in Buffalo. Finally, he asks that the mural not go wall-to-wall; he prefers a border of wall coloring be visible at both ends. Of course, another technical outline and canvas samples are requested and another contract to be developed. Dutifully, Romanelli, who is vacationing at Cranberry Lake on the western slope of the Adirondacks, responds on August 2 in the affirmative to all asked of him. Perhaps, it is the reinvigorating effects of relaxing in a scenic wilderness paradise that allows him to forge on with the project and to put a positive spin upon it. He tells Rowan "I am much more enthusiastic regarding the work since receiving your letter because the suggestions contained fit in perfectly with the manner in which I would prefer to carry out the design."

Rowan writes back on August 7 that he is pleased Romanelli is "working on the drawing of the cattle on the left." Oh, those problematic Homer cows! He, also, provides good news for the artist. He will not need to procure any more approvals from the Postmaster in Homer. Oh, those pesky art critics in Homer! So, can we move forward now? Not so fast. Romanelli tells Rowan he has not received back his pencil sketch and cannot proceed without it. As it turns out, the Buffalo Post Office had failed to forward the returned sketch to his summer address at Cranberry Lake.

On September 26, 1939, Romanelli is given the greenlight to proceed with the creation of a full-size cartoon of the approved design, and he is granted an additional nine months to complete the mural. He is advised to use a heavier quality canvas for the project, but the best he can obtain is the next best grade of canvas samples. In addition, because of a reorganization of federal agencies, Romanelli finds his contract is now with the Acting Commissioner of Public Buildings in the Federal Works Agency. Confused by this and thinking another party is now involved, he needlessly includes that commissioner in his correspondence with Rowan.

On December 28, 1939, Romanelli's full size cartoon is officially approved and the second installment of his pay is authorized. The next day, the Supervising Architect instructs The Fourth Assistant Postmaster General to direct the Homer Postmaster to permit the mural's installation.

On January 4, 1940, Romanelli is requested by the Section to submit a report regarding the lighting fixture's possible obstruction of the view of the mural. No final payment will be made until the report is furnished. Rowan also implores Romanelli "to incorporate more conviction in the drawing of the animals. . . ." Those Homer bovines continue to be the focus of artistic concern, but let's face it, Homer is in "dairy country."

On January 18, Rowan tells Romanelli to commence installation of the mural at the Post Office and to keep him informed of the progress being made. So, all should proceed smoothly now with no more snafus, right?

On April 17, 1940, Romanelli writes to Rowan: "I have since discovered that the glazes laid over the fixed drawing are not adhering as well as I would like them to. And the reason for this I have not been able to satisfactorily discover. I have tried to remedy this without satisfactory results. . . . But in view of this condition of the mural I cannot ask the Section to accept it. Would it be possible for the Section to allow me to do the whole mural over again completely without the necessity of getting the cartoon approved again?" He laments that "No one regrets the necessity of making a report of this kind more than I do. You must know that I have spent almost two years work on this mural. I have tried during that time to evolve a mural that would be a credit to the Section as well as to myself. No doubt my earnestness to give the Section what it deserved as well as what the people of Homer N.Y. wanted and satisfy myself as well, contributed and accounts for the time spent in designing." What Romanelli wrote next summed up the problem quite well: "Perhaps I tried to serve too many masters." He went on to express his indebtedness to Rowan for his cooperation and concludes by stating that his contract is set to terminate in thirteen days and so "obviously under the circumstances I cannot fulfill my contract."

The project seems doomed at this point, but Rowan authorizes the artist to undertake a repainting and to let him know how much of a time extension to the contract he needs to bring the project to completion—a completion that has already been "for several reasons" subjected to "unprecedented delay." Both men are clearly frustrated, but the contracted time frame is expanded to seven hundred and thirty calendar days from August 1, 1938, or three more months.

On July 9, 1940, Romanelli writes to Rowan and includes two photographs of the finished mural that is ready for installation at the Post Office. He explains, "I am glad I re-did the mural because now the tonal quality, color and sensitivity are better than in the previous one." Then, he states that through the Director of the Syracuse Museum of Art he has asked Mr. Lee Browne Coye of Syracuse to install the mural. He highlights Coye's credentials: "highly recommended because of his experience and because he is a mural and easel painter as well (represented in the Metropolitan [Museum of

Art]). Romanelli then asks if Mr. Coye could be permitted to answer the questions regarding the lighting fixtures in relation to the mural since "It would save me a trip to Homer, N.Y." He presses further by inquiring if it is "a fixed rule that the paint must be removed from the mural wall space" since Mr. Coye is of the opinion that "it would take the life out of the plaster." With only twenty-two days left in his contract, Romanelli points out the obvious. "The time is short," and he needs Rowan "to please answer as soon as possible."

Rowan gives his blessing on July 12 to the artist's requests, except for the matter of the removal of the wall paint. He tells Romanelli that "if the paint is a cassin paint it must be entirely removed" and that he disagrees that doing so would affect the life of the plaster. If the wall paint has an oil base, however, "it need not be removed." So, Romanelli avoids making a trip to Homer by engaging the services of another artist to do the actual installation. (In fact, there is no evidence that Romanelli ever made more than the one visit to Homer, even to see his final handiwork on the Post Office wall.) But the project is nearly done now . . . or is it?

October 6, 2016

Correspondence between the mural's artist and patron continues, as the project draws near to its expected close. On July 18, Rowan receives a letter from Romanelli. The artist has yet another request to make. "Mr. Coye has just sent me word that he cannot possibly put up the mural until about August 10." Of course, this is past the contractual deadline of July 31. Romanelli wants to know if the rules can be suspended to allow Coye to do the job about August 10. "I would much rather have him do the work than anyone I know."

What should Rowan do now? Grant the request and have done with this drawn out Homer mural project or put his foot down, say "Enough already!" and terminate the project without a mural to show for it? The request is granted. After all, what is a slight delay in the installation, given the many miserable delays that have plagued the project thus far?

In a letter dated August 23, 1940, Rowan seeks confirmation from the Homer Postmaster that the long delayed mural has finally been installed and states that according to photographs he has received "the mural appears to be a real addition to the decoration of the building." He expresses curiosity about any comments in the local newspapers and asks to see them.

On the same day, August 23, Rowan receives a long letter from Romanelli that he has not actually seen the installed mural, only a photograph of it taken by Mr. Coye (copy enclosed) whom he is sure "has done an expert job." He informs Rowan that he has "taken the liberty of having Mr. Coye touch up the unpainted areas on either side of the door" and a small, round molding placed around the mural. It is his opinion that "the whole thing will be improved by having the molding all the way around." He says, "This molding will be light and with a natural finish to harmonize with the colors of the walls and the mural." Of course, none of these added touches have been authorized by the Feds. And what does Postmaster Newton think of the finished product? According to Romanelli, Coye told him that she "likes the mural very much" and found the colors to be "perfect for its place." Romanelli adds that Coye answered the question of the lighting fixture and found it impossible to take a photograph of the mural without obstruction by the fixture. He says, "I do hope something can be done about this." (Coye's recommendation on Form D-7 was to install flat ceiling lights to fix the problem.) Romanelli concludes by writing that the project has been brought to completion and "consequently my end of the contract with the government fulfilled."

Rowan immediately drafts a polite letter to the artist acknowledging the work that has been done and informing him that his final payment will be pending his office's receipt of "a statement from the Postmaster relative to the satisfactory installation. . . ." Will Mrs. Newton express the approval of the citizens of Homer, or will there be a delay in paying Romanelli?

Rowan receives Mrs. Newton's letter on September 6, 1940. Her opinion? The mural has been "satisfactorily installed" and "seems pleasing," but she says there has been no expected coverage of the newly installed decoration by the local press. (Later, on September 23, she sends in "the bit that was printed in the *Cortland County Advertiser*.") While she includes no rave review of the artist's efforts, it should be noted that she closes with one positive comment: "We can most heartily recommend the work of the young man who installed the mural." Coye, at least, left a positive impression in Homer.

With this statement from Homer's Postmaster, authorization is given for Romanelli to be sent his final payment, and Rowan sends Mrs. Newton a final word of thanks along with instructions on the proper care and continued maintenance of the mural.

While the mural is certainly no sublime Sistine Chapel ceiling and the relationship between Romanelli and Rowan was not nearly as strained as that between Michelangelo and Pope Julius II, the story behind both commissioned works reveals that artists have always been at the mercy of their patrons, and they don't have much, if any, choice in their subject matter.

In his next to last letter to Rowan, Romanelli sincerely asks his patron to "please accept my wholehearted thanks for the trouble you have taken in reference to the mural, for the time extensions allowed me, and for your cooperation." The artist's last correspondence to Rowan is ironic. On October 7, 1940, he sends the two-inch scale color sketch for the mural that he was contracted to provide much earlier. And the reason given for this final long delay? As expected, Romanelli simply states, "the delay was unavoidable." Below his signature he has penned these words: "Thanks for every thing (sic)."

Now you know the story behind the mural in the Homer Post Office, thanks to the paper trail left by the main characters of the story and the school teacher who asked the Homer School District to purchase copies of the archived papers. Romanelli died in 1974. He was 65 years old. Only a portion of his artistic legacy is on the north wall of the post office lobby. Take a good look at it the next time you come to mail something. Admittedly, it looks washed out and monochromatic. Perhaps the colors have faded over time. Seventy-six years can take their toll on paintings. Some feel there is a certain Asiatic influence in the work. And yet the pastoral scene depicted in "Albany Street Bridge over Tioughnioga River" seems to evoke, as through a hazy memory, a more idyllic, agrarian world that may have once existed here in Cortland County—a world of things that FDR said people knew and looked at often "and have touched and loved." And then again, your twenty-first century sensibilities may overpower you and deep down inside, while waiting in line to mail a letter, you find yourself gazing at the mural and almost wishing that Romanelli's original design with the nude was up on that wall.

October 20, 2016

THE STRANGE CASE OF LIEUTENANT COGSWELL

My good friend and fellow Homerite, Ed Raus, is currently undertaking a most ambitious and much anticipated project. He is making a compilation of all the known residents of the county of Cortland who participated in the American Civil War. Brief biographical information will reveal such things as the town in which the man dwelled at the time of enlistment for military service, the nature of the man's occupation at the time, and data about the length and nature of the service rendered. The final compendium will be a useful source for historians and high school history students. This article in two installments, based on primary source material provided by Mr. Raus, is the strange story of one local Civil War participant.

On Saturday, April 13, 1844, a son was born to Linus and Eliza T. (Sparks) Cogswell of the village of Port Watson on the Tioughnioga River in Cortland County. She and her husband named him Wilbur Fisk Cogswell. When Wilbur was six years old, the family moved to Groton City in Tompkins County. The Cogswell family remained there for seven years, after which they took up residence in the village of Homer. In 1860, during Wilbur's sixteenth year, the Cogswells moved to a farm about one mile north of the village of Homer and remained there for about a year. This is where they were living when the Civil War broke out in April of 1861. During the following spring, as best Eliza Cogswell could later recall, the family took up residence in the hamlet of Little York and would stay for some six years. From 1854 to 1862, young Cogswell was enrolled at the Cortland Academy on the Green in Homer. Then, his life took a detour.

The records indicate that Wilbur was eighteen years old in September 1862 when he suddenly left his home in Little York and abandoned his studies at the academy in Homer. He sent word back to his parents that he had the intention of "obtaining a clerkship in some store in Rochester, N. Y." But soon after this correspondence another letter postmarked Washington, D. C. arrived with shocking news. Wilbur had joined the Navy. He wrote that he had enlisted not very long after arriving in the nation's capital.

It was in late September of 1863 that the young sailor returned home. His mother found him to be "reduced almost to a skeleton." Wilbur pointed to a spot on the back of his head that was "as soft as the head of an infant, and could not bear the slightest pressure." His mother would recall years later that her son had experienced an accident on board a ship. She said, "he had fallen from a mast of the vessel a distance of about forty feet, and struck with his head upon a cannon, crushing his skull at the back part of the head just below the crown." The logbook of the *U. S. S. Perry* notes that on July 7, 1863 at 2:10 PM one William (incorrect name recorded) Cogswell fell from the trysail-mast onto the deck of the ship and was carried below to the Surgeon. From there he was taken to a hospital at Beaufort, North Carolina, for an operation, which his mother recalled left "a scar upon the scalp showing where the Surgeons had cut into the skull." She noted that "the hair was quite short over the spot" and that her son told her the area had been "shaved close to the scalp" before surgery.

Despite this unfortunate experience, Cogswell was not apparently so disabled as to be prevented from continuing a career in the Navy. A history of his service provided by the Navy Department in 1875 reveals that on August 17, 1864, he was appointed and ordered to the *Mohican*. Before the end of the year he was transferred from that vessel as Acting 3rd Assistant Engineer. On April 15, 1865, the same day that President Lincoln died at the hand of John Wilkes Booth, Cogswell was listed among the officers of the *Boxer*, formerly known as *Tristram Shandy*. On September 5, 1865, about four months after the end of the Civil War, Cogswell was detached from the *Boxer* and "granted leave of absence." On November 7, 1865, he was honorably discharged, but on July 12, 1866 he was again appointed and ordered to the *Tallahoosa*. On April 10, 1867, he was "detached and ordered to duty in connection with Iron clads at New Orleans." Finally, Lieutenant Cogswell was mustered out of the service on August 28, 1868, at the rank of Third Assistant Engineer. In 1872, he married Frances D. Andrus. Nothing is known about her. The next year, Cogswell remarried. His second wife was Emma S. Soby.

Much of this information comes from a slew of documents generated in 1874 when Emma S. Cogswell filed a petition with A. P. Smith, County

Judge of Cortland County. Subscribed and sworn to on the 20th of August, Mrs. Cogswell of Cortlandville alleged her husband was "a lunatic and in indigent circumstances." She claimed, "that she first discovered such lunacy in the month of March last." The Judge ordered Cogswell to be examined by Franklin Goodyear and Henry T. Dana, "two respectable physicians of the county of Cortland," to ascertain the man's mental state.

What the doctors determined about Cogswell is not known. To complicate matters further, the Treasury Department sent a memo on November 2, 1882, to the Honorable William E. Chandler, Secretary of the Navy, raising another concern about Cogswell. The memo states "that the name of Wilbur F. Cogswell does not appear on the rolls of either the Brig 'Perry' or other vessels mentioned, embracing the period from January 1863 to January 1864." Instead, a William F. Coggswell was found to have enlisted January 23, 1863 as a landsman, or naval recruit with no seafaring experience. He was assigned to the *North Carolina* and served on that vessel until February 28, 1863. Then, he transferred to the Brig *Perry* and saw duty from March 1, 1863 to July 11, 1863 "when he was marked 'sent home sick.'" In addition, the records show he was on board the *William Badger* on July 12, 1863, having been received from a hospital.

November 3, 2016

So, it appears that for some unknown reason young Wilbur Cogswell changed his first name and the spelling of his last name at the time he first enlisted in the Navy and sustained his head injury. This may have hindered any timely bureaucratic granting of a pension. The pension Cogswell sought was not granted until 1897. Much transpired in the interval. Wilbur and Emma must have separated or divorced. Wilbur was residing in Portland, Oregon, when Emma died on July 8, 1897, in her home on Broad Street in Beverly, New Jersey. Her funeral was at the residence four days later, and the interment was private. Three days later, two sons of the Cogswells, Dore and Leon, sent their father a letter from Beverly, NJ. In it they wrote: "Dear mother has gone. Her life seems to have been one of sacrifice, patience, and suffering." They noted how kind she was to all of them and how they hoped in times of adversity that God would "send her kind spirit to watch over and guide us." They also indicated they were responding to a letter Wilbur had sent them on July 9 in which, according to them, they found his "true self speaking." They said it was "that same self which mother loved and knew." Is it possible that Cogswell's trauma to the head caused a personality disorder that adversely impacted his marriage?

On the day after Emma's funeral, Binger Hermann, a Civil War veteran and Commissioner of the General Land Office in the Department of the Interior in the nation's capital, drafted a letter to Lieutenant W. F. Cogswell in Portland. The letter informs Cogswell that the matter of his pension arrears has been resolved by the Assistant Secretary of the Interior. Cogswell is told that "you have been allowed your back pension for four years, leaving ... a difference of $20 per month." Hermann congratulates Cogswell "upon this long-deferred justice in your case" and lets him know that he had gone to bat for him more than once. At these times, Hermann says he spoke of Cogswell's "worthiness as a citizen" and of his standing among his comrades.

Six days later, on July 19, 1897, Cogswell writes a very odd, volatile letter. It starts out with a Scriptural quote: "'Ye have made it a den of thieves.'" This is followed by a paragraph in which he explains the cause of his ire:

"My claim, 2117, hanging since February 4, 1892, in 'the Harrison and Cleveland pillaging administrations,' having sacrificed one pure life in my family (I know not how many others), and made untold suffering, with the mark of Cain upon their foreheads; the mother of my two boys dead, in her coffin, four thousand miles away East; the boys thrown on the charity of the public, and the pension bureau owing me one thousand and forty dollars, by fraud and perjury cut off my pension by a pension examining agent, F. C. Sharp, detailed at Tacoma, Wash., has been allowed and will be paid by the McKinley administration immediately.

The Harrison and Cleveland buzzards, Green B. Raum and Wm. Lochran (sp.), can now take a back seat!" [Raum and Lochren were U.S. Commissioners of Pensions from 1876 to 1883 and 1893 to 1896, respectively.]

Having named and excoriated the perceived source of his family's woes, Cogswell then lists twenty individuals by name and says of them, "I shall ever be thankful for your prompt rendering of justice and quick action in righting a wrong for the sake of the old soldier and my two motherless boys." Among those listed are President William McKinley (whom he refers to as "Major," which was McKinley's rank in the Civil War); the Secretary and Assistant Secretary of the Interior Department; Col. Binger Hermann; the Editor-in-Chief of Portland's *The Oregonian*; seven Congressmen; and the U.S. Senators of Oregon, California, New Hampshire, Kansas, Idaho, Texas, New York, and New Jersey. Cogswell singles out the President by concluding that his sons would "take as their pattern our genuine Christian soldier President, William McKinley, rather than an experiment, Bryan, the pretender." Here he is referring with disdain to William Jennings Bryan, the Democratic candidate for President defeated by McKinley in the election of 1896. Even Cogwell's sons admired McKinley since in the letter to their father they had indicated that "Mother believed in him and had his picture put in its present position on the wall" before the election where it "shall remain."

Records indicate that Cogswell was employed as a newspaper reporter for a time in Washington and went on to marry two more times. In 1901, he married Alverda Gertrude Hawk of Portland, Oregon, at a wedding held in Baltimore, Maryland. On March 27, 1906, Alverda died suddenly in Washington, D.C. Cogswell married for a fourth time on April 11, 1908, at Covington, Kentucky, to Bertha E. Taft, an accomplished soprano and pianist trained in Cincinnati, Ohio.

The life of Wilbur Cogswell is certainly a human-interest story that raises several questions. Why did he run off to join the Navy before finishing his education at the Academy in Homer? Why did he enlist under a different name? Did he have a mental illness directly attributable to the head injury sustained in a fall from a mast, as reported by his mother and second wife in 1874? Or is this a case of what we would now call Post Traumatic Stress Disorder? Why did he continue to seek out a naval career after the war? Why were he and his second wife living a continent apart by 1896? What were the reasons for his pension being deferred for so long? We can only conjecture. We do know this, however: Ex-Lieutenant Wilbur Cogswell died on April 29, 1918, in the famous St. Elizabeths Hospital in Washington, D.C., which was officially known until 1916 as the Government Hospital for the Insane—principally providing care for the insane of the U.S. Army and U.S. Navy. Cogswell is buried at Arlington National Cemetery.

November 17, 2016

THE SIEGE OF STIMSON'S TAVERN

One of the early settlers in the Town of Homer in the 1790s was Major Enos Stimson. Stimson came from Monson, Massachusetts, and settled on property that now comprises 90 South Main Street in the village. Here he built a small house. Being near the road that connected Albany and Buffalo (now Albany Street), he hung out a sign and opened a tavern. The following spring, in order to avoid the scourge of smallpox in the area, his wife and children were sent away. They spent some time at the home of Aaron Knapp and were vaccinated there.

According to H. P. Smith's *History of Cortland County* (1885), it was during this absence of his family in 1800 that Stimson had a most trying experience. It seems that twelve members of the Onondaga Nation to the north patronized Stimson's inn one evening. Drinking freely of the libation at hand, they became inebriated, and Stimson refused to serve them anymore. They became quarrelsome and belligerent and were asked to depart. They would not cooperate, and Stimson felt threatened. For his own safety, he scurried up a ladder to the second floor and pulled the ladder up behind him.

Thinking they had the innkeeper trapped above, a bacchanalian revel ensued. The giddy patrons proceeded to empty the tavern of every jug of whisky they could find. Once the jugs were depleted, they started to scrounge up every bottle in the place. One patron found a bottle labeled "picra," from which he took a big swig before he passed it to his comrade. The two emptied the bottle without knowing it contained a popular laxative of the day. According to H. P. Smith, "The effect was pitiful and at the same time decidedly comical." From his place of both entrapment and safety, Stimson must have witnessed the party below with mixed feelings.

The two sickened men became convinced they were dying of poison, which could have been a distinct possibility, and others tried to tend to them. At this time, one member of the party headed hurriedly out the inn door. In his drunken state, he leaped over what he thought was a stone fence only to find himself at the bottom of a well. The image that historian Smith provides us of the scene that followed is priceless: "This method of diluting the spirits he had swallowed did not please the old warrior, and he yelled and cursed with all the ardor and variations of which the language was capable; but there was too much of similar amusement going on in-doors to make it possible for his companions to hear him for some time."

Eventually his companions used blankets they found to draw him out of the well a wetter but wiser warrior to be sure. At dawn, with the stock of Stimson's libations and medicines gone, the unruly patrons slowly came to their senses and departed in the direction of Syracuse. With the coast clear, the besieged owner of Stimson's Tavern was able to descend and assess the damages. It was a story he would share with his family when they returned and with friends of the wilderness community that would become Homer Village. Before the village was ever incorporated, the tavern was later moved across the street and became part of the front portion of the home at 87 South Main Street. When you stroll or drive by next time, give it a glance and recall the night when Stimson's Tavern was under siege—but on the other side of the road.

December 1, 2016

TWO EARLY SCHOOL TEACHERS IN THE TOWN OF HOMER

Joshua Ballard and Adin Webb were contemporaries during the formative years of Homer and Cortland. Both started out serving the few families residing in Homer back then by teaching their young children. Both dedicated their lives to municipal service, as noted in H. P. Smith's 1885 *History of*

Cortland County, and enjoyed unusual longevity for their time, living well into their eighties.

Homer was first settled in 1791 and the Town of Homer was created in 1795. Joshua Ballard was the first teacher in the town of Homer. He came to Homer in 1797 from Holland, Massachusetts, and for one season taught one of the first schools here (on what is now Hooker Avenue). From 1802 to 1803, he served as supervisor for the Town of Homer and as sheriff in 1810. The fourth "public house" or tavern was built in 1816 by Joshua Ballard. The structure is now a residence located on the southeast corner of Main and Albany Street and was once known as a "temperance tavern" in the 1830s. Ballard moved to Cortland in 1819, the same year he was appointed county clerk and assisted in the founding of the Cortland Academy on the Green in Homer Village. He is said to have raised and commanded the first cavalry company in the county. According to H. P. Smith's history, "Various town offices were conferred upon him and he was an eminently respected and useful citizen."

The next teacher of prominence in the Town of Homer was Adin Webb, a native of Windham County, Connecticut. His father, Christopher Webb, was a hero of the Revolutionary War who participated in the Battle of Bennington on August 16, 1777, and the subsequent capture of the famous British general "Gentleman Johnny" Burgoyne at Saratoga. In 1800, Adin married Deborah Carter, and they traveled to New York State with his parents, Christopher and Olive (Brown) Webb. They settled near Cazenovia Lake. Five years later, Adin was solicited by friends to come to the recently settled Town of Homer to teach in a school on the Commons (where the Methodist Church is now located on the Green) for a term of ten months. He ended up staying on for much longer.

Except for one year, Adin Webb taught seventeen successive years. He was described as "a tall, straight, sprightly young man, dignified in demeanor and with a good education." Being a capable singer, he taught singing school at the same time, and being successful in both vocations, he joined the Congregational Church in Homer in 1813 and directed its choir. In 1809, he was elected to the post of Homer's Town Clerk and held office for twenty years. From 1816 to 1823, he served in the appointed post of surrogate, a judicial officer having jurisdiction over the probate of wills and the administration of estates.

In 1823, the Webbs moved to Cortland, where Adin became a member of the firm of Webb & Bishop. In 1829 he was elected sheriff. In 1840 he was again appointed surrogate, holding the office for four years, and in 1845 he was made town clerk for the Town of Cortlandville, holding this office for eleven years. Upon taking up residence in Cortland, Adin joined the Presbyterian Church and for many years sang in its choir. He died in 1865 and is buried in Cortland Rural Cemetery. This tribute was offered at the time: "It is sufficient praise of Mr. Webb to say that all of the public trusts to which he was called were deserved by him and their duties fulfilled with ability and loyalty to the public good."

Another statement was made about the lives of both Ballard and Webb: "The public confidence in the intelligence, integrity and fidelity of Joshua Ballard and Adin Webb, evidenced in their services in these various civil stations, is a sufficient encomium upon their memory as citizens. One reached in age almost eighty-one, the other eighty-five, and the pilgrimage of each was distinguished by the even tenor of a Christian example." Clearly, these two men should be appreciated and remembered for their efforts when Homer and Cortland were mere fledgling communities.

[Note: A portrait of Adin Webb rendered by Homer-born Francis Bicknell Carpenter is owned by the Cortland County Historical Society on Homer Avenue in Cortland, NY.]

December 16, 2016

THE HOLIDAY SEASON OF YORE

On December 7th the Town Historian made a presentation to the Fortnightly Club at The Sherman House on Main Street. The topic assigned was "The Holiday Season of Yore." He thought he would share it with the readers of this paper, too, in two installments. It is merely a quick overview of how the holiday season has been celebrated in the past—in America in general and here in the Homer-Cortland area more specifically. Perhaps as you read it, you may find yourself calling up from the depths of memory some personal "ghosts of Christmas Past."

Along with religious observances of Christmas, we Americans tend to do the same things every year at this season. We down copious amounts of eggnog; kill a tree and cover it in electric lights; send fruitcake, cards and cookies to our loved ones; kiss under a leafy branch of real or artificial mistletoe; hang colorful socks over the fireplace; and sing off-key demands for figgy pudding at the top of our lungs. Yes, these are our Christmas traditions that have evolved over time. But would you believe Christmas was not a holiday in early America?

This was thanks to the Puritans and their opposition to partying and drinking and apparently all things fun. From 1659 to 1681, the celebration of Christmas was actually outlawed in Boston. Anyone exhibiting the Christmas spirit was fined five shillings. By contrast, in the Jamestown settlement of Virginia, Captain John Smith reported that Christmas was enjoyed by all, especially a drink that combined egg and grog. Grog was rum. In time, the drink "egg and grog" was shortened to "egg nog."

After the American Revolution, English customs fell out of favor, including Christmas. In fact, Congress was in session on December 25, 1789, the first Christmas under America's new constitution. Christmas wasn't declared a federal holiday until June 26, 1870.

So, locally, here in Homer and Cortland, what would the holiday season have looked like in the post-colonial days? Homer was settled in the 1790s by those of Protestant denominations from New England, mainly Massachusetts and Connecticut. There is little to nothing in the records about Christmas because, as you might expect, it would not have been celebrated. That changed slowly with the arrival of immigrant groups who inserted their own traditions. It wasn't until the nineteenth century that Americans began to embrace Christmas. Americans actually re-invented Christmas and made it into a family-centered day of peace and nostalgia.

The early nineteenth century was a period of class conflict and turmoil, but in 1819, best-selling author Washington Irving wrote *The Sketchbook*. The sketches feature a squire who invited the peasants into his home for the Christmas holiday. In Irving's mind, Christmas should be a peaceful, warm-hearted holiday bringing groups together across lines of wealth or social status. Irving's book, however, was not based on any holiday celebration he had ever attended. In fact, many historians say that Irving's account actually "invented" traditions and introduced them into our culture.

Homer merchant William Sherman built this house with its magnificent winding staircase in the late 1820s [11 N. Main Street]. Six years earlier, Clement Moore had published his poem "An Account of a Visit from Saint Nicolas." This became better known as "The Night before Christmas." Moore's Santa is a jolly, old elf clad in red with a miniature sleigh equipped with eight reindeer. It is doubtful, at that time, that a Christmas tree adorned these front parlors. It is more likely that evergreen wreaths decorated the front doors as Christian symbols of eternal life.

But the German custom of a decorated evergreen in the parlor became very popular here through the last half of the nineteenth century. By 1900, it has been estimated that one out of five homes celebrated with a tree. Gifts placed under the tree were predominantly homemade, not store-bought, and were unwrapped. Gifts tended to be exchanged only with family members.

Before the Civil War, the North and South were divided on the issue of Christmas, as well as on the question of slavery. Many Northerners saw the celebration of Thanksgiving as more appropriate than that of Christmas. But in the South, Christmas was an important part of the social season. Not surprisingly, the first three states to make Christmas a legal holiday in the 1830s were Alabama, Louisiana, and Arkansas.

During the Civil War, illustrator Thomas Nast created images of Clement Moore's Santa for the Christmas editions of *Harper's Magazine*. And these continued through the 1890's. President Abraham Lincoln asked Nast to create a drawing of Santa delivering socks and gifts to some Union soldiers. It has been said that this image of Santa supporting the enemy had a demoralizing influence on the Confederate army—an early example of psychological warfare.

After the Civil War, Christmas traditions spread across the country and Central New York. Children's books played an important role in spreading the more secular customs of celebrating Christmas, especially the German tradition of trimmed trees, the Dutch custom of Christmas stockings and gifts delivered by Santa Claus, and the Celtic or Irish focus on mistletoe. Women's magazines were also very important in suggesting ways to decorate for the holidays, as well as how to make these decorations.

By the last quarter of the nineteenth century, America eagerly decorated trees, caroled, baked, and shopped for the Christmas season. Since that time, materialism, media, advertising, and mass marketing have made Christmas the more secularized celebration we have today. But to be fair, it has also become the most significant time of the year for charitable gifting, especially for the homeless, hungry, and unemployed.

Right behind Christmas comes the celebration of New Year's. Consider how the first day of the New Year used to be celebrated in the second half of the nineteenth century. It seems that New Year's Day was a great event in that era—more than New Year's Eve. Even the White House in the Civil War era was open to the public on January 1st, and Mr. and Mrs. Lincoln would stand in a reception line to shake hands with the many callers before they partook of refreshments—just as President Lincoln did for three hours in 1863 before signing the Emancipation Proclamation. He explained at the time to Secretary of State Seward that he had to give his hand some time to regain feeling before he dared pick up the pen to affix his autograph with any authority to the history-making document.

In the mid to late 1800s, New Year's Day was considered a fashionable opportunity for bachelors to call upon the unmarried ladies. Locally, in preparing for this custom, the women of the communities of Cortland County would decorate their homes with evergreens and bake cakes and pastries to serve the gentlemen callers. Sometimes, several young ladies would agree to "receive" at one house, since the traffic of callers could get quite hectic. Despite the pleasant company and the fine refreshments offered, the young men might have twenty or thirty "open houses" to attend in one afternoon.

According to the custom, not only were cakes and cookies served, but wines and other liquors as well. Thus, as the afternoon waned, the young men were known to become tipsy. As one account put it, "the young men were often in a sorry plight and the sweet young girls with hoops and flounces and curls were in a quandary as to what to do about the matter."

By the 1870s, there was a temperance movement astir in the county, led by the area churches. John B. Gough (pronounced "Goff"), a nationally known advocate of abstinence, lectured in the city of Cortland and made quite an impact, at least enough to have the clergy get together to discuss the customs of New Year's Day. It was agreed that something had to be done, and it was. A general letter was sent forth to all the ladies who were known to participate in these receptions. The letter politely and tactfully encouraged them to refrain from serving intoxicating libations to their guests. The plan succeeded. The charming ladies dutifully served tea and coffee instead. And the result? There was a noticeable decline in future New Year's Day receptions. Gradually, the custom of young men racing about from one reception to another on New Year's Day lost its appeal.

December 29, 2016

The local tradition of eligible bachelors calling upon unmarried ladies during New Year's Day died hard for one stalwart. In 1932, Bertha Eveleth Blodgett published *Stories of Cortland County for Boys and Girls*. One of the stories is about her relative, Alonzo Blodgett, a prominent Town of Cortlandville farmer, who continued to make calls on New Year's Day. It was said that "he never forgot the daughters of old Judge Stephens, Miss Vinette and Miss Editha, nor the 'Ives girls,' Miss Ursula and Mrs. Mary Graham, nor the widow of Harvey Greenman." No, on every New Year's Day, Alonzo would put on his best Sunday clothes and go forth to ring the doorbells of the local "girls." This he continued to do long after his contemporaries vanished.

According to Miss Blodgett, by the time he was in his nineties, Alonzo still managed to stop by at the Randall mansion on Main Street, Cortland, on New Year's Day to pay his respects to Miss Wilhelmina Randall, also in her nineties. The pair enjoyed each other's company and seemed to personify the adage that "There may be snow on the roof, but there's still fire in the chimney." The spirit of youth still burned brightly within their hearts as they reminisced and laughed about bygone days. Like old Alonzo and Wilhelmina, may we continue to enjoy the company of others and to laugh and share the stories of bygone days and not just on Facebook.

One story I, as the local historian, have shared is in this book, *Death in the Winter Solstice,* but it is not a pleasant one. Four days before Christmas in 1894, 64-year-old widower and farmer Patrick Quinlan was last seen trudging up James Street, headed for his farm outside of the village. He had just left Doyle's Pub (where Dasher's Corner Pub is now). He never made it home. He was bludgeoned to death half a mile from his home—brutally whacked with a fencepost. Two men were arrested, but no one was ever convicted. It remains an unsolved murder mystery—a "cold case." And it proves you can get away with murder in Homer . . . at least at Christmas. So, if you intend to do homicide, this is the month!

During the Great Depression a child was happy to get a single orange in a Christmas stocking—yes, an orange. Getting an orange was a big deal because oranges weren't affordable during the rest of the year. Other treats in stockings were bananas, nuts, and candy. If the children were *really* fortunate, there may have been a toy such as a doll, or a toy wagon for the very youngest. Gifts were homemade and practical, like scarves, but not whimsical. My parents were children of the Depression, and I can recall that my childhood stocking was filled with many marvelous things, but there was always an orange, that vestige of an earlier Christmas.

Today is the anniversary of the Japanese attack on Pearl Harbor that brought the U.S. into World War II in 1941. That Christmas season, the local Newton Line Company and its president, Ed O'Connell, hosted its seventh annual party at the Capitol Theatre in the Homer Town Hall for its employees and their children. There were party hats for the children and a visit from Santa upon the festively decorated stage. During the war years, there were "shop early" for Christmas campaigns, with the Postmaster General urging Americans in August 1943 to shop "really early, indeed right now." The campaign would be revisited during the Viet Nam War.

I was a post-World War II baby, born at the Cortland Memorial Hospital. One of my earliest recollections of Christmas includes being taken as a four-year-old by my mother to the A. B. Brown Store (where the Central New York Living History Museum is located today). There, I waited in line to sit on Santa's lap and tell him what I wanted for Christmas. It was a clever marketing ploy, for you see this visit with Santa was broadcast live by radio, and my father, back home on Clinton Street, working in his woodshop in the cellar, heard exactly what was on my wish list.

I am sure the radio played two favorite Christmas tunes at the time. While my parents surely preferred "White Christmas," I preferred Gene Autry's version of "Rudolph the Red-Nosed Reindeer." I was three when Johnny Marks wrote the song. It was based on a poem written in 1939 by Robert L. May of the Montgomery Ward Company. May had been "often taunted as a child for being shy, small and slight." He created a ninth, ostracized reindeer with a shiny red nose who became a hero "one foggy Christmas eve." A copy of the poem was given free to Montgomery Ward customers in Cortland (where Marketplace Mall is located now).

And I cannot recall a time when there was not a Crèche on the Green. Folks traveling through Homer are surprised to see a Nativity Set so publicly displayed in an age that subscribes to the practice of separation of church and state. But the Green was deeded to the First Religious Society of the Town of Homer in 1805 and that Society, now the Congregational Church, still owns the Green. They can put anything they want upon it; it's their property. But not without some risk.

I can recall back in December of 1986. The Homer community was churned up upon discovering the statue of the Christ Child was missing from the Green. The police were called in, and everyone was asking "Who would stoop so low as to steal the symbol of the Baby Jesus?" As it turned out, the puppy of David and Margaret Perfetti had absconded with the figure. The Perfetti puppy apparently was addicted to dolls and blankets. Baby Jesus was returned to the manger and the Canine Dollnaper was put on probation. Sgt. Dave Sampson reported that mug shots and paw prints would be kept on file and violation of the probation would mean the loss of dog biscuit privileges.

So, in conclusion, the holiday season has been celebrated through the years in many ways, even by canines. Some customs have become tradition and have survived longer. In recent years, even the political correctness of wishing folks a "Merry Christmas" or "Happy Holidays" has been debated. Whether religious or secular in motive, one holiday tradition is the giving of gifts. As *Harper's* magazine put it in 1856: "Love is the moral of Christmas. . . . What are gifts but the proof and signs of love! I wish you all a love-filled holiday season. And dare I say it? 'Merry Christmas!'"

Image 6.4 Ice skating area on the historic Homer Green. *Courtesy of Harry R. Coleman, Jr.*

Chapter 7

Articles of 2017

January 12, 2017

LINCOLN'S SECRETARY NEEDS A VACATION AND VISITS HOMER

Homer's native-son William Osborn Stoddard (1835–1925) served as assistant personal secretary to President Abraham Lincoln during the Civil War. As such, he observed President Lincoln's anguish over the debacle at Chancellorsville in May of 1863. News of Lee's rout at Gettysburg, Pennsylvania, and of Grant's successful siege of Vicksburg on the Mississippi in early July was welcome relief. The good news arrived during a Fourth of July celebration in Washington that Stoddard had been appointed to organize. He arranged for the Marine Band to perform as regiment upon regiment in Union blue and Zouave red marched smartly down Pennsylvania Avenue. Stoddard, easily putting humility aside, claimed it to be "the grandest Fourth o' July procession that had been seen in Washington since the city was founded."

On the heels of this excitement, Stoddard became ill with Potomac River malaria. He applied for some time away from his job at the Executive Mansion and decided to head for some rest at the seashore. He traveled with his brother, Harry, who was going home to Syracuse. When their train arrived in New York City, the Stoddard brothers found the streets filled with anarchy and confusion. Rioters were outraged over the military draft being instituted that meant they had to fight now to free blacks, not just to save the Union. Impoverished working-class New Yorkers and Irish Catholic immigrants were angered by the conscription law permitting the affluent to avoid the draft by paying three hundred dollars and securing a substitute. Resentment brought terror to the sweltering summer streets of Manhattan. The criminal element of the city took advantage of the situation, and looting, murder, and mayhem occurred for several days in mid-July. Although ill, Stoddard volunteered to help the military defend the Sub-Treasury and the Customhouse from any mob attacks.

When the violence in the streets of New York subsided, an exhausted William Stoddard headed for Syracuse with his brother. Twenty-four years later, back in New York, Stoddard wrote *The Volcano under the City*, an account of the frenzied "upsurging of the criminal classes of the great city" and the near fatal beating sustained by Superintendent of Police Kennedy during the infamous Draft Riots. Using New York City Police Department records, Stoddard helped to document the complex political, class, ethnic, and religious conflicts that contributed to the wanton mob brutality that he and fellow Homerite Francis B. Carpenter witnessed and managed to escape. Neither man knew, at the time, that the other was in New York during what is now considered the largest civil insurrection in American history, aside from the Civil War itself.

On the way from New York to Syracuse, a weary Stoddard stopped at Homer "and spent days in looking around upon the old, familiar places." He visited the Osborn homestead on Albany Street, looking in upon the room where he had been born almost twenty-eight years earlier. He returned to the millponds where he had learned to fish and to swim. It was refreshing to the body and the spirit to return to the river, the woods, the pastures, and the orchards of Homer again, and to gaze upon the verdant, gently rolling hills. Perhaps, given his Baptist upbringing, he was prompted to recall Psalm 121: "I will lift up mine eyes unto the hills, from whence cometh my help. My help cometh from the LORD, which made heaven and earth." Upon walking to the Homer Common, Stoddard found it changed. It was no longer the barely grassy space for pasturing sheep and oxen, as in his childhood. Now an attractive, tree-studded park was in front of the Academy and the churches. Homer's own Paris Barber, at the start of the war, had been a prime mover behind this change.

Stoddard found that the population of the village had grown. More houses had been built along streets west of Main Street, and those under construction had decorative gingerbread along the rooflines and expansive porches in front. The businesses of Main Street were now mostly concentrated northeast of the Green, and another unmistakable sign of progress was the illumination of the streets and dwellings with gas. It was becoming a beautiful little village with streets lined with trees and gaslights, just as Paris Barber imagined it. Just the summer before, the June 26th issue of the *Syracuse Journal* had provided an enthusiastic description of Homer during the Academy's traditional and much expanded annual exhibition of student accomplishments:

> The central week of all the year in this fair village of Homer is now drawing to its close. It has been a week of the highest literary and social enjoyment to the many friends of Cortland Academy, whose history has been closely linked for more than half a century with the growth and prosperity of our churches, our families and our daily avocations. We have had whatever is needed for the refined festivities of the week. We have had cloudless skies and moonlight nights; gardens gay with flowers; streets alive with holiday faces; college boys come back to renew school-day friendships; serenades, vocal and instrumental; hospitality, hearty, refined and enjoyable; essays in racy prose and liquid verse; orators from the school, the college and the church; pleasant talks over mammoth strawberries, and no end of fun for the young, and comfort for 'children of larger growth.'

How peaceful is the scene. Who would have thought that furious battles were being fought at the time and that young men were dying? Who would believe that coffins would soon be transported to grief-stricken families?

Stoddard walked up Cayuga Street to see another of Barber's projects, Glenwood Cemetery. Part of the new Rural Cemetery Movement, Glenwood was more than a graveyard; it was a landscaped, aesthetically pleasing space in which the living could meditate. It was where one could be refreshed in a natural, park-like environment with a gurgling brook making its way down the center of the area. Barber's design called for a flower-lined pool and an ornamental gateway at the entrance. The remains in the cemetery behind the Congregational Church were to be disinterred and respectfully moved to the new site on West Hill. Glenwood would be a suitable place, too, for the community to memorialize their war dead. A section would be set aside for the fallen of the Grand Army of the Republic.

Renewed in spirit by his Homer visit, Stoddard took the train to Syracuse. While only in Syracuse for a couple of days, he found it necessary to bail his father out of one of his all-too-frequent financial difficulties. After paying his father's "considerable" debt, Stoddard headed to New London, Connecticut. He visited his paternal grandparents and enjoyed the restorative powers of the salty air. He enjoyed fishing in the cove, with noisy seagulls darting overhead, as much as he enjoyed the stories he heard at the family farmhouse about the days before the Revolutionary War.

After two months of vacation, a reinvigorated Stoddard returned to his post in Washington, only to be informed that John Nicolay and John Hay, the two personal secretaries to the President, were going to take some vacation time. The assistant secretary found himself having to stand in for Nicolay as "big Private Secretary." He admitted, from the experience, that for this job Nicolay, indeed, "was much better qualified." Perhaps, Stoddard was left wishing he could take another vacation and return to the place of his childhood in Central New York. This is the only known visit he ever made.

The material for this article is taken from Sweeney's book *Lincoln's Gift from Homer, New York: A Painter, an Editor and a Detective* (McFarland & Company, Inc., 2011).

January 26, 2017

ELEANOR ROOSEVELT VISITS HOMER WOMEN IN 1924

The Town of Homer Historian is always receptive to material brought to his attention regarding local history. The following is a gem of historical interest brought to him by the Co-Historians of the Sennightly Literary Club, Gail Bundy and Kathryn Bundy Locke. In doing research on the history of the club, they discovered sources that show Eleanor Roosevelt once visited Homer. Their report is published below, and in the next issue readers can read transcriptions of the three sources they used to document the event.

Mrs. Franklin D. (Eleanor) Roosevelt met with members of the Homer Sennightly Literary Club and their guests from the Homer Leisure Hour Club at the home of Mrs. Jesse (Katherine) Newton on Clinton Street, on October 20, 1924. Mrs. Newton had become friends with Mrs. Roosevelt during shared interests in women's suffrage and other issues when she represented Sennightly in statewide meetings of the General Federation of Women's Clubs, a national organization.

Fall 1924 was only the second presidential election in which women had the vote. Women in Homer's clubs took an active interest in educating themselves on the political issues of the day. This was Sennightly's regular scheduled meeting in which they were exploring the views of the Democratic Party. At the club's previous meeting, the women examined the views of the Republican Party.

Mrs. Roosevelt's presence had several purposes. Yes, she was Mrs. Newton's friend and was in Homer at her invitation. She also was promoting her husband's return to politics after his 1921 bout with polio. At this time, FDR was neither a president nor a governor, but a former Assistant Secretary of the Navy under President Wilson. He had recently made a comeback speech at the June 1924 Democratic Convention.

Eleanor was also in the area serving other purposes of the Democratic Party—namely being a thorn in the side of her cousin, Colonel Theodore Roosevelt, Jr., who was running for governor of New York on the Republican ticket and was making a whistle stop in Cortland at the Lehigh Valley train station. During that campaign year Democrats—already recognizing Eleanor's power to connect with people—often sent her to the same locations to make speeches opposing his election.

While Teddy Jr. gave a 30-minute speech from the back of a train, Mrs. Newton arranged for Eleanor to meet and have extensive conversations with over 300 women in Homer and Cortland, beginning with a luncheon at 1:00 at the Cortland House. This was to be followed by a 2:30 meeting with women in Cortland, the evening meeting in Homer, and a dinner that evening at the home of Mr. and Mrs. R.H. Miller in Homer. One account said: "Her long acquaintance with public affairs . . . and her activities for suffrage, have given Mrs. Roosevelt a grasp of public affairs that is equaled by few, and her Democratic view-point is attained from convictions. She is thus enabled to use most forceful arguments, and at the same time gives a fair hearing to her opponents."

A fascinating account of the long standing conflicts and tensions between the Teddy Roosevelt side of the family (Republican with a home base in Oyster Bay, NY.) and the FDR side (Democrat with a home base at Hyde Park, NY) can be found in the book *Hissing Cousins: The Untold Story of Eleanor Roosevelt and Alice Roosevelt Longworth*. The book is available at the Phillips Free Library in Homer. Mrs. Newton would serve as Homer's Postmistress for many years. To be continued . . .

February 9, 2017

In the last issue, Co-Historians of the local Sennightly Literary Club wrote in this column about a visit to Homer by one who was destined to become a future First Lady. In this column, the two club historians share transcriptions of the news accounts they used as their sources. It is hoped that readers will find these primary sources as fascinating as the Town of Homer Historian did and that others will feel encouraged to share bits of local history they uncover. At least, we all can learn from them how historians go about their craft and make unexpected discoveries when initially researching another topic.

Sources:

1. "Two Roosevelts will Speak Here on Monday Next," *The Cortland Democrat*, October 17, 1924, p. 1. Fultonhistory.com (Cortland NY Democrat 1924-0367.pdf).

In a way next Monday, Oct 20, will be Roosevelt day in Cortland, both Democrats and Republicans having a member of the family here that day. Col. Theodore Roosevelt, Republican candidate for Governar [sic] is booked for ten speeches next Monday and one of them is to be at the tail-end of his train at the Lehigh Valley station. Mrs. Franklin D. Roosevelt will speak for the Democrats at a parlor meeting in Cortland and at a joint meeting of two clubs at Homer.

Mrs. Roosevelt is coming here as the guest of Mrs. Katherine C. Newton of Homer and will speak on national and state politics before the Sennightly club of Homer at Mrs. Newton's home. Members of the Leisure Hour club of Homer have been invited as guests. At the same meeting, Miss Frances Miller of Homer will talk on Democratic local politics.

The Homer clubs are hearing both sides of the political questions this fall. Mrs. Clayton R. Lusk of Cortland was the speaker at a recent meeting and reviewed the Republican Party's platform and candidates.

Mrs. Newton has arranged also for Cortland women to meet Mrs. Roosevelt at a parlor meeting to be held at 2:30 Monday afternoon at the home of Mrs. John A. Wavle, 23 Tompkins street.

Young Teddy Comes at 12:55

Col. Roosevelt's train will arrive at the Lehigh station at 12:55 and it is scheduled to leave at 1:30. The interval is too brief for the Republican candidate for Governor to come up town and the gathering will be at the rear of his car at the Lehigh Valley station.

The candidate's day will begin at Auburn and stops will be made at Moravia and Groton and for fifteen minutes at Freeville, from 12:25 to 12:40, on the way to Cortland. Col. Roosevelt's party upon leaving Cortland will go to East Ithaca and Ithaca, and then to Owego and Waverly, and wind up the day with the tenth speech at Binghamton.

2. "Democratic Rally: Mrs. Franklin D. Roosevelt to speak at Mrs. Newton's Tonight," *Cortland Standard*, October 20, 1924, p. 6. Fultonhistory.com (Cortland NY Standard 1924–2823).

This evening Mrs. Franklin D. Roosevelt of New York, whose husband was assistant secretary of the navy under President Wilson and who is prominent as a Democrat among the women voters of this _____ will speak this evening to the members of the Sennightly club at the home of Mrs. J. C. Newton in Clinton-st. The members of the Leisure Hour club are also invited to share the meeting and hear Mrs. Roosevelt speak. She will present the ____ _____ of the campaign from a Democratic standpoint. [*Note: Some words are missing because the copy is on a fold of the newspaper.*]

3. "Cortland County Women Hear Mrs. Roosevelt's Addresses," *The Cortland Democrat*, Friday, October 27, 1924, p. 1. Fultonhistory.com (Cortland NY Democrat 1924–0375).

Mrs. Franklin D. Roosevelt discussed political issues before some three hundred Cortland county women at meetings last Monday afternoon and evening. About thirty ladies met her at luncheon at the Cortland House at 1o'clock, and at 2:30 the parlors at the home of Mrs. John A. Wavle were filled to listen to Mrs. Roosevelt.

In the evening, Mrs. Jesse C. Newton of Homer entertained the Sennightly club, who had the members of the Leisure Hour club as guests, and Mrs. Roosevelt was the speaker. Her long acquaintance with public affairs, including her residence in Washington where her husband was assistant secretary of the navy during the Wilson administration, and her activities for suffrage, have given Mrs. Roosevelt a grasp of public affairs that is equaled by few, and her Democratic view-point is attained from convictions. She is thus enabled to use most forceful arguments, and at the same time gives a fair hearing to her opponents.

Miss Frances Miller of Homer spoke at both meetings for the local Democratic ticket. Mrs. Roosevelt was entertained at dinner Monday evening at the home of Mr. and Mrs. R.H. Miller in Homer.

Submitted by Gail Bundy and Kathryn Bundy Locke

February 23, 2017

HOMER GIRLS ASK THE PRESIDENT FOR HELP

As part of a recent two-part article on Eleanor Roosevelt's visit to Homer in 1924, I encouraged readers to submit historical material of local interest they come across. One response came in on February 7. Mrs. Jennifer Greenfield, history teacher in the Homer Junior High School, was checking out an online game that day to help her eighth grade students learn about FDR's "New Deal" during the Great Depression of the 1930s. The game made use of primary source documents. One of the documents she found to be especially intriguing. It referred to the Civilian Conservation Corps established in 1933. The CCC put a quarter of a million young men annually to work on conservation and construction projects to help ease the unemployment problem. They lived in military-style camps. This was one of the most popular programs in the "New Deal." However, it did not include young women. First Lady Eleanor Roosevelt advocated for a comparable program for girls, appropriately called "She-She-She camps." Ninety such camps for young women were set up by 1936, with the help of Secretary of Labor Frances Perkins. The letter below, the primary source document discovered by Mrs. Greenfield in the online game, was sent to President Roosevelt and asked for his help in creating just such a program. The letter's original spelling has been preserved here and in the educational game.

Homer, New York

[acknowledged Feb. 11, 1935]

Mr. Roosevelt,

In Homer a lot of us girls think that seeing there is a CCC camp for boys that there should be one for girls. In a book we read about a military camp for girls, it told how in the morning the girls have to attend school for so long and in the afternoon too. They had to learn how to sew and nurse the sick. they had to make clothes for the poor. . . . A camp like that would give young girls a place to go. We are not very old ourselves from 13 on up but we get in a lot of trouble just the same. And we think you might try to do something about it so that girls in our age could do something like we mentioned and not have to wait until they are 17–18 or 19 years of age. We no how to sew and cook we use to belong to "4–H and "Girl Scouts" and in school there are a lot of cranky old teachers, and the children think themselves so high above us girls. If you should care to give us your answer you can broadcast it over the Radio at noon between 5:00–5:30 at station B.E.N. Buffalo if you don't ans. before the 28th of February we will no you aren't going to help us. Why we are writing is because we want to get away from home get a change in life. And we thought maybe you would help us.

Don't put this in the papers. If you do leave out where the Letter came from.

Signed,

The Eight Secret X's

XXX

The letter came from this source: Robert Cohen, ed., *Dear Mrs. Roosevelt: Letters from Children of the Great Depression* (Chapel Hill: University of North Carolina Press, 2007), 222. And it can be found online: Anonymous, "New York Girls Ask the President for a CCC of Their Own," *HERB: Resources for Teachers*, accessed February 7, 2017, https://herb.ashp.cuny.edu/items/show/729.

    I thank Mrs. Greenfield for sharing her discovery which will be added to the Town archives. She and I are both curious if anyone has any idea as to the identities of "The Eight Secret X's." If so, please leave a contact number or email address with the Town Hall.

March 23, 2017

THE TRAGIC DEMISE OF ALTON HOWE

It was June 21, 1925. The schoolyear in Homer had recently come to a close. Fourteen-year-old Alton Howe of 4 Maple Avenue in the village of Homer, had been promoted to the seventh grade at the Homer Academy. His parents, Mr. and Mrs. Worden G. Howe, rewarded him with a new bicycle. On that Sunday afternoon, after finishing his dinner, the boy changed his clothes. He slipped on a pair of overalls and a broad-brimmed hat. The hat was part of a new Boy Scout uniform he had just purchased with money he had saved up from his paper route for the *Syracuse Post-Standard*. Young Alton left his home and sped off on his new wheels. Around 4 PM the boy and his prized possession took in a performance of the Salvation Army Band on the Green. Five hours later, he had not returned home. His parents were perplexed. The boy had never stayed out past 9 PM without calling home and letting them know his whereabouts. And it was getting late.

Alarmed by their son's disappearance, the Howes finally phoned the State Troopers and asked for help in locating the lad. Troopers Rann and Shaeffer searched all night and into Monday but without success. They looked for clues that might explain his whereabouts. His parents reported that he had left his money, watch, and keys on his bedroom dresser. This indicated the boy had not made any preparations to be away from home. Learning that the boy had been swimming much of late at Little York Lake, the two troopers trolled the lake waters. There was no sign of the boy. Boys who were his playmates claimed they had seen him and his bicycle at the band concert on the Green. After that they had seen nothing.

Monday night, the newspaper reported his disappearance. The paper reported that the boy's mother was "on the verge of a nervous breakdown over her son's continued disappearance." She had told the Troopers that "to her knowledge the boy had no quarrels, was in excellent health, [and] had passed his examinations successfully in school." She could offer "no reason why he should purposely remain away from home." The Troopers concluded that they could rule out the possibility that Alton had run off in search of adventure.

After two nights and a full day of fruitless searching, the Howe family, in their desperation, turned to a clairvoyant from Freeville. The clairvoyant claimed the boy was in a dark place and that he had run into foul play "for refusing a pledge of secrecy to bootlegs [those making, transporting, and selling alcohol in violation of the Prohibition law]."

On Tuesday morning, June 23, Leon Witty, a Cortland electrician, reported to work. The worksite was the Homer Academy on the Green. Witty was to work on the wiring for part of a capital project on the high school portion of the Academy. Around 10 AM Witty was making his way back through the false work or timbering in the basement to locate the end of a pipe through which electrical wires were to pass. Upon reaching the corner, he looked up. In the semi-darkness, he spotted a body suspended above him. Unbelievably frightened, Witty made his way out and reported to his superior. The law enforcement and coroner were notified.

Alton's bicycle was found near a pile of bricks at the rear of the high school. As the *Cortland Standard* reported, that afternoon Alton's "lifeless body was found suspended by a rope from a rafter in the west side of the basement of the new Academy High school building now under construction." His feet were just a few inches from the ground. After Coroner Claude E. Chapin arrived on the scene, the body was taken down and delivered by Briggs' ambulance service to the boy's home. Later, an autopsy report showed that "death was due to strangulation and had occurred thirty-six to forty-eight hours prior to the discovery of the body." The only bleeding was from a skinned knee. That had been caused by a fall experienced days before the death. The boy had freshly bandaged the hurt "just before he left home Sunday afternoon . . ." An inquest was ordered. The conclusion reached was that "death was brought about by suicide."

Such a conclusion was totally unacceptable to the grief-stricken parents. They claimed their son had given them no trouble, that he was a "good boy," and that he had gone off that afternoon in a happy frame of mind. They were not going along with the notion that "temporary insanity" was "the only explanation." There was another possible explanation—murder—and they demanded a fuller investigation.

Sheriff Frank Chrisman obliged. Investigators determined the rope used had been discarded by workmen at the worksite. The rope and the stick around which it was knotted were held as evidence and examined for any fingerprints other than the boy's. Occupied houses were within fifty feet of where the body had been found. No one had heard anything. Boys of Alton's age had helped in searching for the missing boy, and Chrisman quizzed several of them. A few reported that Alton had been "tormented by other juveniles with threats to 'get' him."

The village policeman, Legrande Fisher, explained to the investigators that two groups of village boys had been participating in a "sham feud." They had built shacks for their "headquarters," and conducted "raids" on each other. In this era, youngsters played outside a great deal and had play that was rich in fantasizing about "good guys" versus "bad guys" that today manifests itself in videogames played indoors about war or gangs.

This led the investigation to a cache of letters thought to have been written by the boys several weeks before the incident as part of their play life. There were references to "tying up" prisoners. The Syracuse *Herald* published the letters. This is one letter:

> Are you going to raid us tonight at 4 o'clock? We've got three men. We've got a prison and a lot of things. How many men have you got? We'll lick your men.

The letter was signed with initials. Another letter outlined the rules of engagement for the "sham feud":

> Let's have one club like this. If we get you and your men we can tie you up and take your clothes and tie you to a tree or something like that and you can do it to us. We can take you and tie you so long and then do something. We will raid you and you can raid us but have men that won't cry when we get them and have them brave. Don't try to be tied up. You must fight. Make handcuffs and stuff. Start it tomorrow. Get your men. Raid us first at 4 o'clock.

From this evidence, investigators constructed this possible scenario. Alton Howe had participated in this kind of roleplaying, was taken "prisoner" in a "raid," and was the victim of a mock hanging that went tragically wrong. The place where his body was found was at the end of a plank laid on trestles. It was reported that it was "almost an impossibility for anyone to have staged a hanging there against the boy's resistance." Perhaps the boy had willingly played the role of "captured victim" and an accidental strangulation ensued. But would the other boys have made no effort to free him or to get help or to step forward and report it? Would they just walk away without a troubled conscience? Were they so afraid as to keep the tragedy bottled up within and not confide what they knew to anyone? It seems difficult to fathom.

The suspicious circumstances and the parents' insistence that the boy was incapable of such an unaided act led Coroner Chapin to reopen the case. District Attorney Albert Haskell, Jr., was called in to assist in the examination of the evidence at the Homer Town Hall. Seventeen subpoenas were issued for persons thought to have some knowledge to shed on the case.

This writer turned to Haskell's personal papers to find evidence of the outcome of the case but found no mention at all. Otherwise, it must be assumed that the District Attorney let the coroner's verdict stand. If so, then the case of Alton Howe remains a sad and tragic mystery—one of those unexplainable events that continue to cast "doubts in the minds of many."

This article is based on photocopies of clippings from local and Syracuse newspapers provided by Steve Malchak of Marietta, NY, who owns Alton Howe's Boy Scout uniform.

[Thought from 2020: Is it possible that young Alton Howe, alone, fantasized about being taken prisoner, placed the rope around his neck, and lost his footing on the plank, and no one heard a cry for help, if he was able to utter anything at all?]

April 6, 2017

LEARNED YOUNG MAN FROM HOMER BAFFLES PHYSICIANS

Albert Haskell, Jr., was elected the District Attorney for Cortland County in November of 1921. Three months later, Haskell had his first chance to prove his mettle as a prosecuting attorney in the case of The People vs. Arthur Butler. Butler, a young man from Homer, was charged with assault in the second degree. It seems that in August of 1921 Butler had been hired to work for a man named Williams of McGraw. Williams alleged that Butler feigned illness on his second day on the job, and Williams allowed him to remain in the house. For the next ten days, Butler did no work. Then, Mrs. Williams disappeared, and Butler suddenly got well and quit as the hired man. In court, Williams claimed that he tracked his wife to Syracuse and then to her sister's home in Little York. Finding Butler there on November 28, Williams accused the hired man of adultery. Butler responded by using metal knuckles to beat up the offended husband. Williams filed charges of assault. Albert brought this, his first case as a DA, to a successful conclusion when, on the afternoon of February 14, the jury returned a verdict of guilty.

The story does not end there. The court felt compelled to order Butler to be examined by physicians to ascertain his mental state. When brought into court to hear his sentence, Butler was asked if he had any reason why sentence should not be passed. He cried out, "Yes, sir. I have not had a fair trial and, further, I had no confidence in my attorney." Butler went on to insist that he had "a perfect right to try to lead any woman from the path of shame and save her." He carried on some more and admitted that he had been married twice and that his last wife had refused to live with him. His "peculiar answers, and in such unusual verbiage" caused County Judge George M. Champlin to defer sentencing until Butler had been duly examined by physicians.

The testing was a challenging experience on February 17. The physicians reported they had to put off the testing until the next day because their initial efforts were checked by "the young man's brilliant and confounding answers." They claimed that Butler used so many uncommon words—"medical terms and such intensely intellectual phraseology"—that they had to continually interrupt the examination to look up the man's words in a dictionary. Though the newspaper reported the "Homer Subject Is Too Learned For Physicians," the conviction was upheld and sentence delivered on February 25. Albert had no time to celebrate his victory, however, because the next day he had to prosecute the case of The People vs. Dan Patrioco on a violation of the excise-liquor law and after a considerable time had been taken in securing a jury. Between enforcing Prohibition and prosecuting a case of assault by a learned young man from Homer, the new DA was very busy.

May 18, 2017

THE HOMER ARTIST WHO NEVER FORGOT HIS ROOTS

This is the first of three installments.

On Saturday, May 13, 2017, the last two of Homer's "Lincoln men" were inducted into the Homeville Museum's Cortland County Hall of Fame at the CNY Living History Center. Lincoln's assistant personal secretary, William O. Stoddard, was inducted last May. This year, he was joined by two other native sons of Homer: Eli DeVoe and Francis Bicknell Carpenter. DeVoe was the detective who helped to foil a plot to assassinate President-Elect Lincoln when he passed through Baltimore, Maryland, in 1861 to be inaugurated. Carpenter was the portrait painter who captured Lincoln's iconic image in oil on canvas in 1864.

Did any of these "Lincoln men" return to their roots after they left Homer?

We do not know if Eli DeVoe ever did. His work as a detective and a member of the seminal U. S. Secret Service kept him quite occupied when he was not at his residence in New Jersey. We do know that William Stoddard returned to his birthplace at No. 5 Albany Street on at least one occasion during the Civil War. As for Francis Carpenter, he frequently returned to Homer. His residence and a series of studios were in New York City. There he made a name for himself as the portrait-maker for the "movers and shakers" of nineteenth century America. But the place that magnetically drew him back for vacations in August through September was the Carpenter homestead located a few miles north of the Village on what is now Route 11.

After honing his portraiture skills in Homer, rendering the images on canvas of locals like the Jedediah Barber Family and the first trustees of the Academy on the Green, young Frank Carpenter decided to move to New York City in the spring of 1851. In the Borough of Brooklyn the fledgling artist set up his first studio, and the next August the twenty-one-year-old married fifteen-year-old Augusta Prentiss. She was the lovely daughter of a female music teacher at the Academy in Homer. The Carpenters would have two children: a daughter named Florence and a son named Herbert. A third child, Elliott, died in infancy.

The place of Carpenter's birth was never far from his mind. On September 23, 1851, he wrote a letter to Mr. Dalrymple, a dentist in Homer. He wished to ascertain how receptive some of the leading men in Homer might be to a proposal conceived collaboratively with Dr. Fessenden Nott Otis. Otis was the one who had first introduced Carpenter to drawing when both were mere lads attending a one-room school north of the village. The plan of the two men called for painting *A View of Homer* from up on East Hill for the purpose of engraving and publishing. By agreement, Otis did the painting, and a lithograph was made of it by the Endicott and Company of New York City. From that a photomural was made much later in 1946 by Drix Duryea, Inc. of New York for a wall of the lobby of the Homer National Bank. Today, it is most apropos that the 22 foot by 7-foot mural depicting the Village of Homer in 1852 graces the south wall of the Homer History Center at Key Bank on Main Street.

During his illustrious career, Carpenter and his family frequently took the eight-hour train ride from New York to Homer to visit family and friends. Most of his summers were spent at the Carpenter homestead north of the village where he had been born and raised. The farm stayed in the family until it was offered for sale in 1915, and the house still stands with a blue and gold New York State historic marker near the roadside.

With his young son, whom he called "Bertie," Carpenter enjoyed swimming in the Tioughnioga River and fishing in nearby Little York Lake on hot and humid August days. He and Augusta, whom he affectionately referred to as "Gus," traditionally celebrated their wedding anniversaries at Glen Haven, at the southern tip of Skaneateles Lake, in the company of family and close friends. The latter included the Reverend Dr. Theodore Munger, the noted abolitionist and Yale theologian, and Calvin Woolworth, the son of the Academy's first principal and a successful patent attorney. They had all attended the same one-room district school together in the Town of Homer.

Besides portraits of his parents, Carpenter did portraits of other family members. He painted "Gus" twice: in1851 and 1875. He painted his sister Helen, and he did portraits of Florence and "Bertie." Friends he painted included the Reverend Thomas E. Fessenden of the Homer Congregational Church and his supportive neighbors from his youth, Sylvester and Frances Nash. Frances had shown interest because she had been a teacher of painting at the Academy before her marriage in 1837. Judge Henry Stevens, uncle to Cortland's Henry S. Randall, had his portrait done, as did Carpenter's boyhood friends, Calvin C. Woolworth and Martius Lynde, both of whom had also taken up residence in Brooklyn. Lynde was a lawyer and a life member of the Brooklyn Art Association.

Occasionally, Carpenter had visitors from Homer show up at his studio in Brooklyn. One of the visitors, in 1852, was Paris Barber, Carpenter's early benefactor. Paris brought his nine-year-old son Samuel to see the sights of the metropolis. They stayed at his father-in-law's house on Fifth Avenue and called on the great Daniel Webster at the Astor House on Broadway. Then, the boy was taken to see City Hall, the Battery Park, immigrants arriving from Europe at Castle Garden, a museum, and the ferry to Brooklyn. After all that excitement, the lad, as noted by his bemused father, found the long visit at his father's friend's studio to be terribly boring. But the momentous, polarizing events of the 1850s seemed to be on everyone's lips and leading the young and the old toward an "irrepressible conflict."

June 1, 2017

With the attack on Fort Sumter on April 12, 1861, the Civil War commenced. President Lincoln was determined to preserve the Union at all cost. On New Year's Day, 1863, Lincoln provided a secondary reason for the fighting between the North and the South: the abolition of slavery. On that day, he signed the Emancipation Proclamation, freeing all slaves in the rebel states. Back in New York City, Frank Carpenter received word of the proclamation and pronounced it "an act unparalleled for moral grandeur in the history of mankind." Immediately, his artistic muse inspired him to consider rendering a painting in which Secession would be symbolized as a "beast," "offspring of the 'dragon' Slavery," being fatally pierced. In his mind Carpenter saw the war taking on apocalyptic proportions, equal to the battle between the Archangel Michael and Satan. But such an interpretation did not get placed on canvas.

Instead, the national bloodbath hit home. On Sunday, July 12, 1863, Carpenter journeyed to Gettysburg, Pennsylvania, accompanied by his childhood chum, Dr. Fessenden N. Otis. The overpowering stench of death greeted them, and Carpenter noted that "the town and country was one continued battleground." The two men were searching for Carpenter's twenty-seven-year-old brother, William Wallace Carpenter. A private in the 157th Regiment, William, known as "Will," had been caught in a crossfire of rebel bullets and struck on the first day of intense fighting at Gettysburg, July 1. He was in serious need of surgery. He was suffering from a broken leg sustained from a bullet taken just above his left knee. While another brother, Daniel Webster Carpenter, was among the few in the 76th Regiment who survived the first day of the three-day battle at Gettysburg, Will ended up in a deplorable condition. Daily rains pelted the ground that served as the poorly sheltered army field hospital. Will received no medical attention for ten days due to the sheer overwhelming numbers of wounded requiring attention. Extremely distraught over the prospects of needing an amputation of his leg and witnessing "things that would make you crawl all over," Will managed to get letters to his brother in New York City and to family in Homer. He implored them to hurry to his aid.

When Carpenter and Otis came upon Will, they found his leg had been set by a doctor. He was being cared for by an amiable, wounded member of his company, twenty-two-year-old Wesley Huffman of Preble, New York. The next day, with great difficulty, Frank arranged for Will to be transported to a hospital in New York City. There, surgery was performed immediately, but it was too late. Gangrene from the wound left unattended for too long at Gettysburg had spread through Will's body. He succumbed on Friday, July 17, 1863. [*Note: It has been confirmed by Ed Raus of Homer that Confederate soldiers dropped the wounded Private Carpenter off at the makeshift hospital at Gettysburg's Lutheran Seminary, and from there he was transported to the Union field hospital set up at Spangler's Farm. Most likely, that is where Francis Carpenter found him sharing a tent with Private Huffman of Preble.*]

Frank and "Gus" were used to traveling to Homer in the summertime, but that night, wracked with grief, they took an overnight train accompanying Will's casket home. They reached Homer at 8:30 on the morning of July 18. The next day, Sunday, a funeral took place at 12:30 P.M. at the Carpenter homestead followed by a 2 P.M. service at the Congregational Church. This was one of the first funerals to be conducted at the newly built church on the Green. The church had just been dedicated ten days before, just five days after the end of the decisive battle at Gettysburg.

On Thursday, July 23, 1863, needing a burial plot for Will, the Carpenters selected a "beautifully located" family plot in Homer's new Glenwood Cemetery, a beautification project headed up by the civic-minded Paris Barber. Private William Carpenter was buried there on the afternoon of Sunday, July 26. It was the same day as the funerals of Captain George A. Adams and Private Morris I. Shattuck of William's regiment. Frank recorded in his diary that the day was "A solemn time for Homer." Twenty-six days later, on the anniversary of Will's enlistment, another Carpenter brother, Clement DeWitt—known as "Witt"—entered military service.

Four years later, in the summer of 1868, when the dark days had passed, Frank would paint a 16-by-13-inch oval portrait on canvas of his brother Will from a photograph and memory. The portrait now hangs in the fellowship hall of the Homer Congregational Church, where, at the time of his death, William Wallace Carpenter was the Sunday School Superintendent. His last written words, directed to the children, were inscribed on his Glenwood gravestone: "Tell the children of the Sabbath School to meet me in heaven."

In the meanwhile, the war raged on, claiming more lives in order to preserve the Union and abolish human bondage. On a Sabbath near the end of 1863, on his way home from church in New York City, Carpenter's thoughts returned to the Emancipation Proclamation. This time the artist pondered doing a painting commemorating Lincoln and his seven Cabinet members at the moment when the proclamation was first read that would "give freedom to a race." He began to imagine what the event must have looked like that would forever be associated with Lincoln as a moral act. In his diary he wrote "Surely Art should unite with Eloquence and Poetry to celebrate such a theme."

With the President's approval, Carpenter, at the age of thirty-four, left for Washington on February 4, 1864. For the next six months he labored in the White House state dining room on a nine foot by fifteen-foot canvas. By July 22, *The First Reading of the Emancipation Proclamation before the Cabinet* was near completion. Without knowing that his portrait would become the iconic image of "The Great Emancipator," Lincoln expressed his approval of Carpenter's handiwork and admitted that the event depicted was "the central act of my administration."

After exhibition in the East Room of the White House and in the Rotunda of the Capitol, the large, framed, unsigned painting was taken on a successful public tour across the North, including stops in New York, Boston, Chicago, and Milwaukee. A few days after General Robert E. Lee had surrendered his sword, the painting was on exhibit in Pittsburgh, and word arrived of the assassination of the President at Ford's Theater. The public's interest in seeing the painting intensified immediately. At one point, the doors to the exhibit had to be closed, because the crowd pressing forward was becoming unmanageable.

It was a year and a half later when Carpenter brought the painting of "moral grandeur" to Homer from his New York studio at 653 Broadway. He did not fail to include the community of his childhood in seeing his work. On the evening of Saturday, September 29, 1866, the painting was opened to the public at the opera house on the third floor of Jedediah Barber's mercantile establishment on Main Street. Folks from far and near arrived and filed up the long flight of stairs to stand and gaze in awe at the image of the assassinated President captured for all time in oil on canvas. On the same day, Carpenter attended a reception in his honor hosted by the Stone family of Homer. Those who shook the hand that had painted Lincoln's face were also shaking the hand that had clasped Lincoln's hand in friendship—the same hand that had penned the document that initiated the process that led to the passage of the Thirteenth Amendment to the Constitution in the previous December.

June 15, 2017

Before Lincoln's assassination, Carpenter had made a smart business move. He had arranged with New York publisher Derby & Miller to produce a print of the *Emancipation Proclamation* painting for public sale. Alexander Hay Ritchie, a well-known engraver in New York, was contracted to reproduce the painting as a steel engraving for $6,000. To that end, Carpenter started working on a smaller version of the painting—twenty-one by thirty-three inches—for Ritchie's use, and he had brought this smaller painting with him to Homer the summer before the full painting had been exhibited there.

Thus, it was on Saturday, August 19, 1865, during one of his "vacation visits," that Carpenter felt the need for "material assistance." As he noted in his diary, he "went to the village and got a group of men together like [in his] Emancipation picture" and had Homer's photographer, Luther Barker, make him an ambrotype. Homer's very tall butcher, Burdett Newton, was asked to sit at a table as Lincoln. Other locals took their places as directed. Lewis Henry posed for Secretary of War Stanton; "old Mr. Gardner" for Secretary of the Navy Welles; Ki Munger for Secretary of State Seward; Mr. Hicok for Postmaster General Blair; Mr. Wardell for Secretary of the Interior Smith; and Judge Reed for Attorney General Bates. A visitor from New York named Mr. Gillett was commandeered to stand in as Secretary of the Treasury Salmon P. Chase.

From this small painting worked up in Homer, Ritchie produced a high quality print of the *Emancipation Proclamation* painting that the journalist Noah Brooks predicted would be "prized in every liberty-loving household as a work of art . . . a perpetual remembrance of the noblest event in American history." Carpenter gave copies of the print to each Cabinet member depicted in the painting, and an autographed copy was given to his parents in Homer as a Christmas present.

It was during this same "vacation visit" to Homer that Carpenter was working on another Lincoln project. He was endeavoring to do a painting of *The Lincoln Family* in black and white, with the intention of mass producing it as a commercial print by the engraver John Chester Buttre. The subject of the painting was to be the Presidential family as it was in 1861 before eleven-year-old Willie Lincoln's death in 1862 from typhoid fever. However, Carpenter had never met Willie, and the only thing he had to work from was a photograph Mrs. Lincoln had provided of the heads of Willie and Tad Lincoln.

To get a good sense of the bodily proportions of an eleven-year-old boy, Carpenter enlisted the help of a Homer merchant's son, Henry Wheadon. [The three-story Wheadon Block on Main Street was destroyed by a fire in September 2016.] Carpenter had the young lad pose for an ambrotype. From this image he was able to render the Presidential family with Willie's head upon the body of a Homer boy—a task he completed on August 17, 1865, in Homer.

By this time, too, Carpenter was busy writing his reminiscences of Lincoln. They were being published in a series of articles for the New York *Independent.* Like some of his artwork, some of Carpenter's literary work was done while summering in Homer. His diary entry for August 20, 1865, reads: "Commenced my 'No. VII' [installment] for the 'Independent' this evening, under the tree in the southeast corner of the orchard [at the Carpenter homestead]."

His own extended memoir, *Six Months at the White House with Abraham Lincoln: The Story of a Picture*, was completed on the first anniversary of Lincoln's death and published by Hurd and Houghton in 1866. It was a bestseller. It gave readers exactly what they craved after Lincoln's death: personal anecdotes of the man more than critical assessments of his statesmanship.

The next year, Carpenter took time to re-connect not just with the community of his origins but with his artistic mentor. Twenty-two years earlier while in his teens, Carpenter had spent six months studying portraiture under the Syracuse artist Sanford Thayer. Now, on October 4, 1867, Thayer was invited to make the trip from Syracuse to Homer to spend the day with his former and now famous pupil. Carpenter noted in his diary that the two of them "went to the village and sat for pictures at Luther Barker's [photography studio]."

When another native son of Homer, Andrew D. White, became the first President of Cornell University in nearby Ithaca, NY, Carpenter returned for the University's opening in 1868. It was Carpenter that White commissioned to do the portraits of four distinguished intellects of the era: Louis Agassiz, Goldwyn Smith, James Russell Lowell, and George William Curtis.

Ezra Cornell posed, too, for a couple of portraits by Carpenter. One, bigger than life size, showed Cornell standing with his hand resting on a document bearing his time-honored wish of 1868: "I would found an institution where any person can find instruction in any study." In the painting, Carpenter included a bust of Benjamin Franklin, who, among his many accomplishments, was known for experimentation with electricity. This was, at the time, a recognizable symbolic allusion to Cornell's connection to Samuel F. B. Morse's electric telegraph from which the philanthropic Cornell derived his fortune as a contractor for the erection of telegraph lines.

Carpenter continued painting portraits into the 1870s. In July of 1876, the nation was to be one hundred years old. To celebrate, there was to be a Centennial Exposition in Philadelphia, and Homer's Paris Barber engaged Carpenter as a design consultant for "King Corn." This was to be a colossal human figure for the Exposition constructed entirely of the stalks, silk, husks, and tassels of corn. Its base was to be made of agricultural products of all thirty-seven states. Paris planned to travel to Ithaca to seek financial support for the project from Cornell University, but the sixty-one-year-old became ill. Carpenter went in his place. His request was met with disappointment. But it did not matter, for the project died in May of 1876 with the death of Paris, just two weeks after his father, Jedediah, died on April 19. Carpenter attended Paris' funeral and gratefully recalled the inspirational trip he and Paris took to New York in 1847 to see great works of art. He summed up his benefactor this way: "He had so much of the artistic instinct himself, that he could enter perfectly into the aim and ambition of my life."

When Carpenter returned in August for his "usual summer vacation," he took the room over the drugstore and bookshop business of Atwater & Kellogg in the Barber Block on Main Street. He still was managing to combine business with pleasure, finishing up some art projects. Though Homer had not been his primary residence for the past quarter century, the residents of the area still recognized him when he was out in public. The *Cortland Standard* for August 16, 1876, reported "Frank gets a hearty shake from every man he meets."

On February 12, 1878, the sixty-ninth anniversary of Lincoln's birth, a joint session of Congress convened in the House to accept Carpenter's *First Reading of the Emancipation Proclamation before the Cabinet* as a gift to the nation. The credit for this went to the masterful, behind-the-scenes lobbying done for Carpenter by another son of Homer, William Osborn Stoddard. Stoddard had served as President and Mrs. Lincoln's assistant personal secretary, and he had connections in the Reconstruction era capital and was able to remove all financial and political hurdles for "his warm personal friend of long standing." Today, the painting hangs in the west stairway of the Senate chamber. It is said to be "the only nineteenth-century history painting of Abraham Lincoln in the United States Capitol."

Of all the several portrait studies Carpenter did of Lincoln, the best known is the one done for the *Emancipation Proclamation* painting—the one for which Lincoln told his former law partner, William Herndon, "I feel that there is more of me in this portrait than in any representation which has been made." From this portrait, Frederick W. Halpin, the talented engraver, rendered a line-and-stipple adaptation. This amazingly life-like print carried the signatures of both Halpin and Carpenter. Suitable for framing, it made a fine item to give as a gift, which is exactly what Carpenter did. Seven of his friends in Homer received copies of this print as a Christmas present in 1894. The Homer Village Board of Trustees owns one of them today—a symbol of Carpenter's grateful ties to the place of his birth.

Carpenter died in New York City on May 23, 1900, and his funeral was held there two days later. The artist who had gained fame as Lincoln's portraitist could have been buried in New York City or Albany or in the nation's capital. But, no, Carpenter chose to return to his roots in Homer to be buried in the upper, southwest corner of Glenwood Cemetery in the Carpenter family plot.

It is clear that throughout his artistic career Francis Bicknell Carpenter never forgot his roots in Homer. It is also clear that his work was supported by folks from Homer and its environs, and some of his work, artistic and literary, was actually done here. It is fitting and proper that Homer should recognize the historical documentation accomplished by its native son through his public art and writings. This can be done by installing public art as a lasting tribute at the entrance to the Town Hall. Checks can be made out to the Homer Education Foundation, P O Box 174, Historic Homer, NY 13077. Be sure to note on the check that it is for The Lincoln Monument Project. It is a way for Homer to re-connect with Carpenter and its other "Lincoln men."

Material for the three installments on Carpenter was drawn from Sweeney's well-documented book, LINCOLN'S GIFT FROM HOMER, NEW YORK: A PAINTER, AN EDITOR AND A DETECTIVE (McFarland & Company, 2011), which is available through Amazon.com.

June 29, 2017

BOOTLEGGERS ARRESTED IN CORTLAND AND HOMER

The "Roaring Twenties" are often remembered as a time of bathtub gin, bootleggers, and speakeasies because of the 18th amendment prohibiting the manufacture, transportation, and sale of alcoholic beverages. Among the several attempts made in Cortland County to enforce this most unenforceable of federal laws, two stand out for the high level of interest generated in 1922. One happened in the city of Cortland and the other in the Town of Homer. Both were covered by the local press.

The Cortland case saw the jury come in with a verdict of not guilty. It took the jury nearly nine hours to deliberate after the unusual trial of Claude Pickert. On the first ballot the decision was eight to four for acquittal. On the next, it was ten for acquittal. After a time, the jurors were unanimous for acquittal.

Pickert, a restaurant owner on Orchard Street in Cortland, had been charged with selling a half pint of whiskey and two glasses to two roof painters, Fred Anson and Frank Bush. The trial on February 16 and 17 of 1922 had drawn quite the audience because Anson and Pickert had been war buddies overseas in the recently concluded Great War, and the case was the most bitterly fought of all the Prohibition cases the District Attorney's Office had to prosecute. Several times the judge felt compelled to rap his gavel to restore order in the courtroom. At one point he threatened to clear the room. "This court is not putting on a vaudeville performance," he announced.

The cause of the entertainment was, unfortunately, the Prosecution's chief witness, Fred Anson. The case fell apart when Anson was under cross-examination by Pickert's attorney, Elmer Thompson, for whom Anson had worked the past three years. Severely grilled by Thompson, Anson testified that the police commissioners of Cortland had offered him either the office of Chief of the City Police "or something as good" if he succeeded in getting evidence against the defendant. Guffaws erupted in the audience, the jury went into deliberation, and Pickert walked free. And Anson? He received nothing but laughter for his troubles.

Ten days later, another bootlegging incident was brought to District Attorney Albert Haskell's attention. This time Sheriff Frank Henry received a tip from Syracuse early on Saturday night, February 26, 1922. Booze runners were said to be headed toward Cortland County, and law enforcement was urged to be on the watch. A description of the vehicle was provided—a Brockway Big Six Speed Wagon.

According to plans, at 11 PM the law enforcement officers took up positions along Route 11 north of the village of Homer. Under-Sheriff Chrisman and Officer Slocum camped out at the stone bridge north of the village. Frank Miller, on foot, took up a post about a quarter of a mile further north on the highway, and Sheriff Henry went to the intersection of Route 11 and Little York Crossing Road. In the cold and dark, the men waited one hour . . . then two hours . . . and then three.

Around 2 AM, Sunday morning, a vehicle matching the description drove past the Sheriff. The sheriff's car pulled out. At a respectful distance, the sheriff trailed the suspect to prevent any possible retreat. The vehicle in question then passed Mr. Miller's lookout post. As planned, Miller signaled ahead to the men at the bridge, and the men set up a roadblock by positioning the big police truck crosswise at the bridge. The booze runner would be hemmed in.

The south-bound truck driver was surprised. Forced to stop, he asked, "What's the trouble?" Chrisman answered, "I'm broke down." At this point, the Sheriff and Officer Miller pulled up behind the booze runner. Escape would be futile. The trucker was found to be unarmed, and a search was made of the Brockway truck. Under the truck covering, the officers found some fruit baskets and other articles. Under them was found ten big bags of sugar. At least, that was the label on the bags. Further examination revealed that each bag was disguising a twenty-gallon cask suspected of containing liquor. Later, the casks would be determined to hold a total of 200 gallons of high-quality Canadian whisky.

The driver gave his name as Denny Bender of Buffalo, New York. He claimed he was driving the truck for a man named Strauss, also of Buffalo, who was ill. Bender said he had no knowledge of the cargo he was hired to deliver. "I'm just the driver; that's all," professed Bender as he was promptly arrested. He, the truck, and the cargo were taken to the sheriff's office in Cortland, and Bender was jailed overnight. The Brockway truck and half the casks were confiscated.

On Monday morning, Bender was brought before Homer's Justice of the Peace for arraignment. Bender still maintained he was innocent of wrongdoing and refused to tell the Justice the origin or destination of the contraband, though the arresting officers believed the booze was headed through Homer to the city of Cortland or Binghamton. He gave his age as 30 and said he was married. He asked permission to make a phone call to a friend in Buffalo about his plight and to request the friend to not tell his wife of his arrest because she was ill in a Buffalo hospital. Bender, pleading not guilty, was returned to the County jail to be held for the Grand Jury. Bail was set at $1,000.

District Attorney Haskell was informed that the illegal alcohol was "the largest quantity ever seized at one time by an official of the county." For County Sheriff Henry it was the fourth raid made by him since he assumed office the first of January. It had been a busy two months. The exciting events in Cortland and Homer had all the makings of a future Hollywood movie about Prohibition bootleggers in the "Roaring Twenties" minus the use of the "Tommy Guns."

August 24, 2017

"UNCLE JED," THE GREAT WESTERN, AND "CLINTON'S BIG DITCH"

This is the first installment of a three-part article on Homer's first permanent merchant.

A recent two-part article in this column focusing on Homer of the 1840s gave a brief mention of Jedediah Barber and his Great Western Store. Since New York State is at the start of its bicentennial observance of the Erie Canal's construction, it seems appropriate to provide readers with more information about Jedediah and his emporium which benefitted greatly from the creation of this 336 mile, man-made waterway from the Hudson River at Albany to Lake Erie at Buffalo.

The "200th Anniversary" celebration will span from 2017 to 2025, representing the period of construction of the Erie Canal, from the groundbreaking in Rome in 1817 to the fabled "Wedding of the Waters" in New York Harbor in 1825. The canal made New York City a major port and caused a national economic boon. The growth of communities along the canal and the stimulus to business made New York "the Empire State."

The opening of the canal on October 26 of 1825 marked a new era in the development of Cortland County and in an up-tick in trade at The Great Western, the first permanent mercantile establishment in Homer. Jedediah Barber expressed his appreciation by naming a prominent street in the village of Homer after a political friend, the sixth Governor of New York State, DeWitt Clinton. The governor was largely responsible for the construction of the Erie Canal, strongly believing that infrastructure improvements could transform American life, drive economic growth, and encourage political participation. Hence, as Barber expressed in a letter written July 20, 1863, he had memorialized the governor by naming the street north of his farm (that now connects Main Street and West Road/Route 281) "Clinton Street."

Instead of a week's travel in four-horse wagons along the Cherry Valley turnpike to pick up freight in Albany, the canal allowed Barber to travel to Syracuse for his freight and return all within twenty-four hours. It was not unusual to see Barber's carts loaded with pork barrels, grain, tallow, dried apples, and firkins of butter headed for Syracuse. The procession would reach the city by nightfall, remain until morning, and return with hardware, groceries, and other items for the store's shelves. Time and expense were greatly reduced for the merchant by the Erie Canal, and the savings could be passed along to the customers.

Almost immediately, Homer and other inland towns demanded even more transportation improvements to connect them to "Clinton's Big Ditch." They wanted better roads, branch canals, and something new called "railways." On November 26, 1825, a group of Homer citizens met at the home of Levi Bowen. Martin Keep chaired the meeting, and Andrew Dickson (A. D. White's grandfather) served as the secretary. Their purpose was to petition the state legislature for the construction of a turnpike through the Onondaga Reservation in the Town of Onondaga to expedite passenger and freight service to and from the canal.

This turnpike would immensely help Barber's business which was experiencing an increase in demand for goods and would justify the store's expansion to two more stories. One reason for this increase in business was because of an increase in population. When Jedediah and Matilda Barber moved from Tully to Homer in 1811 and set up shop two years later in a structure coated in white paint and named after the nearby Great Western Turnpike (now Route 90), the population of the Town of Homer totaled 2,975. By 1825 the population was 6,128. This represented an increase of 106 percent within fifteen years. Keep in mind that The Great Western and William Sherman's

Exchange, the two earliest general stores, provided for the wants and needs of consumers within a ten-mile radius and beyond. Customers flocked into Homer from Truxton, Tully, Scott, Preble, Little York, Sempronius, Moravia, Groton, Virgil, McLean, Dryden, and McGrawville. It was said that at The Great Western "everything a farmer could raise or a skilled worker could make, found a buyer." It was, indeed, the Walmart of nineteenth century Central New York State.

The second reason Barber's business thrived was because he and others took the necessary steps to encourage folks to settle in Homer and not to move West as new lands opened for settlement. He started up a bank in the back of the store for much needed moneylending services. He advocated with others for the incorporation of the Village in June 1835, thinking correctly that it would be good for development. The matter was consummated in the basement of the new Calvary Episcopal Church. The area in front of the church had been transformed from a six-acre "Common" for grazing the early settlers' cattle to a leveled and fenced-in Green by 1825. The park-like appearance would come later in 1863. The periphery of the early Green was dedicated to the two things which would be most enticing to young couples looking for a place at that time to settle and raise families: religion and education. The original group of churches on the "Common"—Baptist and Congregational-Presbyterian—were joined by the Episcopal Church in 1831 and the Methodist Society two years later. Barber, recognizing his own educational limitations, joined other members of the community in 1819 in successfully gaining a charter from the state for an academy on the Green. By 1838, its faculty consisted of four gentlemen and two ladies, and the facility boasted in the *Family Magazine* (Cincinnati, Ohio, Vol. V, 1837–1838) of having a library and complete equipment of "philosophical and chymical apparatus," minerals, and geological specimens.

The same article emphasized the village's shaded streets and flagstone walkways. It made a boast that would make any developer of today trained in salesmanship proud: "There was in Homer an air of neatness and ostentatious elegance not surpassed by any village in Western New York." What family would not be attracted to such a location with churches and a fine school and an accessible store for all your shopping needs?

A third reason Barber's business increased was Barber himself. Besides the variety of goods offered for cash or barter or credit, the store owner had a reputation for positive customer relations. To be sure, "Uncle Jed" was a taskmaster with his employees. He hated to see any of them idle for even a second and was said by P. C. Kingsbury (Dec. 3, 1935) to even upset piles of goods on the floor, when he thought no one was looking, just to see all his clerks were kept busy. But when it came to his customers, "Uncle Jed" was affable. He knew everybody and lavished personal attention upon them, and they kept coming back and brought others. One customer, a Mrs. C. E. Parmalee Butler, put it this way:

> He knew everybody familiarly for many miles round about and talked freely with them about their family and business affairs. No one at all resented his familiar questions . . . he was kind . . . everybody liked him . . .

Mrs. Butler could be describing the late Roland Fragnoli, don't you think? "Frog" treated the customers who entered his Homer Men's and Boys' Store on Main Street, Homer, the same way. This was part of his commercial success.

And "Uncle Jed" was always on the job, especially when business was brisk. In a letter to his eldest daughter, he described what Monday, November 29, 1841, was like for him:

> . . . so many customers as we have and the most difficult part, 'where is Mr. Barber, I want to see him for a load of lumber, a load of grain, a load of beef or pork' now I don't complain my boys are all good and try to favor me and do as much as I want them to do but this hurry will soon be over we have a great stock of goods a great run of customers and as we have had some sleighing our streets are full every day . . .

Image 7.1 1863 Barber Block as seen today. Third floor opera house has been converted into apartments. *Photo by Don Ferris.*

In another letter, dated Wednesday, December 8, 1841, he wrote:

> ... if we ever had a full store of customers it was Yesterday. I was tired from top to bottom my lungs and all we have so much store trade and produce business at this time that we have to keep additional men to help we are getting
> a good run of trade full enough for our comfort ...

September 7, 2017

Business was normally brisk at The Great Western on Main Street, but it had its challenges. Shoplifting seems to be every merchant's dilemma in every age. It was no less of a problem in Jedediah Barber's day, but the vigilant shopkeeper had a way of dealing with it.

Mrs. Ina Hurlbut Bird once told the story of a woman who entered The Great Western carrying a baby in her arms. The woman wore a long cape which partly concealed the infant. Thinking she was not noticed, she gave into temptation and quickly picked up a Paisley shawl from a counter and tucked it under her cape. Barber spotted the fringe of the shawl hanging down past the cape. Nonchalantly he strolled over to the woman, held out his arms, and cordially called out, "Come, baby; come to Uncle Jed." "Oh, no," said the mother. "Oh, yes, yes," insisted the merchant. "Come, baby; come to Uncle Jed," and he plucked the child from its mother's arms. In doing so, the stolen shawl fell to the floor.

Mrs. Bird told of yet another shoplifter. Missing a roll of butter, Barber invited the suspected customer, a dapper young man in a stylish high plug hat, to tarry awhile and socialize with other customers. He seated him near the pot-bellied stove in the rear of the store and tossed in a big chunk of wood. Soon, "Uncle Jed" knew he had his culprit, as melting butter began to pour out from under the man's top hat and down his face.

A third account of thievery was recalled by Ward A. Woodward of Cortland whose mother knew Barber personally. This story involved the large quantity of barrels of salted pork stacked up along the Wall Street side of the store, behind it, and all the way to the river. One day it seems that Barber was looking over the barrels destined for transport down the Tioughnioga and Susquehanna Rivers, and he found one missing. He told no one but quickly placed an empty barrel in its place. Sometime later, a customer approached Barber and inquired, "Did you ever find out who stole the barrel of pork?" Barber looked the man in the eye and replied, "No, I did not until now. No one knew it but myself and the man who took it."

Other humorous stories, based on fact or lore, made the rounds in Cortland County and contributed to Barber's reputation. Some families preferred to "run an account" at Barber's store if their credit was good. One day, an elderly lady came into the store in an agitated manner. She thrust a lengthy bill across the desk and demanded to know what a mark meant on the bill. "Why, that's a ditto, ma'm," explained Barber. "Look here, Mr. Barber," said she, "you have charged me with several dittoes and I never bought a ditto in my life!" (courtesy of Mrs. Bird, 1935).

Then there is the tale told by Miss Van Buskirk of Preble. She told Mrs. Bird about the couple who came into town from their farm on Mt. Toppin during a severe late winter storm. It was a precarious journey as they guided the team of horses down the slope and over the snow-drifted road into Homer. Their arrival at The Great Western on such a day was met with much excitement. After considerable unwinding and unwrapping, the couple revealed they had a year-old baby daughter with them. "Uncle Jed" immediately came over and took the child in his arms. "How could you bring the baby out on such a day?" he asked. The couple explained they were low on provisions and had to come. "As we could not leave her alone, we brought her along," said the mother. At this, Barber called to one of his clerks and ordered him to cut off a length of high-quality material. And "Uncle Jed" personally presented the baby with the fixings for a new dress. Apparently, "Uncle Jed" and "Frog" were both storeowners with something else in common—generosity.

Clearly, like "Frog," "Uncle Jed" had a patriarchal interest in children. This recalls the story that made its way into Bertha Blodgett's *Stories of Cortland County for Boys and Girls* (1932). It seems that a molasses barrel broke open in the cellar of The Great Western. The floor was said to be covered with two inches of the sweet liquid. Word spread quickly through the village. In no time at all, "all the boys in town tried to get into that cellar to dip their fingers into the molasses and convey it to their mouths." One suspects that "Uncle Jed" did not discourage such an invasion. Why let a sweet go to waste and deny the children the pleasure?

In the days before the railroad came through Homer, The Great Western was the hub of activity for area farmers seeking to sell items to "Uncle Jed." At that time, farmers came into town and received three cents a pound for dried apples and eight to ten cents a dozen for eggs. Barley could fetch $1.75 per bushel. Farmers made butter and packed it away in tubs or firkins. These were kept cool all summer in their cellars and brought in for sale in the fall. A cord of body maple, eighteen inches long with the bark down, would earn you $1.50 in cash or tea or some other trade. Folks could not seem to get along without "Uncle Jed's four-shillin' tea." A common expression heard when someone had behaved strangely was "I ain't had nothing stronger to drink than Jedediah Barber's four-shillin' tea." Jugs of locally made whiskey were commonly purchased or bartered at the store, but "set down and have a dish of tea" from "Uncle Jed's Store" was the cordial invitation Homerites extended to neighbors and strangers alike.

Barber understood well the benefits of advertising. In 1844, he made one of his trips to New York City and returned with a large sign for the storefront. Soon, the other merchants in the village wanted to have similarly impressive signs, but few could afford to import signs as Barber had done. Nevertheless, new signs began to appear. Not to be outdone, the local merchants and a village smithy hired a local teenager to ornament their shops with signs like Barber's. His name was Francis Bicknell Carpenter, who went on to become the friend and famed portraitist of President Lincoln.

Earlier than this, Barber recognized the need to get ads into local newspapers. In the October 4, 1828, issue of the Cortland *Observer*, Barber ran his first full-length Great Western ad and continued to run it for half a year:

NEW GOODS

J. Barber is now receiving his assortment

OF FALL AND WINTER GOODS

which, with his former stock, makes his assortment of

STAPLE AND FANCY DRY GOODS

equal to any in the western country, and as usual

will be sold on liberal terms for Cash, Barter

or approved credit

N B Received, and for sale as above

1 Case Leghorn Hats

1 " "Flats and Crowns

200 pieces paper hangings and bordering

2500 yards brown shirtings

1000 " " sheetings

—also—

Cooking, Franklin and Box Stoves

of almost every size and pattern now in use

POTASH AND CHALDRON KETTLES

together with a complete assortment of

Hollow Ware, Iron, Steel, Nails

Glass, Window Sash, Sole

And Upper Leather

Calf and Morocco

Skins & C

Also, 100 Bbls first quality WHISKEY

September 21, 2017

    Jedediah Barber's Great Western was not without competition. Thanks to the growing population in the area and accessibility to the Erie Canal in Syracuse, others found merchandizing to be lucrative in Homer. Giles Chittenden sold dry goods, leghorn hats (wide-brimmed straw hats for men and women), groceries, crockery, hardware, and fish. W. and J. Sherman sold their famous machine-made "S" nails, hardware, paints, and linseed oil at the Sherman Exchange (just south of the Town Hall today). J. and F. Sherrill had a business on the corner south of the Green. H. Frizell ran a store that had been occupied by Jared Babcock; and McNeil and Rowley purchased their store from another merchant. The sixth competitor was J. Lynde. His stock consisted of 4,000 gallons of old double-rectified whisky. All six businesses advertised in the Cortland *Observer*.

    In addition, from 1830 to 1832, Joel Barber Hibbard and his brother-in-law Oren Stimson operated a store under the name of Stimson and Hibbard. Hibbard was Barber's nephew, and Stimson had married Barber's niece, Rachel Hibbard. Both men moved to Cortland, the rapidly growing county seat.

    Another problem merchants faced, besides dealing with shoplifters, was collecting unpaid debts. "Uncle Jed" had a particularly difficult time getting money owed him by a farmer up on Factory Hill. Barber urged the constable to confiscate a hog as payment. Since the farmer only had one hog the constable refused to attach it. Time passed, and then the farmer's son showed up at the store to buy feed for young piglets. Immediately, Barber and the constable high-tailed it out to the Factory Hill farm. Sure enough, there was a new litter. The constable attached the hog, and Barber's claim was satisfied (told by Richard Price of Homer, 1935).

    One important source of business for The Great Western was the students at the academy, many of whom boarded in the community. Being one of the founders of the Academy, a trustee for fifty consecutive years, and its president for thirty-three years (1836–1869), Barber had an interest in their academic success and "would grant them ample credit" (Miss Sara Kingsbury, in the records of the Academy Centennial, 1919).

On April 1, 1834, Barber took in as a business partner his oldest son George. The twenty-one-year-old was proud to see the storefront sign bear the words "J. Barber and Son." Seven years later, there was another change of title. William Hicok, the bookkeeper, and Watts Barber, the youngest son, entered the firm, and the sign read "J. Barber Sons & Company." For some reason, in April of 1850 The Great Western reverted to its original sole proprietorship, but the former partners continued in the employ of Barber. A third son, Paris Barber, had no interest in merchandizing for a living.

On April 27, 1854, Barber ran an ad of a more personal nature. He announced that $50,000 worth of goods were to be found at The Great Western, and

> This store has been in successful operation for FORTY-TWO YEARS in Homer Village. The proprietor begs leave to express his unfeigned gratification for the long and liberal patronage of numerous customers, and will be extremely happy to see them at all times, and exhibit the largest Stock of Goods ever before offered in this County.

The ad listed three bales of buffalo robes, one thousand butter firkins and tubs, one hundred bushels of clover and grass seed of superior quality, and 200,000 feet of dry white pine boards and planks.

Barber was also determined that his Great Western should keep up with the latest amenities for his customers. So, in 1856, gas lights replaced oil lamps in the store. To help the distributors of the new, improved Benzole Gas Fixtures make more sales, Barber offered a testimonial declaring "the services of one man from five to ten minutes daily sums up the whole expense of maintenance whereas it has been considered the work of one man from one to one and one half hours daily to clean, fill and put in order the lamps necessary in my business."

Perhaps the new type of lighting was responsible for the fire that broke out at The Great Western at 2 AM on Friday, May 10, 1856. The origin of the conflagration was never officially determined, but *Rumsey's Companion* of Dryden attributed it to "the work of an incendiary." The store was a total loss. Nothing was saved except the valuable documents in the store vault. No one was hurt; the clerks sleeping on the second floor managed to escape by jumping out of the second story windows. The newspaper reported that the loss was valued at around $60,000, and that the contents were only insured for half that amount. The paper went on to state that it was doubtful any insurance could be recovered since the newly invented gas fixtures had recently been installed "which is said to be a somewhat dangerous light."

The ringing of the fire bell, the smell of smoke, and the great, red glare in the sky awakened the village. Firefighting apparatus arrived from Cortland to assist. 70-year-old Jedediah Barber hurried down Main Street as fast as his rheumatism permitted. From the front parlor of Judge Reed's house, which was located where the Post Office is now, he sat silently watching the business he had carried on for almost a half-century literally go up in smoke. The next day he would write a painful ten-page letter to his daughter in New York City.

Barber's wife, Matilda, took it the hardest. She was reported to have been running up and down Main Street during the fire, wringing her hands and crying out to everyone she met, "We're ruined! We're ruined! Now we're poor!" The woman was understandably distraught, and no one was able to comfort her (Miss May Buell Barber, 1933).

Eyewitnesses admitted that some of them muttered amongst themselves, "Well, this is the end of old Barber." However, they were too quick to underestimate the resilience of "Uncle Jed" and the Barber family. The old merchant approached the bystanders and in a tremulous voice set them straight: "'Old Jed,' as they call me, will survive the loss and he will someday erect over these ruins a better building."

And Barber did just that. Around 1863, during the Civil War, the indomitable Jedediah Barber rebuilt The Great Western as the three-story brick structure you see on Main Street today. Under different ownership, the third floor with its stage later became known as the Keator Opera House.

Barber faced some serious debts, and his chief local competitor, William Sherman, urged him to call it quits: "Uncle Jed, it's time we closed our businesses and retired—I'm going to." Barber simply replied, "I'm not; you can rust out, but I'll wear out."

And Barber did just that. As infirmities required that he relinquish managerial responsibilities to others, the white-haired, venerable merchant still got about the village by carriage to regularly survey what he had had a hand in creating: his farm, building lots, the railroad, the academy, and his bank building (which still stands) north of his store. He would point to The Great Western, or Barber Block, and tell visitors with justifiable pride, "I built that." Thirteen years after he said he preferred to "wear out," on April 19, 1876, "Uncle Jed" died. Just ten days earlier he had quietly celebrated his eighty-ninth birthday. Matilda Barber had passed four years earlier.

Many well-preserved homes still stand in the village that were once occupied by Barbers, including the brick mansion Jedediah had built on North Main Street in 1825 in the Greek Revival style. Today, Elm Avenue cuts through what was once an impressive, formal flower garden next to the pillared portico along the south side of the edifice. The prosperous owner of The Great Western quite naturally wished for a dwelling that was commensurate with his prosperity—a prosperity made possible in large part by the "Big Ditch" that ran through Syracuse thanks to the man whose name still graces the street near the mansion—Clinton.

The details of this three-part article would not have been possible without the biography of Jedediah Barber written by his great-grandson Herbert Barber Howe (New York: Columbia University Press, 1939).

October 5, 2017

HOMER RESTAURANTEUR FED OUR MILITARY'S "TOP BRASS"

Did you know that a resident of Homer was once responsible for the dining rooms in the Combined Chiefs of Staff Building in Washington, D.C., during World War II? Well, it's a fact, and her name was Nellie Docherty Randall.

Nellie Docherty was born on May 1, 1892, in Motherwell, Scotland, a suburb southeast of Glasgow. Her parents were Patrick and Catherine Hopkins Docherty. In 1909, at the age of 17, Nellie made her way to America—one of 751,786 immigrants that year. Why she left Scotland is not exactly clear, but she did mention being none too fond of having to clean sooty ceilings in an older sister's house.

What is clear is that Nellie chose to settle in Homer, New York, and married a man named Leo Randall. Unfortunately, the marriage only lasted six months. It seems that Leo wandered off, and Nellie Randall was left to fend for herself. This she managed to do quite well. She, also, continued to be close with Leo's sisters, Anna Randall Erhard, and "Allie" Conway. "Allie" was the wife of Pat "Patsy" Conway, the acclaimed American bandleader during the golden era of professional bands. Pat Conway was born in Troy, New York, but moved as an infant to Homer. While he was a young man working at one of Homer's carriage factories, he learned to play the coronet. He joined the popular Homer Coronet Band and then became the leader of the Cortland Band. In 1895, he relocated to Ithaca and was the director of the predecessor of Cornell University's Big Red Marching Band until the year before Nellie came to America. He, also, taught band music at the predecessor of today's Ithaca College. The Ithaca Band he formed in 1895 was better known by 1910 as "Patrick Conway and His Famous Band." The ensemble had a standing contract with Ithaca's trolley company to perform at Stewart Park (then Renwick Park) when they were not on tour around the country. After Pat's death in 1929, "Allie" was known to still visit her sister Anna and their sister-in-law Nellie Randall at the southern end of Skaneateles Lake.

While Pat Conway was making a name for himself in music, Nellie was carving out a niche for herself as a restauranteur. In one of the stores fronting Main Street in Homer, Nellie opened her first restaurant. Well situated on Route 11, the establishment catered to local folks and to the wealthy travelers venturing forth on the highway in the increasingly popular horseless carriages of the day. At some point Nellie moved her restaurant to the old "temperance tavern," once known as "Wisdom's Gate," on the corner of South Main and Albany Street. She named her new restaurant "The Braeside Tearoom," derived from the Scottish word for *hillside*, which was appropriate because of her restaurant's location at the foot of East Hill.

In the 1930s, Nellie partnered with Mary Schermerhorn to operate an additional tearoom. This one was in Tully. It was located in the Cobblestone Lodge, and it was known as "The Glencairn," from the Scottish for *a mound of stones erected as a memorial or marker within a small, secluded valley*. It did not take long for the place in Tully to garner a reputation for requiring a reservation if you hoped to be seated and well fed.

Then World War II broke out, and where do we find Nellie next? She is in the nation's capital and placed in charge of the dining services for the Joint Chiefs of Staff located then on Constitution Avenue between 19th and 20th Streets, NW. Just imagine! One might think the military's "top brass" would expect to be fed by a chef trained in classic French cuisine, along the lines of a Julia Child, not by a fifty-year old woman who learned to cook as a girl in Scotland. How all of this came to pass is uncertain. Perhaps it was Nellie's delightful brogue, which she never lost, along with her people skills and her culinary arts, which captivated the one who interviewed her for the prestigious job.

In this capacity, Nellie made the acquaintance of the Commander-in-Chief, Franklin D. Roosevelt, and the following names from the books of American military history: Admiral William Leahy, Chairman of the Joint Chiefs of Staff; Admiral Ernest King, Commander in Chief of the United States Fleet (COMINCH) and Chief of Naval Operations (CNO); General Henry Harley "Hap" Arnold, General of the Army and General of the Air Force; General George C. Marshall, U.S. Army Chief of Staff and member of the Top Policy Group overseeing the atomic bomb project; and Field Marshall Sir John Greer Dill, Senior British Representative on the Combined Chiefs of Staff. In addition, it is quite possible that Nellie was in the presence of Generals Eisenhower and MacArthur and Admiral Nimitz. And there is some indication that she met the First Lady, Eleanor Roosevelt, and Prime Minister Winston Churchill when he spent three weeks, including Christmas, at the White House in 1941.

One day, Nellie was at the White House. She was in the "Map Room" consulting about menus with "Mac," the overseer of the high security location.

She said to him, "I really should not be in here." "Mac" replied, "Never mind, Nellie, if you were a spy, we would surely know it by now." When she left Washington, Nellie had many stories to share and one much cherished gift: a large, framed photograph of her with the President signed "To Nellie, Franklin D. Roosevelt."

Shortly after the end of World War II, Nellie Randall and Mary Schermerhorn took up residence in Skaneateles and opened up a small diner on Jordan Street. Its seating capacity was a mere ten stools at a counter. Known as "The Penguin," it served lunch and dinner and was described by one patron as "one of the best eating places on earth—or, as far as I know, anywhere else." When the diner opened for the day, one hundred cards with numbers were hung out, and potential customers scrambled to get a number and to wait in line if they were not among the first lucky ten. Promptly at 7 PM, the doors to "The Penguin" closed, no matter how many eager customers were still standing in line.

Later, "The Penguin" was moved to Route 20. Visitors asking for directions were usually told "Just go right through town towards Auburn. Slow down on the top of the first hill and take your appetite inside." Squeezed next to a gas station, the diner could be easily passed by, unless you were intentionally looking for it. And who would have guessed that the diner's proprietor had once cooked for America's World War II generals and admirals?

Mary Schermerhorn died in 1957, and "The Penguin" closed for good in the fall of that year. Two years later, Nellie Randall returned to Scotland. But finding the air around Glasgow to be filled with industrial pollution, she followed the advice of her doctor to move away. She returned to America. Auburn may have been her home for a while. At times she resided with her sister-in-law Anna Randall Erhard at the south end of Skaneateles Lake and wintered in Albuquerque, New Mexico. The last decade of her life was spent at the senior citizen housing at 51 Port Watson Street in Cortland. There she was part of a group of four women who enjoyed celebrating each other's birthdays.

Nellie lived to be 90 years old. On her last birthday, friends feted her at a restaurant in Cortland, "The Community." A telegram was sent to her that day from an old friend from her years in Washington, Edie Jones. Edie had been Admiral Leahy's secretary during the Second World War. Edie congratulated Nellie on attaining her 90th and signed the telegram as follows:

"Grace Kirby, Polly Draper, Gen. Dean, Jessie Dowdy, Mac from the Map Room, Jennie Pratt, Herbert Smellie, [and] In abstentia: Gen. Arnold, Gen. Marshall, Adm. King, Adm. Leahy, Duke of Windsor, Winston Churchill, Franklin & Eleanor, Edie Jones." Telegrams were delivered by phone in 1982, but because the company could not reach Nellie, the message was phoned to a friend, Margaret Frail, who recorded it in her own hand and gave it to a much-surprised Nellie.

Nellie Randall died on January 19, 1983, at Cortland Memorial Hospital, survived by one niece in Philadelphia and several nieces and nephews in Scotland. One nephew paid Nellie the ultimate compliment: "There is nothing any finer than putting one's feet under Aunt Nellie's table." Friends described her as "very independent, well-informed, and an interesting lady" who charmed everyone with stories served up with her rich Scottish brogue. Memories of her culinary arts were not buried with her at St. Mary's Cemetery in Cortland. An article in the *Syracuse Herald American* of Sunday, July 26, 1987, identified "specialties from some of CNY's fondly remembered restaurants." There were the delectable brownies of "The Krebs" of Skaneateles, date-nut bread of "Tubbert's" in Syracuse, lobster thermidor served at the Hotel Syracuse, and Scotch steak pie and biscuits at the "Braelock Inn" of Cazenovia. Among these "popular favorites" was listed one other: Nellie Randall's apricot marmalade made famous at "The Penguin" on Route 20 in Skaneateles. Friends also remembered that when Nellie was invited for a meal, she often brought one of her favorite, easy-to-prepare desserts—date torte.

Nellie kept her recipes in a loose-leaf notebook. That notebook has survived to this day. In the front she had penned a quote attributed to F.D.R. that surely had special significance for Nellie: "When you reach the end of your rope, tie a knot in it and hang on." It was Nellie's recipe for coping with life that she had picked up from one trying to cook up a way to get us out of the Great Depression and World War II.

Some of her special recipes ended up published in *Nellie's Cookbook*, edited anonymously and with a preface written by L. M. B., who is believed to have been a public relations director for Carrier Corp., Leslie M. Beals. The preface to the book of recipes implies that the wives of America's military leaders were a tad jealous of the delicious dishes concocted by Nellie. The World War II heroes would enjoy a repast and then shake their heads as they muttered, "Gad, how does Nellie do it?" According to L. M. B., she did it with "half a scallion, a pinch of this and that and an old kitchen range."

A favorite dish at "The Penguin" was ham in cream and sherry. This was made from baked ham sliced no less than a quarter inch thick. For a single serving, you put a ¼ cup heavy cream into an enamel or Pyrex pan. Let it cook until the cream begins to thicken. Then lay the ham in. It should be ready in 5 to 7 minutes. Add 2 tablespoons sherry wine for each serving. Et voila! Pretty simple, yes? And as you enjoy this dish, you can just imagine Nellie presiding over a steam table wheeled into the map room at the White House and serving those men who had just gathered to confer on strategies for defeating the Axis Powers. Even distinguished men have to eat. And the Scottish lassie who once operated the "Braeside Inn" in Homer knew how to feed them.

Nellie Randall's Recipe for Apricot Marmalade

1 pound dried apricots

2 pounds granulated sugar

1 ounce almonds or pecans

rind of 1 lemon or orange

6 cups water

Wash apricots, cut small, let stand overnight covered with water. Boil slowly until apricots are soft. Add sugar and boil until thick and glazed-looking.

Watch carefully after sugar goes in so it doesn't scorch. When cooked enough, add the nuts, which have been slivered, and the rind, cut very fine. Put in jar and keep in refrigerator. Happy eating!

And do drop in at the History Center at Key Bank in Homer. There you can see on display a dining plate boldly inscribed in blue on white with the word "Braeside" and Nellie Randall's initials: N. E. R.

The sources for this article were photocopies of news clippings and other printed material provided during an interview on July 17, 2017, of Catherine Frail of Cortland, who knew Nellie Randall.

October 19, 2017

TWO HOMER MEN HELPED TO SETTLE NEBRASKA

Former Homer resident Doris Phalen provided this columnist with two news clippings about an interesting former resident of the Town of Homer who was affectionately known to his family and friends as "Uncle Top." His real name was Charles T. Crampton, and he was a relative on Mrs. Phalen's husband's side. Based on the articles from *The Post-Standard* of January 28, 1938, and October 16, 1942, and information accessed online, this is his story:

Mr. Crampton was born on November 21, 1845, to Elijah and Rachael Alvord Crampton of the Scott Road—probably where some Town residents can recall the Spencer poultry farm was once located. His parents were natives of Connecticut and were among the earliest settlers of the town of Homer.

Mr. Crampton's oldest brother, Edmund Crampton, headed out West sometime in the 1880s after the wars with the Plains Indians were winding down. The federal government was granting homesteads of 160 acres at the time, and Edmund obtained a tract of land in unorganized territory near a place today called Burton in Keya Paha County, Nebraska. It is located six miles south of the border with South Dakota. Only a dozen people comprise the village's population today.

At the time, the region was devoid of any villages or roads. There were merely wagon trails. Edmund sent for his brother Charles to join him and his family in his pioneering venture. Charles agreed. He traveled as far as he could by railroad, and Edmund met him with a covered wagon. The trip by wagon to the homestead covered nearly 200 miles.

Soon, in the month of October, the brothers moved in a dozen head of cattle, a yoke of oxen, and some horses. While living in a tent, they had constructed a sod house to accommodate the livestock. By mid-October they were preparing to build a sod house for themselves. On October 15, heavy rains commenced. That night, it turned suddenly colder, and snow began to fall. For the next three days, a howling early blizzard raged across the plains. Their cattle, caught in the fierce storm, fled for protection in gulches miles away.

Edmund, his wife, and their four children abandoned the tent and took up refuge in the sod barn. Charles took up residence in the covered wagon to wait out the blizzard. Decades later he recalled for folks along the Scott Road that for three days "I never slept better." With a smile, he added, "I was young then and didn't mind it."

When the storm subsided, and aware of the onslaught of an early winter, the Cramptons realized they faced a potentially perilous situation. They made the decision to move into a protected gulch about eight miles away. Charles rounded up the cattle, and he and Edmund quickly built a log cabin in the oak thicket in the gulch to get them through the winter.

Supplies ran low, and the family found themselves subsisting mostly on corn. The snow was too deep for them to get out to add to their store of food. Their plan of cutting logs for fuel instead of using hay had to be given up. Starvation seemed to be inevitable. Then, they chanced upon a government supply team that had been caught in the howling storm while headed for Valentine, Nebraska. Miraculously, from this supply train they were able to acquire enough food to see them through the winter.

With the coming of spring, matters changed for the better. The Cramptons started planting, and families from Bradford, Pennsylvania, moved into the area. Soon a sod schoolhouse was constructed, and years after that horrible first winter the early settlers voted, after a bitter rivalry, that nearby Springview, founded in 1885, and not Burton, should be the county seat. The early County Attorney was W. C. Brown, a man who had been born in Syracuse, NY, in 1853.Today, according to the last census, a mere 242 people inhabit the quiet community of Springview.

Realizing the need for a general store in Burton, William Horton and Otto Mutz sold shares—$50 each—to secure the funds to build and stock the store. The post office occupied one end of the store, and mail arrived every three days. Upstairs above the store there was a large public entertainment room. A Christmas program was the first event there. Then there were dances, followed by whatever entertainment the community mustered up. A circuit-riding minister, on horseback, served the spiritual needs of Burton. He resided with members of the community and conducted services of worship in homes or the schoolhouse.

In time Burton had two banks, a millinery shop, John O'Neil's livery barn, and Clint Barrick's creamery. The Crampton brothers could patronize the local harness shop and the hardware store that was added onto the general store. There was even a local newspaper, *The Burton Independent,* until 1919.

Five years earlier, Charles Crampton sold his home in Burton and moved to Texas. He took up residence there with his brother until 1917. That year, he returned to the Scott Road in the Town of Homer, not far from the site of his birth, to live out his days.

Those days were many. Charles, known as "Uncle Top," lived 96 years. At age 92, a news reporter interviewed "Uncle Top" and got him to comment on his rare good health. He told the reporter that he read the newspaper each day without the aid of glasses, was able to eat and sleep well, and took a moderate amount of exercise. The exercise came in the form of caring for the poultry and shoveling a little snow in the winter. He did admit that he was inclined to taking it a little easier now. He, also, stated that he never smoked or consumed coffee or tea. He explained, "I wanted those things when I was younger, but I couldn't have them. Now I don't need them." No doubt, these personal characteristics were born of deprivations endured on the plains of Nebraska.

Amazingly, for a man of his many years, sporting a full snow-white beard and a fringe of equally white hair around his head, he suffered no memory loss. This was a blessing because he left the reporter and all of us a vivid recollection of what his life and that of his brother had been like as pioneers out in Burton, Nebraska.

"Uncle Top" died on October 15, 1942, at the Scott Road home of Mr. and Mrs. Fred Crampton, where he had spent his last 25 years. Funeral services were held at the Briggs Brothers Memorial Home in the village of Homer. Burial was at the Atwater Cemetery—an appropriate site since it is near where his pioneer parents had settled and this Nebraska pioneer had been born.

December 21, 2017

DON BROWN, THE POPCORN MAN

When *The Homer News* was in its infancy, the following article was run in this column. Now that an image of the former Homer resident Don Brown has surfaced, the editor has decided to run both the image and the article, with the insertion of some additional material that has been discovered since.

Back in the pre-Civil War days, an African American gentleman by the name of Don Brown resided in Homer. As a purveyor of peanuts, candy, and popcorn balls the size of volleyballs, he was known as "The Popcorn Man." Little is known of him today except for some news clippings. One is a letter from C. G. Maybury of Winona, Minnesota, that appeared in the December 5th, 1902, edition of the *Cortland Standard*. There, we learn that Don Brown had one leg shorter than the other which caused him to walk with a noticeable up and down movement and that he "was very popular among the residents of Homer." Some days, it was reported, he managed to earn four or five dollars, or approximately $100 to $125 in today's money, from peddling his treats. His popularity among the young people and his business success was not just due to the nature of the enjoyable items he peddled but because of his reputation for generosity and for an occasional antic.

C. G. Maybury explained that Don was quite popular among the young ladies of the village. It seems that he would occasionally charter a large omnibus (stagecoach) and "invite a full load of them to a ride to Little York or Preble, where he would order up a big supper for the young ladies for which Don paid the bill." It was noted that "he always waited until his guests were through their meal before he partook of his repast."

Another account provided by Maybury involves Don's playful interaction with the students of the Academy on the Green. It seems that the students at the Academy got it into their heads that they would take up a new fad. Possibly to mimic the gowns worn by academics, they began wearing a dressing gown, or a tailored robe worn for lounging or for grooming, as they marched from the houses in the village where they resided or boarded to their classes at the Academy. Learning of this fad, Don went to the dressmakers and ordered "a gown like those of the academy boys."

On a selected day, arrayed in his new costume, Don "waited in a hidden corner until the company of students came marching down the sidewalk." Then, he quietly dropped into line behind the boys bedecked in their gowns and joined the parade with his unusual walk, "bobbing up and down like an old fashioned sawmill gate." It must have been quite the sight, for it was said that the boys of the Academy "never again appeared on the streets in their dressing gowns."

In the early 1900s, an issue of the Homer *Republican* reprinted an 1894 letter from the late artist Francis B. Carpenter to his late childhood friend, Coleman Hitchcock. In it he reminded Coleman that Brown was a sawyer who delivered firewood to the district schools when they were young children. He recalled one occasion when the prankster thrust open the schoolhouse door, shouted "I is right," and tumbled a wheelbarrow full of wood noisily into the entryway. Carpenter wrote that "Don Brown frightened us all nearly to death. . . ." Brown undoubtedly took some glee in startling the young scholars and injecting some memorable respite into their well-structured day of recitations. Clearly, Carpenter retained Brown in his memory with a certain fondness.

As evidence of the high esteem in which Don Brown was held by the community, the 1902 article says that "the citizens of Homer have erected a fine monument in the cemetery to his memory. . . ." Now, the question is: Where is this monument? In what cemetery? The records show no such Don Brown buried in Homer's Glenwood Cemetery or in the Cortland Rural Cemetery. Is it in one of the area's smaller, rural cemeteries? So, here's a sleuthing task for you, dear readers. If you locate the burial site of Don Brown the Popcorn Man, please contact the Homer Town Hall.

(Sources of information for this article: Files of the Cortland County Historical Society and news clippings provided to the Town/Village archives by Gail Bundy.)

Image 7.2 Rare photo of Don Brown the Popcorn Man. Note size of popcorn ball. *Photograph from the Archives at Town Hall, Homer, NY.*

Chapter 8

Articles of 2018

January 4, 2018

DON BROWN THE POPCORN MAN: UPDATE

Gravestone Located for Don Brown the Popcorn Man

Eureka! A reader of the column, Ruth Scheetz, has located the gravesite for Don Brown, the subject of an article run in the last issue. By using Ancestry.com and Findagrave.com she easily placed the site in Glenwood Cemetery. The gravestone is located in the upper, southwest corner in a wooded area where the stones are all unfortunately lying flat on the ground. They seem to be the stones for the remains that were disinterred from the cemetery behind the churches on the Green in the late 1860s and reburied in the newly created Glenwood Cemetery west of the village. Though it was thought that Brown did not pass until 1902, the stone indicates the date of death was June 10, 1860. That would place him among those originally buried behind the churches on the Green. Ruth found that he is listed as a "candy peddler" who succumbed to a fever. Many thanks to an avid genealogist for solving the mystery.

February 1, 2018

EARLY SETTLERS: CRANDALL AND ALBRIGHT

In studying the post-Revolutionary War westward migration into the portion of the Military Tract that is now the Town of Homer, you invariably come across the names of the Beebes and the Todds and harrowing accounts of their trials and tribulations. Yet, there were others who followed them after 1791, and they have interesting stories, too. H. P. Smith's *History of Cortland County*, published in 1885, includes accounts of the lives of other early settlers. Two of them were Daniel Crandall and John Albright. Excerpts from that source are printed below.

****

In 1798 [Captain] Daniel Crandall came to Homer and worked for Judge Keep, chopping the timber and clearing ten acres of land on the site of the county poor-house farm. He was a native of Voluntown, Windham County, Conn. He came in alone and it is believed he made the entire journey on foot. Late in the season after his arrival he was seriously wounded by an axe cut in his foot, which made it impossible to continue his labor in the woods. Under these circumstances he collected a few tools and began the business of "cobbling" in Judge Keep's house. Here he was permitted to occupy a small space in one corner of the family room, which was not a large one, and contained a bed, a loom and other domestic furniture, for the use of which and his board he gave the judge one day's work in each week. He soon became sufficiently expert in his new avocation to begin making boots and shoes, and so spent the winter in industry. It is quite probable that this was the first manufacturing of any kind, other than spinning and weaving, carried on in the county. Mr. Crandall subsequently returned to Connecticut, and in the winter of 1799–1800 was married and removed with his wife back to Homer; they made the journey with an ox team, crossed the Hudson river on the ice, opening and breaking his own road a portion of the distance, and being twenty-one days on the way. He afterwards helped to chop the trees from the ground now occupied by the "green" in Homer village, and also to build the structure there for school and religious purposes. He purchased fifty acres of land on lot 38, which included the site of the East River Mills, where he built a log house; he moved into it when it was without a door and the gables were open, and kept his oxen, a cow and a calf through the first winter on "browse." The wolves attempted to kill the calf, but, strange to relate the cow and oxen fought desperately in the feeble animal's defense and came off victorious. Captain Crandall built the first saw-mill at East River, and subsequently, in company with Samuel Griggs, erected the first grist-mill at that point. He was one of the sixteen persons who constituted the first Baptist Church society in Homer.

In the pioneer days Mr. and Mrs. Crandall were in the habit of walking to the house of Judge Keep for the purpose of attending meeting, that being the place where, for some years, religious and other public gatherings were held, Mr. Crandall carrying their first-born child in his arms. On one of these occasions they had proceeded about half a mile, when they came into a small opening in the forest where the water bubbled in several springs from the ground and formed a little rivulet. Here they suddenly encountered a large bear, deeply engaged in digging roots from the soft ground for her cubs; the bear, being a mother and suddenly surprised, instantly reared on her haunches and for a few moments intently surveyed her enemies. It was a critical time; Mr. and Mrs. Crandall confidently expected an attack, and that at the next moment they might be clasped in the too ardent embrace of the animal and their flesh be torn by her teeth. But after a few moments, when her curiosity was apparently satisfied, the bear turned and disappeared in the forest, to the great relief of the churchgoers.

In 1797 John Albright located on lot 29. He was an excellent citizen, respected by his friends, and his experience was of a very interesting character. He passed through much of the severest service in the Revolutionary War, faithfully and honorably serving his country. He was of Swiss parentage and early in life followed the tailoring business; but he did not like the work to which he was apprenticed, and the son of his foster-parent having been drafted, young Albright saw an opportunity of escape from his irksome position by taking the place of the drafted son in the colonial service, surrendering his indentures to the tailor's trade. After his enlistment he was ordered to Fort Montgomery, Orange County, where he was stationed during the siege. He was afterwards engaged in the defense of Fort Stanwix, and was subsequently captured by Tories and Indians and taken as a prisoner to Canada. Afterwards he was a participant in the terrible march of the Continental army from Philadelphia to Valley Forge, where they could have been tracked upon the frozen ground by their bleeding feet. Finally, he was in the siege of Yorktown, which ended in the capitulation of Cornwallis. For his services to his country he drew the military bounty lot on which he located.

March 1, 2018

REMEMBER WHEN ... ?

Surely, there are some locals who can recall when the Town and Village landscape looked differently in several places, such as stores that once existed but have been replaced by other businesses. Memory tends to dim over time and there can even be false memories, so if there is an error or two or more in this piece, let me know. But, better yet, if you recall a story or a description of a site from the town or village's past, jot it down and deliver it to the Town Hall. I'll edit it, if needed, and share it with the readers, young and old. There are some great recollections out there that readers of all ages may find interesting. So, let's take a stroll down Memory Lane, shall we?

Do any of you remember when . . .

Derby's Furniture Store was in the building now housing Schaub Chiropractic, across from the high school on Route 281?

Bill's Sunoco gas and service station was at the intersection of Routes 281 and 90, where the Sunoco Gas Station & Express Mart is located now?

North of that was a very popular diner?

North of that was Sweeney's Variety Store, which sold Borden's ice cream (where Homer Chiropractic is now)? Later it was Woodward's.

A restaurant known as Plummer's Turkey Farm was where HoBo's Bar & Grill is now? Every delicious entrée on the menu was some form of turkey.

A gas station was located where Origins coffee shop is now at the intersection of 281 and 41?

A woolen mill existed across the street where the A-frame building stands on the southeast corner?

R. H. Miller Hardware did business where Copeland Avenue intersects Cortland Street?

The original St. Margaret's Catholic Church was located across the street on the opposite corner and the nuns from St. Mary's in Cortland came every Sunday to provide religious instruction?

The south end of Cortland Street intersected the Homer-Cortland Road before Interstate 81's ramps were constructed and before the Elks' Club was constructed at the road's end?

In the area where the ramp comes off 81 onto South Main Street were located: Mr. and Mrs. Matt Pace's residence; "Slim" Rinaldi's "Gyp Joint," purveyor of fresh fruits and vegetables; and a diner? And was Roy Crandall's Towing service in there, too?

The octagonal Sig Sautelle Circus House on the Homer-Cortland Road was Tracey's Restaurant and Bakery?

The Homer Police Station was on the Water Street side of the Town Hall? And today's Village Police Department on James Street was a train depot, when freight and passenger service were common?

Across the street was Jackson's grocery store?

Across the tracks from the depot was Agway?

Homer Jones Feed Mill was on North Fulton Street until a fire in the early 1950s? (I can still recall a lone firefighter way up high on a tall extension ladder with a hose waging battle with the flames, and burning embers were blowing over the houses on Clinton Street which concerned my mother.)

A milk plant was located where we now have the Homer Intermediate-Junior High School?

And further south on the train tracks was the Sealtest milk plant, with its entrance on Center Street?

You took your trash to the Village Dump on Hooker Avenue?

Homer Laundry dry cleaned clothes just south of the Town Hall on Main Street?

Doc Haverly was a dentist upstairs over what is now First National Bank of Dryden's branch office on Main Street, which was once Briggs' Cadillac? There were gas pumps out front and a service department out back that now houses Upstate Rheumatology.

William G. Crandall's home and real estate office was on Park Place, overlooking the Green? (His rare cigar store Indian, incased in glass, now stands vigil at the Town Hall.)

Public swimming was permitted at the dam at the south end of Little York Lake and at Durkee Park at the north end of the village?

A drive-in movie theater operated just up the Health Camp Rd. off from Rte. 11 north of the village?

You could purchase Comet baseball bats north of the village?

Leonard's Coffee Shop was where the Key Bank parking lot is now on Main Street?

Hefferon's candy store on Main Street was where youngsters obtained toys, paper rolls of caps for cap guns, cherry Cokes, penny candy, baseball cards with gum, cracker jacks, fireballs, candy cigarettes, and flavored wax lips and moustaches? But you could not just drop in to browse and drool; you were expected to buy something. "How much money you got on you?"

Reed's Drugstore where Bev & Co. is now? And his competitor a few stores south, Watson's Drugs? Watson's sold a rectangle of Neopolitan ice cream that was placed in a special cone designed to accommodate the shape (best medicine for whatever ailed you).

Bill Dillon's barber shop on the second floor above the David Harum bar and restaurant (where Edward Jones brokerage firm and the Oh My Goodness Health Foods Store cater to our financial and nutritional health needs today)?

There was a metal drinking fountain at the southeast corner of the Green, which had a container at the base so your pet could slack its thirst, too?

The "Unroom" on South Main was Crozier's gun shop? And across the street was a gas station?

Interstate 81 did not exist, and you took Route 11 north to Syracuse or south to Binghamton?

Durkee's Bakery operated out of the large building on Pine Street?

Denny Cashion served up generous portions of food and tall glasses of iced tea at his diner (where the Village Recreation Office is now)?

Now, do I have you reminiscing about places from "the good ol' days"? Share your stories before the memories fade, folks!

March 15, 2018

AND BE IT FURTHER ORDAINED

Both the Town and the Village of Homer have complete sets of Minutes of their respective Boards. The Minutes reveal the kind of ordinances passed for the welfare and safety of the municipality's inhabitants. Of special interest are the handwritten Minutes and ordinances that were passed in the nineteenth century. By way of example, here are the actions taken by the Village's administration on June 22, 1849. They provide insights as to the problems and concerns of the day.

The Board of Trustees met pursuant to adjournment at O. Bowen's Mansion House.

Present—Edward C. Reed, Oren Bowen—Jacob Sanders Jr & William L. Sherman.

The Com[mittee] appointed to draft the Village ordinances presented the following codes which were acted upon separately and passed unanimously, viz.

HOMER VILLAGE ORDINANCES

Sec. 1. Be it ordained, that Jedediah Barber, Samuel B. Woolworth, Oliver Glover, Samuel Pierce and Sylvester Nash be Fire Wardens & Oren Bowen, Chief Engineer, and Franklin Miller, Assistant Engineer of the Fire Department for the Village of Homer.

Sec. 2. Be it further ordained, that any person who shall disobey the orders of a Fire Warden or Engineer at any Fire shall for such offence forfeit and pay the sum of one dollar [*estimated equivalence of $4,000 in today's currency—See, money went further back then*].

Sec. 3. And be it further ordained, that no person or persons shall permit his or her Cattle, Horses, Geese, Sheep or Swine to run at large within the Corporation of said Village of Homer and that every person offending against said ordinance shall for Each and Every offence forfeit and pay the sum of one dollar, and if any of the above named animals are found running at large in said Village they shall be liable to be impounded in the Village Pound, and said animal or animals shall be kept by the Pound Master until the fine above imposed upon each animal, and the cost of impounding and the charge for keeping, and five cents on a dollar for receiving and paying over the fine, shall be paid by the owner, or until the same shall be sold to pay the same fine, costs and charges of such sale.

Sec. 4. And be it further ordained, that Oren Bowen be Pound Master; and that the Pound Master be entitled to the same fees as are designated by the 61st section of Article 4, Chap. 11, Part 1, of the Revised Statutes, Second Edition.

Sec. 5. Be it further ordained, that any person who shall be guilty of firing any gun, pistol, squib [*a small firework that burns with a hissing sound before exploding*] or [fire] cracker, in any of the streets, alleys, or on the Public Green, except on the 4th of July, without a written permission from the President [*Village Mayor*], shall forfeit and pay the sum of one dollar.

Sec. 6. And be further ordained, that if any person or persons shall obstruct the side or cross-walks of said Village by laying or leaving any lumber, wood, stone, or any other substance, or by hitching a horse or horses, or leaving any team, so as to obstruct or impede the free passage along the same, or riding, leading, or driving any horse or horses, cow or cows, or team, except in necessarily crossing the same upon the sidewalk, shall forfeit and pay the sum of one dollar for each and every offence.

Sec. 7. And be it further ordained, that all running or racing of horses in the streets of said Village, or riding or driving horse or horses for amusement, on the public Green shall be prohibited under the penalty of five dollars for each and every offence.

Sec. 8. And be it further ordained, that any person or persons, willfully or maliciously doing any injury to the public or town pumps, ladders, or other property belonging to the Corporation [*Village*], injuring or destroying any tree or trees upon the public green, or along the sides of the streets, shall forfeit and pay the sum of one dollar over and above the damages done to such property.

Sec. 9. And be it further ordained, that all filth, rubbish, wood or lumber which may be found in the street in front of the premises, occupied by any person or persons in said Village, shall be removed by said person or persons, on being required by the Trustees, or any person acting under their authority; and in case of neglecting to do so, said person or persons shall forfeit and pay such sums as shall be expended by the Trustees in removing the same.

Sec. 10. And be it further ordained, that the occupant of any slaughter house or yard in the Village shall not leave, deposit, or suffer any offensive matter, such as offal, blood, flesh, or other filthy matter, or anything liable to become filthy, to remain in or about said house or yard or in the river, so that the same shall produce any unwholesome scent, or in any way endanger the health of any of the inhabitants of said Village on pain of forfeiting and paying $5.00 for each and every offence.

Sec. 11. And be it further ordained, that every person bathing in the Pond or River within the Corporation between sunrise and one hour after sundown shall forfeit and pay one dollar for each and every offence.

Sec. 12. And be it further ordained, that no person shall be allowed to draw any hand-cart or hand-wagon upon the sidewalks in the Village, or use a wheel-barrow upon the sidewalks; or roll hoops or stones upon the sidewalks in the Village, under the penalty of one dollar for each and every offence.

Sec. 13. And be it further ordained, that all disorderly assemblages of persons, and all vulgar and profane, or obscene language or conduct in any street or public place, and all loud hallooing [*shouting that attracts attention*] in the streets or on the public Green in the evening, are forbidden; and any guilty of either of the said offences shall forfeit and pay the sum of three dollars.

Sec. 14. And be it further ordained, that no person shall keep in any building or other place in the Village, without special permission from the Trustees, over ten pounds of [gun] powder under penalty of five dollars for each and every offence. All powder shall be kept in tin canisters, and every person weighing any powder by candle or other artificial light, shall forfeit and pay the sum of one dollar for each and every offence.

By Order of the Board

E. C. Reed President

Voted. That E. C. Reed & Wm. L. Sherman be a committee to get the Ordinances and Certificates of Membership for the fire companies printed.

The Committee on Fire Buckets made their report which was accepted.

Voted. That Wm. L. Sherman and Jacob Sanders Jr be a committee to put the Corporation Pump in repair.

Adjourned

Homer June 22, 1849   Henry B. Burr Clerk

March 29, 2018

READERS FOLLOW UP TO "REMEMBER WHEN . . . ?"

Two issues ago, this column asked the question "Remember When?" and encouraged readers to provide their reminiscences about Homer in bygone days. They did just that, and I am so appreciative because it satisfied my addiction to all things nostalgic. My neighbor, Al Butler, reminded me of the bridge on Hooker Avenue that allowed pedestrians and motorists to cross over the railroad tracks. Mrs. Betty St. Peter of Scott phoned in her recollection of the

Homer Jones' Feed Mill fire that ended that business. She claims the fire was around midnight on February 7, 1959. She said she remembers because it was her wedding day. Charles "Bud" Jermy remembered walking with his parents from their home on King Street over to North Fulton Street to see the damage. Carolyn (Miller) Dorn of Cortland mailed a photocopy of an ad for Brown's Dairy Bar and this note: "Great trip down memory lane in the last Homer News! Thought I'd add Brown's Dairy Bar at the intersection of Cortland St. (south end) and Homer-Cortland Road. Open from about 1950 to about 1958 and ran by my dad. Crandall's Towing Service was right next door."

Two others, who admitted to having "been around for a while," took the time to provide letters with engaging recollections. They were "Jaff" Harris and Donald Lawson. Below, you will find the content of Mr. Harris' wonderful letter. You will have to wait until the next issue to enjoy Mr. Lawson's equally delightful stories from the past. It is with gratitude to these readers that I share their information with fellow lovers of local history and lore.

From Jaff Harris:

Perhaps I can add a little to your trip down memory lane.

The popular diner just north of Bill's Sunoco was "The 281 Diner" owned by my uncle Merwin "Merv" Randall. He and Eddie Fellows began it (I think after WW2), and after some time Eddie left. In the '40s when I and my friends were teenagers, Merv had owned a gas station on the N/W corner of S. Main and Copeland across from Jerry Crozier's Gunroom, currently a welding materials supply business. Merv's son Robert "Bud" ran the station after school at night and was Crozier's night watchman . . . so to speak. After closing the station, Bud sometimes let two or three of us in the Gunroom to make sure all was well. The collection of Japanese, German, and Italian weapons from World War II was staggering . . . and a delight to touch or handle. There were dirks, swords, pistols, machine guns, flags, mortars, etc.—all of which are nowadays worth a fortune to collectors.

Well, back to the 281 Diner. It did a large "after-hours" business during the late Forties and the Fifties. It was the watering hole we went to after a hard day's night at the Charles Restaurant in Cortland, listening to jazz from the likes of Charles Lines, Ted Hicks, Gordon Huntington, Jim Darby, et al. A classmate, John Kile, was counterman at the diner. We used to marvel at his efficiency. From one end to the other, he was never empty handed and always in motion. We left all this at the outset of the Korean War. When the diner became unprofitable, Uncle Merv changed it into a coin laundromat. He, also, opened a gift shop and converted his repair bay into a liquor store. This was in the '60s.

Yes, there was a gas station where Origins now stands. Among others, it was operated by Paul Stoker in the late Fifties.

Also, in the vicinity of the Route 81 off ramp [onto South Main] was a new building intended for the Nash auto dealership . . . Briggs Bros., I think. It became a farm implement store. Also in that area was Brown's Dairy, an ice cream and sandwich establishment. And, yes, Roy Crandall's business was there.

North of the James Street Agway building and next to the railroad siding was the building material supply store of Maxon and Starin that my father Curtis Harris managed for many years during the Depression. After World War I, Curtis had worked at the Dairymen's League milk plant (Northeast corner of the school on Clinton Street). During his employment at the milk plant, Curt invented a machine to wash milk cans. It worked beautifully. Old Dr. Kelley bought his plans, patented them, and thus sent his son Dr. Kelley to medical school—or so the story goes!

I was a North Main Street kid. We lived next to Factory Brook on a mini-farm that was bound by two waterways—the Brook and the Tioughnioga River. No better place to play for young boys—water and East Hill. The demarcation where Factory Brook emptied into the Tioughnioga was plain to see. The brook was ice cold and the river was pee warm from Little York Lake. Across from the brook on the east side of the river was a favorite swimmin' 'ole. It was called "The Deep" and featured a small boulder where we played "King on the Mountain." There were the usual turf wars between older and younger boys. We were the younger. The older guys would sneak up on the wooded hillside and throw rocks at us until we left. Or, they would sometimes grab our clothes, soak them and then tie them in tight knots. Unknotting them was called "Chaw raw beef." We learned to keep an eye on the hillside . . . something akin to Meer cats perhaps.

Further north on Main Street's west side was a small luncheonette named "Meades" where we could buy small paper cups of ice cream. Under the lid was a photo of some cowboy or movie star. A conversation last year with Dale Hallstead revealed his family owned the establishment. Amazing what a conversation between "old guys" will bring out.

I vaguely remember a baseball field on N. Main. It was called Eldredge Field and owned by Mr. Eldredge who operated a sand and gravel dredging business. Bill Dillon said he and his cohorts played there. This was long before Hudson Street and the Homer Braves, I think. The field was in the area of the present Roy Crandall business. I think Mr. Eldredge is responsible for Casterline Pond and Briggs Pool.

To be continued in the next issue with the letter from Don Lawson

April 12, 2018

READERS FOLLOW UP TO "REMEMBER WHEN . . . ?" (PART 2)

In the last issue, this column focused on readers' responses to an earlier article on "Remember When . . . ?" We got to wax nostalgic when reading material submitted by Mr. "Jaff" Harris. His supposition that Fritz "Fred" Eldredge was responsible for Casterline Pond and Briggs Pool is supported by Betty St. Peter. She reported that her father, Bob Keep, dug both sites.

This time the "guest columnist" is Mr. Donald Lawson. I hope you enjoy the contents of his letter and get a few chuckles as I did.

A few upgrades—

Before Bill's Sunoco on Rte. 281, it was Merv Randall's station earlier. The diner was Eddie's 281 Diner! The owner was Eddie Fellows. Plummers' Turkey Farm Kitchen, the restaurant on 281, probably got their meat from their farm located on Rte. 11, north of Preble. [*However, "Bud" Jermy recalls that the Plummers' farm was on East River Road adjacent to the junction with East River Crossing Road, and his brother-in-law concurs. Isn't memory a wonderful thing?*] You may be thinking of Jack West who raised turkeys at the property just west of Suits Ave. [*And that's my poor memory!*]

Before it was Agway, it was the G.L.F. south of Homer Jones' mill on Fulton Street, and Andrews' Coal, and Maxson & Starin Coal and Lumber.

I remember the village dump on Grove Street. We used to "plink" rats with a 22.

We were known as a "one horse town" because we had a man named "Smitty" who had a horse and wagon, and he collected junk. He lived on Maple Avenue, and he had his horse so well regulated that the creature consistently had his B.M. as he and "Smitty" made their way down Elm Avenue. I lived at 14 Elm and Mr. Armitage [supervising school principal] lived, I believe, at 8 Elm. Mr. Armitage, dressed in his suit and straw hat, would always come out with his shovel and clean up. He had the most beautiful ROSES in town!

Before the dentist Doc Haverly, we had Dr. Haller on the same floor [of the "Union Building" next to the Post Office].

Does anyone remember the polo barn just north of the village?

Before Heffron's [on Main Street], it was Miller's Soda Fountain. Fred had a special sundae, "The Dusty Miller." This consisted of vanilla ice cream, chocolate syrup, and malted milk (the "dust")! In the '40s, having a "Dusty Miller" and playing "In the Mood" on the jukebox was about as good as it gets!!

208   *Chapter 8*

Going back to earlier barbers, the little building just north of the Dillon block was home to two different men who "barbered." First was "Red" Tillyou (Sp?), and then we had a Mr. Pickett (he lived on River Street).

We think we had "Redfield's Diner" on South Main (possibly just north of the "Unroom").

Before the I.G.A. store added on, there was an alley between Burgett's grocery store and Crocker's 5 & 10 store. You could come down James Street and drive through the alleyway and straight into our garage on 7 Wall Street.

Dasher Cox's bar on the corner of James and Main was a friendly bar. I have got a great story about "Ducko" Fellows meeting Ed Peterson one Saturday P.M. at Dasher's. Dasher was an S.U. alumnus and he had many friends in the sporting world. Ed Peterson was a professional basketball player who had played center for Cornell (1945–1948) and then played for the Syracuse Nationals (1948–1950) and the Tri-Cities Blackhawks (1950–1951). Ed was 6'9" tall. "Ducko" was less than 5' or so. When Ed came in to chat with Dasher, we urged "Ducko" to go over and talk with Ed. He did so. Well, Ed looked down and said to "Ducko," "You must be the bouncer here!" Ed then picked "Ducko" up. They were eye to eye, and someone slipped a chair under "Ducko" so he could stand. Wish I had had a camera that day!

Again, much appreciation is extended to each one who provided such interesting and colorful accounts of Homer in yesteryears. Perhaps this will prompt others to come forward with recollections to share with the community. There must be an abundance of tales out there just waiting to be told.

Image 8.1 **Eight ball in the side pocket?** *Courtesy of Jaff Harris.*

April 26, 2018

READERS FOLLOW UP TO "REMEMBER WHEN . . . ?" (PART 3)

In recent issues, this column has presented some readers' recollections of Homer in a bygone time. Yet two more readers have responded to the standing invitation. One of them did so in verse. This time the "guest columnists" are Barb Dowd Gregg of North Lansing, NY, and Gary Weatherby of Homer.

Yes, *The Homer News* is read and appreciated in North Lansing. In her email message Barb wrote, "I love reading this paper and only get it sporadically when I go to Little York a couple times a month, more in the summer. I own two places on the lake [and] I like to shop at Anderson's."

This is what Barb remembers, with a particular focus on the Little York area:

JaLine Togs was in the old Durkee building at one time on Pine Street in Homer; I believe they made kids' clothes.

Sellco Book Binding was located in there as well. I think they are still in business and are now on Grant Street in Cortland near the old milk delivery company—Goodale's Dairy.

The current Sunoco gas station in Little York was once a gas station and small store owned by the Barber Family. You could park your boat in the channel of the lake behind the store near the dam. You could climb up the bank lugging your boat gas can to be filled and carry it back down—not an easy feat for a twelve-year-old girl.

Back in Homer, at the intersection of Route 90 and Route 281, on the left where the car wash is today, there was a diner many kids went to after school and football games. It seems like it was an old trolley car, just like the one that was on North Homer Avenue. And at one time there was the Midway Diner—that was an old trolley—by the viaduct near the A. B. Brown Store that is now the Central New York Living History Museum.

Bob Haskell began selling his barbequed chicken on that corner in Homer on weekends, where the car wash is now, after the diner was gone. I believe he got his chicken from Mr. Munson, who used to butcher chickens where Bob's B-B-Q is located now on 281 and then would sell the fresh chicken door to door from his truck.

And if you went to Little York, there were two trailer parks, one by the dam and one on 281 near the entrance to the Park on the other side of the road. Anna's gift shop was on 281 near the trailer park.

And let's not forget the Little York Hotel on 281, owned at one time by Bud Hall. A boat storage facility occupies the site now.

And there was the Little York Motel, which is now mini-apartments. Sitting between the gas station and motel was an ice cream stand.

The Little York Post Office was in the garage of the house on the corner of 281 and Little York Crossing.

And the hill behind Anderson's was called Anderlan, a place where skiing and tobogganing could be enjoyed during the winter months. A 290-foot vertical drop was served by a Hall T-bar. It was the first site of lift-assisted snow tubing. A rope tow was used in the area designated for this activity. Individuals would sit in their tube and grip the rope running above them. When arriving at the top, an attendant helped them to unload. Then the tube and passengers would skim rapidly down the snow-covered hillside. It seems that Anderlan Ski Center was there before or about the same time that Song Mountain Ski Center was created further north.

Further north in the Town of Preble, Little York Park [now Dwyer Memorial Park] used to have monkeys, a raccoon, peacocks, and a fenced-in area with deer. There were rides for the children, and Friday and Saturday night dances for the teens.

Underwood's huge dairy was where Crane's Little York Plantation now sells plants and things.

Did not mean to go on so. Once I got thinking, so much more came to mind. I had to stop or I would have traveled on through Preble. :) Thanks for the memories!

No, Barb, we the readers thank you for sharing your memories and for helping us to grasp how much things have changed in the Homer and Little York area over a lifetime—let alone over the past 227 years since the early settlers first arrived in an area of only forested, gently rolling hills. Imagine the changes that are in store for our area in the next 227 years!

And to close this article, let's take a moment to savor Gary Weatherby's wonderful poem inspired by a walk he recently took around an area north of the village. His muse was ambling beside him, gifting him and us with memories of summers of our youth.

BRIGGS' POOL

It is smaller than I remember in our summer days
the old bathhouse gone with the shy boys
in the changing room, the numbered metal baskets
with keys on ankle bands, a bronze god on the beach
toys a woman's bare shoulders with oiled hands

Not a pool really just a swimming hole, an old
gravel pit dug for the new highway's base above
filled in by the river and cold springs
we raced ourselves blue chasing the raft's siren call
to reach laughing and haul ourselves up

The skirting rocks on the shore we once stubbed
are dry lichened rip rap against the shallow's
sand pockets where fish brood, a dancing leaf
sails over yielding water grass, there drakes guard
cattails glancing the sky and rainfall ripples wake.

[*Note: Since this poem was published in Homer's community newspaper, Gary Weatherby has graced subsequent pages of the paper with his poetry, usually focused on local places and places in Ireland. Yes, poets and artists and photographers still reside in the Town of Homer, and their imagery is magical.*]

May 19, 2018

READERS FOLLOW UP TO "REMEMBER WHEN . . . ?" (PART 4)

Well, dear readers, we are on a roll as far as jogging people's memories of what the village and town of Homer used to be like. Kathryn "Kay" Bundy Locke sent a couple emails about Briggs Pool, and Jeanette Rood of Homer mailed in some commentary about businesses that once lined Route 281 and allowed cars and people to refuel.

Kay submits the following:

I enjoyed reading Gary Weatherby's memory of Briggs Pool. He graduated with me in 1968, so I thought you would get a kick out of a picture taken around that time when I was life guarding. (I am the one in the boat!). Anyways, out of the six Bundys, four of us life guarded there, beginning with Bob, Gail, myself, and Dick.

Remember when it first opened, the swimming area was at the end of the gravel pit closest to Main Street? Think of all the youngsters who learned how to swim through the free Red Cross swim lessons offered. Think of the thousands of folks that enjoyed their summer days there, keeping out of trouble. I bet it would never happen now because of all the safety issues that plague our thinking.

Doing a little research, I read an article from 1959 that said the bath house was completed, and in 1960 the pool would be moving to the other end of the pit. Also, in the article it said it was estimated that between 30 to 35 thousand swimmers enjoyed the pool that year! Wow! In another article it said that Charlie Briggs bought the land five to six years prior, and as our family lore goes, he gave the property to the village for $1.00.

Kay. . . . living in the past as I often do!

And I thought I alone lived in the past. Nice to know there is company! Here are Jeanette's recollections:

Bill Rice had the Sunoco gas station at the same time as Merv Randall had his station next door.

Eddie Fellows had the 281 Diner in the side of Randall's building closest to Bill's. I know because I worked for Eddie. Bill Rice and George St. John from the farm just up the hill behind came in for coffee often.

I worked there in the mid-fifties when Hurricane Hazel hit. I thought those big windows would blow in.

All that time Sally and Frank Wasley had what is now called "Kory's Diner" on Route 281. Later, the Wasleys opened a diner in the first building north of Clinton Street on 281 on the right. It was once a gas station and the couple who owned it had a pet skunk. They brought it into Eddie's once in a while. I thought that was real neat, but they said skunks didn't make good pets because they were always looking for a place to hide.

I don't know what took place right after Eddie left the diner but in the late '50s or early '60s Merv Randall's wife "Bobbie" ran the diner. I know because I worked for her, also. She also had a gift shop in the middle section of the building—between the diner and Merv's office. I helped her close that up, also.

Later, at least the diner part turned into a laundromat. For how long I do not know, as I was living over in East Freetown and didn't get on 281 very often.

Folks, can you believe that Route 281 once had so many gas stations and diners at the same time? Cars and people need to be fed!

Now, Jeanette mentioned experiencing Hurricane Hazel which passed through Homer in October of 1954. Hazel was the deadliest and costliest hurricane of the 1954 Atlantic hurricane season. The storm killed at least 400 people in Haiti before striking the United States near the border between North and South Carolina, as a Category 4 hurricane. Hazel made her way through Virginia, Washington, D.C., West Virginia, Maryland, Delaware,

New Jersey, Pennsylvania, and New York, bringing gusts near 100 mph and causing $281 million in damages. After causing 95 fatalities in the U.S. and barreling through Central New York, Hazel struck Canada as an extratropical storm, raising the death toll by 81 people, mostly in Toronto. As a result of the high death toll and the damage caused by Hazel, its name was retired from use for North Atlantic hurricanes.

I was elementary school age at the time and residing on Albany Street. My mother had her two boys huddled in the den that night, away from the large picture window in the front living room. I seem to recall thinking the glass was going to buckle in from the gale force winds pounding outside. We were waiting nervously for father to get home from work. He had to drive north on South Main Street. I seem to recall him telling that he had to drive the vehicle up on the sidewalk on Albany Street because trees were down across the road. A lot of damage was done to trees along Main Street. If any readers have recollections of Hazel passing through town, feel free to pass the stories along. She did not stop for gas or food when she came through, and she was in a nasty mood.

May 24, 2018

READERS' RESPONSE TO "REMEMBER WHEN ... ?" (PART 5)

The "guest columnist" for this issue of the paper is Marian (Hudson) Withey. She noticed that in a past issue this column asked about past Homer businesses and their locations. So, she mailed in the following early history of the Economy Paving Company.

Economy Paving started where the Homer Intermediate School is now. My late dad, Harry Hudson, and my uncle, Joe Compagni, began the company after World War II.

My late mother, Frances (Lowie) Hudson, told of how the brothers-in-law decided one day to go into business together when they were sitting on my grandmother Antonia Lowie/Clement's front porch in Cortland.

Dad and Uncle Joe were both fresh out of the Army Air Corps and had that money. Of course, they would need more to buy the dump truck and grader that got Economy Paving started.

I called my Aunt Jane Compagni in Florida to help fill in some blanks. It seems that before the war Dad had worked at Brewer's in Cortland and Uncle Joe at the coal yard with his family. While in the service, Uncle Joe would write home that he wanted to start a new business because he saw that coal was "going out" and gas was "in." I always knew that it was Uncle Joe's idea to go into paving.

Aunt Jane recalled that after the war no one had money, and several banks had turned them down for a loan. They actually found a third "silent partner" who was not interested in doing the work but would put in the start-up money. No one can remember his name now. Finally, the Homer National Bank gave Economy Paving a loan. My mom always spoke fondly of the bank president or loan manager because of that. Aunt Jane said it was because Uncle Joe used to do odd jobs, like mowing the lawn, for the man on North Main Street in Homer when he was a boy.

Economy Paving bought the land with the existing "shop" on Clinton Street. They were there from the mid-1940s to the late Fifties or early Sixties. If my memory serves correctly, there was a workshop on a knoll at the end of a dirt driveway, with wetland and reeds behind it. I think I was seven or eight years old then.

My mother always told that Economy wanted to stay in Homer, but Homer Central School needed land for an Intermediate School. When the business was threatened with "eminent domain," they sold to the school district and moved to Franklin Street in Cortland. The business still owns the property there but is now headquartered at 1819 State Route 13, Cortland, across the road from the Yellow Lantern Kampground.

Thanks, Marian, for sharing the story of the founding of a local business that is thriving today.

[Note: This author's brother Paul Sweeney, a Town of Homer resident, worked for Economy Paving. He started in the spring of 1984 as a project superintendent working in the field. He then moved into the office as a project manager the following season and started helping Joe Compagni with estimating / bidding responsibilities and worked into a more general management role while continuing with specific project management and estimating requirements up to his retirement in December of 2018. He headed up the replacement of the Thurston Avenue bridge spanning the gorge on Cornell University's campus, among other amazing road and bridge projects in the state.]

June 7, 2018

THE LITTLE WHITE CHURCH ON THE GREEN

One of the elements of the village of Homer that is so attractive to its residents and to its visitors is the Homer Green. The Green is a touch of New England nestled in Central New York—a tribute to the early handful of settlers who migrated from Connecticut and Massachusetts in the 1790s and early 1800s and carved out a section of dense woodlands for a "common." This was a place where they could graze their cattle and other livestock "in common." Eventually, the Common was deeded to The First Religious Society of the Town of Homer and an academy and houses of worship appeared along the western periphery since education and religion were valued highly by the early, growing community. Today, the park-like Green is the heart of Homer's Historic District, and community events and ice skating occur there within the shadows of historic architectural treasures.

Imagine for a moment the Green minus the little, white church next to the Elementary School. That's hard to do, isn't it? The white, clapboard covered structure has been standing there in the north-west corner of the Green since it was built in 1832. Generations of Homer residents and visitors (especially history and architecture buffs) have an image fixed firmly in their minds of green space along Main Street backed up by a gray stone Methodist Church, a brick Congregational Church, a public school, and a white clapboard church. The very color—white—leaps out at the eye and contributes greatly to the iconic, New England image that has been enjoyed over time.

If the church were to be razed to make way for a much-needed parking lot or allowed to decay from neglect or burned to the ground by vandals, what would we be losing?

First, we would be losing the oldest edifice on the Green. The other structures along the Green were erected well after 1832. Until recent years, the church was the oldest public structure in the village of Homer still in use. Originally, it was Calvary Episcopal Church, the first meetinghouse for those of the Episcopal fold in Cortland County. In 1849, it organized a mission church in Cortland—Grace Episcopal Church.

The origins of the Homer church go back to 1810. That year, Rev. Reuben Hubbard visited the little community of Homer and lived for a month with relatives on Albany Street. He was permitted to hold Sunday services at the Congregational meetinghouse on the Green. He returned in June of 1812 and baptized five children of Job and Lucy Turrel. It was the first time a sacrament was administered in the county by the Episcopal Church. Hubbard returned in 1823 and again was invited by the Congregationalists to use their church for services. By 1831, the Episcopalians had grown in number and were being served by Rev. Henry Gregory, the missionary to Moravia and Genoa in Cayuga County. Though they were now holding services in the upper room of the Academy on the Green, the faith community wished to have a resident rector and a church building of their own. Thus, the parish was organized and incorporated on June 6, 1831, and The First Religious Society, owner of the Green, granted permission to the Episcopal Society to construct their church on a portion of the Green. It was built in 1831–1832, at a cost of $3,300. The cornerstone was laid on June 20, 1832. Its first service of worship in the completed edifice took place on Advent Sunday, December 2, 1832. On February 14, 1833, Rev. Gregory became their first resident rector with an annual salary of $275. An organ was purchased on January 27, 1834, from a firm in Guilford, Chenango County, for a sum equal to the rector's annual salary. A little later, for the sum of $150, a bell was acquired from the Meneely Bell Company of Troy, New York. On August 1, 1904, a rectory north of the church was completed to house the Episcopal priest.

Of course, as was the custom in the day, the church had a graveyard out back. When the remains in this graveyard were to be removed in the 1860s to Glenwood, a new cemetery west of the village, inadvertently all were not removed. In the early 1990s, an elevator shaft was constructed in the portion of the elementary school that had been built in 1922 over the old graveyard. In the process, the skeletons of two children were unearthed. They had been buried in unmarked graves just a few yards from the southwest corner of the Episcopal Church, probably in the 1830s or 1840s. The remains were properly reinterred in Glenwood in 1994.

During its existence, Calvary Church was under the auspices of three dioceses. First, it was the Diocese of New York. Then, as people migrated west across the state, it was the Diocese of Western New York, formed in 1838. In 1868, after the Civil War, the Diocese of Central New York had jurisdiction.

The parish endured setbacks through the years. More than once they had to close due to a lack of pastors. For example, the Rev. Chester Smith Percival arrived in Homer with his wife and children on April 1, 1861. Eleven days later, Fort Sumter near Charleston, South Carolina, was attacked. One month later, Percival enlisted as a chaplain in the 12th New York Infantry, and the church had no pastor during the Civil War. By 1940, the church had had thirty-two different pastors and pockets of closure, but, to their credit, the faith community always revived. At one point, membership increased amazingly from 22 to 200. Even a fire put them to the test. On February 9, 1932, a defective furnace pipe in the rectory was said to have caused a fire in the study. Great damage was done. There was a loss of 800 books, furnishings, and the personal effects of the pastor, Dr. William Barnes, but Calvary Church persevered.

Secondly, if we lost the church, we would also be losing a site of historic, early secular interest. On March 18, 1833, the Vestry of Calvary Church resolved to establish a library. It was to be known as "The Parish Library of Calvary Church." According to the by-laws, any person could buy for one dollar one share in the Library and be entitled to draw out books subject to the Library regulations outlined in the by-laws. This makes the church the site of the earliest library open to the public in the village of Homer and reveals the high value placed upon the acquisition of knowledge from the printed word back then. In addition, records show that for over fifty years prior to 1890, the nine-foot-tall basement of Calvary Church, used for Sunday School gatherings, also served as a hall for official meetings of both the Town and Village Boards. So, it provided a place for early municipal government. And it was in this hall that the young bandmaster Patsy Conway conducted rehearsals of the popular Homer Cornet Band before he went on to national fame in the early 1900s. Thus, the edifice was an early example of multifunctional built space.

Thirdly, we would be losing a building associated with one of Homer's illustrious native sons. Andrew Dickson White, co-founder and first president of Cornell University in nearby Ithaca, New York, was born on South Main Street in Homer in 1832 and baptized in Calvary Church in 1835. His grandfather was Asa White, one of Homer's early pioneers. Asa owned the local gristmill down by the river at the end of Mill Street [now Water Street] and built a saltbox style house in 1799 on Main Street. The house was later moved to Clinton Street where it still stands and can boast of being the oldest residential dwelling in the village.

In his *Autobiography* published in 1904, A. D. White recalled attending religious services "in the little old Church": ". . . I can remember well, at the age of five, standing between my father and mother, reading the psalter with them as best I could, joining in the chants, and looking with great awe at what went on before my admiring eyes. So much did it impress me that from my sixth to my twelfth year I always looked forward to Sunday Morning with longing."

Years later, White had the opportunity as a diplomat to be "present at the most gorgeous services of the Anglican, Latin, Russian, and Oriental Churches" and had "heard the Pope, surrounded with his cardinals, sing mass at the high altar of St. Peter's . . ." Yet, White maintained "no one of these has ever made so great an impression upon me as that simple Anglo-American Service performed by a surpliced clergyman with a country choir and devout assemblage in this little village Church in Homer."

Finally, we would be losing a real architectural gem. It is of the Gothic Revival style, with the tell-tale pointed arches, and through time has endured alterations by Man and the ravages of Nature. In 1890, three feet in height were removed from the stone foundation wall, and the building was lowered accordingly. In the same year, the roof was shingled with slate and the present stained-glass windows were installed. Some of the original, removed windows were not discarded; they still exist. Inside, a wooden gothic ceiling was installed. In addition, the chancel (the area around the altar used by the clergy during worship) was removed from the traditional east end of the church to the west end, where the rear of the church was extended to receive its depth. New pews of oak were installed, and the bell was re-cast and a new frame supplied. A gothic battlement and railing once adorned the pediment of the roof but had to be removed and the cornice continued across the face of the bell tower. Yes, originally there was a castle-like tower and spire. It was 71 feet in height, with a bell and a clock (with a face seven feet in diameter), but, as can be seen today, a goodly portion of that ultimately was removed due to natural deterioration.

At the time of its completion in 1832, the church was the object of much pride, as evidenced by this description offered by Mr. Hagerman, the architect, on December 15th of that year in the "Gospel Messenger," a diocesan paper:

> [The tower] is surmounted at the four corners by octagonal pyramids 17' high, which are connected with each other by an open gothic framework. The distance from the floor of the basement room to the moulding on the top of the pyramids on the tower is 98 1/2'. The tower is divided by its pediment and the cornice of the bell deck into three compartments. The first, including the space below the pediment, is that which on a front view will soonest attract the eye of the spectator, and be regarded with the most delight. Of this space, a portion 8' wide and 24' high might be taken as one grand entrance. A double door, with gothic panels, occupies the first square of 8', and separated from it only by the mouldings of the window sill is a gothic window 8' wide, 14' high, and divided by mullions into six sections.

The gothic entrance with the large windows above and the range of battlements above that were said then to be "the most attractive objects."

The same description from 1832 also provides an impressive depiction of the interior of the church. So, if you ventured within, this is what you would have found:

> The vestibule occupies the width of the tower and extends into the church 8'. There are no galleries, except one for the organ, which is directly above the vestibule, and extends across the eastern end of the building. The chancel, which is at the same end, is elevated 17" from the floor, has a front of 13' with circular corners, extends forward from the vestibule 14' and is surmounted with a railing of ornamental balusters 20" high. The desk and pulpit (the latter of which is but three feet from the chancel floor) correspond in width and appearance, and are of plain work, like the front of the gallery. The panels, being small and in bold relief, present a specimen of rich neatness. The pulpit rests on heavy pedestals, its square corners project, and access to it is from within the chancel by a winding of stairs. The desk and pulpit are dressed in blue cloth, having a border

of gold lace. These dressings, the chancel cushions of blue marine, the carpeting of the chancel, and the lamps have all been obtained by the zealous exertions of the ladies of the congregation at an expense of upwards of a hundred dollars.

Members of the congregation would point out to you how gratifying it was to have completed the entire building project and be unburdened by debt. This was due to the generous subscriptions and sale of pews to individuals and families.

Through the years, at different times, the church found the resources to repaint inside and out, to do replacements and repairs, and to do a few upgrades. This level of care explains how the structure has managed to endure. In time, an annex was attached for social gatherings, but then the size of the congregation dwindled, and they could no longer afford to maintain the church. Its doors were closed on Easter Sunday, 2005, after 173 years. Dr. Janice Duncan conducted the last, emotional service, and the remaining twenty-five parishioners merged with the parishioners of St. Matthew's Episcopal Church in Moravia, NY.

In recent years, a church in Cortland that was pastored by Rev. Michael Leary—until he moved to pastor a church in Virginia—and a sister church in Vestal, NY, owned and maintained the building. More recently, it has been vacant and has only seen minimal use during a few community celebrations. The interior is still in remarkably good condition, and the acoustics are perfect. The last time this writer was inside, there was a pulpit, handcrafted in wood in the 1840s, that was stunning, and pews were still there. The present owners, however, do not have the wherewithal to keep an unoccupied building heated during Central New York winters.

You must admit that the community of Homer is fortunate to have a structure that has survived for 185 years and has been an integral part of our past and our "sense of place." And it is such a fine example of a religious architectural style associated with a religious tradition that was transported from England by the forbearers of Homer's earliest settlers. The immediate question is: how to preserve it for another 185 years? The Landmark Society of Cortland County, headquartered in Homer at the History Center at Key Bank, thinks it is worth preserving because of its historical and architectural value to the community. Dr. Sam Gruber, a historical preservation expert, expressed agreement during a recent walking tour of Homer's Historic District. The church, he said, is a rare gem that must be saved from neglect, vandalism, the wrecking ball, or the ravaging effects of Nature (a tree is already growing out of the south side of the basement now). The historical/architectural character of this built space contributes to the aesthetic and economic value of the village and promotes the general good, welfare, health, and safety of the village's residents. Just as "it takes a village to raise a child," it takes a village, working together, to preserve its built space.

This columnist is grateful for research material provided by Russ Darr, president of The Landmark Society; Mindy Meisenring Riha, director of the Cortland County Historical Society; Ed Raus, local Civil War historian and preservationist; and the personal effects of the late Anna Morse Hilton, who worked tirelessly in the 1970s to create the Historic District of 220 structures listed in the State and National Registers of Historic Places.

[Note: Not long after this article was published, the Village of Homer acquired this building. The Village has since worked on preserving it and allowing The Landmark Society and the Homer Center for the Arts to use it for educational and entertainment purposes. It is now called the Little White Church Community Center. It has a new lease on life.]

The next several issues of the newspaper saw my articles devoted to presenting A Brief History Of Education in Homer: 1819–2019. *They are not included in this compilation of articles but comprise a bicentennial souvenir booklet available through The History Center at Key Bank in Homer. However, the following two excerpts are among my favorites from the history of the school on the Green in Homer.*

The Honorable Robert G. H. Speed, Class of 1867, a businessman of Ithaca, Cornell Class of 1871, offered lengthy "Reminiscences" of his college preparation days in Homer. He chose this as an opportunity to confess,

Image 8.2 Oldest public building in Homer. *From the postcard collection of Don Ferris.*

after fifty-two years, to an "escapade" in which he and three other boys had participated during the Clark years at the Academy. It seems that Principal Clark and the janitor had gotten into a quarrel over which one of them should be the custodian of the key to the outhouse behind the academy. "The janitor as superintendent of buildings claimed he should control it while the Principal demanded its surrender to him." One morning the Principal found the little building locked. He forcibly broke in the door. Speed and his buddies decided it was time to take matters into their own hands. They would see that each of the "belligerents" had his own privy. They scoured the village for an outhouse comparable to the one at the school. They found one that fit the bill over on the east side of the river. As Speed told it:

> In the small hours of the night we went forth, tipped over the building on its side, carried it over the river bridge, down Main-st. and through the park [the Green] to the rear of the academy and set it up beside the other building, and to prevent any possible misunderstanding, we wrote the principal's name in chalk upon the door.

Needless to say, quite a sensation developed among the students and teachers the next morning when the discovery was made of "the new structure properly labeled and ready for use." At first Principal Clark was furious. No clues as to the culprits could be discovered, and the boys kept the secret through the years until the Jubilee event. Even then, Speed did not reveal the names of the other pranksters. He only said they were now "all honorable and prominent men."

[*This second excerpt is from the account of the third school fire on the Green.*]

On the night of Friday, January 26, 1945, approximately 150 spectators were enjoying a junior varsity basketball game in the Academy gymnasium between two traditional rivals, Homer and Cortland. During the third quarter of the game, Edward Button informed Principal Wolner that there was a fire in the older section of the school, the eighteen-classroom elementary department. At that point, Mr. Wolner instructed Donald Steger to stop the game. Mr. Wolner then stepped forward and quietly told the spectators and players that there was a small fire in the building and he thought it best that they leave. *Cortland Standard* reporter and Homer graduate, John T. Allen, Jr., was present and noted in his coverage that there was no panic. In fact, an unconcerned Don Steger remained behind to shoot baskets in the gym. A fireman came across him and promptly ushered him out of the building. As the crowd proceeded to exit in an orderly manner, they realized it was not a small fire.

The portion of the school that had been built in 1894 was engulfed in flames. The night air registered a temperature of close to zero degrees, which made firefighting a challenge. Strong winds presented another problem. Flaming embers were carried over Main Street and Albany Street and up onto East Hill. The Congregational Church next door was in harm's way. The roof and steeple caught fire half a dozen times. Men and women of the church formed a bucket brigade and passed kettles and pails of water high up within the steeple. They managed to extinguish every blaze. Flames were visible for miles, and thousands of spectators were attracted to the village.

Meanwhile, a hundred firemen from Homer, Cortland, and McGraw were working in the bone-chilling conditions. Fingers froze, and one fireman sustained a head injury. Seven fire trucks were brought into service and 5,150 feet of hose. They pumped about 1,642,000 gallons of water from the village fire hydrants and 120,000 gallons from the Tioughnioga River. During the conflagration, the New York Telephone Company put ten additional telephone operators to work to handle 10,000 extra calls. A Syracuse radio station was enlisted to inform the worried public that all spectators at the game had exited the school safely.

Loss of the older portion of the Academy was estimated to be $100,000 and would have been double that if the fire had spread to the high school annex. Fortunately, the fire did not spread there, and, once again, for a third time in their history, the Carpenter "Trustee Paintings" were miraculously spared.

With the students and teachers ensconced in temporary quarters, the task of rebuilding the school had to be confronted. The fire and a need for a new school building served as the catalyst for serious dialogue about the possibilities of centralizing twenty-eight school districts. Thus, a committee representing the districts was formed and the previous proposals for consolidation were dusted off. Over the course of two days, the committee met in Albany with the State Education Department. A six-year plan for a comprehensive curriculum, construction, and financing was laid out. Then, the proposal was presented for discussion at public meetings held inside and outside the village of Homer. At one meeting at one of the outlying districts, a man arose to state his opposition. Pointing a finger at Wolner, he warned his neighbors, "If we centralize down yonder in Homer, Wolner will put our kids in fancy buildings and give them fancy notions so that they won't want to stay at home." Eventually, the man's sons graduated from Homer Central School, and they remained on the farm.

Chapter 9

Articles of 2019

April 11, 2019

HOMER'S CEMETERY DEEMED TO BE NATIONAL HISTORIC SITE

On March 26, the State Office of Parks, Recreation, and Historic Preservation informed the Village of Homer that Glenwood Cemetery was designated by the National Park Service as a National Historic Site and would be listed on both the State and the National Register of Historic Places. The State Register listing was official as of November 20, 2018, and the National Register listing was done on January 31, 2019.

Glenwood Cemetery was established in 1867 on land donated by Homer-born Paris Barber. He designed the park-like grounds and the Barber Family Mausoleum. A cemetery association managed the cemetery until 1946 when the Village took ownership and has meticulously maintained it since.

Village Historian Martin Sweeney and Dr. Virginia Bartos, a New York State historic preservation analyst, prepared the registration narrative approved at the federal level. The narrative points out Glenwood's three areas of significance for national designation.

First, the landscape design is "a representative intact example of a mid-nineteenth century Rural Cemetery with portions at the extreme east and west ends reflecting twentieth century trends in cemetery management."

Second, Glenwood Cemetery is "significant for architecture with three of its buildings being excellent examples of early twentieth century designs: the Earle Abbey Mausoleum (1923) and receiving vault (1906), both representing the Gothic Revival style, and the 1914 Starin Mausoleum with its Neoclassical revival design."

Third, Glenwood includes the burial sites of Cortland County's first pioneers, many of Homer's prominent citizens, and at least four who "rise to the level of transcendent importance." Buried in section 14 is Francis Bicknell Carpenter (1830–1900). He was a nationally known artist/portrait painter whose painting *First Reading of the Emancipation Proclamation before the Cabinet* is on view in the U.S. Capitol Building in Washington, D.C. Then there is General Willoughby Babcock (1832–1864). He was a lawyer who enlisted in the Union Army and briefly served as military governor of Pensacola, Florida. He died of wounds received at the Battle of Winchester in 1864 and is buried in section 6. David Hannum (1822–1892) is buried in section 11S and was at one time the proud owner of the Cardiff Giant and the model for the lead character in a popular novel, *David Harum*, published in 1899. Last, but not least, is Amelia Stone Quinton (1833–1926), an advocate for universal Indian education and co-founder of the Women's National Indian Association that survived her until 1952. She is buried in section 12.

The designation of "National Historic Place" was granted for all these reasons. The official notice of national designation offered praise to the community and to the cemetery's maintenance staff:

> Glenwood Cemetery is an excellent example of a community's commitment to preserving Glenwood's historic character while adapting to the changes in attitudes toward burials in ways that respect the mid-nineteenth century Rural Cemetery core, originally designed by Homer resident Paris Barber. Historic features such as the curving roads, the stone entrance gate, historic vault, monuments and mausoleums are well preserved. Careful management of the landscapes continues to enhance the stunning vistas from the hillside that Barber and many Homer residents enjoyed, and undoubtedly, current visitors to the cemetery continue to do at present. As a municipally owned property, Glenwood Cemetery is eligible to apply for New York State matching grants and to other organizations that provide assistance for historic resources listed in the State and National Registers of Historic Places.

A marker will be secured to indicate the cemetery's special historic status to residents and visitors alike. [*Note: Through the William G. Pomeroy Foundation of Syracuse, grant money made the creation of this marker and several other historic markers in the village of Homer possible. The community is grateful.*]

April 25, 2019

THE 1950S IN HOMER

Some more readers have come forward with their recollections of the past in Homer, especially back in the 1950s.

Donald Lawson of Tobin Drive dropped off the following note to be shared with the readers:

When Hurricane "Hazel" hit town in 1954, Gloria and I had just rented an apartment on Cortland Street. Our daughter had just been born in September, and we were just getting settled. I was an active Hose No. 1 member of the Homer Fire Department, and when the call came in, we all responded! There were so many trees blown down on Main Street that traffic had to be detoured around them. We had Greyhound buses coming down Cortland Street instead of Main Street, as well as other traffic. There was a live wire on the ground by St. Margaret's Church, and we were monitoring that and trying to keep people away! Our first car was a '49 Studebaker, and I was using the "blue light" on my car to alert people of the danger! There was debris all over the road and yards—tree branches everywhere.

Don told me that he did not think there was such a group as "fire police" at that time. He, also, remembered that he rolled down the window of his car to talk to someone and part of a nearby roof carried by the gale winds almost injured them. Close call!

We finally got through the storm O.K. and kept everyone safe, but my car's battery died, and I got a flat tire for my troubles. (*"No good deed goes unpunished."*)

I also recall that Frank Reagan set up his generator at the "Home for the Aged" (The Elizabeth Brewster House now), and he was there for over a week! That had to be some "service call"!

We should all be appreciative of the "service calls" made through the village's history by the police, fire police, firefighters, and ordinary concerned citizens at times of peril.

Jim Masterson shared by phone some recollections he had been carrying around in his head. He remembers back in the day when the Village had two interesting law enforcement officers. One was "George the Cop" Vernum and the other was known as "Heavy" Taylor. "Heavy" was part of a noteworthy experience in Jim's life. Officer Taylor's real name was Charles Taylor, Sr. His children were Charles, Rachael, and Richard (known as "Dick"). Richard's son is Dale Taylor of Sarvay Shoes fame in Cortland. It seems that Jim was part of a gang of young boys from the Elm Avenue area who liked to venture forth up in the woods of East Hill. On one occasion the boys stumbled upon a guy lying face down on the ground. From all appearances, they assumed he was dead. To make sure, they went and retrieved peashooters. The man made no response when fired upon. So, now the boys were convinced they had discovered a corpse. This had to be reported to the police. They went back into the village in search of "Heavy" Taylor. They found him on Main Street at Heffron's candy store. "There's a dead man up on the hill," they reported. "Show me," demanded a skeptical "cop." And they did. "Why that's just old so-and-so sleeping off a drunk; he's not dead."

Like Don Lawson, Jim has been carrying around memories of Hurricane Hazel. In 1954, young Jim was hired as a pinsetter at the David Harum Bowling Alley *[where the Community Building is now behind the American Legion]* in the village. It was his first time on the job, and the power went off. Jim thought it was something he had done. The high winds of "Hazel" had caused it, bringing down power lines in her path. Everyone was to go home. Someone said, "You are not supposed to be out on the street." So, Jim cut through the back of what is now the Elizabeth Brewster House and the library and the shops on Main Street so as not to be detected. To this day, he remembers just how weird the night sky was. "It was spooky scary—like a sunset over East Hill."

May 9, 2019

A FOWL SMORGASBORD

In reminiscing about life in Homer in the 1950s, community members of a certain age might recall one particularly unique business in the village—Plummer's. Can you believe Homer once had a restaurant that specialized in turkey and only in turkey? Yes, it is true. And it was located where Hobo's 281 Bar & Grill now welcomes its patrons on West Street. For those of you who moved to Homer after Plummer's Turkey Farm Kitchen ceased to be or were born after that, the following article from the front page of the May 20, 1960, issue of the Homer Independent *(courtesy of "Bud" Jermy of Homer) will explain the culinary treats you missed out on—delicious treats that put Homer on the map.*

"UNIQUE SMORGASBORD BRINGS WIDE REPUTATION TO PLUMMER TURKEY FARM"

By Lynn Swan

The drumstick is the yardstick of success for the Plummer Turkey Farm Kitchen in Homer. An ever-expanding business, Plummer's proves that the newer trend of eating turkey year around is gaining more and more in popularity.

The only restaurant in the world serving a turkey smorgasbord, their menu includes more than thirty recipes using turkey products.

G. Dwight Plummer and his wife Doris, after years of research, have developed a wide variety of dishes to tempt the palate, including turkey burgers, boneless rolled turkey, turkey chow mein and "Turkey in the Straw," which is deep fried turkey, served in a basket. One of the most unusual and popular recipes is cranberry ketchup, especially tasteful with the turkey burger.

The [restaurant] was opened by the Plummers in 1952, as the only restaurant in New York State serving turkey exclusively. It was to be just a sideline to their already existing turkey farm. The idea of the restaurant caught on so well, that now it is their main effort.

Catering to parties, weddings, and supplying organizations with prepared turkey, sometimes serving as many as seven hundred at a time, comprises a large part of the business in addition to serving dinner guests at the restaurant. Many Sundays they serve three to four hundred from outside the town of Cortland. Seventy-five percent of their guests come from within a radius of fifty miles and the other twenty-five percent is tourist trade.

Shipping turkeys all over the world is another facet of the business. Each year they ship a batch to the Milwaukee Braves.

Mrs. Plummer, a nutritionist, applauds the merits of the turkey, its high protein content, low fat and cholesterol making it an ideal food.

A home economics graduate of Syracuse University, Mrs. Plummer did home demonstration work during World War II. As a 4-H leader for over twelve years, she imparted her knowledge of the culinary arts to the youngsters.

Mr. and Mrs. Plummer have constantly engaged in experimental and scientific research with turkeys. They were pioneers in the field of cut-up turkeys and developed many recipes in wide use. New breeds, too, have been developed by Mr. Plummer, most noteworthy being a small type, broad breasted bronze turkey.

Chairman of the Cortland County nutrition commission during World War II, Mr. Plummer was also the chairman of the New York State Turkey Association Research committee, and in that capacity worked with Cornell University in turkey research. He is a past elder of the First Presbyterian Church of Cortland, past president of the New York State Turkey Association, is a member of various Masonic bodies and belongs to the Cortland and Homer Chamber of Commerce.

Mrs. Plummer, too, is active civically. She is a past matron of the Eastern Star and the Amaranths and is a representative for New York State to the Grand Lodge of Virginia.

228   Chapter 9

The Plummers enjoy traveling and each year they close the restaurant for three months and tour the countryside.

On display at the Farm Kitchen and at their home is a large collection of turkey figurines Mrs. Plummer has acquired through the years. It is one of the largest collections of its kind.

Claiming their hobby is their business, the Plummers are as enthusiastic about their work today as when they began eight years ago.

As this public historian recalls from childhood, it was always a treat to dine at Plummer's and to enjoy so many entrees prepared from turkey.

May 23, 2019

A NOTABLE GROUP OF HOUSES

"There is a neighborly group of houses in Homer which probably represents more interesting history and personality than any other cluster of houses in New York State." Thus wrote Bertha Eveleth Blodgett in 1932 on page 176 of her book *Stories of Cortland County for Boys and Girls*. She was referring to a nucleus of houses at the intersection of Main and Albany Street in the village of Homer. Through the years, inaccuracies have been found in Blodgett's book, but she admitted in her preface that the book was "merely a collection of old-time true stories strung together on a slender thread of history like beads on a chain" and that ". . . a scholarly historian might find some inaccuracies in historical detail. . . ." Her commendable goal was to try "to reproduce the spirit of the pioneers who helped to build Cortland County."

As a junior high student living on Albany Street in the village, I unknowingly cut my local historian's teeth on Blodgett's fascinating tales of Cortland County. Of particular interest to me were the descriptions of the houses I passed by or near every day on my walk to the school over on S. West Road. I found the information appealing . . . and I still do.

On the northeast corner of Main and Albany is the birthplace of Andrew D. White, co-founder and first President of Cornell University, United States Ambassador to Germany, and "Cortland County's most celebrated citizen," according to Blodgett. A blue and gold New York State historical marker is out front today.

On the southeast corner is a private residence today, but in Blodgett's day it was "The Braeside Inn," a tearoom operated by Nellie Randall, who went on to cook for the Joint Chiefs of Staff in Washington, D.C. during World War II. The building had been known under different names before this. The most notable was "Wisdom's Gate." Blodgett pointed out that it "is a perfect example of Colonial architecture" and that "Homer is to be congratulated that it has been kept in its original lines since 1816, when it was built by Joshua Ballard."

The well-maintained house at number five Albany Street has a marker out front indicating it is the birthplace of William Osborn Stoddard, assistant personal secretary to President and Mrs. Lincoln. Stoddard was an inventor and author, but he is best known for making the first two handwritten copies of Lincoln's Emancipation Proclamation.

South of "The Braeside" is what Blodgett called "the oldest house in Homer." It is not. The oldest house in the village, built in 1799, is located on Clinton Street. The house at 87 S. Main is the second oldest house. Pieced together from two other structures, it was the home for a time of Professor George L. Burr, former librarian and professor of history at Cornell University.

Across the street from "The Braeside" is a beautiful house once known as "The Hedges" and occupied by Jacob M. Schermerhorn, a staunch Republican and acquaintance of President Lincoln.

Three doors north of "The Hedges" is the home once occupied by David Hannum, a figure who gave rise to the fictional protagonist in Edward Noyes Westcott's novel *David Harum: A Story of American Life*. The 1898 novel was a bestseller in its day, only being outsold by Harriet Beecher Stowe's *Uncle Tom's Cabin*. Homer's Jane O'Shea has penned *Westcott's Tale*. She has rewritten Westcott's novel in contemporary language and cleverly interwoven factual material about the author, his motive for writing, and what the folks of Central New York were really like. It is a must read to understand how nineteenth century Homer was the basis for Westcott's "Homeville." You can get your copy at The History Center at Key Bank in Homer.

Now, the helpful thing about Blodgett's book is how she went on to provide young (and not so young) readers with additional, interesting details about the six residential structures—their architectural styles and past residents.

For example, Andrew D. White lived in the house where he was born in 1832 until he was seven years old. At that time, his father, Horace White, moved the family to Syracuse and became "one of its most prominent bankers." The Colonial style house was built in 1819, and according to Blodgett, it "has seen many changes," including the addition in the 1880s of a mansard roof that altered its appearance.

As for "The Braeside Inn," Blodgett raved that "few towns in the State can boast of so fine a Colonial building." She wrote, "How fortunate it is that it has been kept so true to its period—the period of 1816, when it was built by Joshua Ballard, . . . the first school teacher in Homer . . . [who] possessed good taste." As early as 1822, it functioned as a hotel. George Washington Samson was the proprietor when it was called "Wisdom's Gate" and was known as a "Temperance Tavern." Andrew D. White recalled being a curious boy and wanting to know the meaning of the hotel's name. He learned, he said, "that whoever entered that gate would have to drink cold water and no whiskey." From the ceiling in the barroom hung an empty flask, upside down, signifying landlord Samson's view on the issue of temperance. According to Blodgett, Samson edited a paper once a year called *The Bumble Bee,* "and it was a stinger."

Blodgett did not find Stoddard's birthplace at number 5 Albany Street to be architecturally significant. The fact that you can see how Stoddard's grandfather, John Osborn, had built forward toward the street over the years as his family increased in size and wealth and ended up using expensive brick was not noted in her book. She failed, too, to cite how the Stoddard family also moved to Syracuse when the Whites did, and Andrew and William continued to be childhood friends in the growing community on the Erie Canal. Stoddard, wrote Blodgett, "was the first person to suggest [in an Illinois newspaper editorial] that Lincoln would make a good president . . . and the article was copied all over the country." While it is true that Stoddard's pro-Lincoln article did appear in hundreds of periodicals across the country, three other editors had beaten him to the punch in endorsing Lincoln as presidential material. Blodgett claimed that "Lincoln recognized the good turn and asked William Stoddard to go with him to the White House and be one of his secretaries." In fact, the record shows that it was Stoddard who asked Lincoln to take him onto his personal staff in the White House and that Stoddard was first assigned to the Interior Department as a signer of "land patents" before he was "on loan" as an assistant personal secretary at the Civil War White House. But Blodgett got the most important fact correct: "It was William Stoddard who copied the Emancipation Proclamation, fresh from the hand of Abraham Lincoln."

Blodgett called the house just south of "The Braeside" "the Burr Homestead." This is because it was the home of the grandfather of Professor George L. Burr, once the head of the Department of History at Cornell University. She included Burr's own recollection of the house:

> All my life in Homer was spent under a roof which was once that of the first school and first church (built in 1799). This building was on the northeast corner of the Green. My grandmother, who was a girl of nine when she arrived here from Connecticut in 1803, used to tell me, remembering it well, how on Sunday the swinging partition was drawn up to turn the school into a church. The old building stands on the spot to which my grandfather moved it from the corner of the Green down yonder, to just beyond Albany Street, next south of what was called 'the Samson Tavern.'

But it is only the lower part of the structure, for the higher front, with eaves to the street (also added by my grandfather), was the first public house built in Homer, Major Stimson's old tavern. There it stands—church, school, and tavern, a strange union . . .

Across the street is "The Hedges." On this property is where John Ballard, one of five brothers to settle in Homer before 1800, built a log cabin. The structure served as both his home and the first tavern on Main Street. Around 1803 he sold it to Major Enos Stimson, who kept it as an inn. Blodgett tells of the time when Homer's civic-minded Paris Barber set about making the treeless Green into a park. Stimson came along and said, "Golly! Here you are setting out trees and we have just got through cutting them down." Stimson was old enough to recall when Homer was a wilderness of forest trees, and trees were cleared to make a Common for the early settlers to graze their livestock. And in 1863 Barber was putting trees back into the site.

It was Stimson, says Blodgett, who "made the shingles for the first church which the Congregationalists built on the Green, and they remained in good condition as long as the church stood, which was fifty-five years."

In the early 1800s, the center of commerce in Homer was at the intersection of Main and Albany Street. Stimson's Tavern was the hub and well situated to handle the traffic and trade that came into the little community via the Albany Turnpike.

After Stimson's Tavern was moved across the street and attached to the school that had been on the Green, Caleb Ballard built the stately residence that stands now upon the original site of the first tavern. In the 1830s, it was owned by Andrew Dickson, the grandfather of Andrew Dickson White. In his autobiography, White said he was brought up at this site with its spacious flower garden and hedges. Thus, the place became known as "The Hedges." Later, it was called "The Schermerhorn House" because it was occupied by Jacob M. Schermerhorn, who was reported to be the wealthiest man in the county in the 1850s.

Blodgett tells of the time Schermerhorn took his daughter Anna and another Homer girl to the nation's capital. The trio was standing in line at a White House reception when they spotted President Lincoln, Mrs. Lincoln, and William O. Stoddard. Stoddard spied his friends from Homer and excitedly whispered a request to Mrs. Lincoln to be excused long enough to take his Homer acquaintances on a tour of the Executive Mansion. According to Blodgett, Mary Todd "evidently was not so inclined, and young Stoddard was obliged to wait for that pleasure until the reception was over." Years later, Anna Schermerhorn recalled how she was greeted by President Lincoln. Taking both her hands in his, the President said, "It is always a pleasure to me to meet young people." She observed how "his face was full of sincere welcome."

The last of the six Homer houses that Blodgett focused upon was "The David Hannum House." Since Blodgett's book was intended for young readers, she emphasized how "Mr. Hannum was a great lover of young people." She wrote of how "he loved nothing better than to have a crowd of boys and girls around him and to tell them stories." It was well known that "whenever there was a circus in town he would take them to see the show." His young admirers would ask for his photograph and, according to Blodgett, he acquiesced to their pleas and sent them to the photographer's shop to each get a copy. When they arrived, "they found that Mr. Hannum had had his picture taken but only his back was showing." Hannum loved a good practical joke like this one, and copies of this photograph are still in circulation and of value to collectors.

Hannum, also, liked a good practical joke that could make him some money. The best example of this is, of course, the "Cardiff Giant Hoax." A farmer in Cardiff, New York, near Lafayette, was digging a well and discovered a large stone figure. People flocked to see it. Was this a prehistoric giant that had fossilized through time or was it a stone sculpture from antiquity? Learned men from across the nation, including Cornell's President Andrew D. White, came to render their opinions. The farmer who "found" the "giant" charged fifty cents for a peek at the curiosity. Recognizing a business opportunity, Hannum headed up a syndicate of men who bought the giant and took it to Syracuse to make money through a public exhibition. By the time the truth had finally come out that this was "only a make-believe man, carved out of stone," Hannum's name was firmly attached to the story of "The Cardiff Giant."

Blodgett tells a story that may or may not be fact about Hannum's self-promotion. It seems that

> One day a dapper young man entered a passenger car of a D.L.and W. train and tried to get a seat beside a short, thickset man who refused to move over. 'See here, do you know who I am?' said the dapper young man. 'My name is Sloan and my father is the president of this road.'
> 'See here, young man, do you know who I am?' was the ready reply of the occupant of the seat, who did not stir an inch as he spoke. 'My name is David Hannum and I'm the father of the Cardiff Giant.'

Now, Hannum was not the "father of the Cardiff Giant" but he was one of the perpetrators of the hoax that drew national attention and became a money-maker for him and for P. T. Barnum.

In time, built spaces—both residential and commercial—spread out in all directions from this cluster of six notable houses at the intersection of Albany and Main and formed the community incorporated in 1835 as the Village of

Homer. Today, they are six of the 220 dwellings that comprise the Historic District recognized at the State and National level. The Landmark Society of Cortland County, headquartered at the History Center at Key Bank on Main Street, was originally created in the early 1970s to help preserve the well-maintained architecture in the village. Today, the organization has a dual mission that focuses on both local architecture and local history. The Society recognizes that the architectural gems in the village did not build themselves. People did. And the residents have remarkable stories worth sharing and preserving. Blodgett shared the stories attached to six notable houses in early Homer. If the walls of the other 194 dwellings could talk, can you imagine the stories they would tell of the lives of past occupants?

June 6, 2019

FIRES DISCOVERED BY BOYS ON SAME DAY IN 1900

According to the *Cortland Evening Standard* of Saturday, May 12, 1900 (page 5), a fire in Homer and a fire at Glen Haven were discovered by boys within an hour of each other. Both conflagrations had local people deeply concerned.

What might have proven to be a serious fire in the Bennett Block near the intersection of Main and Pine Street in the village was discovered shortly before noon on that Saturday. The three-story wooden structure housed the post office in its southern half of the first floor. Bennett & Starr's shoe store occupied the northern half of the first floor.

A young boy named Bruce Dillenbeck was westbound by foot on Pine Street around ten minutes before noon. As he passed the building, he noticed the blaze had just broken out through the siding on the east end. He immediately hurried to his home just across Main Street and gave the alarm. The fire bell was then rung by Glenn Hicks, and the local fire companies responded. In a matter of minutes, streams of water were directed upon the building.

Both hose companies attached to the hydrant across the street from the building. Hose Company No. 2 succeeded in getting first water on the building. Hose Company No. 1 had first water in their hose but failed to get a stream going on the building as soon as the others because of some delay in getting the nozzle attached. Eventually, Hose No. 1 had a stream directed upon the roof, and Hose No. 2 had a stream directed into the upper two floors. No. 2 also attached another hose to the hydrant in front of Moore's Market at the corner of Main and James Street and soon had a third stream which firefighters took up the front stairway and into the third floor. Orient Hook & Ladder Company was promptly on hand, putting ladders in position to fight the fire.

No one could explain the cause of the fire. It seems that the fire was in the east end of the structure between the siding and plastering and had been burning for some time when it was discovered. In the alleyway behind the building was found a pile of ashes and some papers. It was thought that "the papers close to the building may have caught fire from a cigar stub or in some other way, and set fire to the building." The newspaper reported that a blind resident on the second floor, Miss H. Louise Pierce, said she "smelled smoke all the forenoon but did not know where it came from." It was thought that the fire had most likely been smoldering for a long time under the siding before it was detected by the young boy.

Postmaster W. C. Collins was at his midday meal when the alarm was given. His assistants, Miss Wills and Miss Mary Mahoney, were working in the post office. They were able to transfer stamps and valuables to the Homer National Bank next door. The mail was gathered up and placed in pouches. These, along with fixtures that were all new and had been recently put in place when Mr. Collins became the Postmaster, were removed and taken across the street. Bennett & Starr's store on the ground floor was flooded, and the stock of boots and shoes sustained water damage. Part of the stock and fixtures were taken to the First National Bank building.

The floor directly above the post office was occupied by Andy Johnson. Unfortunately, the rooms had just been fitted up, freshly painted and papered. Mr. and Mrs. Johnson had only moved in three weeks earlier and were just getting nicely settled. Though most of their furniture was removed, their loss was still deemed to be "considerable."

Mrs. C. L. Jones operated a sewing school for children in the rooms above Bennett & Starr's store. Back of her rooms were the living rooms occupied by Miss H. Louise Pierce. Her rooms and furniture were badly damaged by water. She had no insurance.

Mr. A. H. Bennett owned the building. He carried an insurance of $4,000. Of that, $2,500 was with W. C. Collins and $1,500 with W. H. Foster. Postmaster Collins had an insurance of $800 on the post office fixtures. This he had in place with one of his own companies.

Bennett & Starr had their stock insured for $4,000 through agencies operating in Homer, Marathon, and Cortland.

The newspaper reported that it was fortunate that the fire occurred in the daytime. Since the building was of wood, it and adjoining buildings could scarcely have been saved had the fire gotten out of control and gone undetected through the night. There could have been a loss of life with that scenario and much destruction along Main Street.

Another fire on that day had been discovered by a young boy about one hour earlier than the fire on Main Street. This fire was at the Glen Haven Sanitarium at the southwest end of nearby Skaneateles Lake. According to the same newspaper, ". . . for a time it looked as though the big sanitarium was doomed, but by remarkably quick and effective work on the part of the masculine population of the vicinity the building was saved after about three quarters of an hour of the hardest kind of work."

As reported, Robbie Scott, the nine-year old son of Mrs. Scott, an employee of the sanitarium, was playing on the grounds in front of the building at 11 o'clock on Saturday morning. He looked up and discovered smoke and a tiny blaze coming out of the roof near the big cupola over the front of the center portion of the sanitarium. "With a wisdom far beyond that to be expected from a boy of his years he dashed to the nearby cottage of Mr. C. T. Redfield and told him what he had seen. He asked Mr. Redfield to hurry to the sanitarium to help. Then the lad found Fred Randall working on the grounds near the building and told him to follow Mr. Redfield. The two men headed up to the sanitarium's attic. The paper stated that Robbie said not a word "to the feminine part of the residents of the sanitarium" but ran down the road "rousing every man he could find . . ." In less than ten minutes he had assembled fifteen men.

Up in the attic, the men found a considerable portion of the room was ablaze from a fire that had started in the big chimney that went up from the office below. With fire buckets in hand, a bucket brigade was quickly formed down to the lake. For about three quarters of an hour, the men and the fire were locked in a stalemate. Then the tide turned, and the flames were bested. The fire was put out, to everyone's relief.

Then, they took stock of the damages. The cupola was gone, along with about twenty square feet of roof. The rafters and roof boards for some distance back from the hole through the roof were charred and burned. The upper rooms of the sanitarium sustained much smoke and water damage. Ceilings of newly papered rooms were considerably soaked and damaged.

The loss could not be estimated when the paper went to press, but Mr. Mourin, the proprietor of the sanitarium, assured reporters that he had the establishment abundantly insured through G. J. Maycumber and Davis, Jenkins & Hakes of Cortland and W. H. Foster of Homer.

Taken all in all, both Saturday fires could have been much worse and might have been had it not been for two sharp-eyed boys who quickly summoned aid. We can only hope that the boys were rewarded by being taken to the circus the next day in Cincinnatus. An ad published in the same newspaper reporting the fires announced that Homer's Sig Sautelle was putting on a "new, big 25 cent show" on May 12th in Cincinnatus. The show was said to be "The Mightiest Tented Amusement Organization in all the world. A multitudinous, Overwhelming, Indescribable Crush of Amazing Gymnic, Acrobatic, Spectacular, Aerial Sensations by the Greatest array of Circus talent ever assembled under canvas. The most eminent circus the earth has known in any century." The show was said to be presented twice daily, rain or shine, under a mammoth waterproof tent with a seating capacity of 5,000 persons. Wow, what youngster wouldn't want to be treated to this extravaganza?

June 20, 2019

THE SIGNIFICANCE OF THE BRIDGES OF HOMER VILLAGE

Much has been in the news recently about America's crumbling infrastructure and rightly so. Historically, the condition of our highways and bridges has always been a matter of concern to the traveling public. At the grassroots level, here in Homer, we are faced with an interesting situation involving the bridges of wrought iron that span the west branch of the Tioughnioga River which parallels Main Street.

Three bridges were installed in the village by the Town of Homer in 1881. These nineteenth century structures are no longer wide enough or stable enough to accommodate heavy, twenty-first century firefighting apparatuses. Thus, there is a safety factor that urgently needs to be addressed. However, it is complicated by the fact that these bridges are not just any old metal bridges. They are rare parabolic lenticular, or lens-shaped, truss bridges, and William Oscar Douglas of Cortland held the patent on these bridges. They were listed in the National Register of Historic Places in 1977 and are worthy of being preserved for their historical, cultural, and technological value.

According to a representative of the state's Office of Historic Preservation, Homer's three bridges are three of only nine of their type surviving in the state and part of only nineteen in the nation. One of the Homer bridges is a double truss and is the only one of its kind left in the nation. The fact that William Oscar Douglas of Cortland held the patent on such bridges adds yet another layer of local historical importance to the bridges.

The Corrugated Metal Company of East Berlin, Connecticut, originally produced roofing material and metal-clad fire doors and shutters. It branched out into roof trusses but not with great success. Then, in 1877, S. C. Wilcox, a new investor, realized the company had the capacity to manufacture highway bridges. And it was the following year that the company purchased the rights to William O. Douglas' patented "parabolic" truss and started fabricating the first lenticular bridges that began to appear across the Northeast.

Douglas was born in Cortlandville on December 26, 1841, to Limas and Diana (Copeland) Douglas. In 1860 he was a student attending the Cortlandville Academy in Cortlandville. He received further education at West Point and entered military service from Cortland. He was cited for "gallant and meritorious" action during the Civil War. He was wounded slightly at the battle of Chancellorsville and severely in both legs at the battle of Gettysburg on July 3, 1863. After his discharge from the military, he married Amelia Benedict on Christmas Eve, 1863. He went on to join the Corrugated Metal Company as treasurer and executive manager and continued to refine his patented bridge design. In 1885 he was awarded a second patent. By then, the company's name had changed to the Berlin Iron Bridge Company. It was the biggest structural fabricator in New England. Throughout the nation, local highway officials were opting to replace wooden bridges with iron. This was because the price of iron trusses steadily declined and became competitive with wooden spans. They were more durable and much more resistant to damage by floods (wooden bridges typically only lasted 20 to 30 years). Douglas died in Binghamton, New York, on August 16, 1901, and was buried in nearby Port Dickinson's Glenwood Cemetery. This was the year after the Berlin Iron Bridge Company was absorbed by the American Bridge Company during a largely successful attempt by J. P. Morgan to monopolize the nation's structural fabricating industry. However, some of the former employees of Berlin Iron Bridge started up a new, successful firm, the Berlin Construction Company. It remains in business today as Berlin Steel.

Out of a need for safety and convenience in 1881, the Homer bridges which span the river at Water, Wall, and Pine Streets were ordered from the Corrugated Metal Company at a cost of $2,800 payable in full upon completion of the bridge work. The contract was signed April 19, 1881, and the bridges were guaranteed for 25 years. They have been in service since their installation in August of 1881. Despite flood and rust they are a tribute to the engineering and construction ability of the contractor and the Town of Homer that they are still standing after 138 years.

The one-of-a-kind Mill Street (now Water Street) bridge behind the Town Hall is only used for pedestrian traffic today. With its filial capped posts, it is the largest of the three—fourteen feet wide and ninety-seven feet in length. The 58-foot Wall Street bridge and the 71-foot Pine Street bridge are both twelve feet wide. The contract called for joists to be three inches thick and twelve inches wide and made of pitch pine or Norway pine. The floors were to be of good sound hemlock at least two and a half inches thick.

A cast iron plaque on the end of each bridge honored the Village trustees of the day. They were Charles W. Gage (head of one of the local carriage factories), Porter Kingsbury, Phillip Zimmer (German barber residing on Clinton Street), Augustus H. Bennett (head of the Homer National Bank), and Byron Maxson. Supposedly, William O. Douglas' name appeared on a plaque.

Restoration work on the double truss Water Street bridge was completed in 1991 from $25,000 made available by a grant from the 1985 Environmental

Quality Bond Act through the New York State Office of Parks, Recreation and Historic Preservation, which oversaw all the restoration work. The balance of the funds, $25,000, was provided by the Town of Homer. The work on the bridge was engineered by a bridge restoration specialist, Dan Rogers, from the firm of Ryan and Biggs of Troy, NY. The County provided local engineering services under Highway Superintendent Walter Tennant, Jr. Work performed by Town personnel was supervised by Town Highway Superintendent Tom Bell and Village Superintendent Bob Lottridge. At the time, the bridge was believed to be resting on the stone abutments of an earlier bridge built just south of the county's first grist mill. The mill was built by Asa White, the grandfather of Andrew D. White, the co-founder and first president of Cornell University. The mill was the gathering site for the earliest settlers' religious and governmental activities.

The re-opening of the restored Water Street bridge on Saturday, August 17, 1991, included an hour-long program of celebration. The Cortland Old Timers Band, under the direction of Sam Forcucci, played appropriate "bridge music." There was a puppet show of "The Three Billy Goats Gruff" for the children and refreshments for all. Mayor Mary Alice Bellardini explained that after being closed for about 18 years, the pedestrian bridge would give the residents of the senior citizens complex on River Street better access to amenities along Main Street.

At present, the other two bridges at Wall and Pine Streets have been red flagged by state bridge inspectors and closed to both pedestrian and vehicular traffic. That leaves only the Albany Street bridge for emergency vehicles to access River Street. If that bridge should be inaccessible for some reason, one can imagine the perilous problem for residents of River Street. This has necessitated the Town and Village to consider repairs or replacements of the two bridges

The Town wanted to turn the Wall Street bridge into a two-lane bridge to accommodate emergency vehicles, but the $860,000 project was not selected to receive state funding in 2018. The Town wanted to rehabilitate the Pine Street bridge and turn it from accommodating a three-ton load to a five-ton load. That would require state approval and still be insufficient for the fire department's pumper and tanker trucks. For them, the bridge would need a weight limit of 25 to 30 tons. At this writing, the Economy Paving Company of Cortland has begun work on the Pine Street bridge. The wooden decking is all off, and hopefully the bridge will be completely restored by the end of the month, if the weather permits. Then, once again, at least pedestrians, cars, and ambulances will be able to traverse the waterway.

If the Wall Street historic truss bridge is totally replaced, what is to happen to the structure? Should it be consigned to the trash heap? Or should it be removed to another location, preferably within the Town of Homer?

Because of the rarity of the bridges and their rating as "most significant" by the Historic Bridges Organization, the latter choice is more desirable. The Town of Cortlandville and the Central New York Living History Center are among a few local entities that have expressed interest in accepting such a bridge. At a new site, the state requires that the preserved, historic bridge still be used across a body of water to convey pedestrians or small vehicles from one side to the other. A plaque could identify its original location. Imagine the possibility of incorporating the bridge into a trail for walking and biking along the river.

If preserved at another location, the old bridge could receive a new lease on life. It could continue to tell its story of how it was designed by a man from Cortland County and once crossed by horses, stagecoaches, cattle, and early villagers. Mothers with children in tow crossed the bridge to get to the stores at the Barber Block or to the schools on the Green. Soldiers returning home from wars used the bridge as did wedding parties, funeral processions, and young lovers eagerly heading to the Homer Green for a nighttime tryst. The bridge has witnessed generations of Homerites fishing, boating, swimming, playing, and working near its girders and driving all makes of automobiles, trucks, and bicycles across its planks through the years. The beams and braces and rivets hold memories, so to speak, of documented human events, such as the time young pranksters tipped over an outhouse on River Street and carried it over the river and across the Green to the rear of the Academy so the Principal might have his own private privy. The bridge had a key role to play in that escapade.

Saving a Homer lenticular truss bridge is saving a monument—a monument to our technological, architectural, and cultural past. A bridge connecting us to our historic roots is always worth preserving.

Ed Raus of Homer contributed information on the bridges' patent holder and the history of their manufacturer. Additional information was provided by Stephanie Spina of Homer. This author is grateful to them and for their dedication to the preservation of local history and architecture.

July 3, 2019

LIFE IN EARLY NINETEENTH CENTURY TOWN OF HOMER

In the 1930s, Ina Hurlbut Bird was a local historian who had articles published in the Cortland Standard *about her ancestral history on the Scott Road. Fortunately, she kept many of these articles, along with photos, in scrapbooks. These scrapbooks are now part of the Town's archives. From this source we learn what life was like in the early 1800s in the town. This is the first of a two-part installment that draws heavily upon this source.*

It is hard to image that the road between the Village of Homer and the hamlet of Scott, or what appears on the map today as Route 41, was once merely a trail blazed through dense woods. The early trailblazer was Ebenezer Alvord. According to oral tradition, young Sylvester Alvord was sent forth one day to deliver dinner to his father Ebenezer who, with axe in hand, was clearing trees for what would become known as "the Scott Road." For some reason, the lad wandered off the blazed trail and got lost in the forest. Sylvester was later found. From this incident, it has been determined when "the Scott Road" was first blazed through the wilderness. Given that the boy was seven years old at the time and had been born in 1796, we can estimate that the initial creation of "the Scott Road" was in 1803. And there were no chainsaws then.

Five years later, Eliza DeVoe arrived in the Town of Homer. Less than a year old, she was transported by ox-sled, nestled in her mother's arms. Twenty years later, on April 1, 1828, Eliza married a young man named Samuel Smith Hurlbut, who was called by his middle name. As a seven-year-old, he, his parents, and two sisters had migrated to Homer in 1809 from Hartford, Connecticut. They settled on Lot 23 on land owned by Brainard Cleaveland and built a log cabin situated about two and a half miles from Homer village on "the Scott Road."

The newlyweds, Smith and Eliza, took up residence with his parents in this log cabin. What a trying position for a young bride—in any time period!—to be living with the in-laws. As Eliza cooked the samp (porridge made from coarsely ground corn) for breakfast or supper in a huge iron pot hanging from a crane over the fireplace, from the settle (long wooden bench) on either side of the fireplace, her two in-laws kept careful watch. They exchanged curious glances regarding the culinary skills of their son's new wife. She must have been filled with dread the day she overheated the bake oven and burned the first baking of bread. Flour and meal were scarce commodities, and the Hurlbuts could not afford the loss. Thus, Eliza quickly hid the burned loaves in a hollow stump and vowed never to repeat that mistake.

It was in this crowded, little cabin that Eliza gave birth to her three eldest children. Helen Mary was named after the grandmothers, in keeping with the custom of the time for the first daughter. Adelaide Emmalina was given the name that pleased Eliza's ears. A son arrived next, and he was named Eli DeVoe after Eliza's brother, the detective who was destined to help thwart an assassination plot against President-Elect Lincoln in Baltimore in 1861.

There was a log schoolhouse next door to their home. Here, the children received their initial schooling and learned their ABCs. In 1838, Smith Hurlbut purchased two acres of land and erected upon it the iconic little red schoolhouse to replace the one of logs. Until 1890 this was known as the Hurlbut District School. That year, the structure was relocated and known as

District No. 8, until it merged into the Homer Central School District in the mid-1940s.

The customary chores of the women in early nineteenth century Homer included spinning, weaving, and making clothing by hand. Eliza fashioned a gown of linsey-woolsey, a woven material of linen (made from flax) and wool. It was a rather drab looking garb. For her fair-haired girls, she wanted a brighter linsey-woolsey. So, she went into the nearby woods and collected pokeberries. Using the juice, she dyed the homespun fabric a dark red and created low neck, short-sleeved dresses. A suit for Eli was colored dark brown from butternut shells.

According to the custom of the day, when the Hurlbut girls attained the age of six years, they were expected to knit their own stockings. White cotton stockings ringed with blue were worn in the summer. Homespun woolen yarn was used to make winter wear. Two rows of black alternated with two rows of red. Shoes, too, were homemade. Tanneries were common industries at the time. The village of Homer had one down by the river. The skin of a calf raised on the farm was tanned by the tannery and then an itinerant shoemaker would come by and make leather shoes for every member of the family.

Another task that fell to the children of the pioneer household was candle dipping. This was a lengthy process. Into a deep kettle, partly filled with warm water, melted tallow (the white, solid rendered fat of cattle and sheep) was poured nearly to the rim. A dozen or more sticks about 20 inches long had been prepared ahead of time, along with 20-inch lengths of cotton candle wicking. Over each stick was hung a double length of the wicking with the ends twisted. Then the child dipped the wick into the melted tallow and suspended the stick over an empty pan for the grease to harden. The child did the same process again with another stick with wicking. This continued until all the sticks were dipped. Then, the process for all twelve sticks was repeated until all twelve candles had been dipped about 20 times. Twelve dozen candles was an average production rate for a child and quite an object lesson in patience and perseverance.

A large family was considered an asset in those days, and each child was expected "to earn his board and keep" at an early age. Providing the lighting for the family was one way to do that. And a tallow candle gleaming in the window or placed within a tin lantern perforated with holes helped to guide many a person through a Central New York storm to the refuge of his hearth.

From supper time until bedtime, the children were kept busy. The girls were occupied in knitting, piecing patchwork quilts, or making samplers. A sampler was a piece of embroidery worked in various stitches as a specimen of skill, typically containing the alphabet, some mottoes, and some motifs. A motto might be "Friends are Flowers in the Garden of Life." Meanwhile, the boys were engaged in paring and coring apples and stringing them on twine.

The long strings of apples would be hung from the rafters of the cabin near the fireplace to dry.

The year before he married, 1827, Smith Hurlbut owned 17 acres of land. Over time, additional tracts of land were acquired until he had a farm of about 400 acres. As the family grew, the log cabin became too small. In 1834, upon the arrival of another daughter, Elizabeth, Smith built a large frame house just north of the old log cabin. Clad in white paint, it had a central doorway balanced on each side by two windows of small paned glass. With an eye for landscaping, Smith headed off to Bear Swamp and returned with some white pine trees. These he planted around his Colonial-style home, and three of the stately sentinels survived for over a century.

As for the interior of the new residence, Ina Hurlbut Bird described it this way:

> What a jolly place it was for children to play in! There were chimney cupboards and closets and lots of attic cubby holes and four large fire places on the ground floor. Colonial houses were built for children!
>
> The family moved in the same year the nearby Village was incorporated, 1835. They took up residence on the ground floor as the dwelling continued to be a work in progress. The second floor was not plastered and finished off until 1852.

July 18, 2019

This is the second of a two-part series on one typical family's life in nineteenth century Town of Homer.

By 1876, the centennial of the nation, a white picket fence enclosed the yard and garden of the home of Smith and Eliza Hurlbut on the Scott Road. Close by was a peach apple tree bearing a swing for the grandchildren that were beginning to arrive. Purple lilacs shaded the windows, and a boardwalk led visitors from the front gate to the front door. The walkway was bordered by lilies-of-the-valley, sweet fennel, a clump of asparagus fern, red peonies, and perennial phlox. Where the old log cabin had once stood, there was now a well-tended, large vegetable garden. This was bordered by fruit trees, currant and blackberry bushes, and grape vines. Beyond the garden was a row of beehives. To the right of that was Eliza's flower garden, filled with dark blue larkspur, red cock's comb, pinks, Johnny-jump-ups, and more peonies.

Back from the colorful garden was the granary and smokehouse and the woodshed attached to the rear of the house with many cords of wood neatly stacked within. The granary was used for storing wheat and buckwheat.

These were taken to the gristmill at the corner of "the Scott Road" and West Street northwest of the village. What came forth there was the flour for the daily bread and cakes consumed by the family or served to guests. Water was acquired by a hand pump from a well outside the kitchen door.

Cattle and sheep roamed the Hurlbuts' hill pastures. Rail fences and stonewalls did their best to keep the livestock from straying. Pigs rolled in the barnyard mud. Ducks, turkeys, hens, and chickens roamed the grounds freely in their respective flocks. Geese were kept in numbers sufficient to keep the great feather beds well stuffed. There were even peacocks strutting their gorgeous plumage across the grounds. They were the weathermen of the day since their sharp cries were considered a reliable predictor of an incoming storm. Their stunning tail feathers made a fine decorative duster hanging from the knob of the chimney cupboard in the parlor.

Upon entering the front hall, the visitor beheld the steep staircase to the second floor. To the left of the little hallway was a large sitting room. Sunlight poured in through two south windows. A rag carpet with stripes of red and yellow covered the floor. A Staffordshire figurine of Little Red Riding Hood was ensconced upon a long, narrow shelf, along with a china dog and lamb, a glass candlestick, and a copper luster pitcher for flowers. Above the shelf hung a rustic frame embracing the motto "God Bless Our Home," worked in red worsted on silver cardboard. A large map of the United States adorned the south wall, and an Eli Terry clock kept time upon a smaller shelf.

Between the two front windows was a wall mirror in a mahogany frame. Below it, on a maple quartet stand, was a little music box. It could tinkle out three tunes: "The Last Rose of Summer," "The Mockingbird," and "The Lighthouse by the Sea." Spread upon a center table, around the large family Bible, were copies of the *Homer Republican* newspaper and the *New York Weekly Tribune*. Near the kitchen door stood a fine mahogany sideboard. This displayed the family's choice silver teapot, salt cellars, and the kerosene reading lamp.

If you were offered a seat, it might be Eliza's well-padded, calico-covered Boston rocker or Smith's armchair with a cushion of black and red diamond patchwork. Or you might prefer one of the stiff ladder-back chairs or the smaller rocker. All bespoke hospitality, as did the aroma of the room. The scent of rose geranium, fuchsias, and other plants could be detected, along with the slightly tropical scent of an oleander tree with its pink blossoms to one side of the room. The whole effect was enhanced by the presence of a brilliant cardinal bird in a cage at one of the windows.

Chances are you would be ushered across the hallway to the more formal parlor reserved for company. Here the principal pieces of furniture were a mahogany sofa and rocker upholstered in haircloth and matching side chairs.

The earlier fireplace had just been closed off, and a new sheet iron chunk stove took its place and considerable space. There was an Empire table and a what-not, and to finish off the glory of the room, a store-bought carpet. The carpet and the stove had most likely been purchased at Uncle Jed Barber's emporium in the village.

The other floors were all covered with rag carpets. Each room required 25 yards, and there was one carpet for summer and one for winter in each room. During the winter months, clean straw was placed underneath the carpets for warmth. Eliza would sew all the rags, and then Mrs. Samuel Andrews of Homer Gulf wove them into fine carpets.

If you checked out the storeroom, you would find it filled with huge, round, full cream cheeses and an occasional sage cheese. Most of these would be sold, as Eliza's contribution to the family's coffers. She also made butter which was packed in firkins (small, wooden casks) weighing between 50 and 100 pounds each. These, too, were sold. The manual dash churn for making butter was replaced by the rotary churn. The latter was turned by a treadmill. The problem was old Tip, the shepherd dog, sometimes charged off and hid when he saw the harness coming his way. The storeroom was, also, for keeping dried beef, corned beef, hams, barrels of salt pork, dried corn, dried apples, dried pumpkin, crates of honey, mincemeat, plum preserves, and pickles.

On average, about 300 pounds of maple sugar and molasses—enough to last a year—was stored up in the attic. In the same attic, among the cobwebs, hung medicinal herbs, catnip, sage, smartweed, tansy, square stalk, and boneset.

The agrarian lifestyle is very much a gamble in any time period. For the nineteenth century Hurlbuts, there were the bad years of drought and grasshoppers, but the family pulled together, pushed through, and managed to prosper. In the early part of what would be called "the age of homespun," it was their self-sufficiency that saw them through. They could survive because they knew how to make their own food, clothing, and shelter. And they had an abiding faith. "God helps those who help themselves."

In time, interdependency came to be the order of the day, as the Hurlbuts increasingly relied upon others for goods and services. Smith bartered more with other farmers and with the blacksmiths and merchants in the village. Merchants like Jedediah Barber and William Sherman offered items they could not readily make for themselves. Firkins of butter and barrels of salt pork could be exchanged for kegs of nails and rolls of wallpaper for the new home. All in all, the farm produced a good living, and Smith boasted that "a farmer was as nearly independent as it was possible for any man to be."

Yet, truth to be told, Smith Hurlbut's economic success was not due to farming alone. In 1846, he purchased a nearby sawmill on Factory Brook. He owned it until 1852, and during that time was able to pay off the debt on his farm and to finish off the second-floor rooms of his Colonial-style home on "the Scott Road."

Postscript: Smith Hurlbut died on December 7, 1881, at the home of his son-in-law in Toronto, Canada. He was buried in Atwater Cemetery on the Scott Road in the Town of Homer. In 1883, his youngest son Charles bought out his siblings, and Eliza, his mother, returned to her position as matriarch of the Scott Road Hurlbuts. She enjoyed this status and shared her stories with her grandchildren until her death on May 2, 1899, at the ripe old age of 92.

August 1, 2019

RHODA BEEBE'S HEROISM RECOGNIZED

If you have done any traveling recently past the intersection of North Main Street and Hooker Avenue, you may have noticed a new, deep red and beige historical marker there mounted on a pole. Through the auspices of the William G. Pomeroy Foundation of Syracuse, grant money was obtained by the Town of Homer for this marker and the Village installed it.

Unlike the usual blue and gold historical markers, the red and tan markers are part of the Pomeroy Foundation's Legends and Lore grant program. These markers commemorate events or persons that fall in the gray area between historical fact and folklore. Sometimes there is inadequate documentation to prove an event or an individual merit a blue and gold historical marker, but a community has come to accept a story as historical fact that has come down through the ages. Such is the case with the first female of European descent to settle in Cortland County, Rhoda Beebe. This twenty-six-year old woman is said to have survived six wintry weeks alone in the wilderness in 1791–1792. The following is the account and references provided the Pomeroy Foundation when this historian applied for the grant.

"There is disagreement as to the location of the first temporary shelter in Cortland County built by the first settlers of European descent, Rhoda Beebe, her brother Amos Todd, and her husband Joseph Beebe. The trio traveled from New Haven, Connecticut, and set up a temporary shelter on the banks of the Tioughnioga River in what would become the Town of Homer and the County of Cortland in Central New York State. An old resident of Homer, Charles Kingsbury, who knew Mrs. Beebe in her old age, claims she showed him the spot not far from what is now the Port Watson Street Bridge in the city of Cortland. Yet, Mrs. Beebe's son made a chart showing the site to be in Homer where North Main Street crosses the Tioughnioga River. The latter site has become, by tradition, the accepted location. A boulder stands nearby commemorating the residence of the intrepid pioneers until they cleared their farm. It reads:

> NEAR THIS SPOT
>
> IN 1791
>
> A LOG CABIN
>
> WAS BUILT BY THE
>
> FIRST SETTLERS
>
> OF
>
> CORTLAND COUNTY
>
> AMOS TODD
>
> RHODA TODD BEEBE
>
> AND
>
> JOSEPH BEEBE
>
> ERECTED 1924

The three pioneers are buried in Homer's Glenwood Cemetery, which was deemed in September of 2018 to be worthy of listing in the State Register of Historic Places. A decision is expected in December as to its being listed in the National Register of Historic Places. In the "nomination form," Rhoda Beebe is one of the eight names cited among "Persons of Historic Importance."

In the nomination narrative, this remarkable woman is cited by her son Spencer for her bravery when she was left alone in nothing more than a pole lean-to/cabin with a blanket for a door while her husband and brother spent three days rounding up strayed horses. She was said to have endured the long and lonely hours and was able to keep "a tranquil mind and received no annoyance, save such as was caused by the howling wolf and screaming panther . . . she received but one call, and that was from a wolf, who, being rather timid, only displaced the blanket sufficient to introduce his phiz and take a look at her ladyship" (Goodwin, *Pioneer History of Cortland County*, 148, accessible online).

The following winter, the men returned to Windsor, NY, to collect what they had left behind. They were delayed by snow for six weeks. Again, Rhoda was left alone in the makeshift shelter and had to maintain her sanity as she awaited their return. When her food ran out, she resolved to leave and follow the river. She was spared the ordeal by the timely return of the men with cattle and provisions. She was described as "a high-souled, noble-hearted woman, worth more than gaudy gems or golden crowns" (Goodwin, *Pioneer History of Cortland County*, 149–150, accessible online).

The same account of Rhoda Beebe's "womanly heroism" appears in chapter VI (pp. 57–58) of H. P. Smith's *History of Cortland County* published in 1885 (accessible online). It is in chapter XIX that one finds the interesting claim by Charles Kingsbury that Rhoda "had a daughter named Clara, who remained with her" during the delayed absence of the two men. And it is here that one finds the reference to Rhoda's survival skills. "Mrs. Beebe's small stock of provisions was exhausted," stated Kingsbury, "and she was reduced to the necessity of resorting to roots and the barks of trees to appease their hunger and sustain life" (186).

This last fact is unsubstantiated by any other primary source and found its way into local folklore courtesy of Bertha Eveleth Blodgett's *Stories of Cortland County for Boys and Girls* in 1932. She writes that "Mrs. Beebe had been reduced to eating roots and the bark of trees while her husband was away" (40). She mistakenly cites as her source Goodwin's *Pioneer History of Cortland County*, when in fact such an account is only in Smith's history book.

The Blodgett book tends to combine historical fact with historical lore without making a distinction and usually is the first introduction to local history for young people of Cortland County. Nevertheless, it is certain that "Mrs. Beebe was called upon to test her qualifications as a pioneer's wife" (whether as a mother or not) and "to face the privations of the wilderness as best she could" on at least two occasions. This is the lore that makes Rhoda Beebe a "profile in courage" for today's youth. They need to be aware that the nation had persevering "Founding Mothers" and not just "Founding Fathers."

This historian hopes readers agree that Rhoda Beebe merits recognition with signage. Her story is an early part of our local cultural heritage and an indication of how much we value resilience. We hope visitors to Homer will take note upon entering the village from the north and will come to understand how Rhoda Beebe is just one of many individuals of the past who make Homer "Historic."

August 15, 2019

A SIGN OF THE TIMES

Opinion

It is always edifying to a historian when a robust dialogue occurs over the significance of an event or person from the past. It does not happen all that often, at least at the local level. Such is the case now as the community of Homer takes up the matter of new welcoming signage proposed by the Village for its entrances. The question for discussion is this: What should Homer's identity be? What or who merits use as Homer's brand for attracting visitors and especially heritage tourists? What values do we wish to have our name attached to into the foreseeable future?

Some would prefer the Village keep signage referring to Homer as "The Homeville of David Harum"—a reference to a significant novel of the late nineteenth century authored by Edward Noyes Westcott with a colorful, folksy protagonist inspired, it is believed, by Homer's David Hannum. The Hannum-Harum connection served its purpose for the Village's branding for a good many years, but should it continue? Do today's residents of Homer know who Hannum/Harum was? Can they explain to others why the Key Bank on Main Street bears the inscription "Homeville of David Harum"? Would travelers on I-81 be willing to "tarry awhile with us" because of someone named David Harum? Or is it David Hannum? How confusing!

Then, there is the matter of integrity. Do the locals know or care that Homer's Hannum (not the fictional Harum) was convicted of fraud in 1868? The record shows that "Dalrymple, the plaintiff, claimed that Hannum had sold him a completely different piece of land in the Midwest than the piece he had represented. Dalrymple wanted $3500 in damages, but was only awarded $1200." This appears in an article researched and written by Harriet Hamilton, published in *Yesteryears*, "a quarterly magazine for the appreciation and study of New York regional history," Vol. 8, No.29, Sept. 1964, Scipio Center, NY, page 20. Perhaps this explains why Hannum lost in a special election for town supervisor called in 1878. The result was 276 votes for A. Judson Kneeland and 127 for David H. Hannum.

Then, a few months after Westcott's novel came out, the February 16, 1899 issue of *The World* published this: "Hannum's chief claim to a fame wider than this county was his exploitation of the 'Cardiff Giant.' Shortly after the discovery (?) of this huge hoax Hannum happened to be in the vicinity and saw money in it. With two associates he organized a joint stock company to exhibit the graven image. They took it through Central New York and made a pot of money by the deception until some scientific sharps discovered that, instead of a huge human body preserved by percolating limewater, the statue was fairly fresh from the cheating chisel." The same article pointed out that Hannum presented himself to others as the "Father of the Cardiff Giant," which he was not. The hoax was the brainchild of a man named George Hull.

And finally, my opinion of David Hannum (not of the fictional David Harum who used his guiles mostly for good) is aligned with an article by

William Hoge, "The Real David Harum," which appeared in *The Home Magazine* (edited by Arthur Vance), October issue, New York, 1899, p. 303. Hoge wrote, "There are many diverse opinions of David Hannum in Homer. Men to whom he was in debt when he died [in 1892] will tell you that his business transactions were not above reproach . . ."

[After this article was published by the Homer newspaper, it was discovered that Hannum had also been court-martialed for failure to report for annual militia exercises and had lied about the reason for being a no-show. The source is in the Cortland County Historical Society.]

The novel's title character, David Harum, seems to be motivated by this saying of his: "Do unto the other feller the way he'd like to do unto you, an' do it fust." Did this motivate Hannum, too? This is not exactly the traditional Golden Rule, but it is an apt philosophy for the Gilded Age of the 1890s that saw the likes of a John D. Rockefeller stepping on the little oil companies in creating the Standard Oil monopoly. Yet, it seems Americans have always been attracted to "bad boys" who use ethically dubious business practices to rise to the top financially. On the other hand, there are those in the Homer community who would like to see top billing being given now to more admirable figures. This includes Homer's three "Lincoln men": Francis Carpenter, William Stoddard, and Eli DeVoe. Their stories reveal how an earlier Homer had the individuals and the institutions that valued justice and education and gave direction and meaning to the lives of three who would go on to play significant roles with and for Abraham Lincoln. Their stories teach that those from a small community like Homer can go on to important careers at a national level . . . that a small town kid can make good, just as Abraham Lincoln did. And which has the better draw for tourists or economic development grants from Albany—the use of Harum's name or that of Lincoln? Which carries the better cachet?

Still, others in the community have their personal favorites from Homer's past: Amelia Jenks Bloomer, Andrew D. White, Gen. Willoughby Babcock, Rhoda Beebe, Jedediah and Paris Barber, Rev. John Keep, Samuel B. Woolworth, William and George Brockway, Amelia Stone Quinton, Nellie Randall, and others. There is a famous Homerite for every taste and set of values. So many to choose from! What a marvelous dilemma! Every community should be so blessed!

And that is the point of my proposal. While I am biased toward attaching the community's name to that of "The Great Emancipator" and the Homerites who made his painted image iconic, made handwritten copies of his Emancipation Proclamation, and helped to thwart an attempt on his life in 1861, I am pragmatic enough to endorse a compromise design. I would like to see only the words "Welcome to Historic Homer" with one of these three visuals—a background image of the Lincoln penny profile proposed by David Quinlan OR the image designed by Stephanie Spina depicting the Homer Green in the early 1800s OR a blend of both. Without naming individuals, the Quinlan design hints at Homer's attachment to Lincoln, and the Spina design is appropriate as recognition of the "sacred space" trod upon by ALL of Homer's illustrious persons of the past, especially in their formative years, for religious, educational, or leisure-time pursuits. The Green is the heart of the Historic District and Spina's design is already used on the Village letterhead and T-shirts of some Village employees. Should our visual brand be consistent, at least?

Finally, how many villages can boast of TWO Historic Sites listed in the State and National Registers of Historic Places along with ONE Historic District? We have the rare lenticular truss bridges from the 1880s, Glenwood Cemetery, and Old Homer Village (the Historic District). Styles of architecture from the Colonial Period to the Present makes the Historic District (220 structures) a perfect laboratory for the student of historical architecture. This well-preserved array of architectural styles, the exemplary cemetery of the Rural Cemetery Movement, and a slew of famous, accomplished persons, with THREE connecting Homer to President Lincoln, is what makes Homer "Historic" and a source of pride.

It may be problematic to select an individual to represent what Homerites value and respect today, but if we do, which individual(s) should it be? Let the delightful dialogue continue . . . but not forever. We need to get on with promoting what makes Homer a place worth visiting and a place that provides character education instruction for its youth through the local figures of the past it holds up for emulation. While I prefer "Welcome to Historic Homer," I will support whatever wording the Village Board chooses.

[Note: The great Homer signage kerfuffle of 2019 was over what design should be used for the welcoming signs at the entrances to the village. It had been proposed that it was time to replace the one then honoring David Harum, the fictional character in the novel of the same name who was believed to be based on Homer's David Hannum. This generated much contention, which manifested itself in the Homer and Cortland newspapers. A threat of a lawsuit against the Village Administration and the cancellation of an unofficial community opinion referendum over design options caused the Village to decree the wording would be "Welcome to Historic Homer" but not with any of the images this historian preferred. Imagine, all of this over signage and historical identity! At least, for a few weeks, the public got an education about its more significant residents of the past, as shown in the next article.]

August 29, 2019

AND TO THINK IT HAPPENED IN HOMER

In an effort to correct some misinformation and to set the public record straight, I feel compelled to repeat information about Homer's three persons connected to President Lincoln. It is factual content I have already committed to print more than once. I refer to Eli DeVoe, William Stoddard, and Francis B. Carpenter. All three claimed nineteenth century Homer as their birthplace. Each trod the Homer Green to access religious, academic, and leisure-time pursuits. Each was shaped in his formative years by individuals in the Homer community, and one was influenced by the community throughout his lifetime. Each made contributions at the national level in service to Lincoln in the President's lifetime and after, and some of that took place in Homer.

Eli DeVoe was the detective who helped to foil a plot to assassinate President-Elect Lincoln when he passed through Baltimore, Maryland, in 1861 to be inaugurated. DeVoe's report convinced Lincoln to enter the nation's capital via a different train, as detective Allan Pinkerton had urged Lincoln to do. This is no insignificant accomplishment. Indeed, it might well have been a history changing moment in the Abolition Movement.

Francis Bicknell Carpenter was the portrait painter who captured Lincoln's iconic image in oil on canvas in 1864. With Stoddard's assistance, the painting was accepted by Congress and now hangs on the Senate side of the Capitol Building in Washington, D.C.

It has been stated that none of these Homerites accomplished anything of historical significance in Homer. That is not true. Of the three, Carpenter frequently returned to his birthplace and worked on artistic and literary projects related to President Lincoln. While Carpenter had his residence and a series of studios in New York City, where he made a name for himself as the portrait-maker for the "movers and shakers" of nineteenth century America (including five U.S. Presidents), the place that magnetically drew him back for vacations in August through September was the Carpenter homestead located a few miles north of the village on what is now Route 11. A blue and gold historic marker now designates the site.

As a youth, Carpenter first honed his portraiture skills in Homer, rendering the images on canvas of locals like the Jedediah Barber Family and the first trustees of the Academy on the Green. He then moved to New York City in the spring of 1851. In the Borough of Brooklyn, he set up his first studio, and the next August the twenty-one-year-old, fledgling artist married fifteen-year-old Augusta Prentiss. She was the lovely daughter of a female music teacher at the Academy in Homer. Carpenter's portrait of Augusta will soon be placed in a prominent spot in Homer's renovated Town Hall. It is presently one of 23 Carpenter portraits within the community of Homer. Visitors have been known to inquire as to where they might find his artwork on display. Direct them to Phillips Free Library for the most accessible examples.

During his illustrious career, Carpenter and his family frequently took the eight-hour train ride from New York to Homer to visit family and friends. Most of his summers were spent at the Carpenter homestead north of the village where he had been born and raised. With his young son "Bertie," Carpenter enjoyed swimming in the Tioughnioga River and fishing in nearby Little York Lake on hot and humid August days. He and Augusta, whom he affectionately referred to as "Gus," traditionally celebrated their wedding anniversaries at Glen Haven, at the southern tip of Skaneateles Lake, in the company of family and close friends.

During the Civil War, with the President's approval, Carpenter, at the age of thirty-four, spent six months painting in the White House state dining room on a nine foot by fifteen-foot canvas. By July 22, 1864, The First Reading of the Emancipation Proclamation before the Cabinet was near completion. Without knowing that his portrait would become the iconic image of "The Great Emancipator," Lincoln expressed his approval of Carpenter's handiwork and admitted to Carpenter that the event depicted was "the central act of my administration."

It was during his time at the White House that Carpenter walked with Lincoln to Mathew Brady's Photographic Parlor in Washington. There, on February 9, 1864, he arranged how the President should sit for photographs taken by Anthony Berger. No one knew then that the two images would one day grace the Lincoln penny and the American five-dollar bill.

After exhibition in the East Room of the White House and in the Rotunda of the Capitol, the framed, unsigned Emancipation Proclamation masterpiece in oil was taken on a successful public tour across the North. A year and a half later Carpenter brought the painting depicting "moral grandeur" to Homer from his New York studio at 653 Broadway. He did not fail to include the community of his early development. On the evening of Saturday, September 29, 1866, the painting was opened to the public at the opera house on the third floor of Jedediah Barber's mercantile establishment on Main Street. On the same day, Carpenter attended a reception in his honor hosted by the Stone family of Homer. Those who shook the hand that had painted Lincoln's face were also shaking the hand that had clasped Lincoln's hand in friendship—the same hand that had penned the document that initiated the process that led to the passage of the Thirteenth Amendment to the Constitution in the previous December. It was Lincoln who gave new meaning to the words in the Declaration of Independence we publicly recite every July Fourth in Homer: "that all men are created equal."

Before Lincoln's assassination, Carpenter had made a smart business move. He had arranged with New York publisher Derby & Miller to produce a print of the Emancipation Proclamation painting for public sale. Alexander Hay Ritchie, a well-known engraver in New York, was contracted to reproduce the painting as a steel engraving for $6,000. To that end, Carpenter started working on a smaller version of the painting—twenty-one by thirty-three inches—for Ritchie's use. This project was brought to Homer the summer before the full painting had been exhibited here. Thus, it was on Saturday, August 19, 1865, during one of his "vacation visits," that Carpenter felt the need for "material assistance." As he noted in his diary, he "went to the village and got a group of men together like [in his] Emancipation picture" and had the local photographer Luther Barker make him an ambrotype. Homer's very tall butcher, Burdett Newton, was asked to sit at a table as Lincoln. Other locals took their places as directed. Lewis Henry posed for Secretary of War Stanton; "old Mr. Gardner" for Secretary of the Navy Welles; Ki Munger for Secretary of State Seward; Mr. Hicok for Postmaster General Blair; Mr. Wardell for Secretary of the Interior Smith; and Judge Reed for Attorney General Bates. A visitor from New York named Mr. Gillett was commandeered to stand in as Secretary of the Treasury Salmon P. Chase.

From this small painting worked up in Homer, Ritchie produced a high quality print of the Emancipation Proclamation painting that the journalist Noah Brooks predicted would be "prized in every liberty-loving household as a work of art . . . a perpetual remembrance of the noblest event in American history." Carpenter gave copies of the print to each Cabinet member depicted in the painting, and an autographed copy was given to his parents in Homer as a Christmas present.

It was during this same "vacation visit" to Homer that Carpenter was working on another Lincoln project. He was endeavoring to do a painting of the Lincoln family in black and white, with the intention of mass producing it as a commercial print by the engraver John Chester Buttre. The subject of the painting was to be the Presidential family as it was in 1861 before eleven-year-old Willie Lincoln's death in 1862 from typhoid fever. However, Carpenter had never met Willie, and the only thing he had to work from was a photograph Mrs. Lincoln had provided of the heads of Willie and Tad Lincoln. To get a good sense of the bodily proportions of an eleven-year-old boy, Carpenter enlisted the help of a Homer merchant's son, Henry Wheadon. [The three-story Wheadon Block on Main Street was destroyed by a fire in September 2016.] Carpenter had the young lad pose for an ambrotype. From this image he was able to render the Presidential family with Willie's head upon the body of a Homer boy—a task he completed on August 17, 1865, *in Homer*.

By this time, too, Carpenter was busy writing his reminiscences of Lincoln. They were being published in a series of articles for the New York *Independent*. Like some of his artwork, some of Carpenter's literary work was done while vacationing in Homer. His diary entry for August 20, 1865, reads: "Commenced my 'No. VII' [installment] for the 'Independent' this evening, under the tree in the southeast corner of the orchard [at the Carpenter homestead]."

His own extended memoir, *Six Months at the White House with Abraham Lincoln: The Story of a Picture*, was completed on the first anniversary of Lincoln's death and published by Hurd and Houghton in 1866. It was a best-seller. It gave readers exactly what they craved after Lincoln's death: personal anecdotes of the man more than critical assessments of his statesmanship. Carpenter's *The Inner Life of Abraham Lincoln* was published in 1867 and drew critical acclaim from the great English novelist Charles Dickens. These books by a native son of Homer who attended the academy on the Green have become primary sources utilized by historians and Lincoln scholars ever since.

Also, in 1867, Carpenter took time to re-connect not just with the community of his origin but with his artistic mentor. Twenty-two years earlier while in his teens, Carpenter had spent six months studying portraiture under the Syracuse artist Sanford Thayer, and on October 4, 1867, Thayer was invited to make the trip from Syracuse to Homer to spend the day with his former and now famous pupil. Carpenter noted in his diary that the two of them "went to the village and sat for pictures at Luther Barker's [photography studio]."

When Homer's Paris Barber, Carpenter's earliest benefactor, died in May of 1876, Carpenter attended the funeral in Homer and gratefully recalled the inspirational trip he and Paris took to New York City in 1847 to see great works of art. He summed up his benefactor this way: "He had so much of the artistic instinct himself, that he could enter perfectly into the aim and ambition of my life." That is recognizing significant influence from a citizen of Homer.

When Carpenter returned to Homer in August of 1876 for his "usual summer vacation," he took the room over the drugstore and bookshop business of Atwater & Kellogg in the Barber Block on Main Street. He still was managing to combine business with pleasure, finishing up some art projects. Though Homer had not been his primary residence for the past quarter century, the residents of the area still recognized the famous artist when he was out in public. The *Cortland Standard* for August 16, 1876, reported "Frank gets a hearty shake from every man he meets."

On February 12, 1878, the sixty-ninth anniversary of Lincoln's birth, a joint session of Congress convened in the House to accept Carpenter's *First Reading of the Emancipation Proclamation before the Cabinet* as a gift to the nation. The credit for this went to the masterful, behind-the-scene lobbying done for Carpenter by another son of Homer, William Osborn Stoddard.

Of all the several portrait studies Carpenter did of Lincoln, the best known is the one done for the Emancipation Proclamation painting—the one for which Lincoln told his former law partner, William Herndon, "I feel that there is more of me in this portrait than in any representation which has been made." From this portrait, Frederick W. Halpin, the talented engraver, rendered a line-and-stipple adaptation. This amazingly life-like print carried the signatures of both Halpin and Carpenter. Suitable for framing, it made a fine item to give as a gift, which is exactly what Carpenter did. Seven of his friends in Homer received copies of this print as a Christmas present in 1894. The Homer Village Board of Trustees owns one of them today—a symbol of Carpenter's grateful ties to the place of his birth and early artistic development. This writer recently acquired the copy an appreciative Carpenter gave to Stoddard, inscribed in pencil with these words: "To William O. Stoddard, With the affectionate regards of the artist, Frank B. Carpenter, October 20, 1898."

Carpenter died in New York City on May 23, 1900, and his funeral was held there two days later. The artist who had gained fame as Lincoln's portraitist could have been buried in New York City or Albany or in the nation's capital. But, no, Carpenter chose to return to his roots in Homer to be buried in the upper, southwest corner of Glenwood Cemetery in the Carpenter family plot. This fact was not overlooked when Glenwood Cemetery was granted National Historic Site status in late 2018. Carpenter has been called by Lincoln scholar Harold Holzer "the most important artist ever to portray Abraham Lincoln."

It is clear that throughout his artistic career Francis Bicknell Carpenter never forgot his roots in Homer. It is also clear that his work was influenced by and supported by folks from Homer and its environs, and some of his work, artistic and literary, was actually done here. It is fitting and proper that Homer should recognize the historical documentation provided by two of its native sons through public art and writings. And without Detective DeVoe, there may have been nothing for Carpenter and Stoddard to write about and for Homer to celebrate as it did back in 2009.

Carpenter, Stoddard, and DeVoe are not fictional. They are real life figures. They are not folk heroes. Their histories originated in Homer, and because of Homer's citizens and academy they contributed significantly to what we know today of the life and iconography of Abraham Lincoln. Check out scholarly books about Lincoln, such as Doris Kearns Goodwin's *Team of*

Image 9.1 Homer's Green in Carpenter's era. *Combination Atlas Map of Cortland County, New York (Philadelphia: Everts, Ensign & Everts, 1876), p. 19, from archives, Town Hall, Homer, NY.*

Rivals, and you will find the writings of Stoddard and Carpenter in the bibliographies. Homer is the community that truly gifted Lincoln, New York State, the nation, and the world with the timeless image of Lincoln in paint and print as "The Great Emancipator." It is why Homer can boast of being called by Harold Holzer "another Lincoln mecca." It is time to take credit for what our village forebears contributed to the Lincoln legacy. It is time to embrace that which truly makes Homer "Historic" and the wonderful marketing opportunity it presents the village and the county.

September 12, 2019

THE SIGNIFICANCE OF A RUNAWAY SLAVE IN THE CELLAR

History becomes real when it becomes local or personal or both. This municipal historian first became interested in local history through several volumes on the topic discovered in Phillips Free Library when he was in Homer Elementary School on the Green (grades K through 6 at that time). The book Lincoln's Third Secretary *was of great interest. I found it was the memoirs of William O. Stoddard, edited by his son William O. Stoddard, Jr.*

(New York: Exposition Press, 1955). This was the moment that I learned of the first of three native-sons of Homer connected to President Lincoln. What ten-year old would not be captivated by the first chapter of the book describing another discovery made by another ten-year old at No. 5 Albany Street in the village? This is that chapter.

"I thought I heard someone singing. That would be strange enough in Grandfather's house in Homer, New York, where no one sang and only Grandmother sat at home knitting, everlastingly knitting and rocking to and fro on the second floor of the old farmhouse. Yet I did hear singing, and it seemed to come up through the rough boards of the kitchen floor. It could be interesting.

I went outside, threw back the outer cellar doors and went down the stone steps into the cellar. In the half-light I made out a Negro seated on an upturned bushel basket. His eyes were closed, and he swayed back and forth in rhythm as a he sang:

I got a wife, an' she got a baby,
'Way up north in old Canaydy.
Won't they shout when they see Old Shady
Comin', comin'?—Hail, mighty day!

Here was mystery enough for a youngster of ten years. I turned and walked slowly up the cellar stairs, bemused. What did it mean?

At the head of the stairs stood Grandfather [John] Osborn. Though he and I were chums of long standing, I suddenly realized that the tall, gaunt man standing before me was a stranger. His eyes were cold and hard. Stories flashed through my mind about his fights with the Indians as he worked his way along the Mohawk Trail in the westward migration that opened up central New York and the West to the white settlers. He was the embodiment of the explorer, the pioneer, the foreloper. Now frankly I was scared. There was the glitter of ice in his eyes that had always been benevolent, and his voice was hard and fairly cracked with suppressed emotion and purpose. "William," he said, "you have heard *nothing*, and you have seen *nothing*. Remember."

He was a man of few words. This much I understood, and looking in vain for a touch of friendliness in that always kindly face, I answered haltingly, "Yes, Grandfather."

Grandfather Osborn turned and left me without another word.

The next morning the farmhouse was vacant save for Grandmother Osborn, who sat knitting in her room on the second floor. I made a feeble effort to resist the temptation, but finally yielded and crept silently, slowly, down the cellar stairs. Arriving at bottom and pushing the cellar door by inches, I peered in. Nothing. Not a sign. But there was the upturned bushel basket. No, I had not been dreaming.

This was my introduction to the Underground Railroad. This house was one of the "stations"; Grandfather Osborn was one of the "conductors," and very likely a "stockholder." He built the first brick house in Homer—still standing. He was a silversmith, and made silver ornaments. His customers, in the beginning, were mostly the Indians. Long before the town [here he means the village] was called Homer, the Indians had a name for it—*to-wis-ta-no-ont-oa-ne-ha*, which, being interpreted, signifies "the place where the man lives who makes the silver ornaments."

I was a prime favorite with this grand old man. He made me a pair of pistols. They were of the derringer type, muzzle-loaders, with percussion caps. He permitted me to use them freely provided I would go out into the fields alone—strictly alone. Without knowing it, I became an excellent shot. I would aim at the head of a daisy at ten paces, right and left hand, and frequently hit. Any money I might earn or beg went to the purchase of powder and ball. The skill acquired served me in good stead when, twenty years later, I became Marshall of Arkansas [after serving as President Lincoln's assistant personal secretary at the White House and making the first handwritten copies of Lincoln's Emancipation Proclamation]."

Here we see the makings of an Abolitionist right here in Homer. This early event in the adventurous life of William Osborn Stoddard occurred

Image 9.2 **William O. Stoddard, May 4, 1859.** *Courtesy of the author.*

just across the river and on the same street where I was growing up. The fields where young Stoddard had trod were the same ones in which I and my neighborhood friends played. Only, I was permitted to have a cap gun, no pistols, which was a wise parental decision for both my sake and that of my friends.

Years later, I was invited to the Osborn House on Albany Street to meet a special visitor. The house at the time was a bed-and-breakfast owned by the Duane Stevens family. The special guest was a descendant of William O. Stoddard. Of course, I immediately accepted the invitation and took along my personal copy of Lincoln's Third Secretary. *Today, one of my cherished possessions is the book bearing this inscription: "Eleanor H. Stoddard, granddaughter of W.O.S. and niece of W.O.S. Jr. July 11, 1995." In 2009, Eleanor returned to Homer with Lincoln scholar Harold Holzer to participate in Homer's "Celebration of Lincoln in Paint and Print." Then, in 2011, I was honored and pleased to have Eleanor Stoddard write a blurb for the back cover of my book about Homer's three connections to President Abraham Lincoln. Things, sometimes, have a way of coming full cycle, don't they?*

September 26, 2019

THE TOWN OF HOMER IN THE POST-CIVIL WAR ERA

Historians rely upon primary sources for information about the past. One valuable source for this historian has been the GAZETTEER AND BUSINESS DIRECTORY OF CORTLAND COUNTY, N. Y. *for 1869. This was compiled and published by Hamilton Child, Syracuse, NY, in 1869 and contains this description of Homer as seen through the lens of post-Civil War residents.*

"[The Town of] HOMER was formed March 5, 1794. Solon was taken off in 1798, Virgil in 1804 and Cortlandville in 1829. It lies upon the west border of the County, a little north of the center. The surface is uneven and consists of the valleys of the two branches of the Tioughnioga River and the ridges which border upon them. The valley of the western branch is about a. mile in width and elevated 1,096 feet above tide. The eastern valley is narrower. The two valleys are separated by a ridge of hills from 200 to 500 feet above the river, and another similar ridge occupies the south-eastern corner of the town. The western part of the town is a hilly upland, 1,500 to 1,600 feet above tide. The Tioughnioga receives Cold and Factory Brooks from the west, which are its chief tributaries. The valleys of these streams open into corresponding valleys to the northward, through which flow streams emptying into Otisco and Skaneateles Lakes. The soil upon the river flats is a deep, rich alluvial loam, well adapted to tillage; upon the highlands it is a sandy and gravelly loam, better adapted to pasturage.

Homer [Village], (p. v.) incorporated May 11, 1835 [the Village still has the original Charter of Incorporation], is finely situated on the Tioughnioga River and is a station on the Syracuse, Binghamton and New York Railroad. It contains four churches, an academy, a newspaper office, a bank, three hotels, several manufactories and about 2,000 inhabitants. The streets and walks are very broad and ornamented with beautiful shade trees, which add much to the general appearance of the village. There are many very pretty residences and some very fine business blocks. The main street extends nearly north and south, is about a mile in length and embraces most of the business part of the village. Near the center of the village is a beautiful park, upon the west side of which stand the Baptist, Methodist, Congregational and Episcopal churches, and the Cortland Academy, all facing the park. The streets are lighted with gas.

Cortland Academy was incorporated February 4, 1819 [the charter was signed February 2 and Homer Central School has the original]. The course of study includes all the branches usually taught in the common schools, in our best academies, and most of the studies pursued in our colleges. The library numbers over fifteen hundred volumes of choice works in the various departments of literature and science. The philosophical and chemical apparatus is ample for illustrating the principles of these sciences. The geological and mineralogical cabinet has been much enlarged by the liberality of the President of the Academy [Jedediah Barber], and now includes a complete suit[e] of rocks and minerals of this State, and many foreign specimens of great beauty and value. The library, apparatus and cabinet are arranged in a room which has been elegantly fitted up by the citizens of the village and is always open to visitors. A new edifice is in process of erection which will be an ornament to the village and an honor to its projectors. The new edifice occupies the site of the old one, is of brick, ninety-six feet long, and its greatest width seventy-two feet. The corners of the end projections and of the central tower are of hewn stone. The main entrance in the tower is finished in the same way and arched. The windows are all surmounted by cut stone. The lower story is for the heating apparatus and for chemical and lecture rooms. The second story is for the library, the cabinet, the mathematical and two large study rooms. The third story is for chapel and four study and recitation rooms. A Mansard roof gives room in the fourth story for two anterooms and a large hall with a central height of twenty-six feet. There are two rear entrances with staircases communicating with every story. George Almy is the architect.

The village contains two public halls.

Barber's Hall is seventy-five feet by eighty, finished in the most elaborate style and capable of seating 1,000 persons. It is one of the finest halls in Central New York.

Wheadon Hall [burned a few years ago and replaced by developer James Yaman] is forty by fifty feet in size and capable of seating about 700 or 800 people.

Homer Flouring and Gristmill is situated on the west bank of the Tioughnioga River, near the center of the village. It is owned by Messrs. Darby & Son, and is capable of grinding about 300 bushels per day.

An Oil Mill, located in the south-west part of the village, is doing a good business.

The Edge Tool Manufactory of R. Blanshan & Co., upon the east bank of the river, is run by steam and manufactures all kinds of edge tools of an excellent quality.

A Marble Factory, near the depot, turns out very nice work.

A Brewery, upon 'Brewery Hill,' is doing a fair business.

A Flax and Cordage Mill is located a little outside of the corporation, owned by John L. Boorum. This mill produces about a ton of cotton cordage per day, and manufactures the flax from about 1,000 acres per year, valued at forty dollars per acre. There are fifteen tenant houses connected with the factory which employs about thirty-five hands.

Glen Wood Cemetery occupies an elevated position about half a mile west of the village. The grounds include about thirty acres, are laid out with much taste and overlook the villages of Homer and Cortland, and a large extent of surrounding country. The Cemetery is under the control of an association organized February 21, 1862.

Homer Mechanical Brass Band was organized in 1865, and furnishes music for all occasions.

East Homer, (p. v.) situated in the east part of the town, near the Tioughnioga River, contains a church (Methodist Episcopal), a hotel, a blacksmith shop, a carpenter and wagon shop, a school house and about 150 inhabitants. The church was erected in 1841 and dedicated in 1842. Rev. H. Hawley was the first pastor.

Hibbard's Butter and Cheese Factory is situated about one-half mile north-east of East Homer. The building was erected in 1866 and is thirty feet by one hundred and twenty, and two stories high. The milk of from 300 to 500 cows is used, and from 20,000 to 37,000 pounds of butter, and from 55,000 to 100,000 pounds of cheese are made annually. The heating of the vats and the churning are done by steam. Twenty churns can be run at a time and thirty cheeses pressed.

Carpenterville, situated on the east branch of the Tioughnioga River, about four miles from Cortland Village, contains a gristmill, a sawmill, a wagon shop, a blacksmith shop, two turning shops and about a dozen houses.

Mr. V. Carpenter, on lot 47, has a fine trout pond, well stocked with fish of all sizes from the smallest size to two pounds in weight.

Little York, (p. v.) situated on the west branch of Tioughnioga River, in the north part of the town, contains a hotel, a store, a very fine school house, a gristmill, a sawmill, a peg factory, a wagon shop and about twenty dwellings.

Homer Cheese Factory is situated about one and a half miles from Homer Village, it was erected in 1864 and uses the milk of from 600 to 1200 cows. The building is 175 feet by 32, and two stories high. In 1865, 573,868 pounds of cheese were made; in 1866, 382,579 pounds; and in 1867, 233,571 pounds were made.

The population of Homer in 1865 was 3,856 and its area 29,321 acres."

And, thus, you gain some insight as to the Town of Homer 150 years ago, in the post-Civil War era, and how the residents made a living at the time.

[Note: The great Homer signage kerfuffle of 2019 was still being waged in the press. Some residents supporting the David Harum welcoming design called for the mayor's removal in the upcoming November election. The resident of the David Hannum House opined in the Cortland Standard that I was not fit for the historian's post. The following was published in response. And neither the incumbent mayor nor the municipal historian were removed, but the Harum sign was.]

THE LINCOLN FRANCIS B. CARPENTER REVEALED

While there were better painters in the nineteenth century than Homer's native-son Francis B. Carpenter (1830–1900), it is Carpenter who best provided the image of Lincoln that has endured in the American mind. That is the image of the "Great Emancipator" with heavy-lidded, blueish-gray eyes "always in deep shadow" and looking "remarkably pensive and tender, often inexpressively sad, as if the reservoir of tears lay very near the surface . . ." (Carpenter's description). In addition, the only artist involved with President Lincoln to provide posterity an extended memoir is Frank Carpenter. Thus, not only did Homer's Carpenter contribute by paint to the world's understanding of Lincoln, he contributed by print.

Carpenter's reminiscences of Lincoln were first published in a series of articles for the New York *Independent* and then in an afterward—pages 725 to 766—to Henry J. Raymond's *The Life, Public Services and State Papers of Abraham Lincoln* published in New York in 1865. His own book, *Six Months at the White House with Abraham Lincoln: The Story of a Picture,* published by Hurd and Houghton in 1866, was a best-seller. In its preface, Carpenter wrote [and the emphasis is his], "My aim has been throughout these pages to portray *the man* as he was revealed to me, without any attempt at idealization." Carpenter provides a simple, matter-of-fact record of daily experience and observation, fragmentary but true, in all essential particulars of life in the White House as he observed it from February to August 1864.

Carpenter's anecdotes have provided historians many reliable and accurate revelations of Lincoln the man—a man full of brilliance, compassion, humility, and wit. Case in point is his description of the moment when Lincoln signed the document granting emancipation to slaves then held in the rebel states. In modern times, when presidents sign an important document, it is a "photo op" or "photo opportunity." When Lincoln officially signed the *Emancipation Proclamation* at noon on New Year's Day, 1863, no photographer, like Matthew Brady, or reporter, like Noah Brooks, was summoned. Very quietly and without fanfare, Lincoln placed his signature on the document in the presence of only Secretary of State William Seward and Seward's son, Frederick. Through Carpenter's book, it is revealed that when Lincoln went to write his name, he held the steel pen with a well-chewed wooden handle for a moment, and then dropped the pen down. He explained that for the past three hours he had been shaking hands in a presidential New Year's Day "open house" receiving line and could barely feel the pen in his hand. Suffering from the occupational hazard of an accessible president, he expressed his concern: "If my name ever goes into history it will be for this act, and my whole soul is in it. If my hand trembles when I sign the Proclamation, all who examine the document hereafter will say, 'He has hesitated.'" In a while, he picked up the pen, and with firm deliberation wrote "Abraham Lincoln," not his customary "A. Lincoln." Then, looking up with a smile, he said, "That will do." Thus, Carpenter revealed Lincoln the man to be concerned about the judgment of history, at the moment he became the "Great Emancipator."

That evening, again related by Carpenter, Lincoln shared with Congressman Schuyler Colfax his concern that "three hours' handshaking is not calculated to improve a man's chirography [penmanship]." Then, changing to a tone of steady resolve, Lincoln was said to have continued, "The South had fair warning, that if they did not return to their duty, I should strike at this pillar of their strength. The promise must now be kept, and I shall never recall one word."

Carpenter's book reveals, too, the mercy and compassion of Lincoln. When court-martial cases came across his desk requiring the death sentence, Lincoln, as noted by Carpenter, was inclined "to pardon or commute the majority." Carpenter cited Judge-Advocate-General Holt's impression: "The President is without exception the most tender-hearted man I ever knew." One particularly interesting example of Presidential clemency was provided by a letter to Carpenter, and he chose to include its content in his book. It seems that a 23-year-old soldier, Lorenzo Stewart (alias Shear) from Utica, New York—"scarcely more than a boy"—in September of 1863 mustered in as a Private in the 76th New York Regiment. By April 1864, Stewart, now absorbed into the 14th New York Volunteer Artillery, was detained in the military prison camp at Elmira, New York. Charged with multiple attempts at desertion and with the murder of one of his guards by poison, he was sentenced to death and his gibbet was erected. An appeal was made to Secretary of War Edwin Stanton, but he refused to listen. This was, in Stanton's opinion, a case of a hard-core criminal. The boy's mother then appeared before President Lincoln. Upon examining the record, Lincoln told her he concurred with the Secretary of War and that there was nothing he could do. Finally, the assistance of Judge Ira Harris, Senator of New York State, was sought. He prevailed upon the President at the Executive Mansion around midnight, only hours from the scheduled time of execution. Lincoln got up from bed to meet Harris, who explained that the boy was "of unsound mind." Because of insanity, he was not responsible for his actions. Harris did not ask for a pardon but only a reprieve "until a proper medical examination could be made." Finding this reasonable, Lincoln ordered a stay of execution immediately by telegram to Elmira and ordered Dr. John P. Gray of Utica to be commissioned to assess the boy's mental health. Clashing with the direct orders of the Secretary of War, Lincoln, according to Carpenter, "sent no less than *four* [emphasis is Carpenter's] different reprieves, by different lines, to different individuals in Elmira, so fearful was he that the message would fail, or be too late." The boy was saved "from being executed the next day at dawn." On January 25, 1865, Lincoln commuted Stewart's sentence to "imprisonment in the Penitentiary at hard labor for ten years."

According to Carpenter's observations, it would appear that Lincoln possessed what is now called a "photographic memory." He marveled at Lincoln's ability to recite lengthy poems from memory as well as whole passages from *Hamlet* and other works of Shakespeare. In spite of "the multitude of visitors" seen daily by this most accessible of Presidents, Carpenter was "often amazed at the readiness with which he recalled faces and events and even names." A man he had not seen for twelve years presumed the President could not recall his name. Lincoln, in good humor, responded, "Your name is Flood . . . I am glad to see that the *Flood* flows on."

Scattered all through Carpenter's recollections are examples of Lincoln's remarkable sense of humor. Throughout his lifetime, Lincoln demonstrated an ability to commit to memory funny anecdotes. These stories and his own wit were useful upon many an occasion: to put off an irate politician, to socially put someone at ease, or to clinch a point in a lawyerly fashion, such as in Carpenter's famous account of the group that came to the White House just before the fall of Vicksburg. The group urged the President to remove General Grant from his command because of his fondness for whiskey. Lincoln is said to have replied, "By the way, gentlemen, can either of you tell me where General Grant procures his whiskey? Because, if I can find out, I will send every general in the field a barrel of it!"

"In a corner of his desk," wrote Carpenter of Lincoln, "he kept a copy of the latest humorous work; and it was his habit when greatly fatigued, annoyed, or depressed, to take this up and read a chapter, frequently with great relief." Carpenter found that the President had a distinctive laugh: "The 'neigh' of a wild horse on his native prairie is not more undisguised and hearty." During the dark days of the war, a group was waiting to be admitted to see the President when the unmistakable "neigh" could be heard through the partition. One in the group remarked, "That laugh has been the President's life-preserver!" For Lincoln, humor was a "tool" for maintaining his mental health while checking the lengthening mortality lists of a four-year Civil War.

As for Lincoln's physical health, Carpenter expressed surprise at how the President sustained his life, for he noted that it seemed there were weeks in which "he neither ate nor slept," and the President admitted that no amount of rest or recreation "seemed . . . to reach the *tired* spot." Furthermore, Carpenter noted the total disregard Lincoln showed toward his own bodily safety. The President voiced objection to escorts accompanying him on his travels, and he wanted no guards posted outside the Executive Chamber. A Colonel Halpine observed "the utterly unprotected condition of the President's person, and the fact that any assassin or maniac, seeking his life, could enter his presence without the interference of a single armed man to hold him back." When questioned about the wisdom of taking no precautions, Lincoln simply shrugged it off by saying rather prophetically, "if there were such a plot, and they wanted to get at me, no vigilance could keep them out."

The President was the recipient of much hate mail, including death threats. Unnerving as it would seem to be, Lincoln confided to Carpenter how he came to deal with such letters:

> Soon after I was nominated at Chicago, I began to receive letters
> threatening my life. The first one or two made me a little uncomfortable,
> but I came at length to look for a regular installment of this kind of
> correspondence in every week's mail. . . . It is no uncommon thing to receive
> them now; but they have ceased to give me any apprehension. Oh, there
> is nothing like getting *used* to things!

In the same way, Lincoln dealt with the barrage of words his many critics fired at him in the newspapers and through the mail. Through Carpenter, Lincoln's classic philosophy made it into print:

> If I were to try to read, much less answer, all the attacks made on me, this
> shop might as well be closed for any other business. I do the very best I

know how—the very best I can; and I mean to keep doing so until the end. If the end brings me out all right, what is said against me won't amount to anything. If the end brings me out wrong, ten angels swearing I was right would make no difference.

Carpenter had critics, too, and not just art critics. When Carpenter's publishers decided in 1867 to issue a new printing of his memoir under the title *The Inner Life of Abraham Lincoln,* Mrs. Lincoln had harsh words: "To think of this stranger, silly adventurer, daring to write a work entitled, 'The Inner Life of Abraham Lincoln.' Each scribbling writer, almost strangers to Mr. L., subscribe themselves his most intimate friend!" And this was from the same woman who just a year earlier had given Carpenter a memento of the late President as a Christmas present—what she said was a "very plain cane . . . handled by *him*" and inscribed with the President's name.

Praise for *The Inner Life of Abraham Lincoln* did come, however, from one reputable literary figure in 1868. Charles Dickens and Carpenter met for the first time on April 18, 1866. Horace Greeley of the New York *Tribune* feted Dickens at a dinner at Delmonico's in New York City. Among the twenty-four invited guests were the cartoonist Thomas Nast and the artist/biographer, Francis B. Carpenter. On his second tour of America in 1868, Dickens wrote to Carpenter on February 15 from Westminster Notch, NY. The great English author thanked him for the book and commented:

> It has interested me exceedingly. I sat down quietly to
> read some pages of it, an hour after I arrived here: and
> the book did not leave my hand until I had read it
> through to the last word. Believe me, Dear Sir,
> Faithfully yours—Charles Dickens

This was a well-deserved accolade for a painter/biographer of Lincoln who had first learned to draw and write as a child born, raised, and educated in the Town of Homer, New York. This is no "supposed Lincoln connection." It is a documented connection that gives the village of Homer a solid, justifiable claim to calling itself "Historic Homer."

If anyone wishes to question how I have performed my duties as a municipal historian or wishes to challenge anything I have written about Carpenter, Stoddard, DeVoe, or any other individual who ever lived in the town or village of Homer, please feel free to make an appointment. A frank and civil discussion is always welcomed.

October 24, 2019

THE HOMER NATIONAL BANK

This writer can remember when the present-day Key Bank on Main Street was the Homer National Bank, and it took up all the space now occupied by Key Bank and the History Center. As a youngster I could sit on a wooden bench inside the bank and marvel at the mural on the south wall of nineteenth century Homer (now at the History Center) while my mother did her banking at the long counter of tellers along the north wall.

Many years later, when researching about the artist Francis B. Carpenter, I learned that on September 23, 1851, Carpenter wrote a letter to Mr. Dalrymple, a dentist in Homer. He wished to ascertain how receptive some of the leading men in Homer might be to a proposal conceived collaboratively with his life-long friend, Fessenden N. Otis, the one who had first introduced his classmate to the world of art. The plan called for painting *A View of Homer* from up on East Hill for the purpose of engraving and publishing. Otis did the painting, and a lithograph was made of it by Endicott and Company of New York City. From that a photomural was later made in 1946 by Drix Duryea, Inc. of New York for the wall of the bank in Homer. Today, it is most apropos that the 22 foot by 7-foot mural depicting the Village of Homer in 1852 graces the south wall of the Homer History Center at Key Bank in the heart of the Historic District. I still marvel at the mural and how its artist, as a Homer lad, had once inspired Carpenter, another Homer lad, to become an artist, too. It is fun to connect the historical dots.

The early history of the Homer National Bank founded in 1884 appears on the front page of *The Homer Post* for Friday, May 10, 1935, along with other "Highlights of the First Century of Village History." Here is that article:

"A new venture when Homer observed its fiftieth birthday, the Homer National Bank passed its 51st birthday on March 29 [1935]. The first report of conditions for the comptroller of currency in 1884 showed deposits of $1,542.24. The report recently published in The Post showed deposits of $1,275,590.98; capital of $200,000 and total resources of $1,583,904.88.

The late E. G. Ranney was temporary chairman of the meeting held for organization. The bank was first located in the store of George W. Phillips just south of the home of Jesse Jennison. The present building was started the same year.

Mr. Phillips was first president of the bank. The original directors included—Mr. Phillips, J. H. Tripp, Vernon Stone, J. Hill, Mr. Ranney, A. H. Bennett, F. Pierce, M. Van Hoesen, H. Kinney, C. O. Newton, and C. Gay.

James H. Tripp was the first cashier but was replaced soon by Mr. Bennett. Julius S. Pomeroy was the first bookkeeper. Of all the original directors, officers and employees, Mr. Pomeroy is the only survivor. He is now vice-president of the First National Bank and Trust Company of Minneapolis, Minn.

Presidents of the bank in order of service, have been: Mr. Phillips, William H. Crane, A. H. Bennett, George A. Brockway, Randolph H. Miller, and F. R. Thompson. Mr. Thompson has served since 1929.

The cashiers have been: James H. Tripp, Mr. Bennett and C. S. Pomeroy and James E. Ogden. The last three have served over fifty years. Mr. Ogden took the position in 1917.

In 1900 the First National Bank (organized in 1878) and the Homer National were merged and Mr. Crane, cashier of the First National was elected president.

The banking quarters were remodeled in 1921, the space being nearly doubled and a new vault constructed. During this period, business was carried on in the John Briggs block [now the branch office of First National Bank of Dryden] across the street with the money, valuables and books transferred each day under police guard.

W. H. Newcomb who died last year was the last survivor of the original stockholders. Mr. Ranney was a director for 41 years. R. H. Miller was vice-president from 1917 until his untimely death in 1929.

George A. Brockway has served on the board of directors for 45 years. O. B. Andrews has served for 40 years, F. R. Thompson for 32 years. Other directors are: H. K. Alexander, H. H. Blackman, William G. Crandall, H. H. Jones, H. D. Lucy, R. V. Miller, J. E. Ogden and William H. Webster."

This is a reminder of the importance for every organization in the community to keep a record of its institutional history so future residents can understand the origins, growth, and key players in the organization.

The writer of this column is grateful to Shirley Clark for the donation of the local newspaper of 1935 commemorating the hundredth anniversary of the incorporation of the Village of Homer.

November 7, 2019

OUTRAGE OVER CONSTRUCTION OF HOMER TOWN HALL

Several months ago, Russ Darr of Homer brought to my attention an interesting set of copies of letters. They were discovered among the personal effects of the late Anna Hilton of Homer. These were Xerox copies of carbon copies of correspondence sent by the architectural firm of Pierce & Bickford in

Elmira in the spring of 1908 to various persons in Homer. The topic was the proposed building of the Homer Town Hall, which was to be jointly used by the Town and the Village.

Pierce & Bickford was the architecture partnership of Joseph H. Pierce (born 1855) and H. H. Bickford (born 1863). The Elmira firm was active during 1890–1930 and specialized in residential homes and churches. Several of their works are listed on the U.S. National Register of Historic Places. The two were among the co-founders of the Chemung County Historical Society.

The copies of the letters from Pierce & Bickford to Homer were provided Mrs. Hilton on July 20, 1977, by a Tania Werbewsky. Ms. Werbewsky came across the letters in the "Letter books of Pierce & Bickford," Book #32 (Feb. 14, 1908–June 9, 1908) located in the Regional Archives collection of Olin Library at Cornell University. This cache included 51 letter books of outgoing letters and 131 letter boxes of incoming letters. Unfortunately, the incoming letters included no letters to the architectural firm from Homer, but the letters sent to Homer reveal a previously unknown (at least to me) kerfuffle that existed over the architect chosen to construct Homer's Town Hall.

The first letter is dated March 24, 1908 and was drafted by Bickford. It was sent to Mr. Geo. A. Brockway of Homer, who was then serving as the President [Mayor] of the Village. Brockway is informed: "When the writer met four members of the Committee [on Town Hall] in Homer recently, they all agreed that our drawings were the best and the design the most satisfactory of any, but expressed themselves as doubtful as to whether it could be built for the money, their opinions being based, as they stated, upon the opinions of alleged architects, who had submitted sketches in competition, and who had stated that our design could not be carried out within the appropriation . . ."

The letter goes on to indicate that the competing architects had reported that the Pierce & Bickford design was flawed. They claimed, "the water from the roof could not be carried down inside the building, without causing trouble" and "a parapet could not be used around the roof, because it would be necessary to shovel the snow off." Pierce & Bickford claimed these assertions to be ridiculous. To prove it, they stated they had invited the Homer Committee to Elmira and showed them buildings with parapets "which have required no man to go on the roof since they were constructed" and that the water is carried down pipes inside "as it is in every modern building, and never causes the slightest trouble." Furthermore, the Elmira architects claimed to have shown the Committee "better buildings than they had contemplated building" for the same amount of money the Town had appropriated. They said they had told the Committee that they had never failed to construct a building within the designated appropriation and the estimate provided. The letter stated, "This seemed to be satisfactory to [the Committee], but what has transpired since, we know not, but we note that the Cortland papers report the employment of a Syracuse architect."

The letter concludes by stating "we never enter into a competition" and our employment is "conditioned on the appropriation being carried" as the firm maintains was the case with Homer. The firm advised that the matter had been turned over to its legal counsel, and it was necessary for the firm "to get copies of the resolution showing the powers of the Committee to act."

On the same day that Bickford dictated this letter, he dictated and sent a shorter letter to Mr. William H. Foster of Homer. Foster was one of five individuals appointed to supervise the construction project. The other members of the Committee were F. M. Briggs, W. A. Coon, S. F. Andrews, and D. N. Hitchcock. The letter Foster received stated, "We are astonished to note by Cortland Newspaper report that your Committee has commissioned a Syracuse architect to furnish architectural services for the Homer Town Hall" when "we were employed" to furnish such services, and "we stand ready to perform our part of the agreement." The letter closed with this question: "We would respectfully inquire whether your Committee proposes to evade your contract with us, and if so, upon what grounds?"

Next, there is an eight-page letter dated April 9, 1908, dictated by Bickford and sent to Attorney Riley Champlin, legal counsel to the Town of Homer. The letter details the firm's transactions with the Committee in Homer. Starting with a visit by Bickford to the Homer National Bank on March 12, 1907, at the invitation of Brockway, the firm submitted a series of three design sketches. The first was for a building to house the fire department and municipal offices. The firm agreed that if the appropriation for the project was defeated in a public vote, "we were to have no remuneration for our services." If the appropriation carried, "we were to be employed as architects for the proposed building."

After a second meeting in Homer on May 13, 1907, involving Town Supervisor Melvin J. Pratt, Brockway, and others, the firm submitted new sketches. These were to accommodate a change in the building lot. By a letter dated August 13th from W. H. Foster, the firm learned that the proposed Town Hall would not include the fire department. A third sketch was now needed. Bickford indicated confidence that the appropriation for this proposed plan would be carried but requested $100.00 as partial payment for services rendered thus far.

The firm pointed out that at no time during these correspondences or trips to Homer was a "competition" mentioned. According to the firm, by the winter of 1908 they learned from the newspaper that sketches from other firms were being submitted. This caused the Committee to be invited to Elmira and all objections and concerns about the firm's design were unanimously dropped by the Committee. The Committee members praised the superiority of the design, were impressed that the firm "had designed an absolutely fireproof school building . . . in Cortland," and "stated unanimously that they should employ [Pierce & Bickford]."

This lengthy letter of April 9, 1908, continued to explain that "only a short time ago we saw a notice in the Cortland Standard that a Syracuse Architect had been employed, and the building was to be built of concrete blocks made in Syracuse and also of litholite, which is artificial stone, made in Syracuse." The letter then references the letter of March 24 to Mr. Foster and that no response from Homer was received. Then it was noted that a phone call was made to Mr. Foster, and he admitted a Syracuse architect had been hired but not by unanimous vote of the Committee.

Attorney Champlin is then informed that he needs to provide information on any changes that occurred in personnel of the Homer Committee during the time in question and evidence that the Committee was duly authorized to act. Champlin is cautioned that any attempt to alter or conceal the Minutes or evidence of any fraud or collusion will merit "taking action against the Committee as individuals." The letter goes on to imply that Mr. Brockway "was apparently forced off the Committee" for unknown reasons.

Champlin is then urged "to find out who the local stockholders of the Miracle Concrete Block and Litholite Company of Syracuse are at the present time" and to ascertain a motive for arranging architectural services at the same time as the decision was made as to the building material to be used.

A letter dated April 11, 1908, acknowledges that Champlin sent a letter the day before indicating he had received the lengthy letter from the firm. The April 11th letter states: "We know that you will be able to get at the facts in the case, if anyone possibly can. The first of the week will be all right."

Next in the cache is a five-page letter from Bickford sent to Mr. Briggs, Chairman of the Committee, and to each of the four Committee members. The letter lays out in chronological detail again the firm's position that it was never party to a "competition," that the Committee accepted other sketches from other firms after employing the Elmira firm, and that other architects had been allowed to examine the sketches and to render criticisms "which could only spring from hope of personal profit . . ." The letter charges this to be "a gross breach of professional ethics, which no respectable architect would stoop to under any circumstances . . ." Bickford further complains that weeks have passed without a word from the Homer Committee and this after the firm had expended no less than $350.00 on the project. The firm posits they are "entitled to fair treatment" and that the course of action to be taken by the firm depends entirely on the "attitude" assumed by the Committee "upon receipt of this communication." A stamped envelope was said to be enclosed for reply.

Rather stunning, isn't it? But it does not end here.

A letter to Briggs and the other four Committee members is dated May 4, 1908. It acknowledges the receipt of a letter from the Committee dated April 30th and an enclosed check for $100.00. The letter from Homer is purported to clarify that "this Committee is the only committee that was ever empowered to engage an architect" and that "the original committee had no authority to engage, nor as we understand that they did engage any one for the work." Further, the Homer response asserts "Mr. Brockway and Mr. Foster as members of the original Committee understand that you were to receive the sum of One Hundred Dollars ($100.00) in the event of the last plans submitted not being accepted." This follows with words rejecting the accuracy of the facts as presented by the Committee. Rejected, too, is the $100.00 as complete remuneration for the $350.00 expended to design a $20,000 building as part of what was later found to be "an unprofessional scramble" among competing architects. The firm states "therefore, unless we are remunerated for the actual expenses," attorneys will be instructed to act against the Committee members and the Town of Homer.

Now, a separate letter, also dated May 4th, was sent to Village President George Brockway. He is informed of the action taken by the firm but is told "please do not take this as a personal matter, as we are not aiming in your direction, and we certainly appreciate the fair and honorable way, in which you treated us while you were on this committee." He is also told that the firm has no desire of "letting up" on the present committee until the people of Homer know the steps that were initially taken toward building a Town Hall. If they should approve, "they certainly cannot object to publicity, and we think we are in a position to give enough information to make it fairly interesting reading."

How did Mr. Brockway respond? That is not totally clear. All we know is that the Elmira firm did acknowledge a "kind letter of May 5th" from the Village president and stated, "We certainly are not looking for any unnecessary trouble with the committee on Homer Town Hall." Bickford agreed to come to Homer to see Brockway who had offered "assistance to adjust this matter in an equitable manner." Does that mean the remainder of the $350.00 in expenses was paid? If so, by whom?

The exact nature of the resolution of the issue is not clear. Litigation is not noted in either the Town's or the Village's Minutes. All we know for sure is the following: Sixty-year-old Charles F. Colton of Syracuse was the architect selected, beating out the plans submitted by architects from Elmira, Binghamton, New York, and Syracuse. He was a prominent designer whose buildings in Syracuse still stand, including City Hall. Ground for the Town Hall's foundation was broken on May 20, 1908, and "Miracle" cement blocks were used in the construction. The blocks were cast in Syracuse by the "Miracle" Cement Block Manufacturing Company. The company's business manager, E. C. Ide, had come to Homer to tout the block's many points of superiority over other makes of cement work. We, also, know two more things. After one hundred ten years, the Homer Town Hall is still standing. And sometimes, documents surface that shed light on the trials and tribulations that can be part of public administration . . . if only behind the scenes. As Pierce & Bickford noted in 1908, there can be "enough information to make it fairly interesting reading."

November 21, 2019

DISORDERLY CONDUCT IN WINTERS OF YESTERYEAR

The season of holidays is fast approaching. Halloween has passed which means, in short order, Thanksgiving, Christmas, Chanukah, and New Year's Day will be here. And that will next bring Old Man Winter breathing icy air down our necks. Diversions will be found to get us through the cold and snow. Winter Fest and ice skating on the Green will be among the activities to be enjoyed. Back in 1906, according to the Village Minutes, some wintertime activities were frowned upon. Case in point is this small poster fastened into the bound volume of Minutes:

ORDINANCE

Against Snow Balling,

Catching Rides and

Skating on Side Walks

At a regular meeting of the board of Trustees of the Village of Homer, held on the 6th day of December, 1906, the following ordinances were adopted by said Board, and ordered entered on the minutes of said meeting, and published and posted according to law, and to take effect on the 24th day of December, 1906.

FIRST: Snow Balling—All persons are hereby forbidden from snowballing within the corporate limits of the Village of Homer. Every person violating this ordinance shall be liable to a penalty of $1.00 for each and every offense.

SECOND: Catching Rides—All persons are forbidden from getting on or off [street] cars while in motion, and from getting on or off any teams [of horses] or vehicles of any name or nature while in motion, within the corporate limits of the Village of Homer. Every person violating this ordinance shall be liable to a penalty of $1.00 for each and every offense.

THIRD: Skating on Sidewalks—All persons are hereby forbidden from skating, sliding or coasting upon any of the sidewalks or cross walks within the corporate limits of the Village of Homer. Every person violating this ordinance shall be liable to a penalty of $1.00 for each and every offense.

FOURTH: Misdemeanor—It is further ordained that a violation of any of the foregoing ordinances, or any of the provisions thereof, shall constitute disorderly conduct, and any person violating the same, or any of the provisions thereof, shall be a disorderly person and shall be dealt with according to the provisions of the Village law of the State of New York, applicable thereto.

Dated, Homer, N. Y., December 6th, 1906.
By order of the Board of Trustees,
C. O. Newton, President

L. P. MERRILL, Clerk.

The above ordinance in 1906 must have been deemed necessary to deal with a problematic issue in the village. The culprits most likely were young people and matters of safety were of concern. Note, too, that the ordinance was to be enforced starting on Christmas Eve Day, which must have been a dubious holiday present for the Chief of Police and local constables charged with dealing with "disorderly persons." The enforcers of the law may have already had their hands full dealing with older citizens of the community, since the next regular meeting of the Board on January 4, 1907, reveals the following action taken:

> "On motion the Chief of Police was instructed to notify the hotel and saloon keepers to comply with the Sunday and night closing laws and enforce the same."

Oh, what an unruly lot our forebears must have been, especially when it came to wintertime diversions!

December 5, 2019

VILLAGE ORDINANCES IN 1897

My column in the last issue of this paper, you may recall, was focused on some wintertime public behaviors that were prohibited in the Village of

Homer in the early twentieth century. The topic peaked my curiosity about other ordinances enacted a tad earlier in the 1890s. I was not disappointed. I came across forty-one ordinances that were all to take effect the first of June 1897. The bulk of these ordinances are described below. They reveal much about the culture (way of life) and especially the norms and mores of good behavior of the community in that era.

The mayor was called "The President of the Board of Trustees" in the 1890s and was designated the head of the police department. He "shall from time to time take such measures as he may deem necessary for the preservation of peace and good order" and the enforcement of village ordinances. It was considered the duty of all persons in the village, if called upon for assistance by any police officer, to "promptly aid and assist him." Failure to comply could mean a fine "not exceeding $25." Refusal to obey the orders of the Chief Engineer or Assistant Engineer at any fire in the village was punishable by a $5 fine.

Any person participating in "any improper noise, riot, disturbance or breach of the peace . . . to the annoyance or disturbance of the village or travelers, shall be subject to a fine of $5." The fine was double for anyone who disturbed an assembly for religious worship "by making a noise, or by rude and indecent behavior, or by profane language, within the place of worship, or so near the same as to disturb the order and solemnity of the meeting . . ." Any person found to be intoxicated within the village limits was "subject to a fine of not less than $3 nor more than $10" and would be detained by the police constables until a justice of the peace could be found to hear the case.

The making of a bonfire on the public Park [Green] could result in "a fine of $2 for each offense." Playing ball on the public Park or on any street was forbidden as was the use of the Park and streets "as play-grounds for any purpose." Riding or driving a horse or horses across the Park was expressly forbidden, "except to pass along the roadway commencing at the N.E. corner of said Park and running thence west to and along the south side of the building known as Homer Academy, and from the south side of said Academy building south along the roadway to Cayuga street . . ." [Today the one-way street is paved and officially known as Central Park Place.]

Expressly prohibited was permitting your "cattle, horses, sheep, swine or geese to run at large" within the village limits. Each offense could set you back $1. In addition, "the excretion of any horse, cow, ox or other cattle upon any sidewalk" would be deemed "a public nuisance," and the owner of the offending animal was to remove the excrement "at once" or be penalized $1 for each offense. There was no mention of dogs running loose or leaving feces on sidewalks or neighbors' properties.

If one was found guilty of keeping or maintaining a "place for the purpose of prostitution" or for the purpose of gaming or gambling, the fine was to be $25. Further, any person found guilty of "vulgar, profane or obscene language or conduct in any street or public place in the village" would be subject to a fine of $3 for each offense.

The sum of $30 was to be exacted from anyone who failed to obtain a license from the President of the Board of Trustees (the price of which was set by the Board) before exhibiting for money "any theatrical representation, caravan, circus, feats of horsemanship, or natural or artificial curiosity."

A license was to be procured, too, by any person or business located outside the village limits before selling, peddling, or soliciting "for the retail sale of groceries, dry goods, tea, coffee or meat, or any other merchandise." Excluded from this ordinance were any farmers selling produce of their own farms within the village. Included in this prohibition was the auctioning of any merchandise within the village limits.

Any physician practicing in the village who found one of his patients to be harboring an "infectious, contagious or pestilential disease" was required to report the existence of such a disease within twenty-four hours to one of the Village Trustees. Negligence in doing so meant forfeiting the sum of $10. Anyone who was not a resident of the village and found to have an infectious or pestilential disease was to leave the village within twenty-four hours upon notice provided by a Village Trustee. Failure to leave meant a fine of $25 and an additional $10 for each succeeding twenty-four hours of non-compliance. Question to consider here: Would a quarantine of the ill individual have been better than sending him/her forth to spread the contagion to other communities?

The penalty was $5 for anyone found to have willfully damaged "any bridge, fence, railing, trees, shrubbery, public or town pumps, ladders, wells, or fixtures" in the village. The same fine applied to anyone causing damage to "any gas-pipe or tube, gas-burner, street lamp or lamp-post" belonging to the Village of Homer.

If you left a horse or team of horses hitched in such a way as to obstruct the free passage of pedestrians along the village's streets, sidewalks or crosswalks, you could face a fine of $2.

All occupants of residences, owners of businesses, and owners of vacant lots were required by 10 o'clock A.M. each morning to remove snow that may have fallen the night before upon any public sidewalks adjacent to or opposite said premises. Any person failing to comply with this ordinance was to be fined the sum of $2.50 and to be liable for any expense incurred by the Village in removing the snow.

Then there was the fine of $1 to be imposed upon any person caught bathing in any stream or pond within the village limits "between the hours of 5 o'clock A.M. and 8 o'clock P.M." So, apparently it was acceptable for someone to bath in these natural waterways say at 4:45 A.M. or 8:15 P.M.

All boys were cautioned to refrain from getting on or off the streetcars while in motion. Failing to obey this ordinance did not carry a fine. The culpable lad was "liable to *arrest and imprisonment* not to exceed ten days." [The emphasis is mine.]

If an individual lodged a complaint with any Village Board Trustee that a train passing through the village caused an obstruction to James, Cayuga, Clinton or Warren Streets for a period of time longer than five minutes, the conductor or engineer of the train would be subject to a penalty not to exceed $10.

The posting of handbills upon any of the shade trees of the village was liable for a $1 penalty for each offense. The wheeling or carting of swill or other garbage on the village sidewalks could be met with the same fine. The riding of bicycles or tricycles "at a rapid rate of speed" upon the village sidewalks or the riding of the same upon the sidewalks "when the highways are in a proper condition for riding thereon" would require the forfeiture of $5 for each and every offense. And anyone caught riding said vehicles on the sidewalks on a Sunday between the hours of 9 A.M. and 2 P.M. would face the same fine.

Anyone found guilty of owning or maintaining a slaughterhouse within the limits of the village without the consent of the Board of Trustees was to be fined $5. The same fine was exacted of anyone throwing into the Tioughnioga River "any offal or dead animal, or spoiled fish, or other impurities."

And finally, no fine or penalty for a violation of these ordinances enacted on May 7th of 1897 was to be remitted without a majority vote of all the Trustees at a regular or special meeting of the Village Board.

The posting of the Ordinances was authorized by William J. Watson, President, and Edward W. Hyatt, Clerk.

Now, the fines cited seem ridiculously low, don't they? You may want to read this article again, keeping in mind that $1 in 1897 is equivalent in purchasing power to about $31.01 in 2019. So, a fine of $30 in 1897 would be roughly equivalent to a fine of $900 today. Would you have liked being a village resident in 1897? What ordinance would you personally have found to be problematic? Would you find the regulations too harsh, not harsh enough, or just right? Do you think folks were economically motivated in 1897 to comply with the Village's ordinances and to behave accordingly?

December 19, 2019

THE EVOLUTION OF FIREFIGHTING IN HOMER

Did you know that Thanksgiving is the single worst day of the year for cooking-related house fires? And that is followed closely by Christmas Day, Christmas Eve, and the day before Thanksgiving. Distracted and unattended cooking is a primary contributor to most Thanksgiving house fires. Learning this information got me to thinking about how our predecessors coped with fires and how our local fire department came into being and has evolved.

Consider for a moment what it was like in Homer when it was just a wilderness and still part of Onondaga County. Roads were mere trails through the dense forest. Fire was humanity's best friend—for heating and cooking—but what did they do when fire became a deadly enemy? You grabbed a bucket of water and attempted to douse the flames. A larger conflagration required several buckets of water being passed from hand to hand. Family and neighbors formed a "bucket brigade" to fight a fire. The fire frequently won such a battle.

In 1815 the citizens of Homer purchased a "squat pump." This was operated by four men. The way it worked was water would be pumped onto the blaze as water was poured in the tub or box. Local homes, shops, grist mills, and sawmills were made of wood. Roofs were hand-split shingles of wood. Lighting was by candles and whale oil lamps. Heat was supplied via fireplaces and wood burning stoves. Opportunities for combustion were plentiful, and water came from the Tioughnioga River or wells. No village water system existed yet. As the population of the community expanded, more squat pumps were needed, and they were placed about to be at the ready.

The Village of Homer was officially incorporated in May of 1835. Two months later, at a special meeting of the Board of Trustees, a decision was made regarding better firefighting. A hand pump with leather hose was to be acquired, along with pike polls and hooks. In addition, they voted to build a suitable building not to exceed $150 in the middle of the Green. This was to accommodate two engines

Over time a hand-pulled apparatus was replaced with the horse-pulled engine, and more efficient equipment for firefighting was introduced. But firefighting, like battling any enemy, requires organization of manpower, not improved equipment alone. In the nineteenth century, the job of fighting fires was the responsibility of the Village Trustees. They appointed citizens to be fire fighters. These individuals did their best, without success, to save a hotel that once stood where the fire station is today. Three grist mills, responsible for turning out 85,000 barrels of floor annually, were lost. Jedediah Barber's Great Western emporium was destroyed by fire in 1856 and later replaced during the Civil War era with the three-story building of brick on Main Street. Fire took a wooden structure named Mechanics Hall. That site is now occupied by the Homer Center for the Arts, formerly a church built of brick.

Better equipment kept on being invented, and in 1873 a mass meeting was held to demand the Trustees do something immediately to acquire a state-of-the-art apparatus. In response, the Gilsby Steam Fire Engine Company of Auburn, New York, brought to Homer a rotary engine on trial. It ran all day at the Pine Street bridge, pumping water through one thousand feet of hose and throwing streams of water to different parts of the Green and even over the Congregational Church steeple. The demonstration was quite impressive—so much so that the people voted to allocate $10,000 for firefighting purposes. After seeing other types and makes of pumps at Albany, Hudson, and Waterford, New York, the Trustees bought the model from Auburn on April 10, 1873, along with two hose carts, one thousand feet of hose, and other accessories. The cost was $5,600, payable over five years. Then, too, cobblestone cisterns, 10 by 20 by 8 feet deep, were to be built at Clinton, James, and Cortland Streets and at the intersection of Cayuga and Cortland Streets. The cost was $175 each, plus an additional $66 for railroad iron. These were installed and ready by July 1, 1873. At the end of the month, a leak in the Cayuga Street cistern meant no water was available for a house fire that broke out. The house burned.

It was shortly after this that the Homer Volunteer Fire Department was organized, with two companies: Tioughnioga Steamer Co. No. 1 and Tioughnioga Hose Co. No. 1. These were composed of the businessmen and more prominent young men of the village. One of Jedediah Barber's grandsons, Samuel McClellan Barber, was elected Chief of the Fire Department. W. H. Harrison Blaney was elected Assistant Chief. John J. Arnold was Secretary, and George W. Cottrell was Treasurer. The Village Trustees appointed Hoel C. Pierce engineer for the steamer at an annual salary of $125. Each of the two Companies had their own officers, headed by a Foreman or Captain.

In 1874, the Fire Department provided uniforms for the men. Thirty men marching in several parades that year were a sight to behold as were the men when they assembled for the funeral of a valued member.

In September of 1877 an independent fire company was formed. This was Tempest Hose Co. No. 2. It was made up of men between the ages of sixteen and twenty who were to help the Fire Department when necessary. They bought some of the old equipment and a discarded hand pumper and was said to be a great asset to the community at the time of disastrous fires. Their first elected officers were: Foreman, George A. Brockway; Assistant Foreman, LeGrand A. Brainard; Secretary, Frank M. Newton; and Treasurer, F. Eugene Stone. When this Company disbanded in 1898, it was known as Tempest Hose Co. No. 3.

By 1878, the village was expanding westward across the railroad tracks. Residents there started complaining of inadequate fire protection because of the distance from the water source—the river. Thus, the decision was made to dig wells for fire use only. One was at the corner of James and Fulton. Another was east of the tracks on Cayuga, and there were others. In the same year, Tempest Hose Co. No. 2 was taken into the Department as a regular company, and the Village saw that they received more equipment. At one point, as West Road (now Route 281) became lined with homes and a Woolen Factory, West Side Hose Company No. 3 had a fire house on the west side of the artery. The structure has since been renovated into a residential dwelling.

Due to some internal discord, Tempest Hose Co. No. 1 split up. One part formed a new company and took the name Tioughnioga Hose Co. No. 2. So, as of 1878, the Homer Fire Department consisted of four companies. At this time, an alarm system was instituted, with different numbers of strokes on the fire bell used to summon the various companies. The system was soon abandoned because some companies felt they were being treated unfairly.

1882 was a busy year. One company changed its name, one disbanded, and two new ones formed. Tempest Hose Co. No. 2 became Tempest Hose Co. No. 3. Tempest Engine Co. No. 4 was created, and Tioughnioga Hose Co. No. 1 disbanded. Members of the latter company formed a new company, the Orient Hook and Ladder Co. No. 5. When their hook and ladder truck, purchased by the Village, finally arrived on September 8, 1882, it was said to be "a gala day."

December 16, 1882 was not a celebratory day in Homer. A disastrous fire caused the demise of P. F. Smith's grocery store. It was reported that "someone goofed" and allowed Company 4's hand engine and some of their leather hose to freeze up. In any time period, winter can be the most difficult season for a fire fighter. Icy temperatures, high winds, and blinding snowstorms present challenges. It was not unusual in such circumstances for non-member citizens to be asked to give a hand. Records indicate that some young men started as "torch boys" with uniforms like those of the firemen they hoped to become. Many a meal prepared for a husband was for naught when a local factory whistle was sounded and a fireman had to dash off to save someone's building from a chimney fire. The fire whistle indicated there was a fire; it did not tell you where the fire was.

In 1884, Homer voted to install a water system. This was about the time that insurance companies were refusing to do business in municipalities with no fire protection. The next year the waterworks were started, mains laid, hydrants put in, pumps installed, and a tank constructed on East Hill. The tank had a single line acting as both supply and offtake, giving a static pressure head downtown of some ninety pounds per square inch. The system was first tested on October 29, 1885. The first fire afterward was in the ceiling and roof of the Homer Wagon Company on Albany Street. Although the men had had little practice in the use of hydrants, it was reported that they put out the fire with only minimal loss.

In 1887, according to the Warden's report, members of the hose companies found it very inconvenient to hang up the hoses at the fire house on James Street, which is now occupied by Heritage Realtors of Central New York. It was recommended that a gas jet be placed up in the tower so the men could see what they were doing.

In 1893, when the Academy on the Green burned, the Fire Department had a hand-drawn hook and ladder truck. Later it was stored in the Village Garage on Fulton Street and fell into disrepair over time. The Department bought its first motorized truck in 1920. It was a chain-driven, high wheeled, hard rubber-tired vehicle manufactured by Brockway Motors. It had to be cranked, and it just had a soda-acid tank. A pump was put on it, and it stayed in service until the motor burned out.

In 1933, the Department built a hook and ladder truck on a Cadillac chassis donated by John Briggs. The 55-foot ladder took three men to lift and five to hoist, using poles that fit into recesses at the top and center. But the single greatest boost to the Department came in June 5, 1941, when the present fire station on Main Street was dedicated. The cost was $60,000.

Through the decades, many prominent men have served as Fire Chiefs and other officers. Names like Darby, Burgett, Riter, Crosley, and Irish, among others, readily come to the minds of those who have lived in Homer for much of their lives. By 1973, a dedicated John T. Allen had been in active service for over fifty years.

Over time, firefighting has improved and become big business, and heavier trucks and more modern equipment have become expensive but necessary. Fire prevention education and rescue are part of the mission today. Training is now mandatory. And the area served by the Homer Fire Department now extends outside the village into surrounding rural territory. One must keep in mind that the Homer Fire Department has always been a volunteer fire department. The department, like those across the nation, is now facing a serious shortage of personnel willing to serve voluntarily. That creates additional burdens going forward.

So, folks, do enjoy this holiday season, but please exercise caution in the kitchen, with the fireplace, with candles and with electrically powered decorations. Failure to do so may put not only you in jeopardy but the volunteer firefighters of Homer who risk life and limb to keep us all safe throughout the years. Let us tip our hats in gratitude to a department that originated 146 years ago and is still going strong!

The major source for this article: Burden, Howard W. "History of the Homer Fire Department" in a booklet prepared in observance of the centennial of the Homer Fire Department and the 80th Annual Central New York's Firemen's Convention held in Homer from July 18–21, 1973. Printed by the Cortland Press.

Image 9.3 The old James Street Firehouse still stands. *Illustration from an old Homer bank calendar archived in Homer Town Hall.*

Chapter 10

Articles of 2020

January 16, 2020

INTERESTING FEATURES OF LIFE IN POST-CIVIL WAR HOMER

How much do you know about activities in Homer after the Civil War? Pouring over the Village Board Minutes for the years 1866 through 1871 allows one to discover some interesting things that went on in the post-Civil War era in Homer. Here are several items for your edification. Does anything surprise you as you read along? Be sure to read to the end where a local lawsuit reached the State Supreme Court. The case and its participants just might astonish you.

1866: On May 4th the Village allocated $800 for the building of bridges on Pine and Wall Streets. These were not the lenticular truss bridges of iron we have today. Those were erected by the Town Government in 1881. No, wood, masonry and paint were called for in 1866 for bridge building.

At the same meeting, funds were provided for a "Lock Up." This term meant a Jail. Later records indicate that local attorney John Patten was paid rent for a "Lock Up" he provided the Village. Perhaps it was an unoccupied horse stable?

It was decided that the gas streetlamps be allowed to burn until half past ten o'clock P.M., and in cases of "Public Exhibitions or services of any kind" the lamps were to be allowed to burn until 11 P.M. The services of a lamplighter were to be secured. The pay was not to exceed six shillings per night. At the next meeting, Board member Alphonso Stone reported that he had engaged William C. Lewis to perform the duties of the Village lamplighter at five shillings per night.

On May 9, Dr. George W. Bradford appeared before the Board and "made some suggestions in regard to what ought to be done to put the Village in a good sanitary condition." On the motion of Charles O. Newton, the Board voted in favor of authorizing Dr. Bradford "to visit each house in town and examine into its sanitary conditions."

On May 28, a poll tax of fifty cents was added to the other taxes imposed upon village residents.

On June 6, the Board voted that the Secretary should "notify the owners or occupants of Mechanics Hall and the Ice House located on James Street to put said premises in a sanitary condition at once."

At the next Board meeting, on June 15th, a vote was passed upon a motion made by John Patten, Esq. that the Board should "prosecute Matilda Lamberson for keeping a house of ill-fame." At the same meeting, Village Clerk Harrison Hoyt was appointed Corporation [i.e. Village] Attorney for the ensuing year. Trustees C. O. Newton and John L. Boorum were appointed as a committee "to act in conjunction with the Corporation Attorney in the prosecution" of Matilda Lamberson. They were ordered to compel Lamberson "to give bonds for her good behavior for the ensuing year."

On July 2, William Haight was granted permission to erect a tent between the Academy and the Congregational-Presbyterian Church on the Green for "the purpose of giving an Exhibition on the 4th Day of July." Three men were appointed as "special policemen" for the Fourth.

On August 7, the Board approved payment of the $4.00 bill submitted by Timothy Burr for cleaning the premises of William Joy.

On October 16, the Board approved removal from the table and payment of a bill for five dollars submitted by John S. Smith "for conveying Cortland Firemen home after the Sherman Buildings burned in 1864." No explanation was given for the long delay in payment.

In November, the Village paid the gas bill for lighting the village streets for the month of August: $57.30.

1867: In February, a bill in the amount of $12.50 was to be paid for care of the Town Clock. This may have been the clock in the Congregational Church steeple. When this writer was a child, he recalls the clock, which worked then and rang out the hours, being called "the Town Clock."

On March 4, the Board authorized the payment of twenty dollars to Harrison Hoyt for his services during the past year as Village Clerk and as Corporate Attorney "in the case of The People vs Lamberson." At the same meeting, a committee was appointed to negotiate with Charles H. Wheadon and Thomas D. Chollar about the matter of widening James Street. The result was $300 being paid to Wheadon and Chollar for the purpose of purchasing land so that the east end of James Street could be widened.

On September 12, the Board directed Street Commissioner Samuel Bean to see that all trees along the streets of the village where there were gaslights be trimmed to a height of at least twelve feet from the ground.

1868: On March 10th, a committee of three—Wheadon, Stone, and Clark—was charged with conferring with the Trustees of the Academy to "ascertain on what terms the main building of Cortland Academy can be purchased to be used as an Engine House and Town Hall." Nothing seems to have come of this endeavor. Instead, the Academy building was demolished and replaced with a new school edifice.

On June 26, the Corporation Attorney was authorized to notify Levi Rockefeller "to put his meat market in a sanitary condition."

At the same time, Trustee Stone was authorized to notify Nelson. G. Burr that "his premises must be cleaned up."

On September 10, Mr. J. R. Dixon and Mr. Wheadon presented a petition setting forth the claim that the building owned and occupied by Nelson G. Burr was "a nuisance by reason of its being a residence and resort of prostitutes and bad characters of both sexes." The petition was referred to Corporate Lawyer Hoyt "for his examination and opinion as to the power of the Board to act." The existence of "houses of ill repute" in Homer may seem scandalous to modern sensibilities, but it should be noted here that women turned to prostitution on a casual or steady basis as a survival strategy in a sex segregated labor market that paid women perilously low wages, or in response to family disruptions such as paternal or spousal abandonment. Though there were risks of disease, harassment by law enforcement, and unintended pregnancy, prostitution could be profitable, and it provided some women with a path towards economic independence at a time of limited economic opportunities for females.

1869: On April 7th, the Board voted to notify the owners of the plank road between Homer and Cortland to put the road in good order within the Village of Homer or "to give up their pretended rights to control any portion of the street." The plank road had previously been deemed a nuisance.

On September 6th, $30 was to be paid to architect George Almy for the lettering of the corner stone of the new Academy that had been constructed upon the Green.

1870: On March 18, the Board accepted Mr. William Wakeley's proposition "to wind and keep in repair the Town Clock . . . for the sum of $15 per year . . ."

On July 16, Newell Jones and Moses Gale were directed to visit the "Village Green" and to report "any trespasses thereon." If they were unable to attend to it, the President [Mayor] was authorized to "appoint other parties." On August 6, the Board appointed Stone, Augustus Kingsbury, and Hoyt "to take counsel in relation to the Village Green."

1871: March 11th, J. M. Coats was to be compensated $5 for making a map of "The Green" to be used "in the case of The Village of Homer vs Wm Ives."

At a meeting of the Village Board on May 26, with all members present, this resolution was passed: "... the Corporation Attorney H. Hoyt be and he is hereby authorized and directed to commence an action in the name of the Village of Homer against The First Religious Society of Homer to restrain the members of said society from building or grading a road on or across the public Park or Green and he is further directed to prosecute said action to judgment and procure a decision as to the legal rights of the respective parties, and the Pres't [Mayor] is hereby authorized to employ counsel in this case." Alphonso Stone was the duly elected Village President. The Village Trustees were Augustus H. Kingsbury, Amory W. Hobart, Oliver Glover, and David H. Hannum. On October 3rd, $128.44 was allocated for costs incurred by M. M. Waters in the injunction Suit of Village of Homer vs First Religious Society of Homer.

Unfortunately, the Minutes for the remainder of the year and next year, 1872, are practically indecipherable, but another source does make mention of what happened in 1871 regarding litigation over the Green. While the six-acre Green was deeded to The First Religious Society in 1805 for religious and educational purposes (thirty years before the Village was incorporated), down through time the piece of real estate was permitted to be put to public use. This included drills and practices conducted by the early Fire Department, exercises conducted by the local Militia, public exhibitions, and musical concerts on a Village-owned bandstand. According to Howard Burden's brief history of the fire department (1973),

> Because of this public use, and the fact that records were seldom seen ... the village assumed it owned the Green and it took a State Supreme Court decision in 1871 stating that the First Religious Society had title thereto by Fee Simple, in perpetuity.

Thus, today the Village is the steward of the historic Green, but The First Religious Society owns it and determines its use. There are some today who object to the heart of the Historic District being called "the Village Green," when it is not the Village's Green. At one time, the Native Americans who hunted through this region would have been surprised by the European notion of land ownership. For them, land was owned by the Great Spirit, and humans merely its temporary stewards.

So, the Village Board continues to take actions it deems to be in the best interests of the health, security, and economic interests of the community just as the Village Board did in the post-Civil War era. And what will future inhabitants of Homer find surprising about today's Municipal actions and our lifestyle?

January 30, 2020

ALBERT BIGELOW: THE MUGWUMP MINISTER

The present Congregational Church building was constructed in 1863 and dedicated on July 14, not long after the battle of Gettysburg was fought. The pastor at the time was Rev. Albert Bigelow. He served in Homer from 1858 to 1863 and resided in the house just west of what was then Watts Barber's house. The house is the one at No. 27 Clinton Street. He was, to say the least, an interesting person. He was an accomplished artist, poet, musician, historian, and preacher—sort of a "Renaissance man." He, also, was part of a group of prominent clergymen who later called out Presidential candidate Grover Cleveland for a sex scandal. This is Bigelow's story.

Albert was born in Stafford, NY (east of Batavia), on October 11, 1827, to Samuel and Maria Bigelow. He graduated Yale Divinity School in 1852 and married Maria Storrs the next year on April 18. During his senior year at Yale he was director of the Beethoven Society, of which all the best singers of the college were said to be members. He was also one of the editors of the Yale Literary Magazine—"Yale Lit.," as it was familiarly known.

As a painter, he rendered four of the portraits now hanging in the gallery of the Buffalo Historical Society; they are the portraits of Judge Samuel Wilkeson, Judge Joseph C. Masten, Samuel A. Bigelow and Lucius Storrs. Perhaps, his best success in painting was a portrait of the novelist James Fenimore Cooper. From a daguerreotype of him, and two or three paintings of him by well-known artists, and from what he said he imagined Cooper "ought to look like" through acquaintance with his literary works, Bigelow painted what was accepted by the Cooper family as "the best likeness of the novelist."

As a historian, he served as the secretary of the Buffalo Historical Society and contributed several important papers to the archives there. Three sons operated the Bigelow Brothers printing house—Allen, Walter, and Lucius Seymour (who was born in Homer September 6, c. 1859)—and when they conceived and carried out the publication of the Society's papers, it was their father who did the daunting task of thoroughly editing the two volumes.

Though the bulk of his sixty-five years were spent in or near Buffalo, he did serve as a minister in North Bergen, NY; Brooklyn; Homer; Jackson, Michigan; and Silver Creek, NY. He was pastoring in Homer when the Civil War broke out. On the afternoon of Monday, April 22, 1861, there was a "packed" meeting at Wheadon Hall on Main Street in Homer. The purpose was to support the local men who had shown up to organize Company D of the 12th New York Regiment to preserve the Union "at any cost." A band played "Yankee Doodle" as names were called to sign up for service.

An immense send-off meeting was held the next Wednesday at the old wooden Congregational Church that students of the Academy referred to as "God's Old Barn" and was soon to be replaced with an edifice of brick. The highlight of the program came when Rev. Albert Bigelow stood to address the volunteer soldiers and to present them with the national flag draped over the pulpit from which he spoke. When he directly asked Captain Stone and his men if the coming horrors of war would deter them in performing their duties as soldiers in a noble cause, they shouted in unison, "No!" The minister continued, "in the name then of the ladies of Homer, I commit to you this flag; and I charge you not to dishonor it." Then, Bigelow asked to speak directly to two in the assemblage—his wife Maria's brothers, Lucius and Origen Storrs. Oddly, he began to lecture them about honoring their ancestors who had fought in both the Revolution and the War of 1812. "Remember too," he added, "your sister, the wife of my heart, and let your conduct be such as will not discredit them." The Homer *Republican* newspaper reported that "many eyes were moistened during this part of the exercise."

However, in the anniversary sermon of July 14, 1963, delivered in the Homer Congregational Church by Rev. James H. Russell, we learn that "while the Trustees were building the [new] church the Deacons were dealing with their minister." It seems "at the Annual meeting in 1863 there was some misunderstanding, so that Mr. Bigelow resigned in the spring, and was dismissed in October, three months after the dedication." The noted theologian and abolitionist Theodore Munger was Bigelow's classmate at Yale, and he attempted to explain that Bigelow was "versatile, brilliant, successful, except that he spread himself over too wide a variety of work" both in college and during his ministry in Homer. "He loved his violin, and he paid the penalty." His sermons were written in great haste and failed to leave a "strong and definite impression," unlike the exhortation of the troops he gave in 1861. Munger credited Bigelow with broadening "the channels of human interests in a community that required such an influence in order to keep abreast of the age," but he was "a man of rather too fine a nature for the rough and tumble of everyday life." Bigelow, in modern parlance, was "not a fit," or as Munger put it, "Homer never quite understood him."

An increasing deafness forced Bigelow to give up pastoral duties, and in 1869 the family returned to Buffalo. Later he accepted resident charge of the Congregational Church at North Evans, a few miles west of Buffalo, where he remained until poor health overtook him. He died in Harrisburg, PA, on June 7, 1892, at the home of his son Lucius Seymour Bigelow. He was returned to Buffalo for burial in Forest Lawn Cemetery.

Of special note is the role Bigelow played in 1884 during a tumultuous run for the Presidency of the United States by Buffalo's former mayor and the state's governor, Stephen Grover Cleveland. Cleveland was a genial, burly, mustachioed bachelor, attorney, and son of a Presbyterian minister. His father died when he was sixteen, and it fell to Grover to provide for his mother and some of his eight siblings. As Democratic governor he challenged the Tammany Hall political machine and opposed the corrupt spoils system. A reputation for personally being a straight arrow stood in marked contrast to his Republican challenger for the Presidency, James G. Blaine. Blaine had better political credentials—Speaker of the House, senator, and Secretary of State—but had a tarnished reputation as "Slippery Jim." The Democrats called him "Blaine, Blaine, James G. Blaine, continental liar from the state of Maine." Even the famous cartoonist Thomas Nast unmercifully lampooned him in the papers.

Then, several days after Cleveland's nomination at the Democratic Party convention, the bombshell hit. The *Buffalo Evening Telegraph* published an exposé based on information brought forward by the Reverend George H. Ball of the Hudson Street Baptist Church, a staunch Republican crusader for morals and decency. Titled "A Terrible Tale: A Dark Chapter in a Public Man's History," the article alleged Cleveland had fathered an illegitimate child, had refused to marry the mother, and had been paying the mother for nine years to keep her quiet. After the birth of the child, the mother was admitted under murky circumstances to a local asylum for the insane. Doctors from that institution, when interviewed by the press during the 1884 campaign, corroborated her insistence that she was not, in fact, in need of committing. She was released. And the child was placed in an orphanage for a while. Republican newspapers eagerly picked up on the tawdry tale, and Blaine's supporters started up a jeer of their own: "Ma, Ma, where's my pa?"

Bigelow was one of a group of ministers who publicly opposed Cleveland in 1884 because of the revealed salacious account involving the 38-year old widow Maria Halpin. The *Owego Evening Blade* of October 31, 1884, reported that Rev. Albert Bigelow had "turned from Cleveland." Bigelow declared he was a "mugwump," i.e. a reform-minded Republican who voted for Cleveland for mayor and governor because of the politician's reputation for being incorruptible, and "intended to vote for him for president until the truth of the damning charges against the Democratic candidate became irrefutably convincing."

What happened next became a textbook example of crisis management. Cleveland himself made no attempt to deny the charges. He had accepted responsibility for the child and had helped in naming him—Oscar Folsom Cleveland. He had paid for the support of the mother and child. He instructed his aides to "tell the truth" and to refrain from mudslinging. When a packet of papers impugning Blaine's personal life was offered to him, Cleveland paid for it, then shredded and burned the papers without reading them.

The event that many agree was the deciding factor in the election was a last minute Republican rally in New York City. One of the speakers, Presbyterian minister Samuel D. Burchard, called the Democrats "the party of rum,

Romanism, and rebellion." In other words, drunkenness, Catholicism, and Confederate ideals. This was said right in front of Blaine, who didn't think to respond to the slur about Catholicism at a rally full of Irish Catholics. This would cost Blaine votes.

The campaign was ugly, and the election was tight. The voters were torn. Who was the more trustworthy candidate to vote for? Who was the lesser of two evils? Cleveland did not carry his hometown of Buffalo. He carried New York State by a mere 1,047 votes and won with 219 electoral votes to Blaine's 182. He was the first Democrat to occupy the White House since before the Civil War. His jubilant supporters took to the streets, chanting "Ma, Ma, where's my pa? Gone to the White House, ha, ha, ha!" Another celebratory chant by the Democrats was: "Hurray for Maria! Hurray for the kid! I voted for Cleveland, and I'm damned glad I did!" When he ran for President again in 1892, he became the only President elected to two non-consecutive terms.

In the election of 1884, the Mugwumps chose to hold their noses and cast their votes for Cleveland, but it is doubtful if one vote was among them—that of Homer's former clergyman, Rev. Albert Bigelow.

Sources used for this article:

The Bigelow Society, Director Rod Bigelow. Online material.
"The Charges Swept Away," *New-York Times*, August 12, 1884.
"Cleveland: History of Wicked Maria Halpin," *Chicago Daily Tribune*, August 13, 1884.
"The Cleveland Scandal: A Fresh Scrutiny of the Charges Affecting the New York Governor," *Chicago Tribune*, October 31, 1884.
"The Cleveland Scandal: What Three Buffalo Clergymen Say of Grover Cleveland—Will Any Clergymen Testify on the Other Side?" in *Chicago Daily Tribune*, August 11, 1884.
"Corroboration: A Physician's Statement. Seeking Redress," in *Chicago Daily Tribune,* September 19, 1884.
"Cortland County Aroused!" *The Republican*, April 25, 1861. In Blodgett Scrapbook, Vol. 2, page 19, Cortland County Historical Society, Cortland, NY.
"The Defense: A Man of 40 Lusty Summers 'Sowing His Wild Oats'," in *Chicago Daily Tribune*, August 13, 1884.
Furgurson, Ernest B. "Moment of Truth: Scandal in the Election of 1884." Accessed online at https://www.historynet.com/moment-of-truth-the-election-of-1884.htm.
Russell, James H. "Anniversary Sermon" observing the 100th anniversary of the dedication of the Homer Congregational Church. Sunday, July 14, 1963. Copy in Town of Homer's archives.
"Turned from Cleveland," *Owego Evening Blade,* October 31, 1884.

The writer wishes to thank Homer's Ed Raus for recommending some research on Bigelow and for pointing out the article in The Republican *newspaper of 1861.*

February 13, 2020

A BRIEF HISTORY OF THE VILLAGE POLICE DEPARTMENT

A brief history of Homer's Volunteer Fire Department recently appeared in this column. It came to mind that a similar piece ought to be run on the history of another local protective organization—the Village's Police Department. Relying heavily on information the Department provided along with early Village Minutes and local news articles, here is an attempt to pay tribute and express gratitude to those who have enforced the law for the safety of the village's residents down through the ages.

On March 5, 1794, the Town of Homer was organized as a huge township of Onondaga County. It included what is now Cortlandville, Solon, Cincinnatus, Virgil, Harford, Lapeer, Taylor, and the southern halves of Truxton and Cuyler. The few residents of this 300 square mile township in the wilderness were to be served by town officers appointed by three Onondaga County judges.

On April 5, 1795, these town officers met at the home of "Squire" John Miller, and the next year, the first election of a Homer Town Board was held. Only white males who owned property were legally eligible to vote then. The "Squire" was elected the first supervisor of the Town of Homer. John Keep was "judge" and Peter Ingersoll was the first town clerk. As with any society, there had to be more than an organized government; there had to be a means of getting and keeping social order. To that end, there was a "constable" and "collector" [of taxes]. Two men were elected to perform these combined roles: Barzilla Russell and Roderick Beebe. Each "constable" was tasked with seeing that town and state regulations were carried out by what would be 97 inhabitants in 1797 and 2,975 by 1810. The following Town ordinance, for example, was passed in 1812, four years after Cortland County broke off from Onondaga County: "That horses, cattle, sheep & hogs be not suffered to run at large within half a mile of any meeting house, mill stone or tavern."

Not until 1835 did the Village of Homer become incorporated and begin passing municipal ordinances for what was approaching 1,625 residents. It appears from the Minutes that the Board President [Mayor] and trustees were responsible for enforcing the ordinances along with the Town's constable. The Village Minutes show that by May 5, 1857, the elected Village officers included the combined position of "Constable and [Tax] Collector." The first village constable elected to "keep order" was Simon P. Miller. This generally meant he and J. R. Dixon, the elected "Police Justice" [Justice of the Peace], were to settle local disputes and see that the local merchants received protection.

One example involved Jedediah Barber, proprietor of The Great Western emporium on Main Street. It seems "Uncle Jed" had a particularly difficult time getting money owed him by a farmer up on Factory Hill. Barber urged the constable to confiscate a hog as payment. Since the farmer only had one hog the constable refused to attach it. Time passed, and then the farmer's son showed up at the store to buy feed for young piglets. Immediately, Barber and the constable high-tailed it out to the Factory Hill farm. Sure enough, there was a new litter. The constable attached the hog, and Barber's claim was satisfied (told by Richard Price of Homer, 1935).

The first printed and published set of Village Ordinances to be included in the Village Minutes were to take effect on July 2, 1857. They make clear that the President of the Corporation [Village] "shall be the head of the police department, and shall from time to time take such measures as he may deem necessary for the preservation of peace" and the enforcement of ordinances. And there we have the origins of today's Police Department being accountable to the elected Village Mayor. The same document of 1857 clearly vested the police constable with the power to arrest and detain violators of the peace and village ordinances. For a while in 1858, Constable Miller was also the "Pound Master" responsible for impounding stray animals and exacting a fine from their owners.

In 1866 Isaac W. Brown was the elected constable, and the Village Board voted for a designated "Lock-Up" (most likely an unused horse stable) and two "special policemen" for the Fourth of July. Between 1868 and 1877, the following were elected as "Constable": Isaac S. Crofoot, Newell Jones, William H. Cobb, Moses Gale, Frank D. Carpenter, Addison Northrup, and William A. Shirley. The turnover seems to indicate that the post was political in nature and required no special training.

The term "constable" started to disappear in early 1884 when Homer's "Protective Police" was organized on February 19th to patrol the village streets, and "Special Police" were appointed by the Village Board in March of 1886. Constable Shirley was still on the force in 1895 because newspapers report he was part of the investigation that year into the never solved murder of Homer farmer Patrick Quinlan. In June of 1917, Dell Carson assumed the appointed post of "Police Officer" and was reappointed in March of 1919. William Fitzgerald succeeded Carson in April of 1920, and there was a Chief Harwood around 1929. Of course, as changes came along in transportation, communication, and the storage and retrieval of information, policing required the use of patrol cars, phones, computers, and ever more sophisticated means of maintaining social order.

Homer's most notable village police officer was George Vernum, better known affectionately as "George the Cop." Born in Greenwich Village in New York City, Vernum went on to join the Army and to serve overseas during World War I. From 1921 to 1924 he served with the Marine Corps in Haiti and the West Indies. He was next appointed to the New York State Police (mounted division) and assigned to Oneida, NY. He was stationed in Homer in 1925, and six years later quit the troopers to join the Homer Police. This man with a distinctive down-state accent was appointed Homer's police chief in 1932 and served for the next 24 years. In 1937, the additional task of "Dog Warden" fell to Vernum (remember the post of "Pound Master" in the 1800s?). In 1939, he became the school attendance officer. Children would be admonished, "Don't be caught playing hooky by 'George the Cop.'" Those whose memories can stretch back to the 1950s can tell you stories of the Homer Police Department's dynamic duo of "Heavy Taylor" and "George the Cop." They can tell you of George's dedication to the safety of children crossing Main Street to and from the school on the Green for eighteen uninterrupted years. They can tell you about the time some youngsters led "Heavy Taylor" up on East Hill to see a "corpse" they had discovered, only to learn it was a local "sleeping off a drunk." Officer Taylor's real name was Charles Taylor, Sr., but everyone called him "Heavy."

Chief Vernum retired in 1956, after a total of thirty-six years in police work, and was soon replaced by Tom Davis. Others employed on the police force included Officer Hill, Officer Dehart, and George's son Ed Vernum. Davis' tenure as chief was also a lengthy one. In 1985 Sgt. David Sampson of the Cortland County Sheriff's Department took over the Homer Police Department. During Chief Sampson's tenure the department grew. Daniel D. Mack, Dave VanOrden, and Bob Pitman were hired. They joined part-time officer John Evans, whose years of service encompassed 1983 through 1996. First employed as a patrol man in July of 1986, Mack rose to the rank of Sergeant and took over as Chief when Sampson retired in 1999. He served the community until his retirement in 2014. At that point, Mark Helms, a captain with the Cortland County Sheriff's Office, became Homer's Chief of Police. He served until his election in 2016 as the Sheriff of Cortland County. Bob Pitman next took on the role of Chief of Police. Previously, he had worked for police agencies, including the Village, the City of Cortland, and the Onondaga County Sheriff's Office.

Through the years, headquarters of the H.P.D. has been at different locations: the Town Hall, the little brick building at the intersection of Main and Cayuga Street, and now the historic train station on James Street, where one can find Kimberly Reitano, the Administrative Assistant, willing to be of help.

Today, the Village police department provides 24-hour police service throughout the year for a population of 3,291 (2010 census). That requires substantial personnel and technical expertise. Chief Pitman is ably assisted by Sgt. R. J. Eckard and three Patrol Officers: C. Parrow, M. Compton, and K. Forney. There are nine part-time patrol officers: T. Huttleston, D. Warner, M. Howell, A. SanJule, J. Valetin, F. Forbes, T. Huff, K. Natoli, and B. Gilbert The main function of the police department is patrol where they detect and prevent crime while providing traffic safety through enforcement. In addition to patrol, certain officers in the department provide additional police services to the residents. Officers are certified evidence technicians, trained to respond to crime scenes and to properly document and collect evidence in ways that did not exist back at the time of the Quinlan murder case in 1894–1895. Certain officers are also trained forensic interviewers. They are specially trained to interview children that have been traumatized. Also, some of the officers are certified police instructors. They conduct in-service training to the department members and sometimes teach at local police academies.

The department also has a police bike patrol unit. It was initially started by Chief Mack who purchased two police patrol bikes. The police bike patrol was formalized under Chief Pitman, who has had officers become certified as bike patrol officers through the State of New York.

In 2016 and 2019, officers provided security during the summertime military training at the Intermediate / Junior High School. People from Cortland County came to avail themselves of no cost medical, dental, vision and veterinary services provided by members of the military.

Yearly, officers provide traffic safety during annual events, such as the Winterfest Parade, the Memorial Day Parade, the Fireman's Field Days Parade, the Homecoming Parade, Holiday in Homer, and Magic on Main Street. Officers also participate in events such as Cops on Top, a fundraising event for the Special Olympics and the Drug Take Back Event that allows residents to safely dispose of unwanted or un-used medications.

Then there is the School Resource Officer (SRO) program that expanded in 2018. It went from two officers to five: D. VanOrden, M. Bort, Q. Giles, K. Soderholm, and S. Morgan. Currently there is an officer in each of the schools and during the evening for after school events and meetings. SROs are not only enforcement officers; they are law-related counselors and educators. They work in collaboration with the school and the community as a resource for maintaining a safe and secure environment. School administrators benefit from the SROs' training, knowledge and experience in handling situations involving possible weapons violations or in the identification of controlled dangerous substances. The SRO provides a highly visible presence to deter or identify trespassers on campus.

Given today's environment, all officers within the department train annually with outside agencies for active shooter incidents. They are properly trained and equipped to respond to incidents and to take the appropriate action to save lives. Officers are also trained to teach civilians on how to respond to active shooter events. They provide this training free of cost whenever requested.

Homer's police officers have been cited for outstanding, even heroic, service. Most recently, Officer Michael Howell was honored by the Red Cross for entering a burning building four times on April 5, 2019, to bring out residents who might otherwise have perished. Chief Pitman was honored this past December by the Cortland County Adult Services and New York State Office of Children and Family Services for his advocacy for elder abuse prevention. The previous June he had worked with Postal Service inspectors to prevent an elderly villager from being scammed out of $9,000.

Thus, the Village of Homer Police Department has a rich history dating back to the middle of the nineteenth century when they were constables and tax collectors. The department has grown over the years in the quantity and quality of protective services provided. It has evolved into today's dedicated, trained professionals who are committed to working with the community to make the village of Homer a safe and desirable place in which to live, work or visit. According to Chief Pitman, "The department's mission is to partner with the community to solve problems, improve public safety, and reduce crime in a manner that is fair, impartial, transparent, and consistent—all with respect for human dignity according to the highest standards of professionalism, integrity and accountability."

February 27, 2020

PLEASE GET OFF THE PHONE, BERTHA; I'M TRYING TO REACH BURGETT'S

One hundred forty-four years ago, the idea of using a device to instantly chat with someone anywhere in the world seemed impossible. Alexander Graham Bell's invention of the telephone in 1876 and his patents on transmitting equipment led to the incorporation of the Bell Telephone Company in 1877 in Massachusetts. The introduction of Bell's machine at the Centennial Exhibition created interest and awareness of the new system, convincing the earliest investors of the value of the revolutionary technology. Originally, the telephone system connected users by a single line from one point to another. The limitations of this arrangement quickly became clear, and led to the introduction, in 1878, of the telephone switch and central exchange (or switchboard with operators). With this arrangement, local telephones within a service area were connected at the exchange to all others served by the same provider, and through them, were eventually able to connect with other exchanges to provide unlimited service.

Telephone service must have arrived in Cortland and the village of Homer sometime around 1884. Homer's *Republican* newspaper of December 18, 1884, reported the line operated by the Cortland and Homer telephone exchange "has worked admirably, and the management are entitled to much credit for the efficient service." Ten years later, two telephone companies were in existence in the Homer-Cortland area and beyond: The Empire State Telephone Company and the Central New York Telephone Company. The former had less than 15 telephones in Cortland and a half dozen in Homer. By May 1, 1897, a "List of Subscribers of Cortland and Homer Telephone Exchange" showed 89 telephones connected to the telephone exchange in Cortland and Homer. That number would be up to 13,000 by late 1959.

Telephone No. 1 was not listed in the 1897 directory, but 2 was the telephone number of the Kellogg-Van Hoesen Law Office; 3 for Keator, Wells & Co.; 4 was the Cortland Forging Co.; and 5 the Wickwire Roller Mill. You could get a horse-drawn ambulance by calling 61 and horse powered fire wagons by asking the operator for 137. Some of the other enterprises with telephones were The First National Bank (134), F. H. Cobb & Co. Wholesale Fruit and Confectionery (39), Cooper Bros. Foundry (84), County Poor House (50), *Democrat* Printing Office (41), D. L. & W. Freight Office (30), Electric Light Co. (11), Lehigh Valley (8), Maxson & Starin's Homer Coal Office (45), Police Office (137), Sheriff's Office (87), F. D. Smith Hardware (82), Standard Oil Co. of N. Y. (68), *Standard* Printing Co. (52), Western Union (10), and Wickwire Bros. (36).

A telephone could operate on a desk or mounted upon a wall and be "wired" to a telephone cable strung along poles by the roadside. The device consisted of a transmitter and a listening device, and a crank to ring for the operator. At the exchange, a "shield" would drop down for the number making the call, and the operator would intone "Number, please." The caller would give the number, and the operator would plug the cord into the appropriately numbered hole on the board of the party being called. At first, some men were hired as operators. They performed the connections while standing before the switchboard. By the early 1900s, women were predominantly hired (having performed more reliably and courteously), and they were seated before the board.

Among the instructions in a caller's directory were: "Ring off when through talking," "Do not use the telephone during thunder storms," "During conversation face squarely the front of the transmitter with lips close to the opening," "Any telephone can be used to report a fire or call a doctor." A telephone subscriber in Cortland could call one in Homer for 10 cents. Little York was 15 cents, Preble and Scott 20 cents, and a call to Virgil cost 15 cents. By the 1950s, these points were toll free.

People residing outside the village without phones would often have to journey into town to a store or some other central location to be able to make and receive calls. Eavesdroppers could hear you conduct your personal business as you used a public phone. Switchboard operators who connected the calls were known to sometimes invade people's privacy. The early house-to-house phone systems were often "party lines" on which several families would receive calls, and neighbors were free to listen in and often chose to do so. It was not unusual for a disgruntled caller to shout into the transmitter, "Bertha, will you get off the phone. I know you are listening in!"

By February 2, 1901, the Cortland Home Telephone Company, operating out of the Wickwire Block on Main Street in Cortland, advertised in the *Cortland Evening Standard* that its service was "Not an Experiment; But a Success." They claimed they had more than 200 telephones connected and in operation 24 hours around the clock every day of the week. They announced that their Homer exchange had about 40 advance subscribers and would be opened in a few days and connected with the Cortland exchange. They touted that "Each telephone is absolutely private. No party lines. $2 per month for business service. $1 per month for residence service. A postal card will bring our solicitor to you, or you are invited to call us up over the nearest telephone and try our service . . ." The Cortland Home Telephone Co. was "owned and operated by home people. Dr. Chas. D. VerNooy, Pres.; Calvin P. Walrad, V. Pres.; Herbert L. Smith, Sec'y; Geo. J. Magrer, Treas.; Wlllard H. Jones, Mgr." Christmas of 1901 saw the new technology figuring prominently in an entertainment put on for the Homer Congregational Sunday school. The title was "Telephoning Santa Claus" (*Cortland Evening Standard*, December 16, 1901).

On June 7, 1906, *The Homer Republican* reported that Homer was to have a new telephone exchange. The entire second floor of the Homer National Bank Block [now the Key Bank] had been leased by the Cortland Home Telephone Company. Near the Pine Street side of the floor "a full lamp-signal, multiple switch board" was to be installed with natural light from the windows coming in over the operators' shoulders. A public station was to be located on this floor, along with "living rooms for a manager of the Homer exchange lines who will look after repairs, etc." Manager Bennett informed the newspaper that the completed exchange "will be first class and modern in every particular and a model one for a town of Homer's size. Work upon stringing the telephone cables which are to replace largely the open wires now in use here, will be commenced within the coming week."

It took almost a year to complete the installation. Not until May 10, 1907, did *The Cortland Democrat* announce that the "very modern and up-to-date" telephone exchange in Homer "went into use on Saturday night last." However, the public was forewarned "The new board is quite different from the old one and the operator will need some time to learn the new apparatus, so that the service may be affected at first."

Early telephone service had an impact upon life in Homer, especially on the conduct of business. Around 1908 (from an article in the *Cortland Standard* of December 20, 1978), Burgett's IGA at 7 S. Main Street became the sixty-first phone in Homer. Its number was 61. A second phone was added, number 69, with an extension from the office to the meat cutter in the back of the store. Operators at the exchange were instructed to ring 69 automatically anytime 61 was busy. Later, a third line was added, number 92. This led to the store's slogan: "Three Phones, Always Busy." In those days, almost everyone with a phone called in their grocery orders. Deliveries were made within minutes or hours by a horse-pulled wagon. Remember, now, there was no refrigeration in this era, except for ice boxes in families' kitchens. So, prompt delivery of fresh produce was welcomed. You might say it was the local forerunner of Amazon.com.

According to Howard W. Burden's "History of the Homer Fire Department" (in a 1975 booklet), sometime after 1908, a contract was drawn up between the Telephone Company and the Homer Volunteer Fire Department for the fire alarm to be rung from the exchange office when a call came in reporting a fire.

The *Cortland Standard* of April 8, 1909, reported that the number of local telephone subscribers was expanding rapidly, and efforts were being made to gain more. As an experiment for use of the long-distance toll lines, a little incentive was put out. When the bills were sent out April 1, a coupon was

Image 10.1 Early telecommunication in Homer. *Courtesy of the Cortland County Historical Society.*

enclosed with each bill, entitling the holder to one free toll message that month to any point on the lines of the Empire State or Central New York Telephone companies. These two companies covered eighteen counties. The goal was to show "how easy it is to talk with Watertown, for instance, or Utica or some other remote point . . ."

The Homer *Republican* of April 4, 1912, ran this blurb: "The Homer telephone exchange is giving prompt and efficient service and its patrons ought to appreciate the good work of the telephone girls who are so prompt and courteous, sometimes under trying conditions, for they have to deal with all sorts and conditions of cranks who never think telephone girls are entitled to courteous treatment." Operators worked nine-hour shifts, but that was reduced to eight in 1913.

In 1933, according to *The Homer Post* of April 21, a survey of the Homer exchange by the New York Telephone Company was conducted at the request of the Homer Chamber of Commerce. This was done in response to several complaints being lodged with the Chamber about the telephone service in Homer. A traffic expert was brought in to look over the situation. A few minor changes were made, but the careful investigation revealed most of the complaints "arose from the condition which can be corrected by the subscribers themselves." The condition was said to exist on multi-party lines. A diplomatic and defensive solution was offered:

> Thoughtlessness of the rights and conveniences of our neighbors too often leads to over lengthy conversations, which upset a smooth working telephone service and bring inconvenience, which may be serious, to ourselves as well as our fellow subscribers. . . . Most telephone subscribers are reasonable telephone conversationalists. They say what they have to say and get it over. There still are those who . . . inconvenience others and disrupt the service of a whole section of the country that daily calls the butcher, the baker, the doctor and sometimes the ambulance and the fire company and that depends upon instantly cleared lines to protect lives and property. . . . Let's try as a community to use our telephone system fairly.
> Then if we can't get good service, we'll know we're not at fault.

The survey found that 4,400 calls were made per day or about five calls a day per telephone served by the Homer exchange. The peak hours of the day, when the call load was greatest, were the hours between 9 a. m. and 10 a. m. and 6 p. m. to 7 p. m. These were local calls only. Toll calls were handled out of the Cortland exchange. Besides the "busy wires" caused by overlong conversations on party lines, the report explained the local exchange employed a small staff of nine local girls trained to telephone work but due to the economic constraints of the Depression "it had been necessary to reduce working hours to spread the work among telephone-trained employees." This was the same throughout the country, officials said. The telephone company "has maintained a policy of spreading work among employees rather than firing them . . ."

Miss Margaret Harris graduated Homer Academy in 1938. After a couple months of training in Cortland, she started work as an operator at the Homer exchange in September of 1941, just a few months before the Japanese attack on Pearl Harbor. By then the telephone exchange over the bank was part of New York Telephone Company. Margaret joined about ten women who manned 200 lines in an eight-hour shift for twelve dollars a week. One woman worked the overnight shift. With the end of World War II and the Depression, the pay increased markedly, and the number of lines increased steadily and reached 800. The work could become "boring during slack times," but Margaret found she liked best the camaraderie she enjoyed with her fellow workers. The downside of the job were such "inconveniences" as having to work seven Christmases before having that religious holiday off with family. Holidays and blizzards did not bring a halt to the need for communication.

Today, Margaret Harris Fiske is a 99-year-old resident of Walden Place and in possession of an amazing memory and an equally sharp wit. She can recall the night of Friday, January 26, 1945, when the school across from the exchange was engulfed in fire during a basketball game and everyone evacuated safely. She says, "The event caused us to be busier than usual at the board but not as bad as we anticipated." Margaret can readily recall the names of other Homer and Cortland operators—names like Charlotte Angel, Aletha Crosley, and Linda Belden.

With a twinkle in her eye, she recalls Denis Hartnett, the confirmed bachelor who spent over four decades stringing wires inside and cables outside for the company, installing phones, making repairs, and making friends. Margaret agreed he was "a character" who in the early days of his career would hop up on his wagon seat, slap the reins, and give the horse a verbal command, "Commence!" And off the Irishman would go to commence his workday of climbing telephone poles and being the face of the company. She laughingly told of how "The girls would cajole Deny into buying us ice cream sundaes on hot summer days." Deny retired after 45 years of being "Mr. Telephone" in Homer. The genial William G. Crandall, whose real estate agency overlooked the Green, placed an ad of appreciation in a local paper citing Deny's many years of "accented, booming, happy tone of big-hearted, courteous, good nature . . ." The Bell Telephone System included the tribute in a nationally-run ad and added "The story of Deny Hartnett illustrates the local character of the telephone business"—a business not distant "but right on the main street . . . managed and operated by home-town people." Deny, who took his meals at Denny Cashion's Diner between the fire station and the American Legion, retired when dial service came into use.

As of Nov. 27, 1952 (as cited in the November 20, 2002, issue of the *Cortland Standard*), work had begun on an expansion of the Homer central telephone office "to take care of the needs of telephone users here until the dial service is introduced." This was announced by Kenneth R. Archibald, "manager here for the New York Telephone Company."

A new building was constructed at 58 N. Main Street (now owned by Verizon). It housed the "Pioneer" dial equipment, and there was to be an open house on January 14 and 15, 1954, between the hours of 2–5 PM and 7–9 PM. A cable splicing display was to be on view in a tent next to the telephone office. Homer school children were invited to the open house as well as the general public. Phone service and its employees were in transition across the land. Only a change in technology could keep pace with the mushrooming demand for tele-communication services.

And so, we come to December 4, 1959. On this date *The Cortland Democrat* reported that the "well preserved 'List of Subscribers of Cortland and Homer Telephone Exchange'" dated May 1, 1897, had been presented to Kenneth Archibald, telephone manager, by W. W. Doolittle, a retired executive of the company, then living in Binghamton. The directory in turn was destined to be loaned by Mr. Archibald to the Cortland County Historical Society. At that point, early telephone companies and switch board operators in Homer were consigned to the pages of history . . . but their dedicated service must not be forgotten.

Thanks goes to Don Lawson of Homer for suggesting research be done on early telephone service in Homer and to Margaret Fiske (daughter of Homer's former local historian R. Curtis Harris and sole survivor of the Homer Class of 1938) for an amazing and most helpful interview on February 5, 2020.

March 12, 2020

THE TRIALS AND TRIBULATIONS OF HOMER'S CIRCUS OWNER, SIG SAUTELLE

Over a hundred years ago, there must have been something thrilling about a circus coming to town and perhaps something even more enthralling about a circus coming to town to spend the winter. Such must have been the case for young people in the Cortland County village of Homer in the 1890s when Sig Sautelle's Circus came parading down Main Street. There were cavorting clowns, bareback riders, trapeze artists, tumblers, high-wire performers and exotic animals. The Circus had 225 people on the payroll; boasted two elephants, 14 cages of animals and 150 horses, and ponies (according to John C. Kunzog's book *Tan Bark and Tinsel*, 1970). For twenty-five cents one

Image 10.2 Sig Sautelle. *Photograph from the Library of Congress.*

could enjoy one of two performances per day in one ring under one big tent set up on a large lot at the corner of Cortland Street and Copeland Avenue.

Then, starting in 1900, some of the performers and animals took up headquarters for the winter months at three red-painted, octagon-shaped buildings (one with a cupola still stands) and other structures at the south end of Main Street. Circus employees filled up the hotels in Homer, and their children attended the academy on the Green. "Sig," its popular owner, was known for his big cigar, a diamond pin in his lapel, and ventriloquism skills he had learned while a drummer boy during the Civil War.

According to James P. Hughes ("Homer's Sig Sautelle." *Life in the Finger Lakes*. Summer, 2008),

> In Homer's confectionary store, to give the impression of a man
> trapped in the basement, he would carry on a conversation through
> a hot-air register in the floor with a helpless voice below howling,
> "Let me out, let me out!" As the children gazed through the grate
> bewildered, Sig stood by with a twinkle in his eye.

With these tantalizing influences, how many local boys contemplated running away with the circus come spring? Perhaps they would have reconsidered if they knew what events lurked ahead.

Judging by the newspaper accounts of the day, circus life, at least outside the ring, was not all that glamorous. For George Satterly (Sept. 22, 1848–June 21, 1928)—sometimes spelled Satterlee and better known as "Sig Sautelle"—there seemed to be plenty of unwelcomed, even dangerous, challenges for a flamboyant circus showman whose show traveled via road, the Erie Canal, and railway to communities primarily in New York State. While his ads, such as one in *The Daily Argus* of July 5, 1901, enticed the people of Mount Vernon, NY, and elsewhere to take in "A Vast All-Star Programme of sensational and exclusive features in its arenic department," other newspaper articles present a sampling of the traumatic events associated with Sautelle's traveling entertainment extravaganza.

For example, there was the negative reputation borne by circus people that comes through in *The Port Chester Journal's* reporting of an incident (Thursday, July 18, 1901). It seems that during the evening show at Port Chester, Sautelle ordered a police officer to arrest a lad named Eddie Hutchins, a Port Chester lad "who had been with the circus for some time" as it made its way through the Hudson Valley. Sautelle claimed "he had discharged him in Albany and that he had followed the circus ever since and he wanted him arrested and taken off the grounds." Sautelle further maintained he had paid Hutchins upon termination and had the receipt. However, Hutchins countered that Sig Sautelle had "fired" him without paying him what was his due and that "he had followed the circus around in the hope of getting his money."

The officer believed that in ordering the arrest of Hutchins, Sautelle would appear in court against him. He claimed Sautelle had vouched "his lawyer" would be present and appear against Hutchins. The lad was locked up for twenty-four hours before a justice of the peace was available to hear the case. At the hearing, neither Sautelle nor "his lawyer" appeared. Without a complaint brought forward, Hutchins was released. And Sautelle's Circus had already departed, leaving the lad in the dust.

The newspaper went on to state that while Hutchins was admittedly an unsavory character, "this does not alter the case. . . . There was no warrant for his arrest and the officer was clearly in error in arresting him on the word of a circus-man. The integrity of Sautelle may be all right, but circus men are birds of passage and the officer should have known this. He should not have taken as gospel what Sautelle told him." The paper further noted that "in the wake of all circuses there is a miscellaneous following which drift in with the vans of the road." The paper called them "camp followers," but maintained that Hutchins [mind you, a local boy] had an "outrage" imposed upon him. "Hereafter," the paper concluded, with a stereotypical bias, "there should be some discretion used in making arrests of persons on the order of circus men. As a class we are not stuck on the Canvass Knights who are not loath to resort to all kinds of acts to gather in the shekels."

The next incident, as reported by the Syracuse *Evening Herald* on August 17, 1901, occurred in Saratoga, NY. This time, J. Charles Banks of Seneca Falls, the manager of Sig Sautelle's circus, shot and killed Herbert Tackaberry of Ottawa, Canada at 8 P. M. on the 16th at the South Broadway circus ground. "Tackaberry had been following the circus, running a gambling outfit," reported the paper, "and for some reason left, it is supposed, because his presence was not desired." He returned on the 16th, the shooting resulted, and Banks claimed it was in self-defense.

The coroner was summoned. He examined the body. One of the shots took effect in the right temple and went clear through the head. The other entered just below the ear, severing the jugular vein and carotid artery. The coroner concluded death must have occurred within five minutes after the shooting. Banks was arrested on the charge of murder in the first degree.

Banks was taken to police headquarters and jailed. The examination of Banks took place around midnight that night before Justice Delaney. C. B. Kilmer and W. P. Butler appeared for the defendant, and Assistant District Attorney McKnight for the people. To take the testimony of several employees who had been subpoenaed, the examination was not held until after the circus' evening performance. The court room was filled with a good many of Sautelle's employees when the proceedings commenced.

After the formal charge of murder in the first degree was read and a plea of not guilty entered, Richard Raymond, ticket seller for Sautelle's show, was called to the stand. He stated that he knew Banks and Tackaberry and was standing at the entrance to the main tent when he saw Tackaberry sitting to one side of the entrance and Banks opposite him on the other side. He said Tackaberry got up and started towards Banks with his hand at his hip pocket. Banks then took hold of Tackaberry. A scuffle ensued and shots fired. Tackaberry fell to the ground. Raymond testified he heard nothing said between the men and "it was only an instant between the time of the scuffle and the firing of the shot."

Under cross-examination, Raymond said that he had been with the show since the 10th of May and knew both men personally. He said that Tackaberry followed the show with a "gambling game" and was a "grifter." He had remained with the show two weeks, but on the 16th came as a visitor. Raymond said on one occasion he had been shown a revolver by Tackaberry and was told that if ever Banks told anything about him, he would "croak" him. On another occasion he had said that if he (Tackaberry) should be obliged to leave the show he would get even. Raymond stated, "Tackaberry carried two revolvers, one in his hip pocket and the other in his vest pocket, wore brass knuckles at times, and carried a cane and a lead Billy club. Some witnesses testified that the weapon was in Tackaberry's possession and that he "was loading it apparently for use when Banks snatched it and fired the two shots." Hearing the shots, a crowd collected in time to see Tackaberry fall and Banks start to run away. Chase was given, and Banks was readily captured when he saw that escape was impossible. But he managed to dispose of the weapon, which had yet to be found. Circus employees called Banks "an inoffensive sort of fellow." They were surprised he had even resisted.

After the People rested their case, Clarence B. Kilmer for the defendant moved to discharge the defendant on the grounds that the shooting was justified. It was overruled by the court, and the District Attorney would not accept a plea of manslaughter. It was ultimately determined that Banks be held to await the action of the grand jury on the original charge of murder in the first degree. During the coroner's inquest, about fifteen witnesses testified Tackaberry had at various times threatened Banks with violence, which was similar to that brought out in the Police court examination. The coroner exonerated Banks.

Residents of Homer, New York, must have found some irony in the *Cortland Evening Standard* of Monday, August 19, 1901. The paper noted Banks was to stand trial and added the following: "It will be remembered that the grand jury of Cortland County on Feb. 4, 1901, reported six indictments, two of which were sealed. One of these was against Tackaberry for assault on the person of a man by the name of Morrison. Tackaberry then worked in Thurston's winter garden. He was given a hint of the indictment before the grand jury reported and he skipped to Canada and had not been found by the officers."

Banks was acquitted November 15, 1901. The following notice appeared that day in the *Waterloo Observer*: "The many friends of J. Charles Banks, of Seneca Falls, were pleased to note this morning that his trial for the murder of Herbert Tackaberry . . . had been finished and that the jury, after being out five hours, had returned a verdict of not guilty." The verdict must have been a relief for Sig Sautelle as well, whose business had moved on since the incident, following the adage "The show must go on."

It was not just the humans associated with Sautelle's Circus that got into deadly scuffles; the animal performers did, too. On June 4, 1902, the *Cortland Evening Standard* reported that a tiger in the Sautelle menagerie had escaped from his cage while on a moving train and got into a horse car. A terrible fight occurred between the tiger and the frightened horses. Several horses were badly lacerated and bitten. A horse named Toby fared the worst but managed to kill the tiger, breaking its ribs and neck. *The Poughkeepsie Eagle* of May 31 described the ferocious attacker as a year-old, 400 pound Bengal tiger in Sautelle's circus and said, "It is fortunate the tiger in escaping entered the horse car instead of jumping off the train and taking to the woods where he would probably soon have attacked people." The *Eagle* said the circus train was headed for Poughkeepsie when the battle occurred and that it was "a bloodcurdling affair while it lasted."

There has always been conjecture regarding the fate of some of Sautelle's elephants. According to local lore, some were buried in the field in Homer that was once known as Contento's junkyard. Judging by the following article in *The Cortland Republican* for November 30, 1905, Sautelle may have, indeed, pondered burying one problematic pachyderm in Homer.

BIG ELEPHANT BREAKS LOOSE

"Duke," Sig Sautelle's Ugly African Elephant Breaks from His Moorings at Headquarters and One of His Keepers Narrowly Escapes His Murderous Attack.

There was plenty doing at the animal house at Sig Sautelle's headquarters last Monday morning. Soon after daylight, "Duke," the big and ugly African elephant which was chained to a big post in the animal house, made a lunge at one of his keepers. The post to which he was attached broke off under the strain and liberated him. Mr. Marrow, the expert animal man and manager, was quickly summoned and hastened to the quarters. "Duke" had chased one of his attendants into a corner, knocked him down and made a vicious lunge at him with his single tusk. The tusk providentially missed the man's body and went below his legs. Other attendants with pikes, attacked the elephant and made him back away and Mr. Morrow secured a long pike in use by telephone linemen, who were working close by, and hastening to the rescue drove it into the elephant's trunk. As soon as the man was rescued from his perilous position and the others had found places of safety, about 100 grains of morphine was administered to the elephant. It was given in water first, but "Duke" detected something wrong with the water and drank only a few swallows. Then bread was soaked in the water and fed to him and more was placed in apples which he seemed to relish. About fifteen minutes were required to get the desired amount of the drug down the big brute. Fortunately, with the exception of smashing up some woodwork, little damage was done. The stoves, fortunately, were not overturned and as soon as possible the fires in them were extinguished. After some time the morphine began to take effect and along in the afternoon "Duke" became drowsy enough so that he was able to be again chained securely to a post which it will be very difficult for him to break. The other animals in the house were greatly excited during the elephant's rampage and there was a lively time all around till the morphine took effect and quieted the angry elephant. The beast has been Sautelle's property for about a year and has given much trouble by his treacherous and ugly disposition. Mr. Morrow said he was a sorry looking beast Tuesday morning, the morphine having evidently given him considerable distress. Mr. Morrow said enough was administered to kill 150 men.

Marital spats among circus employees are hard to ignore when traveling and living in close quarters. One such conflict made it into the May 22, 1903, issue of *The Waterville Times:* "One of Sig Sautelle's hyenas was devoured by its mate, while en route from Oneida to Rome. When the cage was opened, the blood spatters were seen and naught remained but the bones."

The same newspaper revealed on January 26, 1912, that a circus performer had such a disagreeable personality he simply had to be terminated:

> "Kruger," the African lion which was purchased last spring for $1,000 by Sig Sautelle and kept in winter quarters at Homer, was shot last week having become so viciously ugly that he fought his keepers and no one could be hired to longer care for him. "Kruger" had killed two keepers and injured others. An attempt was made to put him to death by poison, but he detected an unusual smell in the meat and refused to eat. Chloroform was then tried but he knocked away the saturated sponge with his paw as fast as it was shoved under his nose and finally he was shot.

The following from *The Waterville Times* of October 4, 1912, presents a concise summation of how Sautelle dealt with the trials and tribulations of being a showman, including inclement weather:

> Sautelle appeared in Waterville on Wednesday afternoon and evening according to schedule, giving two excellent performances. The circus travels by wagon and had experienced some very bad roads during the past week. On the way from Worcester to Cooperstown, where the company showed last Saturday, one of the lion cages toppled over and turned a complete somersault down an embankment, breaking the reach and otherwise damaging it. The circus is now on the way to winter quarters in Homer, after a most successful tour. Sig Sautelle is one of the oldest circus men on the road and small disasters like a deluge of rain or the tipping over of the menagerie merely cause him to puff a little harder on the cigar and gaze quizzically out over the rim of his glasses. The circus left Cooperstown in the pouring rain on Sunday, Richfield Springs being their next stop. They came here from New Berlin and left yesterday morning for Morrisville.

Circuses faced incredible expenses and that could have devastating economic consequences, as *The Holley Standard* of Holley, NY, (December 17, 1914) posted in this notice:

> George C. Satterlee, better known as Sig Sautelle, the circus man, who resides at Homer, Cortland county, and was in this section with

his circus for several seasons past, filed a petition in bankruptcy in Utica Saturday with unsecured liabilities of $33,103 and nominal assets of $3,815. His fifty creditors are scattered. All that is left of the circus is a spotted horse and mule.

George Satterly and his ailing wife, Ida Belle, took up residence in 1915 on a small farm outside of Homer. That was about the time, according to the late Homer historian R. Curtis Harris, that the Wharton Moving Picture Company of Ithaca (the Hollywood of the silent film era) came to Homer to film a segment with the famous actress Pearl White. Extras were the many circus performers who still made Homer their home. Sig must have enjoyed it. For three days the glory of his old Circus was reenacted, if only for the camera ("Sig Sautelle: A Circus and an Era." *The Crooked Lake Review.* October, 1995).

In 1927, the year before he died, Sautelle, then a widower, tried to give it another go. With the improvement in roads, he decided to use the new large, motorized trucks to move his new show. Caught in a downward whirlwind of credit and a fluctuation of prices, Sig's show failed the first year. To the end of his five-decade career in entertainment, Sautelle contended with ups and downs, earning his rightful place in the Circus Hall of Fame, and, for a while, Homer's fame was tied to that of Sig Sautelle's highly respected traveling circus.

[2020 Note: This article was selected for inclusion in the April 9, 2020 online issue of New York History Review *and the hard copy published at year's end.]*

Image 10.3 Sautelle's circus house on Route 11 has seen many uses. *Courtesy of The Landmark Society of Cortland County.*

March 26, 2020

THE GREAT INFLUENZA PANDEMIC OF 1918–1919

Given the recent, rampant spread of the coronavirus, or COVID-19, one may hearken back to a pandemic of just a little over one hundred years ago. In World War I, neutral Spain was the first to report flu deaths in its newspapers, so commentators soon nicknamed the pandemic "Spanish flu." However, the exact origins of the global pandemic remain a mystery. Ironically, some experts believe it may have originated in China. Sound familiar? Yet, some studies indicate a U.S. origin, perhaps in hog farms in Kansas followed by camps of soldiers in Kansas readying for shipment "over there" to the Great War in Europe.

The influenza pandemic commenced in 1918 and by the spring of 1919 had sickened an estimated one-third of the world's population and may have killed as many as 50 million people. It claimed more lives in a single year than either the First World War or the four-year-long bubonic plague, or "Black Death," that swept through Europe and Asia in the Middle Ages. According to today's Center for Disease Control and Prevention, that influenza pandemic was caused by an H1N1 virus with genes of avian origin. In the United States, it was first identified in military personnel in the spring of 1918. It is estimated that about 675,000 deaths occurred in the United States. Mortality was high then in people younger than 5 years old, 20–40 years old [the age of U.S. "doughboys"], and 65 years and older. The high mortality in healthy people, including those in the 20–40-year age group, was a unique feature of that pandemic. With no vaccine then to protect against influenza infection and no antibiotics to treat secondary bacterial infections that can be associated with influenza infections, control efforts worldwide were limited to non-pharmaceutical interventions as is the case now with COVID-19. Those interventions included isolation, quarantine, good personal hygiene, use of disinfectants, and limitations of public gatherings, which were applied unevenly. It has been pointed out that St. Louis fared better than Philadelphia because they did a better job of practicing these interventions. St. Louis shut down, but Philly hosted a wartime parade, which 200,000 people packed the sidewalks to view. Therein lies a lesson for all of us. What was lacking then but not now was the rapid means of educating communities on how to mitigate against human to human transmission. Of course, with faster means of transportation now, communicable contagions spread more rapidly than a hundred years ago.

It is interesting to look at a small sampling of the news coverage of the pandemic of 1918 in the *Homer Republican*. This is from the issue of Thursday, August 1, 1918:

Is the world face to face with another international epidemic of influenza, commonly known in America as 'the grippe?' The obnoxious disease first became epidemic in Spain a few months ago. Even King Alfonso fell victim to it. Hardly a city or town in Spain escaped. Then it spread to Germany, and the German army became infected. So widespread was the epidemic in Hunland that the delay in resuming the German drive on the Western front has been ascribed to it. Now the influenza has spread to England, and whole counties are suffering from it. The epidemic has reached the midlands, schools have been closed to prevent its further spread and many mines and factories are in danger of shutting down. It seems likely that the epidemic will soon assume the proportions of a panic, as in Spain and Germany. Will the disease spread to the United States and cripple this country's war industries also? The present prevalence of the disease is the most widespread since the worldwide epidemic of 1889, when every country on the globe was affected. There were recurring epidemics in 1893, 1894, and 1895, but they were viewed as recrudescences of the persisting epidemic of several years before. The grippe plague seems to have no system in spreading itself. It jumps from one country to another, over seas and mountains. That was the case in 1899. In the present epidemic it has jumped from France over the English Channel to England. Of course, there is always more or less of grippe in America, both winter and summer. But English physicians are warning their brothers in the United States to be on the lookout for a real epidemic. Influenza is extremely infectious and is caused by a microbe known to scientists as "Pfeiffer's bacillus." The fact that it has a German name is no guaranty that its present spread is due to a German plot to make the whole world sick, for Germany was one of the first nations attacked. Everybody knows—to his sorrow—the symptoms of the disease, and it is important, if the spread is to be checked, to consult a physician and dose up with quinine immediately they are felt coming on.

Two months later, the *Homer Republican* began to report daily the names of those in the community who had come down with the flu and the names of those who had died from the malady. The October 3, 1918, paper, for example, announced the death of Mrs. Harold Andrews:

F. M. and W D. Briggs were called to Syracuse as undertakers, this morning, by the death of Mrs. Harold Andrews, wife of the son of O. B. Andrews [prominent grocer] of this village. It is reported that her death was due to influenza, but no particulars could be learned here this morning. The remains will be brought to Homer for burial but when could not be learned.

Seven days later, subscribers of the *Homer Republican* read this:

INFLUENZA RAMPANT IN HOMER

The influenza epidemic has hit Homer hard during the past week and cases have been and still are very numerous and some have been severe and a few deaths from it in Homer and vicinity have resulted. Physicians are taxed to the utmost to attend to the calls made upon them, and help to care for the sick has been impossible to secure in many cases where help outside the family was necessary, so that many who should be in bed themselves have been keeping about to care for other members of the family who were totally unable to leave their beds. All public meetings, church services and school sessions have been put under ban by the village health board since last Saturday and people are urged to take all possible precautions against contracting the disease, or if they have it or symptoms of it, to avoid communicating it to others as far as they can. The epidemic is serious, and no one can afford to be careless in relation to it in any way. Miss Helen Eldred, a sister of Mrs. P. W. Warner of this village, who is a trained nurse, has been engaged as a visiting nurse and for the past few days has very materially helped the overworked physicians in caring for their patients in a number of the most severe cases.

Another article in this edition of the paper explained the impact of influenza on nearby Syracuse, NY, where Mrs. Andrews had died:

SYRACUSE BANS PUBLIC MEETINGS

Monday Mayor Stone of Syracuse ordered closed all places of popular assembly including churches, schools, theaters, Liberty Loan mass meetings, etc. Public funerals are also to be banned and all possible precautions taken to check the influenza epidemic which has already cost many lives in that city, nineteen deaths being recorded Sunday as plague victims. The order will remain in effect until the epidemic is checked.

On the day after Christmas, using an emotionally laden noun to reference the epidemic, the *Homer Republican* ran this article:

PLAGUE DEADLIER THAN WAR

Influenza Killed 6,000,000 Persons in Three Months

The London *Times* medical correspondent says that it seems reasonable to believe that throughout the world about 6,000,000 persons perished from influenza and pneumonia during the last three months. It has been estimated that the war caused the death of 20,000,000 persons in 4 years. Thus, the correspondent points out, influenza has proved itself five times deadlier than war, because in the same period, at its epidemic ratio, influenza would have killed 100,000,000. Never since the black death has such a plague swept over the world, he says, adding that the need of a new survey of public health measures have never been more forcibly illustrated.

While the epidemic was subsiding in December 1918, the U. S. Health Service issued warnings that there could be an increase in serious cases of "pneumonia, bronchitis and other diseases of the respiratory system" during the winter and that precautions needed to be taken.

The epidemic had economic consequences, as well, as revealed in another article from the December 26th issue:

> The United States fuel administration has found that a plentiful supply of egg and pea coal is available at the present. The influenza epidemic in the Pennsylvanian anthracite fields has broken out again with renewed virulence and has cut down anthracite production to a degree that necessitates the use of broken (grate), egg and pea sizes in lieu of chestnut.

In scanning through the columns listing the local people stricken with influenza, I was surprised to come across the name of Ralph McConnell, an active member of the Homer Grange. All ten members of his family were sick with influenza in 1918. Ralph was my maternal great-grandfather. He lived until 1959. And then there was this for December 26th: "Carrie and Lillian McConnell are ill with influenza. It is hoped that the flu and scarlet fever will not get mixed up." I took a special interest in this notice because 17-year-old Carrie McConnell would later become my maternal grandmother. It dawned on me that had she not survived in 1918, I would not be writing this column today because, quite simply, I would not be. Each of us can imagine times in our family tree where war, genocide, disease, and forces of nature could have impacted in a similar manner. Rarely do we take time to ponder just how fragile and miraculous Each Life really is.

News reports tout how we are now in uncharted territory. That is not exactly true. We are facing a different kind of contagion, to be sure, but we have faced pandemics before. At this critical time in our history, we should learn from the lessons of the health crises of the past. We can each protect our lives and that of others by taking proactive, common sense, aggressive measures regarding personal hygiene and social distancing. We humans have historically been involved in a never-ending war of the worlds—humans vs viruses. This is another moment where we are all in the trenches together. It is a time at the grassroots level for solidarity. Like other wars we have been engaged in, "this too shall pass away," and there is no need to give up on the joy, resilience, and hope of life. In the words of Lincoln on February 11, 1861:

> Trusting in Him who can go with me and
> remain with you and be everywhere for good,
> let us confidently hope all will yet be well.

April 9, 2020

A SALUTE TO HOMER SCHOOL SECRETARIES

As this column was being written, the COVID-19 pandemic caused schools across the state to go on "pause" as far as the traditional means of delivering education in a brick-and-mortar building. Everyone has been impacted—students (most unfairly), faculty, administrators, and non-instructional staff. It might be a good time to pause and ask this question: Who really keeps a school running smoothly? Anyone who works in a school or, like this writer, has worked in a school knows the answer. The administrative professional, commonly called the secretary, is the one who keeps things running smoothly by doing a lot of the up-front *and* behind-the-scenes "heavy lifting."

"If you want to know what's really going on in any school in the Homer Central School District, just ask the secretary."

Frequently, that line has been spoken with a soft chuckle, but most teachers and principals know it's no joke. The statement is probably one of the common truisms spoken in school hallways across the nation, not just in Homer. Well, think about it. The principal assumes the lead with school-wide instruction and staff evaluation and sets the overall climate in the school. The teachers are responsible for day-to-day classroom planning, instruction, and discipline. The custodians hold "the keys to the kingdom" and keep the physical plant safe and clean. The cafeteria personnel keep everyone fed. But the secretary is usually the keeper of the pulse of the entire school.

In that regard, consider this:

Who is at the front lines of school communication—answering the phones, greeting visitors, welcoming new families, scheduling appointments, and acting as "gatekeeper?" The secretary.

Who generally works with little direct supervision, must be a good problem solver, and capable of handling several tasks at once, especially during the busiest, most stressful times—the first and last hours of the school day? The secretary.

At some point in the past, as the local school increased in enrollment, in curricular offerings, and in the number of state-imposed regulations and mandates, the school administration required assistance with the surging paperwork and recordkeeping. Who supplied that? The secretary.

With the introduction of guidance departments, special education, school psychologists and social workers, who had the skills needed to maintain records by hand and later by computer? The secretary.

Who have I seen with a tissue when a child's feelings were hurt or with a calm voice when parents were upset about something? The secretary.

Who is frequently the first to deal with a student sent to the principal's office for some disruptive behavior and elicits the "background story?" The secretary.

Who is always there lending a sympathetic ear and dispensing sage advice when teachers and teacher aides are stressed? From my experience, it has been the secretary.

Again, from my experience and that of others, the Homer schools have been blessed with excellent administrative professionals in recent decades: Tammy Alger, Nancy Barrows, Amy Bauer, Connie Becker, Colleen Bentley, Barb Brady, Gerry Diamond, Susan Downes, Gerry Duane, Patti Durkee, Bonnie Eckard, Nancy Greggins, Barb Hale, Trina Hapgood, Freida Jacobi, Janet Julian, Mary Kabat, Katie Kerr, Joy Lawler, Melissa Meriwether, Ahren Morse, Carol Musson, Alice O'Donnell, Emily Olsenwik, Linda Robison, Judy Smith, Peggy Strauf, Arlene Thomas, Kim Vitello, Joyce Watrous, and Kelli Yacavone. Additional names appear below. Some names may have been overlooked due to poor memory or inadequate access to primary sources, and apologies are offered. These Homer secretaries garnered reputations for being efficient, warm and caring individuals but strong enough not to allow others to run over them.

Trust me, that trait is especially needed of secretaries working in a challenging junior high school environment. These secretaries could be in training for a juggling act in a Sig Sautelle circus. This is because they are required to multi-task and to keep on top of a million things in the course of a work day/week/month/year . . . and enjoy, along with the faculty, working with emerging adolescents said to be "experiencing raging hormones and dying brain cells" and "searching for their identities and values." It is a real test of one's character and stamina.

And finally, the ultimate, essential quality that gets a secretary in any school—elementary, intermediate, junior high, or high school—through the ups and downs of a school year is a sense of humor. You will understand why that trait is needed when you read this semi-humorous suggestion found online for schools to use:

Hello! You have reached the automated answering service of your school. In order to assist you in connecting to the right staff member, please listen to all the options before making a selection:

To lie about why your child is absent: Press 1
To make excuses for why your child did not do his/her work: Press 2
To complain about what we do: Press 3
To swear at the Superintendent or staff members: Press 4
To ask why you didn't get information that was already enclosed in your Newsletter and several letters posted to you: Press 5
If you want us to bring up your child: Press 6
To complain about school lunches: Press 7
To complain about bus transport: Press 8

Lastly, if you realize this is the real world, and your child must be accountable and responsible for his or her own behavior, class work, homework and that it's not the teacher's fault for your child's lack of effort: Hang up and have a really wonderful day!

On the serious side, the history of public-school secretaries is imbedded in the history of clerical workers in America. Originally, clerical workers were males. During the Civil War federal government officials were plagued by the labor shortage caused by the war, and the first female clerks were hired in Washington, D. C. under "experimental conditions" (See Davies, M. *Woman's place is at the typewriter: Office work and office workers 1870–1930.* Philadelphia, PA: Temple Univ. Press., 1982, p. 51). The initial role of the female clerks was limited to the completion of rudimentary tasks like sorting and packaging currency for the U.S. Treasury.

The "experiment" was deemed to be a success, and by 1869 women were being recruited as stenographers, bookkeepers, and typists, as well, in both the public and private sector. Salary was the most notable factor for hiring women. Employers discovered that they could save money by paying women lower wages than their male counterparts. It made good business sense to hire a woman who was willing to accept a yearly wage of $500 for doing the same job a man had been doing for $1800 per year (Davies, p. 52). Wages were kept low because of the high turnover rate. Young women would marry and move on to raise a family. Other less experienced, younger women would take their places in the office. The practice of hiring female clerical workers rather than males was firmly established by the late 1890s.

By the turn of the century, public high schools throughout America, including the Homer Academy and Union School, offered courses in "commercial education" which prepared students—primarily females—to use new office machines (typewriters) and techniques (shorthand). Increasingly, clerical work was considered "women's work." This "feminization of the office" continued steadily. According to a 1992 report from the Bureau of Labor Statistics, 4.2 million secretaries were employed in the United States in that year and 98 percent of them were women (Waldrop, J. "More than a typist." *American Demographics.* 1994). The trend persisted in public schools as well.

The earliest known Homer school secretary was Miss Victoria Gordon, who was the secretary to Principal Louis J. Wolner in 1936. It is quite likely individuals in secretarial/assistant roles in Homer Academy and Union School existed earlier than 1936. However, the existing yearbooks mention Gordon and indicate she was followed by Miss Rena Williams, Miss Shirley Brower, Miss Eleanor McAuliffe, and Miss "Margie" Blanden.

These young ladies were all Homer graduates who had gone on for further education in Syracuse at Central City Business Institute or Powelson Business Institute. Post-high school training could be received at the Cortland Business Institute between 1896 and the 1950s. Located on the second floor at 12-14 Railroad Street (now Central Avenue), it provided a two-year course of study leading to a diploma in either bookkeeping, cashiering, stenography (which required 150 words per minute typing), or general business. This writer's mother was a graduate.

In 1945, Blanden was married and still on the job as Mrs. Charlie Alexander. She was joined by Sally Beard. By 1946, the year the District "centralized," "office secretaries" were Mrs. Francis Riley and Carolyn Downing. Two years later, the secretaries were Bette Hazzard and Peggy Gower. In 1949 and 1950, the names of Hazzard and Helen Leonard appeared in school yearbooks. In 1951, Shirley Knapp joined the "office staff," and the next schoolyear she was appointed Clerk of the Board. She served for many years, amassing in her head much institutional history. She missed reaching the school's bicentennial milestone by five days when she passed on January 28, 2019, at age 94.

The National Secretaries Association was founded in 1942, and U.S. Secretary of Commerce Charles W. Sawyer proclaimed June 1–7, 1952, to be "National Secretaries Week" with Wednesday, June 4 designated as "National Secretaries' Day." In 1955, the observance date of "National Secretaries Week" was moved to the last full week of April, with Wednesday designated as "Administrative Professionals Day." In 1973, Hallmark saw a marketing opportunity and began producing Administrative Professionals Day cards. The name was changed to "Professional Secretaries Week" in 1981 and became "Administrative Professionals Week" in 2000 to encompass the expanding responsibilities and wide-ranging job titles of administrative support staff in the modern economy. At present, National Administrative Professionals' Day, or "Secretaries Day," is observed each year on the Wednesday of the last full week in April. This year, that would be Wednesday, April 22nd.

Through the history of Homer Central Schools, the following has been said of each of its secretaries and administrative assistants: "She helps in any way that anyone needs. We all treasure her and the hard work she does." This next statement may not sound like high praise, but it is: "I would *never* want her job." The only other school employee job this writer would never want is bus driver. Just imagine the responsibility of having a classroom of multi-age pupils on wheels, in motion, and seated (supposedly) *behind* you as you navigate some of the District's backroads on a blustery and icy winter's day. No thank you! Hats off to those men and women who perform this important transportation service for our children every school day. Like the secretaries, the bus drivers are expected to perform their jobs with a smile on their faces. Some days that can be a challenge. But the driver's face for some children is the first and last face of the District they see each school day.

And the secretary's face? This is the first face that greets the public in the main office, Superintendent's office, Guidance office, or Business office and provides the information being requested. In short, the school secretary is the face of the District, and first impressions are critical. Is the impression made positive or negative? Is it welcoming? A good school secretary helps build relationships, reflects by word and deed the values of the school, and is an integral part of the school climate.

Do school secretaries in Homer, or anywhere for that matter, receive the credit they deserve? History reveals school secretaries as a group have not been singled out for academic study. That's hard to believe. They are "invisible;" they are essentially missing from the vast body of research literature related to public education, school administration, or school improvement and reform. If you need to have your eyes opened as to the importance of their impactful role in school culture, go visit a school on the first week of school at bus dismissal. That should convince you. Even in the face of the current pandemic, some Homer School secretaries are reporting off and on to their posts for "essential" business or working from their homes to keep the gears turning under trying circumstances. So, as we come upon Secretaries Day 2020, this writer hopes all our past Homer school secretaries have felt appreciated and that all our current school secretaries have been told, "We cannot function without you."

Thanks goes to Kelli Yacavone, Kathy Beardsley, and Harry Coleman for providing some of the information needed for this article.

April 23, 2020

EARLY HOMER PHYSICIANS AND THE COUNTY MEDICAL SOCIETY

Given the current heroic battle being waged by health care providers across the nation and world against the coronavirus, it seems appropriate at this time to offer this tribute to Homer's earliest doctors. Surely, in their time, they were on the front lines confronting epidemics of cholera, smallpox, and scarlet fever, and equipped with far less knowledge, technology and medicine than found in today's arsenal.

According to its website, "The Cortland County Medical Society represents the interests of patients and physicians in Cortland County in an ongoing effort to assure quality health care services for all. The county society provides resources for physicians, including continuing medical education, practice and professional guidelines, legal support, and a patient referral service. For the general public, the county medical society is a source for physician referrals and guidance on patient rights." The organization has a long history, and Homer doctors were instrumental in its founding and early success.

The Cortland County Medical Society was organized in 1808 in accordance with a law, enacted by the Legislature in 1806, incorporating the New York State Medical Society. Approved by Governor Morgan Lewis on April 4, 1806, the law also required medical societies to be formed in every county of the State.

Cortland County was organized in the spring of 1808, having until that time been a part of Onondaga County. Soon after this, on August 10, 1808, the following gentlemen, legally qualified to practice medicine and surgery, convened at the house of Captain Enos Stimson in Homer village: Drs. Lewis S. Owen, Luther Rice, John Miller, Elijah G. Wheeler, Robert D. Taggart, Ezra Pannel, Allen Barney and Jesse Searl. These men took on the responsibility of forming a medical association under the name "Cortland County Medical Society."

The following members were elected as the officers of the society: Dr. Lewis S. Owen, president; Dr. John Miller, vice-president; Dr. Jesse Searl, secretary; and Dr. Robert D. Taggart, treasurer. Drs. Miller, Barney and Taggart were appointed a committee to draft a code of by-laws for the government and regulation of the society.

Fifty years later, when the society celebrated its semi-centennial anniversary, only one of the founders of the society was still living in the county. That was the venerable Dr. John Miller, of Truxton, who was serving as the society's president. It is believed that the society was not represented in the State Medical Society until 1814, when Dr. Miller was sent as delegate.

You may be surprised to learn not one of the founders of the society had graduated in medicine. Opportunities for a thorough medical education were limited at the time. Only those of affluence or those residing conveniently near the few medical colleges then in existence in the country could avail themselves of systematic, medical instruction. It is true that Dr. Miller had been a private pupil of Dr. Benjamin Rush in Philadelphia (signer of the Declaration of Independence) and had attended the lectures of Rush and Shippen, two of the founders of the medical department of the University of Pennsylvania, but Miller never completed a university course. As with the legal profession of that era, you prepared for the medical profession simply by finding a practitioner willing to mentor you and by reading what books were available.

Around 1814 steps were taken by the society to establish a library for its use, and Drs. Owen and Miller were appointed a committee to select such books as they had the means to purchase. Sometimes, surplus funds in the treasury were expended to acquire books. The library of standard books and periodicals eventually reached a total of about two hundred volumes. After 1845, this cooperative plan of keeping up a central library, by additions to it, was discontinued. Each member was expected to supply himself with the most recent and best periodicals and books and thus keep up with the latest advances in medicine.

Of the first officers of the new society, two of the four resided in Homer: Dr. Owen and Dr. Searl. Two other Homer doctors who played significant roles in the early success of the society were Dr. Lewis Riggs and Dr. George W. Bradford.

Dr. Lewis S. Owen was elected the first president of the society and held that office by annual election until 1820. He was born in the town of New Lebanon, Columbia County, NY, in 1772. His early education was obtained in the common schools of his native town. For a short time, he attended the academic department of Williams College. This was preparatory to commencing the study of medicine around 1795 under Dr. Stringer, a prominent practitioner of Albany, NY. His final mentoring was with Dr. McClellan, also of Albany. He then was licensed by the courts of Albany County in 1798. The next year, he came to the town of Homer. Here he continued to reside until his death in 1849—short by one month of fifty years.

It is believed that Dr. Owen was the first physician who permanently located in the county of Cortland. The country was new, and the roads were bad—often mere paths through the woods—and doctors commonly made house calls at that time. These wilderness conditions made a physician's labors severe and fatiguing, but Owen pursued the practice of his profession steadily and successfully for nearly twenty-five years. In addition, Dr. Owen was one of the founders of the Academy in Homer chartered by the state in 1819, one of its trustees during the remainder of his life, and president of the board of trustees for several years. The last twenty or more years of his life were mainly devoted to agricultural pursuits.

Dr. Jesse Searl, the society's first secretary, was born in 1767 and raised in Southampton, Massachusetts. He was educated in the common schools of his native town before pursuing his medical studies with Dr. Woodbridge of Southampton. He commenced practice in the vicinity of his native town and then came to New York State sometime around 1800. He took up residence in Fabius, Onondaga County. He came to Homer either in 1803 or 1804 and diligently pursued the practice of medicine until the year 1812. That was when he purchased and assumed the editorship of the *Cortland Repository*, at that time the only newspaper published in the county.

Being a frail man physically, Searl chose to give up his medical practice for a less strenuous occupation. It was said that he showed sympathy with the sick and possessed an education, general and professional, that was somewhat in advance of most of his contemporaries. He was reported to have the best private medical library in the county and to be a subscriber to the only medical periodical then published in the country—the *Medical Repository*, published in New York. He kept up interest in medicine and continued to be a regular attendant upon all the meetings of the County Society and to be its secretary until 1820. He died in 1834, at the age of sixty-eight years. His obituary described him in these flattering terms: "In all of the affairs of life, as a man, a Christian, a conductor of a public newspaper, and as a physician, Dr. Searl was consistent and faithful in their varied duties, and the poor always found in him a friend in time of need."

Dr. Lewis Riggs was born in Norfolk, CT, on January 16, 1789. His aptitude for mechanical employment led to his apprenticeship to the carpenter's trade to Mr. Samuel N. Gaylord, with whom he came to Cortland in the spring of 1805. In after years, when riding over the country as a practitioner of medicine, he was able to point to not a few houses and barns which he helped to build. In the spring of 1809, he decided on the profession of medicine and commenced his studies in the office of Dr. Samuel Woodward of Torringford, Connecticut. In May of 1812, he received a county license to practice, and in October he went to Philadelphia to attend a course of medical lectures by Dr. Rush, "the father of American medicine," and Dr. Philip Syng Physic, "the father of American surgery."

In 1818, Riggs moved to Homer and opened a drug store. He soon found himself engaged more fully in the practice of medicine and joined the County Medical Society. Oddly, in the summer of 1828 he sold his practice to a Dr. Metcalf and went to Trumansburg. There he and a partner entered the dry goods business. When Dr. Metcalf left Homer, Riggs was persuaded to return to Homer and to the profession for which he was best suited. In 1834 Dr. Riggs formed a partnership with Dr. Ashbel Patterson, formerly of Danby, Tompkins County, and continued the association for about seven years.

After the dissolution of the partnership, Riggs was nominated in the fall of 1840 to represent the Twenty-second district in Congress from 1841–1842. He was elected, which led to his retirement from practice and to his engagement in other enterprises. He purchased the flouring mill south of the village and erected a new stone building on its site, superintending its construction and planning many of the details of its machinery. Still, he did not forsake his interest in medicine entirely and frequently responded to professional calls from his old friends in the village and beyond who insisted on a consultation with "the old doctor." He died about midnight on November 7, 1870, at the age of 82. Much of what we know of this Homer doctor is from the biographical sketch read at the annual meeting of the County Society in December 1870 by Dr. H. O. Jewett of Cortland.

The fourth early Homer doctor of note is Dr. George W. Bradford. Born in the town of Otsego, near Cooperstown, NY, on May 9th, 1796, he was of the seventh generation in direct descent from the famous William Bradford, the second governor of Plymouth colony. He early acquired a taste for books and became a devoted reader of the best literature accessible. In 1812 he was sent to an academy at Woodstock, Connecticut. Among his schoolmates was the afterwards celebrated surgeon and clinical teacher, Dr. George McClellan, the father of Civil War General George B. McClellan. In 1814 he was sent to a classical school at Clinton, NY. In the fall of 1816, he entered as a student the office of Dr. Thomas Fuller of Cooperstown, the leading physician of that vicinity. He always lamented not receiving a structured medical education from a college.

In 1819 Bradford moved to Preble and commenced the practice of medicine. In February of 1820, he returned to Cooperstown and was licensed to practice medicine by the Otsego County Medical Society. About 1821 or 1822, he came to Homer and continued the practice of medicine for the next sixty years. He was elected a member of the Cortland County Medical Society, and six years afterward he was chosen its secretary. He held this office for an astounding forty-five consecutive years. Only an increasing disability from deafness caused him to resign from this post, but he continued in the office of treasurer until 1881. He declined a re-election upon having permanently relocated to Syracuse. At the time of his resignation as secretary the society attributed much of its prosperity to his "vigilant administration."

In 1841 Bradford was elected a delegate to the State Medical Society for four years, and in 1847 was elected a permanent member of that society. In the same year he was elected one of the delegates to the American Medical Association, which then met in Philadelphia and where he became a permanent member at the time of its permanent organization. In 1858 he was elected vice-president of the State Medical Society, having declined the nomination for the presidency.

In 1851 he was elected to the New York State Assembly and served on several committees, especially one on medical colleges and societies. In November of 1853, he was elected to the State Senate, and re-elected two years later. He showed perseverance and tact in securing the passage of a bill providing for anatomical matériel for medical colleges—appropriately called the "Bone Bill." He was the author of the Prohibition law passed by the Legislature in 1854, which was declared unconstitutional by the New York Court of Appeals in 1855. In 1856 he was elected a member of the American Association for the Advancement of Science.

In addition, he was elected in 1832 as a trustee of the academy in Homer and continued for thirty-eight years, serving alongside Principal Samuel Woolworth. He had a huge medical library the contents of which he was more than happy to share with others. It should be noted, too, that he was a member of the Electoral College in 1864 and cast his vote for Abraham Lincoln.

In July 1863, while treating the gangrenous wound of a soldier just returned from the field of Gettysburg, he suffered septic poisoning through an abrasion on his right hand. This resulted in a continued inflammation with thecal abscesses of the palm and fingers, loss of tendons, and a stiffness of joints—collateral damage from a battle waged just one state away. Still, he persevered and, in the words of his pastor, Rev. T. K. Fessenden, "people of Homer then employed him and regarded him as a wise, skillful, entirely trustworthy and successful physician."

In 1881, he retired to Syracuse and died on October 30, 1883, at the home of his granddaughter. The funeral services were held in the Congregational Church in Homer in the afternoon of November 2nd. He is buried in Glenwood Cemetery.

Of the four early physicians in Homer, it can truly be said that they showed an exemplary fidelity to their profession and to the organization they helped to create—the Cortland County Medical Society.

Source: Smith, H. P., editor. *History of Cortland County.* Chapter XVI. Syracuse, NY: D. Mason & Co., Publishers, 1885.

May 21, 2020

PAST MEMORIAL DAYS IN HOMER

Memorial Day is fast approaching. Since 1970, the last Monday of May has been set aside for this national holiday. That was not always the case. May

30th was the date for the observance from 1868 to 1970, no matter the day of the week upon which it fell. Originally called "Decoration Day," the first national celebration of Memorial Day took place May 30, 1868, at Arlington National Cemetery. Since then, the tradition has been for many people to visit cemeteries and memorials on Memorial Day to honor and mourn those who had died in military service. Many volunteers, such as Boy Scouts in Homer, usually place an American flag on each grave in cemeteries. From its post-Civil War origins, veterans' organizations in communities have encouraged school children, even in Homer, to bring flowers to "decorate" the graves.

Because of the coronavirus pandemic, this year's Memorial Day will be like no other. The Homer American Legion Post will be having a virtual ceremony at the cemetery Memorial Day morning. Police Chief Bob Pittman and Post Commander Paul Powers came up with a good plan. There will be no parade, and the main speaker will hopefully be a nurse who has been on the frontlines of the war against COVID-19. The ceremony will be broadcast on X101. The community is urged to participate from the safety of home.

Meanwhile, here are some examples of how the Homer community observed Memorial Day in the past. What traditions have continued, and which ones have not? See if you can find similarities and differences.

> On May 25, 1877, the *Homer Republican* made this announcement:
> The exercises of Memorial Day, Wednesday, May 30th, will commence on the Public Square [the Green] at 8:30 a. m. Comrade Captain J. C. Atwater is detailed as Marshal of the Day. Comrade H. Fuller, Officer of the Day, will take command of the Post. The procession will be formed at 9 o'clock a. m. in the following order: Homer Cornet Band. Post Willoughby Babcock and soldiers [veterans of the war for the Union]. Speaker and Clergy. Trustees of the Village. Fraternities. Fire Department. Citizens.

At Glenwood Cemetery, the following was to be the program:

> Decoration of graves. Music by the Band. Prayer. Singing. Address by Rev. Wm. A. Robinson. Music. Benediction. Comrades J. K. Miller, G. W. Dayton, and Horton Bates will receive and take charge of contributions of flowers.

The ladies of Homer were "urgently requested to prepare and send bouquets to the town hall [Episcopal Church] at eight o'clock a. m." Businessmen and citizens of the village and vicinity, were "earnestly invited to lay aside the ordinary pursuits and share with us in the performance of a sacred duty." The invitation to the community was signed by E. J Peck, Commander of

W. Babcock Post of the Grand Army of the Republic and W. D. Brooks, Adjutant.

Sometime around 1913, Memorial Day leaned more in a religious direction in Homer. The *Homer Republican* reported that a well-attended joint church service was held on a Sunday evening at the Methodist Episcopal church "in honor of the veterans of the civil war, living and dead . . ." The local Grand Army post and Sons of Veterans arrived in a body. The twenty-six veterans in attendance and sons of veterans were given seats of honor. The churches were represented by Rev. E. E. Merring, Rev. B. L. Herr and Rev. F. W. Dickinson. A choir led the singing and a trio consisting of Mrs. Chauncy Baker, Mrs. F. M. Briggs and Mrs. W. B. Newcomb performed two selections and Mrs. Baker sang "a familiar civil war song." Rev. Mr. Merring delivered the sermon. His text was "What Mean Ye by These Stones?" (Joshua, iv, 6).

The newspaper commented that Merring "spoke in an interesting and effective manner of memorial day set apart as a sacred day of remembrance and honor to the nation's dead and of honor also to the survivors of the Grand Army of the Republic, who fought for noble principles and a united nation." The pastor went on to emphasize "the duty of a proper observance of the day and of teaching the children patriotism and true love and appreciation of our nation, and those who had suffered to make it what it is." He said he wanted the next generation to be fighters—"fighters for the right, fighters in the battle against the great wrongs existing in our national and social life of to-day." Chiefly, he pointed to "the liquor question and the taking from any person the right to a fair chance in life." He appealed to the veterans assembled "to live the Christian life of service and by righteous living to set a worthy example to the rising generation who look upon them with reverence as the nation's heroes."

The *Homer Republican* of June 5, 1913, noted that Memorial Day itself in Homer was "fittingly observed" that year "in accordance with the program published in the *Republican* last week." Because the weather was "fine and bright and not too cool for comfort," the attendance "was larger than usual, many young men and women being present." Over forty Grand Army veterans attended, along with twenty Sons of Veterans. The memorial services took place at the usual place in Glenwood Cemetery at 10:30 a. m. The veterans were conveyed there by automobiles courtesy of local citizens. The parade had formed at 10 a. m., under the command of H. H. Harrington and the Marshall of the Day, C. H. Stevens. The column was headed by "an excellent fife and drum corps from Cortland."

Upon reaching the cemetery the veterans were "seated in chairs provided on the soldiers' plot where these services have long been held." The extensive services were opened by the reading of the G. A. R. ritual by Commander Harrington and officers of the post. The command was then turned over to the

President of the Day, W. G. Crandall. What followed was: Memorial Hymn. Male Quartet (Messrs. Schaeffer and Ralph Bennett of Cortland, Prof. J. M. Round [of the Academy] and Fred T. Newcomb of Homer). Prayer offered by Rev. E. E. Merring. Remarks by the President of the Day W. G. Crandall. Reading of Lincoln's Gettysburg Address by Dr. G. A. Burdick. Reading by W. G. Crandall of G.A.R. Commander-in-Chief Logan's 1868 Order calling for a national day of remembrance for the nation's Civil War dead. Song "Rock of Ages" by the Quartet. Address by Rev. B. L. Herr. Singing of "America" by the Quartet. Benediction offered by Chaplain Rev. F. W. Dickinson.

The newspaper observed that "The program was very effectively given and the address by Rev. Benjamin L. Herr was most able, appropriate, eloquent and inspiring." The paper summed up the contents of the speech in one long sentence:

> It was full of patriotic sentiment and appreciation of the brave and noble deeds of the soldiers of the Civil War, living and dead, and of sane and timely thought for the future and the type of bravery required to solve our grave and insistent problems, which must be worked out by strong, high minded, God fearing men.

It is interesting to note that Homer's Grand Army post had a membership at the time of thirty-five. It had been organized in 1870 with Prof. E. J. Peck, then Principal of Homer Academy, as its first commander. The members in 1913 were Charles S. Brown, F. D. Carpenter, Sr., Frank Corl, Rev. F. W. Dickinson, H. H. Harrington, C. O. Newton, Lewellyn P. Norton [Congressional Medal of Honor recipient], P. A. Norton, M. J. Pratt, R. C. Shattuck, William Simpson, Charles H. Stevens, George W. Stebbins, Henry Walton, E. A, Williams, Myron Wooster, Charles W. Hutchings, L. Stebbins, Harrison Chapman, Frederick Monk, William Sweet, David B. Chapman, John Y. Simmons, George Satterlee [also known as "Sig Sautelle"], W. A. Brink, Theron Gutchess, E. F. Whitcomb, Charles Lawson, J. S. McMaster, Robert Nixon, E. W. Clark, H. A. Smith, C. E. Haight, Smith S. Wright, and John Tuthill.

The Sons of Veterans had organized only a few months earlier during the winter, and its charter members included F. A. Crosley, William G. Crandall, D. F. Shattuck, F. H. Alvord, Charles Creque, Dr. G. A. Burdick, Arthur Stebbins, Fred Stebbins, Wilbur Gutchess, Melvin Pratt, Fred T. Newcomb, R. J. Simpson, John Marble, F. D. Miller, Roy McMaster, Earl Smith, and Herman Miles.

On that Memorial Day, one hundred graves of soldiers in Glenwood Cemetery were decorated with the national flag, and several graves of soldiers in Atwater Cemetery on the Scott Road and the Goodale Cemetery on West Hill were similarly honored.

The next year, 1914, the newspaper informed its readers on May 28, that Homer's "Grocery stores will be closed from 12:30 to 5 p. m. on Memorial Day, [but] will be open morning and evening." The paper's June 4th issue described the special day's events. It noted "There was a little rain during the forenoon but before noon the skies had cleared, and the afternoon was an ideal one for the parade to the cemetery and the out-of-door exercises." At 2 p. m. the veterans, Sons of Veterans, and Village officers in automobiles formed in line on Main Street under command of John Y. Simmons and, headed by a Cortland drum corps, paraded to Glenwood Cemetery. Marshal of the Day was F. A. Crosley, and "the exercises were held in the usual place on the plot in the center of the cemetery." The program was quite like the previous year, including the Grand Army ritual, prayers, recitation of the Gettysburg Address, and a main speaker. This time, however, singing was provided by "the girls of the sixth, seventh, and eighth grades and academic department of the Academy, led by Choir Director Cook of the Congregational choir."

Rev. J. H. Olmstead, pastor of the Congregational Church, was the main speaker, his subject being "Trophies." He spoke of the visible trophies of the Civil War, "treasured in many places in our nation and . . . stored in the hearts of our citizens." He pointed out "many lessons taught by the brave and self-sacrificing soldiers of our Civil War, which should be treasured as priceless trophies of that great and bloody conflict which cost this nation so dearly but left to it heritage of union and freedom beyond price." Interestingly, there was no mention of lessons taught by those involved in the more recent war with Spain or the prospects of any future lessons looming on the horizon. The Great War in Europe would break out the next month. In just a few years, offspring of Civil War veterans would ship "over there" for another "great and bloody conflict."

Led by the girls' choir, the services of 1914 were closed by singing "America." The graves had been previously decorated on Sunday by a committee from the Sons of Veterans led by a G. A. R. member. At the conclusion of the exercises the G. A. R. veterans and Sons of Veterans again entered the automobiles and were taken to Post headquarters.

One cannot help but notice the emphasis that was placed on vocal music at the earlier Memorial Day observances. Some patriotic songs were written for the day's purpose and for commercial interests. A publisher in Toledo, Ohio, ran a notice that appeared in the May 11, 1877, edition of the *Homer Republican*. For thirty cents, one could order a copy of a new song, "No More the Bugle's Stirring Blast." With lyrics by Samuel N. Mitchell and music by Charles E. Prior, the piece was arranged to be sung either as solo and chorus, or as a quartet. Emphasis was placed on it having been "written expressly for Memorial Day, May 30th, 1877, and will be sung in every State, where there is a soldier's grave to honor." But the publisher was offering a special deal. Those ordering for the memorial exercises could have one single copy for 25 cents or five copies mailed postpaid for $1.00.

We know, as mentioned above, that there was "singing" at the cemetery in Homer on May 30, 1877, and if this proposed "National Memorial Song" was included in the program, those in attendance would have heard this opening stanza:

No more the bugle's stirring blast
Will call our heroes to the fray;
For they have found a rest at last
And at their graves we pause to-day.
The buds brought forth by April show'rs
We've woven into garlands gay.
And on each mound we strew the flow'rs
Fresh with the breath of May.

June 4, 2020

DENNIS DOBBINS AND THE HOUSE THAT CABBAGE BUILT

The Landmark Society of Cortland County, now headquartered at the History Center at Key Bank in Homer, was originally created in the early 1970s by Anna Hilton, Mary Alice Bellardini, and other Homer citizens. Originally, the goal was to foster the designation of a proud "historic district" in the village and the preservation of the 220 structures within it

Houses do not build themselves. Behind every edifice, be it large or small, residential or commercial, there is a story—a story of the people responsible for this built space. Thus, in the past couple years, the Society has transitioned from a singular mission to a dual mission: the preservation of local architecture *and* local history.

An excellent example of a built space in the Historic District with an interesting history behind it is the picturesque house at 16 North Main Street occupied by Barry and Pat Ryan. Their Queen Anne style home was originally built by an Irish immigrant named Dennis Dobbins who made a name for himself locally as "the cabbage king." This is his story as gleaned from multiple issues of over ten newspapers of his era.

Image 10.4 One of the architectural gems in Old Homer Village historic district. *From the picture postcard collection of Kelly Preston.*

Dennis Dobbins was born in 1847 in Cork, Ireland, one of nine children of John and Mary Crimmins Dobbins. When Dennis was ten years old, the family immigrated to America and soon settled in Homer. In 1871 Dennis married Johanna Barry (called "Hannah"), who also had been born in Ireland in 1847 and came to this country when a child. Her family came to Marathon. This is where she first met her future husband. The couple would spend the rest of their lives in the village of Homer and raise five children. Only two of the children outlived their parents—one son, Joseph, who always remained at the parental home, and a daughter, Rosa. Maurice died in infancy. Then there was Ella and a second son named Maurice.

Little is known about Dennis Dobbins until his name starts to appear in local papers in the 1880s, and then it is because of his political life. *The Republican* newspaper of August 14, 1884 lists him among fifty men who signed up to establish a club to support the Democratic Party presidential ticket of Cleveland and Hendricks. Three years later, he was reported to be active in Democratic Party politics at the county level.

Homer Village Minutes for 1885 reveal the 38-year-old Dobbins was hired by the municipality to "cart timber, coal, etc." and to provide wood. This ad in *The Republican* on July 22, 1886, shows him to be a hardworking member of the community:

Fire Wood of All Kinds at DENNIS DOBBINS' WOOD YARD!
CORTLAND ST., HOMER, N. Y.

All kinds of firewood delivered promptly

to any place in the village at reasonable prices.

I am also prepared to do teaming, trucking,

moving, etc., in the lowest rates.

He must have been successful at his earliest vocation. By March 3, 1887, he was building two new homes on Cortland Street on a lot he had purchased earlier. The next year, he bought four building lots on Copeland Avenue, and in August he bought a team of trucking horses and continued to advertise his trucking business. In May of 1889, he bought a house on James Street, and two months later bought a lot on Cayuga Street with intent to build a new residence for his family.

It is presumed that it was at this Cayuga Street residence that Ella, the youngest daughter, was nearly suffocated by coal gas on a December night in 1890. Hannah arose in the night to see if Ella was properly covered and found her unconscious and the room filled with gas from a coal stove. Dr. Stone was summoned. Only after working over the child for hours did he manage to revive her, but word circulated that she was dead. Other members of the family also suffered from the gas but were not seriously affected.

Then, on New Year's Day, 1891, the *Republican* reported: "Ella, youngest daughter of Dennis Dobbins, who was reported to have been poisoned by coal gas on the night of December 16th, died Friday night. It is now learned that she had been ill for some time previous to the gas poisoning and it is thought that her death was not due to that accident. The child was thirteen years old and was very bright and intelligent."

Little is known about the other daughter, Rosa. On May 13, 1892, *The Cortland Democrat* noted that a twenty-two year old Miss Rosa Dobbins "has commenced a civil action in the supreme court against Joseph Pickett and Byron Maxson to recover damages to the amount of nearly $4,000 for alleged mismanagement of the Fisher manufacturing company [of Homer], limited, of which the plaintiff is the largest stock holder." Other than that, we know she outlived her parents and siblings. She died in 1933 and is buried in St. Mary's Cemetery in Cortland.

On the night of January 17, 1893, either the house on Cayuga Street or the next Dobbins' residence at the northwest corner of the Green became the destination for books, pictures, and every object that could be safely removed from the nearby Homer Academy being engulfed in flames. In the fire's aftermath, it was Dennis Dobbins who cleared the stones and iron from the site and became a scrap iron dealer if he was not already engaged in the business.

Sometime in 1897, Dobbins partnered with one of his brothers and together they parlayed their hard-earned capital into the next Dobbins business venture: the erection of two cabbage warehouses in the village. One storage house was built at the end of South Main Street. Another, with a capacity of 900 tons, was constructed on property Dobbins had purchased on the south end of West Road. As *The Cortland Democrat* for April 9, 1897 noted: "Dennis intends to purchase [cabbage]in the fall at a low figure, then store them and sell at a margin later." Dobbins must have already garnered a reputation as a shrewd dealer because the paper added with tongue in cheek "He has a terrible eye for business."

But agricultural markets can be risky, and in March of 1898, Dobbins sold the locally grown cabbage stored in his cabbage house in the south-western part of the village to F. X. Litz for 1 and 1/4 cents per head. This sale of nearly 300 tons of cabbage represented a loss for the Dobbins men, but it was said they more than made up for it the next year. Meanwhile, Dennis continued to buy and sell real estate in the area and to build homes on Cortland, Cayuga, and James streets in the village.

The Dobbins Family still resided in their house at the northwest corner of the Green in 1899. This is known because the Thursday, April 20th issue of *The Homer Republican* reported a burglary had been thwarted at this residence about a week before. Son Joseph Dobbins, who resided with his parents,

> was aroused from his slumbers by footsteps in the house, and soon saw a man cautiously stealing into his room. He sprang out of bed and his nocturnal visitor turned and ran downstairs with Joseph after him. "Joe" grasped a chair and sent it flying after the would-be burglar, who quickly made his escape through a rear door. It is thought that the man made his entrance through a front window. Nothing was found missing the next morning.

Dobbins sold this home [no longer standing]in the summer of 1902 for $1,900. The purchaser had it remodeled into a rectory and donated it to the Episcopal Church next door. And the Dobbins Family moved again—this time to a house on James Street.

Meanwhile, Dobbins had been doing very well in the cabbage market. On March 15, 1900, the *Cortland County Sentinel* ran this notice: "Thirty dollars per ton is the price received by Dennis Dobbins for seventy-five tons of cabbage last week. He still has sixty tons left for which he expects to receive a still higher price." Two months later, Dennis Dobbins & Sons [Maurice and Joe] bought the lot where C. O. Newton's hay barn once stood, between Fulton Street and the railroad. The goal was to begin building a cabbage house, 82 feet by 72 feet, and with three air chambers on all four sides to prevent the contents from freezing. The strategy was obviously to buy and sell huge amounts of cabbage grown by farmers in the cabbage belt stretching from Tully and Preble south to Homer and into south Cortland. Over time, Dobbins had cabbage storage facilities not just in Homer but in Tully, Preble, and Little York.

It was said of Dobbins that he was "well-known and had many friends but a man always busily occupied with his own affairs." Perhaps he overextended himself. In May of 1902, while on a business trip to New York City, he suffered a stroke and was hospitalized. Once he improved, he returned to his home on James Street to resume his usual business activities.

Adversity struck next on January 2, 1904. The fire bell at the James Street firehouse commenced ringing at 8 o'clock that night. Fire had broken out in Dobbins' large cabbage house on South Main Street. A defective stovepipe in the basement was believed to be the cause. $10,000 worth of cabbage was threatened, but the firemen, contending with a temperature of 14 below zero, gale winds, and snowfall, managed to get the fire under control in short order. Little damage was done, and Dobbins had insurance.

The next month, on the 18th, *The Gazette and Farmer's Journal* made this announcement:

"Cortland—The shipment of about forty tons of cabbage from Blodgett's Mills recently exhausted the supply in the southern part of this county. The price received was $45 a ton. Dennis Dobbins of Homer now owns the largest stock in this territory, which amounts to about 900 tons. At the present price it is figured that he could reap a profit of about $40,000 on his cabbage, but he is holding out for a further advance in the price."

It is believed that on this occasion and in other seasons, Dobbins bought local cabbage at a price of $12 and $14 a ton and then in the winter sold at $50 a ton. At one time he was known to have refused an offer of $15,000 profit, and since he had a corner on the local cabbage market, he was able to rake in a fortune.

It was at this time, in 1905, that Dobbins determined the time had come to build another residence for his family. This built space on Main Street was to reflect the level of affluence his family had attained through hard work and good luck. Prosperity made possible the building of this pretentious house, and Dobbins took great pride in it. It took two years to construct, and while artists were at work painting murals on the interior walls and ceilings, it was said that Dennis and his sons would go across the street to stand and admire their prized creation. For them, it was the American Dream come true.

In the spring of 1907, Dennis and Hannah and their two sons, Maurice and Joe, moved into their "dream house." Unfortunately, soon after moving into the new residence, Maurice became seriously ill and at age 32 succumbed there to a pulmonary disease on October 16. Not quite four years later, the *Cortland Standard* for February 23, 1911, was raving about the Dobbins "palace." It called it "one of the finest and most expensive houses in central New York, one whose interior is the best finished, and most elaborately decorated."

Interestingly, the house was never completely furnished. It may have been because sixty-four-year-old Hannah Dobbins died in the fall of 1911 "after a protracted illness of several months," and her husband and son could not bring themselves to follow through with any plans Hannah had for furnishings. Now, alone in the big house, Joe and his father spent their days over an oil lamp, living mostly in the kitchen, while the gorgeously decorated rooms, barren of furniture, were permitted to be inspected by any who wanted to see them, and many did.

For some reason, in the summer before Hannah's passing, Dennis and Joe began excavations for the erection of another dwelling on Elm Avenue, in the rear of the corner lot on which their palatial residence stood. The plans called for a nine-room house with all modern conveniences and a broad porch across the entire front. A news reporter for the *Cortland Standard* (August 29, 1911) predicted "The house, when completed, will be a handsome residence and an ornament to the street." But it would be no match for the home of the "Cabbage Kings" next door.

Back in 1893, Dennis had contemplated making a trip back "home" to Cork, but in 1912, as a sixty-five-year-old widower of means, he must have decided it was now or never for a trip to Ireland and Europe. Thus, as reported in the *Skaneateles Free Press,* "Dennis and Joseph Dobbins, the cabbage kings" departed New York City on May 30 onboard the *Carpathia*, the British passenger liner that rescued the survivors of the "unsinkable" *RMS Titanic* the month before (April 15, 1912). What was to be a two-month tour turned into four, as the "cabbage kings" took in Europe, England, Ireland, and the Holy Land. They docked back in New York on September 6 on the *Mauretania.* The next day, they arrived back in Homer, where the *Cortland Standard* reported "They received many a cordial greeting and hearty handshake from old friends as they passed through the streets to their home." The *Homer Republican* quoted the travelers: "[We are] both in good health and ready to go to buying cabbage as soon as the market opens." And that they did, among other transactions.

As the "Tin Lizzie" was replacing the horse as a means of transportation, the Dobbins men sold Skahan's blacksmith shop at 19 James Street. This was "one of the landmarks of this village" (*The Cortland Democrat* July 4, 1913), and the Dobbins family had owned it "for a number of years." The buyer, George Ryder of Dresserville, planned to move his family into the rooms on the second floor.

Selling cabbage to out-of-town kraut makers required shipping via rail, and that could be problematic, as was indicated in *The Homer Republican* of

September 18, 1913: "Joseph Dobbins, the Homer cabbage king, has thirteen actions against the Delaware, Lackawanna and Western railroad for alleged negligent carrying of property." The same paper noted "Cabbage is quoted in the New York market at from $15 to $20 per ton."

Then, cabbage production in New York State hit a slump. Poor prices—$4 per ton—received for good crops of winter cabbage during 1914 and 1915 discouraged farmers from planting again. In many instances large quantities were fed to the cattle, farmers preferring the stuff as fodder to carting to market for low prices. As a substitute for cabbage many turned to raising peas for canning factories in the area. A fifty percent decline in cabbage production was predicted for 1916 (*Homer Republican,* June 15, 1916).

What happened next was an upswing in demand for cabbage. With a low supply by early winter 1917, there was a phenomenal uptick in the price of cabbage, a rise from $30 in the fall to $90 in the winter and prospects of a high mark at $100 a ton. Dealers like the Dobbins men, who were wise enough to have bought heavily in the fall, cornered the market again and stood to make unprecedented fortunes. Even cabbage of poor quality sold for $85 a ton in 1917, and cabbage men did not anticipate a drop in the prices until the next season's crop (*Homer Republican,* January 18, 1917).

When Dennis Dobbins died at age 82 in 1929, funeral services were held at the home and at St. Margaret's Church in Homer, and burial was in Cortland's St. Mary's Cemetery. His obituary in the January 25th *Cortland Democrat* referred to him as "THE CABBAGE KING OF HOMER . . . reputed to have made a fortune." The house he built was described as "a show place of this part of the country" in which "he and his one surviving son, Joseph, have resided . . . ever since its completion."

Joe continued living in the house until his death in 1932. The March 18th issue of *The Homer Post* noted his passing and that "Good fortune and canny handling of sales outweighed occasional misfortune and the Dobbins bankroll grew to comfortable proportions." The paper noted, too, that Joe never married and "was a willing contributor to charity and although quiet and reserved, he was friendly and warmhearted" with a cheerful Irish lilt in his voice. Further, it was noted that Joe was a graduate of Homer Academy and known, in an era where it really mattered, for his beautiful penmanship.

A week later, the same newspaper informed its readers: "The settlement of the estate of Joe Dobbins son of the late Dennis Dobbins, the "cabbage king", awaits the receipt of signed waivers from more than thirty cousins. Only one waiver had been received this week. The Homer National Bank safe deposit box which holds Joe's securities, in which much of the money was invested, cannot be opened until these waivers have been received." The securities may not have been worth much since "it is known that Joe had been a heavy loser in the stock market during the past two years." Joe left all he possessed to his cousin Abbie Dobbins, who had come to Homer eleven years earlier to look after Dennis and Joe at "their beautiful house at Elm Avenue and Main Street." The only other provisions in his will were for a monument for his grave and a bequest of $200 to St. Margaret's Church on Copeland Avenue.

Later, Abbie Dobbins sold the house to Charles and Ruth Kellogg. After his parents died, Ernest Kellogg owned the house. Then, in 1993, Barry and Pat Ryan purchased the house from him, making them only the third family to reside there since 1907. The Ryans found the exterior needed paint, a new roof, gutters, and some serious landscaping. Amazingly, the interior required no repairs. The original murals were all intact—walls and ceilings—depicting cherubs, birds, and flowers! There was stenciling on the walls, and some on the ceilings. Over time, the artwork had lost some of its luster. "It would have been wonderful," said Pat, "to be in the house when the artwork was completed in 1906, with all the brilliant colors!! If we were able to have the paintings conserved, it would have cost a huge fortune." Fortunately, the Ryans deemed it important to preserve the murals as they found them—with the age of the house. They sought the opinion of a professional preservationist, Ted Bartlett of Crawford and Sterns, a Syracuse architectural firm. He made a studied examination of the murals. He was impressed. He said, "You have Metropolitan Museum quality of Art in all the murals and frescos!" The Ryans have been a welcomed addition to The Landmark Society, and Pat is now an active member of the Board of Directors.

So, there's the story behind one of the finest architectural gems in Homer and one of three clear cut favorites of this writer. Perhaps the next time you walk or drive by and admire the Corinthian columns, the balustrades, and the Sheraton fans at the second-floor opening, you will recall the "cabbage kings" that built it and appreciate the owners who have done their best to preserve it. You will have to admit that candles in the windows of the Dobbins House add to the elegance and ambiance of our historic Main Street.

June 18, 2020

PAST JULY FOURTHS IN THE TOWN OF HOMER

For more than two decades, the anniversary of colonial America's severing of ties with Great Britain and the birth of the United States of America has been celebrated in Homer with a community reading of the Declaration of Independence. This annual event on July Fourth has been led by Homer's Charles "Bud" Jermy II and his son Charles "Chip" Jermy III. Both gentlemen have immersed themselves in the background story leading to the historic July days in 1776 and in the lives of the document's signers. Prior to the reading, the Jermys have shared this interesting information, and after the reading there has been the ringing of local church and school bells. All of this has been done with patriotic reverence, and then participants disperse to their homes to further celebrate with family and friends and perhaps take in firework displays outside of Homer.

This year marks the 25th anniversary of this unique Homer observance. Due to the pandemic, an abbreviated program will take place at a location on the Green at 10 AM. On July 4th. Be sure to check the Village website for exact details as the event draws near.

In the meanwhile, compare the present-day means of honoring Independence Day in the town and village of Homer with those from the past.

On July 4th, 1776, the Continental Congress formally adopted the Declaration of Independence. Though the vote for actual independence took place on July 2nd, from then on, the 4th became the day for celebration. The first public readings of the document included concerts, bonfires, parades and the firing of cannons and muskets. Philadelphia held the first annual commemoration of independence on July 4, 1777, while Congress was still occupied with waging the war for freedom. Fireworks were set off, and a tradition was born.

Massachusetts became the first state to make July 4th an official state holiday. This is appropriate given the fact one of the signers, John Adams, was from Massachusetts, but Adams thought July 2nd should be the day for celebration, and he predicted the way it would be celebrated. In his letter to his wife Abigail, dated July 3, 1776, he stated: "The Second Day of July 1776, will be the most memorable Epocha, in the History of America. . . . I am apt to believe that it will be celebrated, by succeeding Generations, as the great anniversary Festival. It ought to be commemorated, as the Day of Deliverance by solemn Acts of Devotion to God Almighty. *It ought to be solemnized with Pomp and Parade, with Shews, Games, Sports, Guns, Bells, Bonfires and Illuminations from one End of this Continent to the other from this Time forward forever more.*" (The emphasis is mine.)

With the successful conclusion of the Revolutionary War, Americans continued to commemorate Independence Day every year on July 4th, but it evolved into an opportunity for the new nation's emerging political leaders to address citizens. The oratory was customarily marked by an appeal to patriotism and a feeling of unity. For example, a young Millard Fillmore of New York State first made a name for himself as a rising political star upon giving a stirring Fourth of July public oration.

The *Republican & Eagle* newspaper for Tuesday, June 25, 1830, announced the Celebration of the Fourth of July in Homer Village was to be kicked off with firing "a national salute of 20 guns . . . accompanied with the ringing of bells, at the rising of the sun." This was to be followed at 10 A.M. with "a federal salute of 13 Guns"—one for each of the original thirteen states. Then, the paper explained, "A procession will be formed under the direction of Major General Samuel G. Hathaway [of the New York State Militia] and Brigadier General Austin W. Otis, with their respective staffs, at 11 o'clock A. M. in front of the Mansion House hotel [on South Main Street]. This procession was to march to the Presbyterian Church [now Congregational Church] in the following order: Martial Music. Uniform Companies. Military Officers in uniform. Revolutionary soldiers. Clergy. Orator and Reader. President and Vice President of the Day. Principal, Teachers, and Students of Cortland Academy [on the Green]. American Standards. Committee of Arrangements. Civil Officers. Citizens. Once all had assembled at the church, there was to be "singing by the Homer Association under the direction of Mr. E. Bernent (sp?)."

Now, another community in the town of Homer seems to have offered an alternative that conflicted timewise with the Homer Village festivities. The same newspaper explained that, in addition, "a patriotic, rational, and temperate celebration of the coming anniversary of our Nation's birthday will be held at Little York. This event was to include the following:

> A procession of carriages containing the teachers and pupils in the several Sabbath schools, with their banners, together with the teachers and pupils of Cortland Academy and the citizens, as choose to unite in the celebration, will start from the head of Main Street, in Homer Village, at half past 9 o'clock A. M., and proceed to the parade ground, near the school house [for planned commemorative exercises].

Note that the event in the hamlet of Little York was to be "temperate," i.e. no consumption of alcoholic libations. However, on the One Hundred and First Anniversary of our independence, at least one individual chose to ignore the admonitions of the local chapter of the Women's Christian Temperance Union. He created his own "fireworks":

> The Fourth of July passed quietly in Homer, except for the actions of one young man who got crazy-drunk. He had a skirmish back of Babcock and Gilkerson's store, which was squelched by J. Gilkerson taking him by the throat and pinching him a little. On going out-doors, he kicked open a sack of flour, drew his revolver and ran up James Street. He fired once at Joseph Watson, missed; ran on to the residence of Leander Tracy, not being able to break in the door, he broke a window and fired through it, not hitting anyone of the three people in the room. He was caught by Officer Bigsby who took him to Cortland. When in jail, his irons were removed; whereupon he knocked another man down and bit off the end

of Bigsby's finger, before he was locked up.
County Republican, July 1877

This was seven years after Congress voted to officially make July Fourth a federal holiday.

One decade later, as reported by the *Homer Republican*, July 1887:

> Fourth of July was observed with a big celebration. It began at midnight Sunday night, with cannon booming, bellringing, and bonfires. There was a parade at 10:30 a.m. led by Marshall Pembroke Pierce and staff, followed by the Homer Protective Police, the Homer Cornet Band, the Village President and Trustees of Homer and Cortland in carriages, the Fire Department, the Grand Army of the Republic, and others including floats. After the parade, there were exercises on the Green, and speakers from Syracuse. At 3:00 p.m. the Fusilier parade was held. "Dide" Ripley was the Fusiliers' orator. There were many take-offs on the Village Board, the "Fossil" Croquet club, the new village fire alarm, and etc. A traction engine pulled a wagon with eight steam whistles on it. Frank Rice and Tommy Fairbanks held a traction engine race, from the Windsor Hotel on N. Main street, to the Mansion House on S. Main street. It was an exciting race; the engines went flying down the street at seven or eight miles per hour, puffing steam and filling the street with smoke. It was a close race until near the finish, when the Rice machine blew off an elbow in the steam line. There were running races, sack races, and wheelbarrow races. A large crowd witnessed fireworks on the Green. The crowd in Homer was estimated at 10,000 [seems too high unless people came from all over]; there was a minimum of disturbance and the village was quiet at 11:00 p.m.

Eleven years later, on July 1, 1898, *The Cortland Democrat* posted a one sentence announcement: "Little York will have a Fourth of July Celebration with a boat and tub race, greased pig, etc." "Greased pig" refers to a once popular type of game, sometimes played at agricultural shows such as state and county fairs, in which contestants, usually children or young adults, tried to grab a squealing pig covered with lard. Such an event was ultimately frowned upon by animal rights organizations. This writer is not sure what the event has to do with marking our Independence Day. He would like to think that perhaps it is a metaphor for the difficulty Britain had in keeping the Thirteen Colonies from slipping away.

And the "etc." could refer to most anything, but it would be nice if it included a community reading of the document largely drafted by Thomas Jefferson that launched "the Great Experiment" we call American democratic government. It and the Constitution and the Bill of Rights are America's founding documents. They are what the French intellectual Alexis de Tocqueville referred to as the sacred texts of the "transcendent universal religion of the nation." If we value them, we should find a way to honor them, besides with a barbeque. Don't you agree? Do consider the public reading on the Green of the United States Declaration of Independence on our nation's upcoming 224th birthday.

July 16, 2020

[*Note: As of the publication of this issue, coronavirus cases had soared more than one million in five days. Miami, not New York City, was now the epicenter of the pandemic in the U.S. One in every 100 Americans had been infected to date. Given this grim news, it seemed this column should run something lighter.*]

THE DARNEDEST THINGS ONE COMES ACROSS WHEN RESEARCHING

My favorite source for researching local history has become *The Homer Republican* which was published by William O. Bunn from 1877 to 1919. When digging in on a topic, trust me, one can get easily distracted by unrelated material. This is material that is humorous, of human interest, or just insightful as to what Homer residents were reading in the newspaper of their day. Below are a few examples listed in chronological order. My comments are in brackets. In these days of stress, may these accounts from the past bring you a momentary distraction and perhaps a smile to your lips.

October 7, 1886: The Alabama Slave troupe [name used by several vaudeville touring groups composed of African American entertainers and/or whites in "blackface"] played at Keator opera house [on Main Street in Homer] last Saturday and Monday evenings. They attracted a crowd to be victimized by a medicine peddler. The minstrel part of the entertainment was fair. [Apparently, before television, even live entertainment had unwanted commercial interruptions.]

June 21, 1888: A tin cart peddler was arrested on Saturday last, on complaint of one Shearer, of Freeville, N.Y., who claimed that the man had stolen his dog, which was then in the peddler's possession. The peddler proved that the dog was his property by putting him through several tricks, much to the amusement of the spectators in Justice Bouton's court. He had lost the dog, he said, a year or more ago and had but just found him. [Just when the news was going to the dogs, there was a doggone happy ending.]

Image 10.5 Charles W. (Bud) Jermy, Jr. and Charles W. (Chip) Jermy III lead a community reading of the United States Declaration of Independence at a church on the Green. *Photo by Don Ferris.*

March 9, 1905: About noon yesterday Harrison Dewitt of Marietta, who drives a peddler's wagon, drove his team and cart through Main street, Homer, on a furious run, yelling and swinging his hands. In turning up Clinton street his wheels caught in the streetcar tracks, turning the cart completely over and making a total wreck of it. The horses broke away and ran into Justin Pierce's barn and through the back door where the harness caught and stopped them. Dewitt was thrown violently from the wagon and badly bruised. He was taken into the Windsor house [hotel], and everyone supposed he was intoxicated, but it was afterwards learned from one who knew him that he was subject to temporary crazy spells, and that he was demented instead of drunk. He has some land near Cortland which he had been working in the morning and was driving back to Marietta, having come by way of light-house hill and while coming down the hill lost his hat. A man who was with him got out to get his hat when Dewitt whipped up the horses and ran them till he met with the accident at the corner of Clinton and Main streets. He had been suffering from a fever sore on one leg and this was badly hurt by his fall. He was taken home in the afternoon by Officer Phillips. [Now, honestly, haven't you ever had a day where you wanted to just drive furiously down Main Street yelling and swinging your hands? Aw, come on; admit it! If not, you obviously have never served on a school board.]

April 17, 1913: It was voted to accept with the thanks of the board of trustees [of Phillips Free Library] the gift of some relics from General Washington's headquarters at Valley Forge, from George VanMeter of New York, a former student of Homer academy, and to give them a place in the library and the secretary was instructed to communicate with Mr. VanMeter concerning the action of the library trustees and to express to him their appreciation of his valuable gift and of his interest in the library thus manifested. [How is that for a long sentence? And wouldn't you like to know where these artifacts are now? I would.]

February 26, 1914: Leo Gilleran of Auburn, N.Y., after two years of blindness was restored to sight by the pulling of a tooth. [Must have been an "eye tooth."]

April 30, 1914: A wineglass of hard cider each day is good for rheumatism. [And other things]

May 7, 1914: One hundred sparrows painted yellow to resemble canary birds and guaranteed as singers were sold at Hastings, N. Y., Monday, for $1.00 each by a peddler who had them in neat wooden cases. The birds refused to sing but took a bath whenever water was offered them. The bath removed the disguise. [the original "Angry Birds"?]

August 1, 1918: A skunk attended the [silent] movies at Hamilton, New York, the other night and almost succeeded in having the entire opera house to himself. [The show was a real stinker.]

January 2, 1919:
AVIATOR WHO SHOT DOWN QUENTIN ROOSEVELT [youngest son of President Theodore Roosevelt]

With the American Army of Occupation, Coblenz, Dec. 30: Christian Donhauser, the German aviator who is said to be the man who killed Lieut. Quentin Roosevelt of the American army in an air duel near Chambray, France, on July 14th, arrived at Coblenz yesterday.

He is one of a bunch of fliers sent by the German army to repair and deliver to the Americans about forty chasse planes, which have been turned over to them in accordance with the terms of the armistice.

Donhauser is a little fellow [and] about as cocky as they come. He was strutting around town today in full uniform, with his blue cap slanted over his ear and his head half buried in a fur collar. On his chest he wears the gold insignia of a flier, along with black and white ribbons, indicating that he has won the Iron Cross of the first and second class. He is said to admit frankly that he is the best flier in the German army.

Quentin Roosevelt was flying with a party of four or five other American aviators in the vicinity of Fere en Tardenois in France, when they encountered a party of German machines. Roosevelt left his group and made a fearless dash at the bunch of Boches. One of them pulled off from the group and met him.

In the fight which followed the young American was shot down. His body was later recovered, having been buried by the Germans, who have always expressed their greatest admiration for his bravery.

Quentin Roosevelt's eldest brother, Theodore Roosevelt, Jr., is today commanding the Twenty-six infantry, across the Rhine.

Donhauser told the correspondent today of the battle. He said: " I was one of a party of six German aviators and on July 14th sighted six American machines east of Fere en Tardenois. One American, who, I learned later, was Quentin Roosevelt, was ahead of the rest of his squadron and off to one side. He came straight at me and I swooped down under his machine. We seesawed back and forth, peppering away, and each trying to gain the advantage by climbing above the other. Roosevelt made several loops and I admired his gameness. Once I thought his machine gun was jammed, but a second later he began again to shoot and I felt the bullets striking my plane. Then I mounted above him and swooped down to within twenty meters of him, firing all the time. Then I saw my opponent collapse and his machine began to fall."

Donhauser, who is a non-commissioned officer and speaks English, has relatives living in Michigan. He was credited with thirty aerial victories in the fighting after July 1st, when he entered the German air service. [How popular do you think this made the relatives in Michigan at the time?]

January 16, 1919: London, Dec. 26—The remarkable story of a British soldier who for over two years escaped capture from the Huns by dressing as a girl has just been told by a Britisher returned from Belgium. He was taken prisoner in 1916 and finally escaped. For six days he hid in ditches, but he became so exhausted that he decided to risk capture by asking for food at a small farmhouse. He entered half expecting to find soldiers billeted in the house. The only occupant was an old woman who was wailing at the bedside of her daughter, who had died that morning. Able to speak a little French he persuaded the old woman to let him impersonate the daughter. He buried the girl in the garden that night and for six months wore her clothes and worked in the fields. A few of the neighbors were told, but they kept the secret. [Who says neighbors can't keep a secret about a cross-dresser?]

In the same issue: More than two years ago, Charlie, an old fire department horse at Greencastle, left the station, his place there having been taken by a new motortruck. Since that time Charlie has been doing heavy hauling for his present owner. The other day Charley and his working mate were stopped near the fire department station, and one of the firemen ventured the statement that Charlie would still make a good fire horse if the old equipment should have to be resorted to. To prove his contention the fireman unhitched Charlie, led him to his old stall, adjusted the harness above the old wagon and sounded the alarm. The door opened and just as of old Charlie trotted out and ran under the harness ready to make a run. In two years, he had not forgotten his lesson. —Indianapolis News. [And you thought it was elephants that never forgot.]

January 30, 1919: The Selective Service Headquarters in Albany received letters requesting deferment from the draft during World War I. Among them, one "registrant replied that his dependents were father and mother and an orphan brother and sister." [No comment.]

August 13, 2020

MAN'S BEST FRIEND AS REPORTED IN THE NEWSPAPERS

(Before Used for Paper Training)

The recent razing of the long-standing Homer Animal Clinic on West Road in the village caused this writer to wax nostalgic and prompted the following article.

A dog is said to be "man's best friend." Let's see if that adage holds true upon examining some excerpts from past local newspapers and a few other sources.

What do dogs have in common with lawyers, imported liquors, and bars in the year of the nation's centennial? The answer is revealed in an 1876 issue (month and day indecipherable) of *The Cortland County Republican* newspaper:

"Hadn't we better cut off some of our useless expenditures before we scold about the hard times? It costs $70,000,000 per annum, to keep dogs in this country; lawyers' fees for litigation cost $35,000,000; importation of liquors costs $50,000,000, and the support of grog shops [bars], three times the last sum." [Source of statistics was not given.]

Next, we come across a case of mistaken identity reported in *The Cortland County Republican* on September 22, 1876:

"A four-year-old boy, . . . [in] Vermont, was lost in the woods last week, and had a play spell with two "dogs." They came up to him as he sat on the grass in an open glade and smell[ed] of him. He patted them on their heads . . . and they then walked away into the forest." Their footprints disclosed that they were not "dogs" the boy had told about encountering. They were black bears.

Apparently, not all breeds of dogs are herders; some have "prey drive" and kill. *The Cortland County Republican* of April 6, 1877, contained a report of damage done to sheep in the nearby Town of Truxton by dogs. The report listed the names of eight individuals assessed a fine for the damage done. The fines ranged between 3 and 20 dollars.

Vaccinating dogs is very effective in preventing the spread of rabies to humans. The first rabies vaccine was introduced in 1885, and an improved version did not come along until 1908. Thus, the following remedy was urged to readers of *The Cortland County Republican* on April 13, 1877, under "Local Matters":

"Almost every paper contains accounts of deaths from hydrophobia [rabies]. Better clean out the dogs."

Pet dogs are invariably listed as "lost" in local papers, even back on May 11, 1877, in *The Cortland County Republican*:

"Local Notices: LOST DOG. On Friday, April 27, in this village, A BLACK SHEPHERD DOG, Red spots over eyes, red legs, answers to name of 'JIP.' Finder will be liberally rewarded by bringing to this [newspaper] office." [Hope the finder did not experience the owner living up to the dog's name.]

Did you know that New York State was the first state to legally require a dog to be licensed? New York around the turn of the twentieth century was rife with wild dogs, the result of an unchecked population. To help curb the dog growth, the state passed the first animal control ordinance in the United States. On March 8, in 1894, New York announced that dog owners were required to obtain a yearly permit for ownership, at the cost of 2 dollars (about $50 in today's money). The ASPCA was entrusted with enforcing the new statute.

The village seems to have been going to the dogs as of February 6, 1919, in the *Homer Republican:*

"Police Officer Carson has been instructed by the village board of trustees to seize all unlicensed dogs found in Homer village and see that they are killed. Persons owning or harboring such dogs are violating the state dog law and are liable to arrest and fine as well as the loss of their dogs, and they must secure licenses for those animals or take the consequences. Dogs have become a great nuisance in Homer and the action of the village trustees is fully justified and it is hoped that it will speedily result in lessening the number of these worthless animals which have been roaming the village streets. Strict enforcement of the board's directions will surely accomplish this end and officer Carson will see to it that unlicensed dogs are quickly disposed of."

Here are two more notices about licensing dogs in Homer:

Cortland Standard, February 9, 1955:

"Feb. 10, Thursday, is the deadline for obtaining dog licenses. After this date delinquency lists will be made out. To date, there are 300 out of a possible 780 dogs licensed."

Cortland Standard, February 28, 1964:

On this date, it was announced twenty-four Homer dog owners had failed to obtain the legally required dog license. Names had been filed by the Town

Clerk. Justice R. Curtis Harris said he would issue summonses next week for all who had not taken care of the matter. The law provided for the confiscation and disposal of dogs not licensed. The penalty was $10 for the failure to license a dog. Additional costs could be imposed: court costs, costs of the constable's service for serving summonses, and the cost for retrieving an impounded dog. Harris said that some costs could be lessened by the owner coming in and obtaining a license before the return date on the summons.

Must be there were too many dogs in the village as of March 3, 1971. Carefully read the following from the *Cortland Standard* of that date. Villagers were seemingly putting dogs out to the curb for pick-up, along with their garbage, but not confining the dogs in "tightly covered containers." Is that how you read this?

"Police Chief Thomas Davis has received numerous complaints concerning dogs tearing open garbage containers when they are put out at the curb for weekly pick-up. He suggests that owners confine the dogs until after pick-up time in the area and if possible residents should use tightly covered containers."

Of course, if a canine is truly "man's best friend," then that canine deserves quality health care. This is where professionals come in. However, it wasn't until Dr. James Law began teaching at Cornell University in Ithaca in the mid-nineteenth century that veterinary medicine became a topic of study in the United States. He was the first professor to introduce veterinary medicine to American students. Following Law's introduction, practitioners in the U.S. established The American Veterinary Medical Association in 1863. Still, paid veterinarians were rare in America until after World War II. Before this time, most household pets were not given proper medical attention.

Today, with 62 percent of American households owning a pet, it is no secret that veterinarians are in high demand. Veterinary care accounted for $14.37 billion of the total amount of money spent on pet care in 2013, so investing in an experienced vet is a must for the overall health and safety of our furry friends.

Homer has been blessed with outstanding veterinarians. In the twentieth century, two readily come to mind. Doctor Carleton Potter had a general veterinary practice from 1943 to 2008. "Doc's" large animal veterinary practice took him to dairy farms across Cortland County and neighboring counties until the 1980s. He continued his small animal practice from his home on South Main Street in Homer for another 20 years. His highly respected practice overlapped that of Doctor William Cadwallader.

From 1967 to 2005 Bill and Jean Cadwallader operated the Homer Animal Clinic located on West Road, adding the Tully Animal Clinic in 1985. Bill was a remarkably skilled veterinarian, surgeon and diagnostician. He always took time to educate his clients, especially children. Many years ago, he allowed this writer's children to be present at the autopsy of a pet turtle that had died suddenly.

The *Cortland Standard* for August 10, 1973, reported that Dr. Cadwallader was . . .

"talking to some of the children who attended the pet clinic held yesterday in Homer at the elementary school. Cadwallader spoke on the care and grooming of pets and how to take care of young animals including puppies, kittens, and rabbits. He also distributed literature to the youngsters and explained the recommended diet for pets, the shots which are needed, first aid measures to deal with minor injuries, what to do in case of a major accident involving a pet, and the general health of various pets."

At the time of his retirement, "Bill" said he always wondered whose pet would be the last on whom he would perform surgery. As it turned out, it was a cocker spaniel belonging to the family of this writer. Dr. Cadwallader proved himself to be the "best friend" to "man's best friend."

Realistically however, no matter how well behaved a dog can be, there is no way of telling what can happen on a veterinary exam table. Statistically speaking, more than half of all vets will get seriously injured in their line of work. This is according to "Fun Facts about Veterinarians" (found online at https://www.dentalplanet.com/blog/dental-news), though it is unclear how this fact can be "fun" for those vets who care for a ferocious Fido. Nevertheless, it points up the risks we will go to in maintaining companion canines. What is given in return is called love, and it is usually of the unconditional variety, as Priscilla Berggren-Thomas, Phillips Free Library Director, can attest to and does so well in a contemporary news column.

Incidentally, the name of Fido was made popular, according to the American Kennel Club, because Abraham Lincoln had a friendly yellow lab mix of that name. Lincoln did not take Fido to the White House. The pet remained in Springfield in the care of a friend. Ironically, Fido met a similar fate as his master. A year after Lincoln's assassination, Fido, with dirty paws, jumped up on an inebriated Civil War veteran (Company G, 114th Illinois Infantry Regiment, from 1862–1865) sitting on a curb. In a drunken rage, the man knifed the dog. The dog's body was found about a month afterwards where he had lain down to die behind the chimney of the old Universalist church. The first presidential dog to be photographed and assassinated was reported by the press, and thus the canine name of Fido was catapulted into popularity. [See Matthew Algeo, *Abe & Fido: Lincoln's Love of Animals and the Touching Story of His Favorite Canine Companion*, Chicago Review Press, 2015.]

August 27, 2020

We are revisiting a column written by Martin Sweeney that appeared in the October 22, 2015 issue of The Homer News. *Why? you may ask.*

Well, the editor went searching for the most recent article that Martin sent, and could only find the one that ran in the August 13, 2020 issue. What happened?

I really don't know. Maybe Martin is "On Strike" for more pay. I'd double what I pay him, but 2 times nothing is still nothing.

Most likely a computer gremlin has been messing with my email. It happens quite frequently. In any case, I hope you enjoy a reprise of the column from the past. Ed.

THE GREAT CORTLAND ROTARY HIJINKS OF 1921

Because of the enthusiastic response to the installments recently appearing here about the driving of the Ku Klux Klan out of Cortland County in 1924 by District Attorney Albert Haskell, Jr., allow me to share with you another story about Haskell. This, too, involves the Klan but almost two and a half years before the courtroom drama. This involved a well-staged series of dramatic stunts that reveals another side to the character of the 30-year-old Haskell and something about the times in which he lived. This account was researched from news clippings, copies of letters, and "The Klan Episode" written in longhand by Albert Haskell—all found in a scrapbook that the man had created, and his descendants have kept.

Let me take you back in time . . . back to Cortland in 1921 . . . a mere two years after the Cortland Rotary Club was founded. Step into the beginning of the era known now as the "Roaring Twenties." Can you hear the Charleston and Black Bottom dance music? Can you see the young women in their straight-line chemises and close-fitting cloche hats over bobbed hair? Note how the men are giving up creased pants and ties and sporting colorful suits and patterned socks. But no fashionable male would dare leave his house without wearing a fedora, especially when going off to a Rotary Club meeting.

Imagine, if you would, that you are one of those early Rotarians. It is the evening of September 28, 1921. Rotary is exclusively a male membership at this time. You have been instructed to report to Rotary President Tyler's dry-cleaning establishment on Court Street in Cortland by 6:15 PM. As directed, you show up in old, worn-out clothes. Stiff collars are barred. You gain entry upon giving the password: "Kalzuka."

Shortly, you board one of 20 automobiles. The "Tin Lizzies" head down Tompkins Street to the city limits, where all but the drivers are asked to put on blindfolds. You and your fellow Rotarians, blindfolded, are transported along the Virgil Road, then a right turn and up a hill a short distance and then to the left and onto a farm road. Unknown to you, while the motorcade was turning onto the Virgil Road, a Ford had cut in, and the last four or five cars followed the Ford to Virgil. You, however, are part of the motorcade that has ended up on a back road. The cars come to a stop.

You are ordered to get out and to remove your blindfold. As you do, trumpets blare, and standing in front of you are seven men in the white hooded regalia of the Ku Klux Klan. Two are mounted on horses. The ghostly figures lead you into the woods by torchlight—oil-soaked cattails set ablaze. You march for half a mile. An occasional gunshot can be heard. They take you to a clearing and a small hunting lodge. Food awaits you. Sitting around a campfire, you are invited to partake of hotdogs, pickles, doughnuts, and hot coffee served in tin cups. You and your fellow Rotarians are surrounded by dark woods, and every once in a while, the night air is punctuated by the sound of a gunshot. You look apprehensively about you and notice there are Klansmen lurking in the woods about you.

Suddenly, someone realizes that some Rotarians are missing. Nineteen of them had been part of the motorcade. Where are they now? Should we look for them? A search party is organized and sent down the road. The "lost battalion" is found, escorted back to the clearing, and offered food. Bang! Bang! Guns go off again. Everybody looks up the hill. Through the woods you see seven or eight Klansmen approaching. One of them is holding a burning cross. They march right up to where your group is sitting, and the leader begins to read an Imperial Proclamation by order of Colonel William J. Simmons, Imperial Wizard and Emperor of The Ku Klux Klan, of Atlanta, Georgia:

"Gentlemen of the Cortland Rotary Club: Believing that you gentlemen are interested in the principles of true Americanism and are aware that the principles of our order are similar to the principles of Rotary, a delegation is here this evening to solicit your interest and cooperation in our cause. We believe, as did our forefathers, in maintaining white supremacy. We believe that the Jews of this country are an overwhelming menace to capital business. We believe that the greatest threat to our beloved country comes from the Roman Catholic Church. Now, my friends, I want you to listen while I conclusively prove to you these contentions.

In your own community, consider for a moment the insidious influence of that hideous, creeping, crawling, hissing, pie-eating Parsons, better known as 'Pa.' What more safe and sure method could be devised to forever banish from your midst this miserable specimen of humanity? I answer—the Klu (sic) Klux Klan!

Personally, I know you would welcome the opportunity to rid your club and community of a certain wooly haired, foul-mouthed, blatting Hebrew of musical comedy fame. Though he bears the name of the Apostle Paul, he is but a sheep in wolf's clothing. You know who I mean—'Old Carp.'

Do you approve of the way 'Pop DeGroat' gives hand-in-hand with the Bootleggers, with a gun on one hip and a pint bottle on the other? Can the law reach this man? No!! The Klu (sic) Klux Klan is your only remedy.

Haven't you noticed of late how chummy Charlie Wickwire, Ed Stilson, 'Ted' Brewer and Doc Scovel have been? They meet regularly on pretense of perfecting plans for the new Presbyterian Church annex. Are you blind? Remove the cataract from your eyes!! It's wine, women, and song! Call in the Klan and clean them out!

Do you know that 'Chris' Tyler, who is a neighbor of 'Al' Haskell, positively knows that said Haskell is secretly a Catholic and has recently installed and purchased a wireless outfit for the sole purpose of communicating with Rome after January 1st, when he becomes District Attorney? How can you expect justice under these conditions? Down with his wireless program; let him beware of the Klu (sic) Klux Klan!

Think what it would mean for you to silence forever 'Bill' Walsh. Will you endure forever the discords which this whiskey soaked, cigarette smoking, card-playing, nasal toned, would-be Caruso thrusts upon you? Leave him to the Klan!

Do you know that Floyd Wood, Harold Helm, and Ben Hilton, known in police circles as 'The Hill Gang,' are terrorizing the community and must be wiped out before your Normal School is completed? Why not introduce them to a coat of tar and feathers at the hands of the Ku Klux Klan! How much longer will you allow 'Tookie' Newcomb, that mellow toned fat Irish hypocrite, to persecute the unfortunate element of this beautiful valley? Do you not know that he drags down thousands of dollars in private contributions to the Cause of the Poor? What does he do with this vast wealth? Poker, is the answer! Call out the Klan!!

Finally, is there an 'honest' physician in your fair community? If so, we would like to know who. These uneducated parasites are lopping off the lives of your healthy wives and children at an outstanding rate. Would you consult 'Higgins' on a case of diphtheria? Or 'Kelly' with his keen edged sword, when life is so sweet? Protect your lives, and call on the Klu (sic) Klux Klan!"

With that last statement—"Bang! Bang!"—gunfire is heard again, and into view come three deputies of the Sheriff's Department. They bark out, "Alright, you're all under arrest." Some Rotarians step forward immediately. They explain that the whole sordid affair has been a hoax. They own up that Rotarians Lloyd S. Ingalls, Merle S. Nye, and Albert Haskell, Jr. had secretly planned this burlesque Klan meeting for weeks. The "Klansmen" were members of the Ithaca Rotary Club, except for the men on horseback who were local farm boys dressed up and hired for realism. The nearby rustic cottage was owned by Rotarian Ray Wiltsie.

Then followed the Club's business meeting and the adoption of a new by-law, in accordance with Rotary International, that a member is to be automatically dropped if at the end of six months, his attendance record falls below 60 percent. Attendance is one of the cardinal rules of Rotary in the 1920s. The only excuses accepted are illness and absence from the city. What comes next is an hour of entertainment and a running line of laughter furnished by the Ithaca Rotarians.

Then all made their way back to the cars by lantern light, concluding that the monthly evening meeting of the Cortland Rotary Club had tried the members nerves at the beginning but turned out to be one of the most enjoyable they ever had.

[2020 Note: Homer residents have been members of the Cortland Noontime Rotary Club since its founding over a hundred years ago. This article was a portion of a speech the author, a member of the Rotary Club, gave at the Club's 90th Anniversary Gala Dinner at Tinelli's Hathaway House in Solon, New York, on April 14, 2010. At the conclusion of the speech, a Klansman burst into the banquet hall shouting words to the effect "This is a big lie! The Rotary Club continues to badmouth the Klan. Good luck trying to get back to Cortland tonight." The author, from the podium, responded, "I demand that you unmask yourself!" The Klansman removed his hood to reveal Tom Haskell, a Cortland Rotarian and the grandson of Albert Haskell, Jr. And, thus, the Rotarian Haskell tradition of pranking was kept alive!]

September 10, 2020

HOMER'S AFFINITY FOR ULYSSES S. GRANT

As every student of U. S. history knows, Ulysses S. Grant (born Hiram Ulysses Grant on April 27, 1822) was an American soldier and politician who served as the 18th President of the United States from 1869 to 1877. He is better known as the general selected by President Lincoln to lead the Union Army to victory in the American Civil War. A war hero but a reluctant politician, Grant was unanimously nominated by the Republican Party and was elected president in 1868. He was a natural leader on the battlefield but was not an especially effective leader of his country and admitted to making "errors of judgement."

Nevertheless, as president, Grant worked with the Radical Republicans in the Reconstruction of the Union while dealing with corruption in his administration. In addition, Grant stabilized the post-war national economy, created the Department of Justice, and prosecuted the Ku Klux Klan. He appointed

African Americans and Jewish Americans to prominent federal offices. In 1871, he created the first Civil Service Commission.

Scandals during the Grant administration were often used to stigmatize his political reputation, though he was not personally responsible for any of them. However, historical assessments of Grant's presidency and integrity have improved over time. Grant was ranked 38th in 1994 and 1996, but ranked 21st in 2018. Recent historians have emphasized Grant's presidential accomplishments.

One of President Grant's successes was the *Alabama* claims settlement. This was the most pressing diplomatic problem in 1869: the matter of depredations caused to the Union by the Confederate warship CSS *Alabama*, built in a British shipyard in violation of neutrality rules. The issue was resolved when the Senate approved the Treaty of Washington by a 50–12 vote. Signed on May 8, 1871, it settled various disputes through arbitration. Besides the *Alabama* claims for damages to American shipping caused by British-built warships, it addressed illegal fishing in Canadian waters and British civilian losses in the American Civil War.

After the arbitrators endorsed the American position, Britain settled the matter by paying the United States $15.5 million (approximately $295 million in today's currency). The Treaty inaugurated permanent peaceful relations between the United States and Canada, and United States and Britain. That international arbitration established a precedent, and the case aroused interest in codifying public international law. The *Alabama* claims settlement proved to be Grant's most successful foreign policy achievement.

To commemorate this precedent-setting accomplishment, Homer's native-son Francis Bicknell Carpenter produced what he called his *Arbitration Picture*. He started the huge painting in 1871 and completed it in 1891. In oil on canvas, Carpenter depicted the American and British signers of the May 8, 1871 Treaty of Washington gathered around a table in the manner of the men in his more famous *Emancipation Proclamation* painting.

To mark the successful completion of this artistic project, a dinner in Carpenter's honor was held at Sherry's, an elite New York restaurant. The toastmaster for this special occasion was none other than another native son of Homer, Andrew D. White. Among the twenty-seven guests were New York Senator Frank Hiscock of Tully, NY, and alumni of Homer's academy: Dr. Stephen Smith, Calvin C. Woolworth, and Rev. Theodore T. Munger.

In 1892, the *Arbitration Picture* was presented to Queen Victoria and accepted through Robert Todd Lincoln, who was then the American Minister to the British Court. For a while, the painting hung in St. George's Hall, the Royal Banqueting Room, at Windsor Castle. No one knows its whereabouts today.

Upon Grant's death from esophageal cancer on July 23, 1885, plans were made in Republican dominated Homer to memorialize the man with ceremonies. Businesses and offices in the village shuttered their doors on the appointed day, Saturday, August 6, and the *Republican* newspaper described the day's event one week later:

"The day for the burial of the nation's great hero opened dark and dismal. The heavens, drab and angry, had every appearance of rain. The town had laid aside its business air, and scarcely a pedestrian or vehicle were seen upon the streets, and the serenity of the village indicated that the great national calamity shrouded it in mourning. Nature in her quiet mood apparently sympathized with the people in their great bereavement. At about eleven o'clock the clouds cleared away and the people thronged the streets until one o'clock, when a line of parade was formed on Main street, with right resting on James, in the following order: Homer Cornet Band, Willoughby Babcock Post, G. A. R., Homer Fire Department, comprising its first, second, third, fourth and fifth divisions, and in the rear were the Village Council and speakers in carriages. The line with heads reverentially bowed, slowly proceeded up Main street to the strains of a funeral dirge. At Warren street the order was given to countermarch down Main to Copeland avenue and thence back to Keator hall [the opera house on the third floor of the former Barber Block]. The church bells tolled as the column trailed slowly its line of march. The walks on either side were thronged with people, who watched in respectful silence the progress of the procession. The larger portion of buildings along the line of march were heavily draped [in black crepe]; here and there a flag was gracefully festooned and draped in mourning. The great throng of people attended the exercises at the hall. The services were opened by the President of the Day, Mr. W. H. Crane, who announced that the band would play the 'Soldier's Dream.' Dr, E. W. Hitchcock then read the XC Psalm, which was followed by an impressive prayer by Rev. J. B. French, and the song 'Tenting on the Old Camp Ground' was sung by a male quartette with fine effect. Rev. Dr. Hitchcock then came forward and delivered an impressive and eloquent address—which will be found in another column. 'Nearer My God to Thee' was then rendered by the quartette after which Rev, J. B. French, a member of the G. A. R., extemporaneously addressed the assemblage. He carried his hearers with him through the eloquent and appropriate discourse of nearly an hour's length, speaking largely upon General Grant's military career, statesmanship and life as a citizen. And, in closing his address, he urged the people to cultivate the spirit of fraternity in their relations with men as the dead General had done. At the conclusion of the discourse the band played 'Dreams of Childhood' after which the services were closed by the benediction."

The lengthy eulogy, printed up in the same newspaper, was offered by Rev. Hitchcock. He claimed, "It was my privilege to know General Grant personally and to meet and converse with him on various occasions." The minister focused mostly on Grant the general. Using the flowery pathos typical of sermons and orations of the day, Hitchcock virtually deified the "war hero," vesting him with a messianic aura that was likely agreeable to the residents of Homer:

"The deadly struggle was joined, The land shook beneath the tread of armed men. Defeat after defeat pursued the loyal arms. Disappointment, consternation, despair wore on their track. 'Give us a leader,' cried the patriots of the North, 'a leader worthy this holy cause.' Heaven heard the cry and from his obscurity christened the man he had chosen and prepared. You shall know him by his works. Unbroken victory shall attend his onward march . . . the South shall crumble beneath his mighty blows. The shackles of 4,000,000 slaves shall snap asunder. Their civil and political rights shall be acknowledged and maintained. The nation shall live. The union, in its integrity, shall be restored and peace with union. Sectional bitterness shall die out. The conquered shall bless their conquerors for the new and better civilization wrought out for them, and on his burial day shall rank themselves among his sincerest mourners. . . . They shall recognize him as their champion, and hail him as their savior."

Continuing, Hitchcock admitted that time must pass for humanity to fully grasp Grant's place in history. He states, "Like the lofty mountains, they must be looked at and studied from a distance to rightly appreciate their greatness. At some future time the historian will be raised up and qualified for his task, and with the aid of those "personal memoirs" which we await, will assign Ulysses S. Grant his rightful place among our nation's benefactors and the world's heroes and great men."

Hitchcock proceeds next to speak of Grant the two-term President and again prophetically looks to the future for his rightful assessment:

"Then the historian of that calmer age will wonder how a soldier by endowment and education, accustomed only to camp and field, unlearned in State-craft, unfamiliar with political science, unacquainted with the methods of civil administration, could have displayed such breadth of statesmanship in the measures which be originated and approved."

Hitchcock enumerates those "measures" and includes the Treaty of Washington. He lauds "the concessions he compelled foreign powers to make" and the precedent set so "all international disputes may be adjusted by peaceful arbitration when 'nations should learn war no more.'"

In closing his oration, Hitchcock addresses how a terminally ill Grant struggled against the clock to get his memoir manuscript written and published in time so his family might draw upon the royalties for income:

". . . bearing torturing pain without a murmur, facing certain death with unflinching fortitude and giving his waning strength to the composition of his 'Personal Memoirs' that the facts he knew might find their true place in history, and that the family he left behind him might share the needed pecuniary fruits of his labors."

With help from his friend Mark Twain, Grant completed the two-volume book one week before his death. With Twain's promotion of the book, it became a bestseller and is considered one of the finest military autobiographies ever written. Grant's wife Julia would eventually earn some $450,000 (more than $11 million in today's money) from sales of the book. The *Republican* of Nov. 5, 1885, informed the residents of Homer that "The agent for 'Grant's Memoirs' will be in town as soon as possible after the issue of the books and will then be glad to furnish the book to any who may desire it. Communications will reach her if addressed to Mrs. E. M. Dates, box 757, Homer."

Surely, Ron Chernow's definitive biography of *Grant* (2017) drew upon these memoirs and contributed to the recent elevation of Grant's historical reputation. However, on this past June 19, protesters toppled a bronze bust of Grant that was erected in 1896 at Golden Gate Park in San Francisco. Grant had been stationed in northern California from 1852 to 1854. The cause of the bust's removal is likely the little-known fact that Grant did own an enslaved person named William Jones for about a year on the eve of the Civil War. In 1859, Grant either bought or was given the 35-year-old Jones, who was in Grant's service until he freed him before the start of the War. In addition, Grant, ironically, did marry into a slave-owning family and never touted himself as an anti-slavery man.

The nineteenth century community of Homer most likely was not aware of this other side of Grant. They chose, as did many communities, to focus on the positives of the deceased man, who with President Lincoln "saved the Union." Since then, both Grant and Lincoln have been deified and vilified by historians. Like all of us, Grant was human, not a deity. He was flawed, multi-faceted, and evolving. Grant is an example of many in the past who were ordinary persons who accomplished extraordinary things. Stately statues, framed paintings, and fine tombs are created for those Americans who, with warts and all, made a remarkable difference, moving us toward "a more perfect Union" and perhaps a better world.

[2020 note: The article for September 24, 2020, was a brief history of North West Street in Homer by Ward Dukelow. It was a fine example of how a resident of the village could research his former neighborhood's history and present it to the community via the public historian's news column. It was one of several goal-satisfying moments for this public historian.]

October 8, 2020

A RAILROAD RUNS THROUGH IT

As every Homer villager knows, a railroad cuts through our community. Freight trains of the New York, Susquehanna and Western Railway use it now, but passenger trains operated by the Delaware, Lackawanna and Western once used the rails and made regular stops in Homer until the end of the day on July 12, 1957. Do you know how a rail line through Homer ever came to be?

Homer's first permanent merchant, Jedediah Barber, deserves much credit. According to Herbert Barber Howe's biography of his ancestor, Jedediah Barber, along with his three sons, George, Watts, and Paris, played a significant role in Cortland County's efforts to secure a railroad. The Erie Canal was barely opened before Homer's Barber and Andrew Dickson advocated a Salina and Port Watson Railroad. They envisioned the benefits to be accrued by Homer merchants and farmers by a rail line that could connect to the Canal, the Hudson River and New York City. The project was organized April 27, 1829. $375,000 in capital was required for a seven-year undertaking. The cars were to operate by steam or animal power. It all sounded good on paper, but that is where it stayed. Nothing ever came of this first attempt at a railway through Homer.

Efforts revived in 1836. A more ambitious project was proposed with the organization of the Syracuse, Cortland and Binghamton Company. This was to require $500,000 but only four years to construct. The county committee spearheading this included Homer's Judge Edward C. Reed. This time, however, the north-south route through Cortland County was deemed to be too visionary. Again, it was postponed.

A third attempt was made in the 1840s, marked by serious opposition and competition among Central New Yorkers. The *Mc'Grawville Express* of July 27, 1845, cited this opinion from the *Cortland Whig*:

> The Auburn people have discovered a new route to Binghamton. The dear good people of the infant city, have not yet discovered that it is easier to clothe themselves with the high honors of a municipality than to build a railroad.

The same issue quoted the sarcasm-tinged opinion of the *Syracuse Star*:

> We have been well aware that it would be about as easy a task to build a railroad over the Alps as to construct one from Auburn to Cortland, except by way of Skaneateles or Syracuse. The ridge of mountains lying

between Auburn and Cortland is rather a formidable obstacle in the way of Railroads; but since our neighbors have made their thriving little village a city, we have made up our minds that wonders will not cease, and a rail may be constructed to the moon, some time or other, commencing or terminating at Auburn.

Some folks must have questioned the wisdom of constructing railroads anywhere, since the newspapers reported with some regularity on accidents involving trains. This appeared in the *Mc'Grawville Express* of October 7, 1847:

An accident happened on the western railroad, on Friday evening. —As the night train was on its way down, an Irishman, who had been spending the day at a "corn husking," laid himself out alongside the track, and in thrashing about, got his hand upon the rail, and in a short time the train came along and cut it off near the wrist. Yesterday forenoon, a second accident happened upon the same road. The morning train ran over a cow, a few miles west of the city [of Rochester], which threw off a couple of cars, and smashed them up.

One of the first rallies to promote a railroad through the county took place at the Mansion House in Homer on February 25, 1848. Dr. Lewis Riggs chaired the meeting, and George J. J. Barber (Jedediah's son) and Oren Stimson served as secretaries. The building of the New York and Erie Railroad through the southern tier motivated this gathering to pass a resolution calling for "the construction of a railroad through this county from Syracuse to Binghamton." A Central Correspondence Committee was selected to shepherd the bill. Its chairman was Cortland's Henry Stephens, and its secretary was Homer's George J. J. Barber.

McGrawville (now known as McGraw) saw the advantage for them to support this third attempt, and a meeting was held on Saturday evening, March 4, 1848. Gilmore H. Kinney, Esq. was chosen chairman and P. Bacon Davis secretary. O. H. Salisbury, G. H. Kinney, and J. P. Holmes were appointed to draft resolutions "expressive of the sense of the meeting." The resolutions adopted after free discussion were published in the *Mc'Grawville Express*, March 16, 1848:

Resolved: That the citizens of this county, in view of their own interests are called upon to make a vigorous effort for the construction of a Rail Road from Syracuse to Binghamton.

Resolved: That we believe a Rail Road through this county will prove a great and lasting benefit, that it will ultimately give a new impulse to every interest connected with its prosperity.

Resolved : That the citizens of Mc'Grawville and vicinity use all honorable means to procure the construction of the Railroad through this village, if compatible with the public interest but if not we will as citizens use our utmost efforts to promote said road through the county.

On the 6th of the next month, the same paper published the opinion of the *Oswego Daily Times*. Oswego endorsed the railroad proposed from Syracuse to Binghamton as ranking "among those most feasible and most likely to succeed." The paper listed several routes that had been proposed for a road branching off from the New York and Erie at some point in the southern tier of counties to intersect with the main rail route from Albany to Buffalo. The route from Binghamton to Syracuse by way of Cortland was touted as "the best route of them all." It was deemed to be a separate link "strengthening the entire chain" of railroads "from Boston and New York to the Mississippi River." A link between Binghamton and Syracuse and on to Oswego would unite the Great West with New York and afford another "mode of conveyance for the transmission of freight." Goods could be transported to the Great Lakes through Oswego. As for passenger service, "if a man desired to leave New York for Rochester, he comes on the Erie Road to Binghamton, thence to Syracuse, and then to Rochester" and on to Buffalo or Niagara Falls and other western destinations. Having offered these "considerations in favor of this road," the Oswego and McGrawville papers indicated their "hope to see steps taken to insure the construction of the road."

On April 20, 1848, the *Mc'Grawville Express* was again effusive in its praise of the project:

> It has been for some time in contemplation to construct a railroad from Syracuse, on the Boston and Buffalo, to Binghamton on the New York and Erie railroad route, passing through Tully, Homer, Cortlandville, McGrawville, Freetown Corners, Marathon, etc. The surface of the country is extremely favorable, and the benefits to be anticipated, both for internal convenience and general travel, peculiarly great. It is believed that, when this road shall have been completed from Lake Ontario (where it is already begun from Oswego to Syracuse) to Pittston in Pennsylvania (where, also, a section is already graded, some sixteen miles northward and twenty miles more under contract towards Binghamton in New York) the route will be second to few others in the country. It will be the Great North and South Railroad, opening by far the shortest passage from Buffalo, Rochester, Syracuse and Canada to Baltimore, Washington, &c. The road will pass down the Susquehanna valley from Binghamton, which is on that river, to the Chesapeake Bay, through the great coal region of Pennsylvania. By this means coal may be transported to the Syracuse and Salina salt works where the price of wood for evaporation is already so high as to increase the

expense of salt-making almost to the point of no profit.
This road will, moreover, open convenient emission of the immense quantities of salt needed all the way through that vast interior country, &c, &c,! It is, also, needed for the transportation of the abundant products of that country. A plank road is already in process of construction, the materials having been brought upon the ground during the last winter, from Syracuse to Homer, thirty-two miles, nearly halfway to Binghamton; but this, it is thought, will but partially answer the demands for a general thoroughfare through that important part of the country.
We observe that the New York Legislature has recently declared for "the public use of a road from Binghamton to Syracuse." When this work shall have been accomplished, Cortland county, now untouched by any great thoroughfare, will be opened to all the advantages of the most favored counties. It is a rich, beautiful and very healthy section, and is inhabited by virtuous, intelligent and enterprising people. The proposed locality for the FREE LITERARY INSTITUTION [believed to be a reference to the New York Central College that opened its doors in 1849 in what is now called McGraw] is precisely in the centre of the county and on the line of the proposed railroad. We believe no better spot could have been selected in the United States.

Other newspapers solicited the support of all the communities in the area. And the communities did not disappoint. At S. S. Hart's Inn in Preble, a large gathering was held on March 27, 1851. The *Cortland County Whig* reported the meeting was "very eloquently addressed" by the project's supporters, including George J. J. Barber of Homer. Two days later, Homer's town hall [basement level of the Episcopal Church on the Green] was the site of another meeting. For this one, Watts Barber was the secretary, and addresses favoring the railroad were made by Paris Barber, Henry Stephens, John Miller, and Principal Woolworth of the academy on the Green. Syracuse hosted a meeting on April 16, 1851. Delegations from Oswego and Cortland attended, and Watts Barber of Homer was one of the secretaries. After construction began, a large meeting occurred at Binghamton's courthouse on February 12, 1852. The Homer representatives were William Sherman, David Coye, and Watts Barber.

Jedediah Barber was present at these various rallies but left the public speaking to his sons, especially to George. Here was a project that took the elder Barber away from his Great Western store, but as his descendant Herbert Barber Howe put it, "Maybe he thought that after forty years in business he could stand it or maybe he considered the goal more important to the community than anything else."

On July 2, 1851, the Syracuse and Binghamton Railroad Company was finally organized and was to run through the counties of Onondaga, Cortland,

and Broome. The capital stock was $1,200,000, issued in 12,000 shares of $100 each. Jedediah Barber was quick to kick in $500. Thirteen men would comprise the board of directors presided over by Cortland's Henry Stephens. Homer's representatives would be Israel Boies and Jedediah Barber. The stockholder's report of 1853 announced a roadbed, practically completed, of 79.64 miles between Binghamton and Syracuse at a cost of $22,728 per mile. Homer was to have a passenger house sixty-six by twenty-five feet and a freight house one hundred by twenty-five feet. By the Fourth of July 1854, the tracks were almost all laid. The *Cortland County Whig* announced that Homer would honor Jedediah Barber by making him President of the Day at a celebration to be held at the Homer Fair Grounds on the Fourth.

October 18, 1854 was the grand opening day. A train of twenty-seven passenger cars, loaded with guests, made the first run from Binghamton to Syracuse. Along the way was much rejoicing in communities like Homer. Church bells pealed forth, and cannons fired a celebratory welcome. There were bonfires and fireworks to mark the auspicious event, for it had been exactly a quarter of a century since Barber and Dickson had proposed the first railroad project for Cortland County.

Over the long run, the community in Cortland County that would economically benefit the most from a railway was Cortland, the county seat. Homer experienced no markedly significant monetary gains. Yes, local farmers and merchants found it easier and relatively cheaper to transport goods, and the local academy benefitted from the ease with which students from all over could enter and leave the village hosting their schooling. Fortunately, by agreement with the company, all trains had to stop in Homer ten minutes for luncheon. As later recalled by a Homer resident in 1901, there was an African American handyman at the depot named Kendall, and he would call out to passengers: "Right here is your fine stall-fed eggs and time enough to come and get 'em." It was said that this lunch counter became one of the important local institutions.

Sadly, the terminal at Syracuse was just that—a dead end. There was no right of way granted to the port of Oswego nor was there a direct rail link to the Erie Canal—two serious economic defects, to be sure. Cartage was an added expense. The whole railroad venture had been too local in character, and the joy of the opening was all too quickly replaced by the disappointment of bankruptcy for the company. In 1855, Jedediah Barber suffered a loss of $10,000. Large numbers of county residents had invested their savings in the project. Their stock certificates, like Barber's, were reduced to souvenirs. The coming of the "Iron Horse," in the words of Herbert Barber Howe, led to "Homer's first general financial crash." To compound matters for Barber, this was just a few months before his emporium on Main Street was destroyed in a fire and would not be rebuilt until 1863.

Image 10.6 **DL&W passenger station on James St. in Homer prior to 1910.** This building was moved to 11 Wall St., where it is being renovated. *From Ken Eaton's collection at the Homeville Museum at the CNY Living History Center, Cortland, NY.*

Facing the loss of his investment, Jedediah Barber's son-in-law, Jacob M. Schermerhorn, a former resident of "The Hedges" on South Main Street, took the lead in a company reorganization. The result was a re-named railroad—the Syracuse and Southern. Very shortly, with Schermerhorn having controlling interest, the name changed again. The Syracuse *Daily Journal* announced on June 27, 1857, that Schermerhorn was to be the Superintendent and President of the Syracuse, Binghamton and New York Railroad. In due course, Schermerhorn managed to get the road through to Lake Ontario. Successful operation of the 110 miles allowed the company to be sold after a few years to the Delaware, Lackawanna and Western Railroad. No one rejoiced more than Jedediah Barber. In 1863, he reported to a friend that his new store was "doing a heavy business," dealing in 700 tons of [Scranton] coal daily, sending Syracuse hemlock lumber, and bringing back from Oswego stone, salt, pine lumber, and sacks of flour.

Jedediah Barber took the S. B. and N. Railroad and other rail lines for a trip out west in 1857. Perhaps Homer's transportation visionary concurred with a lengthy poem from the *Knickerbocker Magazine* reprinted in the October 27, 1847, issue of the *Mc'Grawville Express*. Let's close with an excerpt:

> Singing through the forests, Rattling over ridges,
> Shouting under arches, Rumbling over bridges;

Whizzing through the mountains, Buzzing o'er the vale
—Bless me!—this is pleasant, Riding on a rail!
Men of different "stations"' In the eye of Fame,
Here are very quickly Coming to the same!
High and lowly people, Birds of every feather,
On a common level, Traveling together.
Woman with her baby, Sitting vis-a-vis;
Baby keeps a squalling; Woman looks at me;
Asks about the distance, Says it's tiresome talking,
Noises of the cars Are so very shocking!
Singing through the forests, Rattling over ridges,
Shooting under arches, Rumbling over bridges;
Whizzing through the mountains, Buzzing o'er the vale
—Bless me,—this is pleasant, Riding on a rail!

Research assistance on this topic was graciously provided by a former student Joshua Blay, Museum Collections Manager for City of Philadelphia and railroad enthusiast; Mary Kimberly, McGraw's Historian; and Sharon Stevans, creator of an outstanding documentary on the New York Central College of McGrawville that was gifted to the Smithsonian.

October 22, 2020

HOMER AND THE GOLDEN AGE OF THE BICYCLE

In recent months, there has been renewed discussion about creating a Tioughnioga River Trail through Homer to Cortland for walking and biking. What you may not realize is that interest in a local man-made path for cyclists is not new; it has a history. Ever since the invention of the wheel, humans have tried to find versatile ways to use wheels for recreation as well as industry and transportation.

First, consider the attachment of wheels to the foot. In the 1880s, according to the late R. Curtis Harris, roller skating was a huge fad. The third floor of the Barber Block was the scene of such activity, first made popular locally in 1879 by Jake Metzgar. Then, in 1884, a large rink—50 ft. by 110 ft.—was constructed on Wall Street. Can you picture it? I wish I had a photograph! It should be noted that certain clergymen condemned the activity. Harris reported that one minister "was allowed by the wily promoters to preach a sermon against it within the rink itself" (*Homer Independent,* December 1, 1961).

Locally, LeGrand Fisher and Charles Creque were accomplished at racing on skates. One was a champion long distance (five miles) racer, and the other was a champion at short distance racing (two and a half miles).

After about seven years, the fad died out, and the building was moved to the southwest corner of Cortland Street and Copeland Avenue. There, it became part of the Phoenix Hardware Company's plant.

The fad that took the place of roller skating was bicycling. The first true bicycle was created in France in the 1860s. Early bikes had enormous front wheels and were called "ordinary bicycles" or "high wheels." Ordinary bicycles were dangerous due to their forward center of gravity. These bikes, also appropriately known as "bone-shakers," were ridden primarily by wealthy young men that were physically fit enough to take a "header" (the term used to describe when one flew over the front of the handlebars). Most were not willing to take the risk of riding a high wheel.

The invention of the "safety" bicycle in the 1880s prompted a worldwide bicycle craze. The safety bicycle had two wheels of equal size and used a chain drive to prevent loss of speed. In the 1890s, Syracuse was the bicycle manufacturing hub of America. There were no fewer than nineteen companies building safety bicycles in the city. Without the dangers of being thrown over the handlebars from a great height, the idea of bicycling began to develop broader appeal among both sexes and all ages. At some point, in Barber's Hall, N. H. Waters offered instruction in the art of riding a bicycle, and the Cortland Wagon Company was a local seller of bicycles. For forty dollars, one could buy their wheels which came with a one-year guarantee (according to the April 16, 1896 issue of the *Cortland Standard*). New language was invented to describe bikers. Fast bikers were called "scorchers," and bicyclists in general were called "wheelmen."

Locally, a club was formed—"The Homer Wheelmen"—and they proudly wore their club's colors: ribbons of red, olive, and yellow. The *Homer Republican* in 1895 reported that "the first of a series of four races for the October Handicap road race of the Homer Wheelmen . . . was run from the Union Block [now owned by the First National Bank of Dryden on Main Street] up the west Little York road and back on the east road, a distance of ten miles. Leslie Tucker won it in a time of 31 minutes." In June of 1896, the Homer Wheelmen donned their colors and met at the Green to ride to Groton to attend a Sunday morning church service. This expedition saw 500 wheelmen attending. The Homer club was joined by riders from Auburn, Ithaca, Elmira, Geneva, Owego, Waterloo, Moravia, and Cortland. About 225 registered at the church.

Three years earlier, a Cortland club of nine men and four guests, attired in black caps and black and tan uniforms said to be "very nobby" [meaning "chic"], made a twelve-mile ride to Truxton in one hour and fifteen minutes. Rain showers, as reported by the May 15th *Cortland Standard*, forced them to return to Cortland via the train.

It should be noted that in some communities across the nation, bicycling, like roller skating, was condemned by clergy. The recreational activity on the Sabbath, the only non-workday of the week, caused a temporary decline in church attendance. Shop owners and saloon keepers voiced opposition. Consumers saved up their money to buy wheels rather than other goods offered by businesses. Cycling replaced frequenting the pubs for recreation and socializing. The growing demand for two-wheelers saw 1,200,000 bicycles produced in 1896 alone. Of course, adding to the controversy was the sight of females invading the cycling world of men. How un-lady-like! How radical! A Homer poet and innkeeper, Isaac Marshall Sampson, described the situation this way:

> The bicycle is all the rage,
> Without regard to sex or age.
> The ladies mount the wheel astride,
> And arch their necks with stoic pride.
> And like an Albatross begin to paddle.
> The wheels our mothers used to run
> Were for the flax and wool they spun.
> "The wheel! The wheel!" the people cry,
> O credit you the wheel can buy.
> Unless that craze soon doth stop,
> It will bankrupt every store and shop.
> Ancient Rome ran too fast,
> In pride and luxury, it could not last.

In an age where women lacked the legal right to vote and hold public office enjoyed by men, here, at last, was something with which females could publicly hold parity with males. They, too, could operate a bicycle. In fact, the bicycle figured prominently in the changing of women's lives. The cycling craze and the women's rights movement of the 1890s became so inextricably intertwined that Susan B. Anthony in 1896 told the *New York World*'s Nellie Bly that cycling had "done more to emancipate women than anything else in the world." For the woman who wished to break with convention and demand political equality with men, the "freedom machine" became a new tool of personal expression and political power. With the bicycle, a sense of independence was experienced by women, and, of course, some men resented it. Why, just look at them peddling around town on that "Yellow Fellow" (popular model made in Syracuse by E. C. Stearns and Company) and wearing shorter skirts, knickers, and "bloomers." What is the world coming to? What will they demand a right to do next? Will it never end?

While some bicycle clubs were "males only," the Homer club may have accepted females. After all, Homer's academy on the Green had accepted female students as early as 1821 and was apparently more liberal then than many other communities. As early as 1887, a Floral Cycle parade was held. This event kicked-off the second annual Flower Show, held in the Baptist Church barn. Women were seen cycling among the male riders. There is a photo that purports to be of a club on the Homer Green (but the exact site cannot be confirmed) which includes all ages and sexes and what appears to be a black woman.

Indeed, cycling seems to have had a democratizing effect in the region. An amusing article on the egalitarian aspect of the pastime appeared in the May 3, 1901 issue of the *Cortland Democrat*. It observed that all types of people—"the rich and poor, the very young, the middle-aged and the old, the handsome and the plain-looking, all classes"—had been afflicted with "the bicycle fever." The author wrote of watching "a lady whose back hair is rolled up in a knot about the size of a two-cent orange, the seat being so low that with every revolution of the pedals her knees reach the level of her last year's sailor hat." Then he adds the seemingly snide comment that "if I couldn't make a more presentable appearance on a wheel than she, I would walk or hire a cab."

On May 30, 1880, the League of American Wheelmen was founded in Newport, Rhode Island. It soon became a prominent advocacy group for improved roads and highways, well before the advent of the automobile. In June of 1897, as reported by the *Cortland Democrat*, the Homer Wheelmen met at the Cortland Y.M.C.A. and raised $600 toward the construction of a $1,000 cycle path from Cortland to Little York. It ran through Homer and next to the west fence along the East Little York Road (now Route 11). Two furrows were turned, about five feet apart, and the space in between was filled with cinders. Riders were urged to join the "Cortland County Side-path Association" and to pay annual dues of one dollar. Members were issued badges to wear while riding on the path. Anyone caught riding on the path without the badge was liable to a fine of five dollars. Highly popular bicycle races (against time) were held from Cortland or Homer to Little York and back. The bicycle store sold handlebars of various designs along with "anatomical saddles," ammonia syringes (guns) to ward off dogs, and toe, pants, and dress guards.

It is interesting to note that the June 11, 1897 issue of the *Cortland Democrat* made this observation about the bicycle path: "When completed no rain can make disagreeable riding to Little York and probably in two years Syracuse and Binghamton will be interested enough to work from each way and complete over eighty miles of cinder path, running through Cortland."

Fourteen days later, the same newspaper reported that construction of the cinder path had begun under the direction of D. M. Totman at the second bridge north of Homer. Teams of horses were donated to draw the cinders. In addition, the directors of the association had met to elect officers and to adopt by-laws. It was decided that after the first year, the annual dues exacted of members would be fifty cents, which would "entitle them to all privileges of the side path."

By July 2, with less than two miles to go to finish the path from Homer to Little York, they ran out of cinders. The work was delayed until several carloads of cinders could be brought down from the Solvay Works in Syracuse. The *Cortland Democrat* reported that "Twenty teams were drawing until the cinders gave out."

The bicycle path must have been completed and viewed as a success because the newspaper of April 22, 1898, reported a strong probability that the Homer-Little York path might be extended south and north. At a meeting of the Cortland County Cycle Path Association, two proposals were made. A delegation from South Cortland expressed a desire to see a path extended to their village, and they were willing to commit 22 teams of horses for two days work each if the association would invest $75. The association approved the proposed extension.

Another project was proposed by the community of Preble. They were eager to see the path extended from Little York to their town and expressed a willingness "to do much to get it there." The association agreed to confer with Preble and Tully enthusiasts. There was hopeful talk that if the path reached Tully, "it is probable that Syracuse will meet it."

By 1898, the height of the bicycle craze, the Cortland County Cycle Path Association had 450 members. Their dues were to go for path maintenance and "new work." Members were urged to leave their money with George I. Watson, G. F. Beaudry, C. F. Thompson, or T. J. Kennedy. Those not members were "cordially invited to join and thus enjoy the privilege of the paths."

As R. Curtis Harris reported in Volume Two of *Cortland County Chronicles* (1958), in 1902, Homer's Dr. H. S. Brauman cycled to Little York on the side-path in eighteen minutes to answer an emergency call. So, the pathway was not used merely for recreation.

Perhaps, it is time to resurrect the Little York to Homer biking trail—but with something better than cinders—and have it intersect with a Tioughnioga River Trail. Then, too, what about a canal from the gravel pit north of the village to connect to the river for canoes and kayaks? Just consider the possibilities of another "golden age" of cycling and recreation in Historic Homer, NY.

Primary source material for this article was graciously provided by Homer's Ed Raus, who upon occasion takes a bicycle trip to Little York and back, enjoying the verdant scenery along the way and imagining a time when the bicycle reigned supreme through the valley.

[2020 note: Next to the column about the bicycle craze appeared the following notice written by the author, which supports the idea that the community of Homer had established a name for itself as the place that gave rise to the famed portraitist Francis B. Carpenter.]

CARPENTER DESCENDANT VISITS HOMER

On Saturday, October 10th, one of the great-great-great granddaughters of Homer's famous portrait painter Francis Bicknell Carpenter paid a visit to Homer. Traveling with her husband, son, and two dogs from Manhattan, Cynthia Romaine Milstead, a New York City kindergarten teacher, arrived at the Homer Town Hall. There the group was met by Homer's David Quinlan, who was instrumental in arranging this meeting. As an expert on the life and artistry of Carpenter, Quinlan graciously represented the town historian Martin Sweeney and took them on a tour of historic Homer, showing them Carpenter's birthplace and gravesite, the Stoddard birthplace, and portraits at the Phillips Free Library rendered by Carpenter.

At the Town Hall, Cynthia viewed her ancestor's portrait in oil of his fiancée, Augusta Prentiss Carpenter, from whom she descended. Quinlan offered his assessment of items brought by the Milsteads, including a watercolor that is only one of two known that Carpenter ever painted and a rare portrait of William Sydney Mount rendered in oil by Charles Loring Elliott. Both Mount and Elliott were artists and friends of Carpenter. The Stony Brook Museum holds a major collection of William Sydney Mount's genre paintings of early rural American life. One portrait there matches perfectly with the one the Milsteads brought to Homer to show Quinlan. The director of the Stony Brook Museum theorizes the one owned by the Milsteads was a second or first study done to compliment a larger portrait of William Sydney Mount.

Before departing, Cynthia provided the Town of Homer, on temporary loan, a family album and a family scrapbook for perusal by the town's historian. Also, on temporary loan, were two framed pastel portraits by Juliet Thompson. One from 1910 depicts a noted New York City suffragist, Cora Anderson Carpenter, who was the wife of Carpenter's son Herbert Sanford Carpenter. The second is a beautiful 1912 image of Herbert and Cora's daughter, Cora Carpenter Legg. At some point, the two portraits will be exhibited at the Town Hall, most likely to the right of the old stage and fittingly opposite Carpenter's portrait of his future wife. This way the public will have an opportunity to appreciate artwork from the period and to learn more about a family rooted in Homer who advocated for the rights of blacks and the rights of women.

By phone, the Milsteads later acknowledged the fine hospitality they received in Homer, and the Town Historian expressed appreciation for the items entrusted to the Town credited with launching Carpenter on his career as a nineteenth century portrait painter of renown.

November 5, 2020

THE HOMER ROAD PRISONERS BUILT

Many readers have undoubtedly traveled by car along Route 41A. The portion near the southern terminus winds through a ravine just off the Atwater Cemetery and is called by the locals "Homer Gulf Road." Originally, this portion was a mere path through the wilderness used by our earliest settlers. Trees were cleared to make a roadway for farmers to move their goods via teams of horses to the Great Western store or the Sherman Exchange in Homer village. With the advent of the automobile, a paved surface was called for. But did you know that the first paved road through Homer Gulf was constructed through the labor of convicts? Using information found in ten issues of the *Homer Republican* newspaper from 1914 to 1917, this is the story of the road prisoners built in the Town of Homer.

The road through Homer Gulf was not paved at the start of the twentieth century. By 1914, repairs were being called for. One local businessman, F. X. Litz, finding the dirt road to be "of much importance to Homer Business men," decided to take matters into his own hands. He proposed "with the consent of the town authorities to spend some of his own money in putting this road in better condition." The *Homer Republican* on August 6, 1914, supported Mr. Litz' project and wrote that it was "worthy of emulation by other business men of Homer."

It is uncertain that any meaningful action was taken to carry out this ambitious project. It is known, however, that word arrived in Homer on Monday, May 8, 1916, that the state had made an appropriation of $50,000 for the construction of a number of state roads, and "it was suggested that if Homer would send in a petition at once for the construction of the Homer gulf road under this act and appropriation it was probable that this piece of road would be designated for construction this year." Immediately, copies of such a petition were circulated through the village and town of Homer by F. M. Briggs, W. G. Crandall, and a dozen other members of Homer's Commercial Club [comparable to today's Cortland Chamber of Commerce]. The newspaper reported:

> ... all the people were more than willing to sign it as Homer people have long been anxious to have the road improved. It is an important highway to Homer from Auburn, Moravia, Dresserville, Como and Sempronius. It is also a picturesque route which will be much enjoyed by motorists. It is hoped that the prayer of the petition will be granted.

Town Supervisor L. M. Austin and Postmaster Samuel Andrews left that Monday evening for Albany, carrying with them the signed petition requesting "a state road be built from the Homer-Scott state road through Homer gulf to the Summer Hill town line—a distance of between two and a half miles."

Mr. Andrews and Mr. Austin returned Tuesday night from Albany with encouraging news. They reported they met with State Highway Commissioner Edwin Duffey, "who received them cordially and was surprised at the size of the petition, which contained about 500 names of Homer citizens, all obtained in a half days' time." While the governor had not yet signed the appropriation bill, the committee from Homer was informed that the bill would be approved at once, that "engineers from the highway department will be here within a week or ten days to look over the Homer gulf road and consult with the town board on the matter," and that roadwork could likely commence that summer "as soon as preliminaries can be arranged."

By summer, it was clear that the state would build the road but not pick up the full cost. The state would bear the cost of labor and some material, but the Town would have to pay for paving material, necessary tools, and team work [horses] to construct the top course of the road, and to furnish necessary sluices and guard rails for the highway. This meant that a special public vote had to be held to authorize expenditures by the Town and to issue bonds to finance the proposed project.

Two items appeared in the newspaper of August 3, 1916. The first was the officially required notice that the vote would be held at the Town Hall on August 24 on expending an amount not to exceed $9,000. Financing would be through serial bonds, payable $1,000 each year, beginning with the year 1917, until fully paid. The second item was an article in which the paper urged readers to "VOTE FOR THIS PROPOSITION":

> This road will be valuable to this town and village as a feeder to trade and a convenience to those who drive horses or cars. Homer people are anxious that their town and village should prosper and the building of this fine road will open up the most direct, easy and convenient inlet

for a large section of country west and north of Homer Gulf to Homer markets to deliver their produce to our buyer and to patronize Homer's business places. Every loyal Homer voter should be at the polls on Thursday, August 24:

A positive outcome to the vote must have been well anticipated because on Wednesday, August 16, laborers were delivered by the state. They arrived on the Lehigh Valley train to Cortland, where six or seven Homer automobiles met them and took them to the Samuel Andrews farmhouse in Homer Gulf, where they were to be quartered during the construction project. This work force consisted of thirty-one prisoners from the Auburn State Penitentiary. The newspaper explained that "A single guard will take charge of the men who will sleep in the Andrews house and do their cooking there. Milk, eggs and butter have been arranged for from neighboring farmers and bread, groceries and other necessaries will be purchased in Homer."

It may be presumed that the convicts were treated the same as those doing similar roadwork at the time in Erie County. A report of the State Commission of Prisons indicates such workers were to be paid ten cents per day, which would considerably reduce the cost if contract laborers were employed. They were issued work garb that did not distinguish them from ordinary workers. The report maintained the work benefited the men physically and morally. They enjoyed working outdoors and "consider it a privilege to be selected for road work."

Mr. P. G. Murphy of Troy, an expert road builder in the employ of the State Highway Department, was to board with Mr. and Mrs. George Langdon and oversee the road work. He planned to blast out the south west side of the shale rock bordering the road to widen it and to raise the roadbed about four feet in places where elevation was needed. The plan called for "a water bound macadam road 12 feet wide with 3-foot shoulders, making the total width of the road 18 feet." Cement sluices and retaining walls were be constructed where necessary and a large amount of posts and guard rails erected to make safe the sides of the road next to the creek. Besides providing residents in the environs northwest of Homer "a direct and almost hill less road to this village and beyond" and "the most direct and shortest route from Homer and Cortland to Auburn," the newspaper predicted "it will be the most scenic route in this part of the state and will be the mecca of automobile tourists for miles around . . ." Highway Commissioner Duffey was said to have ordered the work be done "in the best and most durable manner possible." Also, it was reported that the Homer Gulf road would have the added distinction of being "the first original road construction to be done by prison labor."

"So, it is up to Homer to carry this appropriation," stated the newspaper of August 16, "if the town's people want this fine, macadam road completed—and they do." To campaign for the passage of the vote, the Commercial Club, presided over by G. Howard Miller, called for a meeting at the Town Hall on the Monday evening before the vote: "All loyal members who can, will attend the meeting and help to organize and carry this project to a successful termination. It is the most important and beneficial one that Homer people have had an opportunity to support for many years and all should pull together for its success at the polls."

The day of the big vote arrived, August 24th, and by 10 AM 150 votes were already cast. The day's paper made a point to note "Many women who were interested voted for the appropriation." Note that this was 1916 and women of New York State could not yet legally vote in a Presidential election, but they could vote on a local highway proposition. The proposal passed by "a large majority," as was expected. After all, once the road became a state highway, the townspeople could benefit from it, but the Town would not have to maintain it.

By September 14, more than 500 Auburn prison convicts were reported to be then engaged in repairing and building state roads in various parts of the state. Obviously, the state had found a way to keep the cost of labor on these projects to a minimum. "Most of the men are engaged in re-surfacing jobs," stated the paper, "and the Homer gulf road is the first one to be built from the bottom by prison labor." This historical first may be considered a dubious honor.

The next week, the paper informed its readers that "The Homer gulf road grading is progressing steadily and satisfactorily. The grading is done from the west end of the road to about the Andrews farm. The men are nearly all working efficiently and satisfactorily." "Nearly all" was an appropriate description of the amount of manpower involved, because this appeared on the same page:

> Five prisoners working on the Homer gulf road escaped about 10 days ago and three of the men have been recaptured and returned to Auburn prison to serve a much longer sentence for their foolish attempt to escape. They lose all credits for good behavior. Does it pay?

The paper made no mention of the other two escaped prisoners. Are we to assume they made a successful getaway and returned to a life of crime?

By July of 1917, the original work force was cut in half, since "only a short distance remains of the grading work to reach the Homer-Scott state road." The laying down of the stone courses would be next. The Homer paper of October 25, 1917, posted this notice:

Work on the Homer gulf state road is finished for this year and the prison laborers have returned to Auburn. The subbase of the road has been completed from the Homer-Scott state road west to the town line. This winter the top-dressing stone will be hauled from this village ready to be spread in the spring. The road is left in fairly good condition for travel this fall and winter, it is reported.

By early November of 1917, the Auburn prisoners were transferred to Camp Coleman near Messengerville and were scheduled to work on the road through the narrows during the winter.

So, as you travel through "this gulf where the road is heavily shaded by the precipitous, wooded banks and ridges on either side," remember the first paved road there was put down by convicts who might not have thought they were rendering a great service to the people of Homer. We know that five of them saw it as their opportunity for an escape route.

November 19, 2020

HOMER'S CONNECTION TO A CIVIL WAR NURSE

While men from the Town of Homer served in the military during the Civil War, was there any woman connected to Homer who served as a nurse for the Union Army during the conflict? The answer is yes, and I am indebted, once again, to Homer's Ed Raus for the information. Ed donated to the municipal archives a booklet he had published in 2004 by Thomas Publications of Gettysburg, Pennsylvania. The title is *Ministering Angel: The Reminiscences of Harriet A. Dada, a Union Army Nurse in the Civil War.*

It has been estimated that 3,214 women were appointed and paid by the federal government to serve as nurses in Union Army hospitals, on medical ships, and near battlefield sites during the Civil War. They received forty cents a day, one ration, and transportation. For four long years, 1861–1865, these nurses endured horrible hardships: scenes of human carnage, ravaging effects of gangrene and disease (measles, small pox, pneumonia), the unsanitary and disorganized conditions of the military hospitals, and, at times, the "unkind words and sneers" of prejudiced male surgeons and hospital administrators. It was thought that no "proper" woman should or would take on the role of nurse. Not until twenty-seven years after the war ended did Congress pass the Army Nurse Pension Act. This gave the nurses the status of military veterans and the ability, upon proof of service, to receive a federal pension amounting to twelve dollars a month. 2,448 women applied for the pension. One of those nurses was Harriet A. Dada.

Harriet was the daughter of Lemuel and Merinda Budlong Dada. The couple lived on West Hill in the Town of Homer before moving to Cortland in 1825. Lemuel was a cabinetmaker and minister and one of the first trustees of the First Presbyterian Church in Cortland. Harriet was the youngest of their three children. Her older siblings were Samuel and Elizabeth. Harriet was born 1835 in Hannibal, New York, which is in Oswego County. When Harriet was ten years old, the Dada family moved yet again. This time it was to Fulton, New York. There, she attended local schools and graduated in 1854 from the local academy (later the Falley Seminary).

At age 20, Harriet began a life dedicated to serving others. She became a teacher to the Choctaws, under the auspices of the American Board of Commissioners for Foreign Missions. She became proficient with the Choctaw language and was given the name "Imponna" which meant "skillful." However, during the winter of 1860, Harriet and other Northern teachers left their posts and returned home because of threats and hostile actions by local pro-Southern individuals. Living with her father in Fulton, she fully intended to return to the Indian Territory, but plans changed when the Civil War broke out in April of 1861. Harriet chose to be among the first to respond to the call for army nurses.

Elizabeth Blackwell, America's first female to earn a medical degree (Geneva Medical College, 1849), spearheaded the organization of the Women's Central Association of Relief (WCAR), a forerunner of the U.S. Sanitary Commission. WCAR registered and examined volunteer nurses and sponsored their training in New York City hospitals. Then, they were referred to the superintendent of the United States Army Nurses in Washington, D.C. At that time the appointed post was held by the famous reformer Dorothea Lynde Dix.

When Harriet applied, she received the endorsement of Homer's prominent physician and Academy trustee Caleb Green. Dr. Green wrote that she was "eminently qualified for the duties of Hospital Nurse." Once accepted, Harriet spent six weeks in New York City attending lectures by prominent surgeons and working as a nurse at Bellevue Hospital. Two days after the First Battle of Bull Run, Harriet and a fellow missionary to the Choctaws, Susan Hall, arrived in Washington, D.C. Immediately, they received a directive from Dorothea Dix: "You are needed in Alexandria."

Although she did not keep a daily journal of her wartime experiences, Harriet did save her letters from the field. From them, we learn from July 21, 1861 through September 19, 1865 she was posted to several hospitals in Virginia, such as at Harpers Ferry, twice to the nation's capital, to Gettysburg after the three-day battle, and finished up in Murfreesboro and Chattanooga in Tennessee. On one occasion, she and her fellow nurses found themselves in enemy hands at Winchester, Virginia.

In 1884, her letters were the basis for her ten-part series of articles published in the *National Tribune* under the heading "Ministering Angels." Ed Raus states in his annotated version of Dada's series: "These reminiscences provide a historically significant and poignant story of a woman's self-sacrifice, devotion to duty, and struggle in the face of great adversity." The following are excerpts from her reminiscences.

"At first the food was pretty poor, but it could not be helped. The soldiers would get so tired of bread, butter, and tea for supper, and bread and coffee for breakfast! This was all they had, and we had just the same."

"None of the pastors of the churches in town ever came to visit the sick and wounded, except one Roman Catholic priest. Neither did the white people come in, but many good Christian colored people often came and brought something good for the soldiers, saying as they did so, 'I pray for you every day.'"

"[A soldier] of the 1st Minnesota, who had been wounded through the neck, the ball coming out of his mouth and knocking out several teeth, was the first [to die in the ward]. . . . He suffered patiently, and, at last, bled to death."

"One of the surgeons in this new hospital said to one of the ladies: 'A lady ceases to be a lady when she becomes a nurse.'"

"In the ward to which I was assigned were eight who had been severely wounded, and the nurses had been bathing all their wounds from one basin of water, which set on a table in the center of the room. . . . Why the surgeon had not instructed them to do differently, I never knew."

"We were told that surgeons were known to stop and dispute as to which of them should perform the operation, and then, after the amputation, instead of attending to the sufferer, they would play with the dismembered hand, foot or limb. Such surgeons should have been summarily discharged. Fortunately they were in the minority, for many were true and noble gentlemen, and very skillful."

"'What, will you take care of me, too, lady?' was the inquiry of a wounded Confederate. 'Yes,' said I, 'we treat you just as we want our boys treated when they are taken prisoners.'"

"On the 22nd of March 1865, a man named Ellis, belonging to the 1st Wisconsin battery, died in my ward. His younger brother, a member of the same battery, came to the hospital in great distress, as this was the third brother he had lost in the army. He said he wished to send the body home, but he had not been paid off in a long time and did not have enough money. His home was in Moravia, near Auburn, N.Y. It happened that I had some money with me, . . . so I let him have it, and directed him to Mr. Reed, . . . knowing he would render him assistance in getting a coffin."

"If a patient gave up all hope he was almost sure to die; therefore, it was necessary to inspire courage."

Harriet brought her deep religious faith to bear in her nursing. In her reminiscences, she points out several cases where she assisted her patients in renewing their faith in God. She supported the work of hospital chaplains and used her contacts with upstate New York churches to enlist their aid in her efforts. For example, while stationed at Aquia Creek in the spring of 1863, Harriet's sister Elizabeth asked the children of Homer's Congregational Church to make cloth "comfort bags" for the sick and lonely soldiers to store their keepsakes. The children were to include personal notes as well. This was done, and in a letter of thanks to the children, Harriet explained that many of the soldiers had acquired the bad habits of smoking and drinking whiskey to cope with their loneliness. "If any of you have brothers in the army," she wrote, "I hope you will send them so many letters and [news]papers that they will have no excuses." She added that the pillow included in the box of "comfort bags" "was placed under the head of a Mr. Holland from Chenango Forks and he thought it softer because it came from Cortland Co."

This assistance provided by Homer and Harriet's written response was noted sometime in the 1950s by the presentation of a short play by a Homer Congregational Sunday School class. Titled "A Cortland County Nurse in Action" and paying tribute to Nurse Dada, the typewritten script is in the municipal archives. This writer suspects it was researched at the Cortland County Historical Society and written by the late Betty Haller, a grade six teacher at the Homer Elementary School at the time.

Blessed with good health and stamina, Harriet Dada survived her stint as a Civil War nurse and went on to earn a degree in 1868 from the New York Medical College for Women in New York City. A few months later she became a homeopathic physician in Syracuse, specializing in diseases of women and children. In December 1873, she married Rev. Peter Walter Emens. Upon her death on September 1, 1909, she was buried in Syracuse's Oakwood Cemetery. The grave is identified by simply a small stone bearing her three initials. It is interesting to note that the Daughters of Union Veterans of the Civil War in Cortland County chose to honor her by naming themselves the Harriet Dada Emens Tent 63.

Perhaps, the greatest recognition Nurse Dada received was from former patients. They sent letters expressing gratitude for her years of exceptional army service, and some submitted testimonials when she applied for the federal pension. This is one representative example:

> The doctors . . . said I could not live and I was indifferent whether
> I lived or died, and she . . . bid me live. To her, more than to all else,
> I owe the life and strength and happiness which I now enjoy. [. . .]
> What she did for me she did for hundreds of others as helpless and
> hopeless. [. . .] She did for us all that a sister, wife or mother could do.

William H. Bright
Company C.
22nd Wisconsin Infantry

One of the more overlooked aspects of the Civil War has been the role played by female nurses, such as Harriet Dada. Through her letters, even that sent to a Sunday School class in Homer, she documented for history the needs of those struck down while fighting to preserve the Union and to end human bondage. With humility she wrote in 1884, "Surely, I did receive my reward . . . it had been my privilege to minister to the sick and wounded soldiers—one of the greatest privileges given to an American woman."

Edmund J. Raus, Jr., of the village of Homer, served as a historian at Manassas National Battlefield Park, at Gettysburg, and at Fredericksburg-Spotsylvania. He is the author of A Generation on the March: The Union Army at Gettysburg *(Thomas Publications, 1966),* Where Duty Called Them: The Story of the Samuel Babcock Family of Homer, New York in the Civil War *(Schroeder Publications, 2001), and* Banners South: A Northern Community at War *(Kent State University Press, 2005) in which Ed states, "Cortland County has left future generations of its sons and daughters something to think about" (p. 257).*

December 3, 2020

SHOPPING IN HOMER: WHAT'S CHANGED?

With the rapid approach of Christmas and Hanukkah, the secular side of the holiday season finds folks thinking of shopping to satisfy our wants and needs and those of others. Other than prescription drugs in recent years, most all of one's essentials have always been readily available for purchase in the village of Homer. As revealed in the following ads posted in the *Cortland County Republican* newspaper between 1876 (the nation's centennial year) and 1880, one could find establishments on Main Street and James Street selling a long list of goods and services: groceries, barbering services, train tickets, men's clothing, women's wear, footwear, toys, hardware, tools, books, picture frames, and everyone's favorite essential—fresh brewed coffee. Unlike today, back then cash was preferred, not credit. Plastic did not exist yet as a medium of commercial transactions, and some folks would even engage in bartering.

August 18, 1876:

CANES! CENTENNIAL CANES.
THE BEST CANE ever made.

Sticks from all parts of the world
And prices to suit the buyer.
Gents' Furn'g Goods
A large Stock of Gents' hosiery, Gents' jewelry,
Gents' neckwear, shirts, ties, bows, collars, cuffs, suspenders
And CHOICE BRANDS OF CIGARS,
At JACOB METZGER'S BARBER SHOP James Street
[*This is the same Jake Metzger who introduced Homer to roller-skating.*]

W. M. Haynes GROCER in the Brown Block
Credit played out!
Having seen the evils of a credit business, I shall henceforth sell goods for cash only.

In all credit business good paying customers are taxed a percent on their goods to make up for losses on poor accounts which will accumulate in the best conducted firms. To do justice to myself and customers I shall henceforth offer my goods at GREATLY REDUCED PRICES and for value received. SAVING of over 25 per cent!

Right below Haynes' ad appeared this ad from a competitor:
BABCOCK & GILKERSON, THE LIVE GROCERS
Ask special attention to their choice stock of TEAS, SUGARS, COFFEES, SPICES, WOODEN-WARE, ETC. which in Price and Quality are as low as the LOWEST! We do not take off 25 per cent for cash, but we do sell goods for the smallest living profit as our many customers of the past nine years can testify.
Attached to our store we have a neat LUNCH ROOM!
where will be found at all hours
PORK AND BEANS, COLD MEATS, OYSTERS, PIE AND CHEESE
No, 1 Sherman Block. Homer, NY

BOOTS AND SHOES!
T. D. Chollar
Manufacturer. Wholesale and Retail Dealer in
BOOTS, SHOES,
Leather and Findings
Main Street, Homer Village
I WILL NOT BE UNDERSOLD!

January 2, 1879:
GAMES, DOLLS, TOYS, BOOKS,
MUSICAL goods etc., at E. Loomis & Son's

December 18, 1879:
WESTCOTT's FOUNDRY and MACHINE SHOP
Westcott, Noyes, and Pierce, Proprietors
Water Powered Manufacturers of CASTINGS & GENERAL MACHINE WORK
South Main Street, Homer

December 25, 1879:
MRS. G. E. T0RRY and Co.
Keeps the largest and best selected stock of
MILLINERY GOODS
PATTERN BONNETS,
FLOWERS, SILKS, LACES,
And all Novelties necessary to produce
FIRST-CLASS WORK
Also a large stock of
FANCY GOODS
WORSTED in all Colors,
at our store on MAIN STREET, Homer
January 8, 1880:
New BRICK STORE on James street
with a dollar in your pocket, prepare to take away
$2 worth of Goods. Good Butter, Eggs, Lard, Dried Apples,
Berries, Beans and Oats, and in fact any and everything
but skunk skins taken in exchange for Groceries.
O. C. CHURCHILL

March 12, 1880:
STOVES AND RANGES
At Old Prices
HARDWARE
House furnishing Goods
G. & J. Murray

May 27, 1880:
ATWATER & KELLOGG,
DRUGGISTS AND BOOKSELLERS
Manufacturers of
Picture Frames
A complete stock of
MOULDINGS, RUSTIC FRAMES,
BLACK WALNUT BRACKETS

FANCY GOODS A Specialty
We have a circulating library.
Western and Southern Ticket Agency
Round trip tickets to prominent points
No. 2 Barber Block, Homer, NY.

Miss M. L. CONINE has established a shop over Allen & Shattuck's store, and is now ready to do Fashionable Dress-Making at reasonable prices and Invites the ladies of Homer and vicinity to give her a call [meaning a visit].

Ladles', Gents' and Children's Hosiery and Gloves
cheap at P. R. BREWSTER'S, Barber Block.

What is better than a cup of GOOD HOT COFFEE?
And how unsatisfactory to the taste if the coffee
used is of poor quality or stale. I roast coffee and peanuts
at the store twice a week, and know the coffee used is the BEST.
Try It. Found at P. F. SMITH'S [*Can't you almost smell the aroma upon entering?*]

December 17, 2020

"THE QUEEN OF VAUDEVILLE" PERFORMED IN HOMER

We are rapidly approaching the 126th anniversary of two remarkable events from Homer's past. On the night of December 21, 1894, Homer farmer Patrick Quinlan had two drinks at Doyle's Pub [now Dasher's Corner Pub] on Main Street and headed on foot up James Street. His home was at the end of what is now Bishop's Hill Road. He never made it. He was bludgeoned to death along the way. No one was ever convicted. The heinous crime remains a "cold case" and proves you could get away with murder once upon a time in Homer. The event fell into oblivion over time as did another event that night across the street from the pub in Homer.

While Quinlan had made his brags about making a lucrative sale that day in Christmas turkeys at O. B. Andrews' grocery store, some of the conversation in the pub must have focused on the show scheduled for that evening at the third-floor opera house across the street. Sixteen-year-old Eva Tanguay (pronounced "tang gway") was in town for one performance and was destined to go on to become the highest paid performer in vaudeville.

This entertainment event at the Keator Opera House may have been possible because of George W. Ripley, who was a Homer resident and Tanguay's advance man. He resigned from the post soon after the Homer performance. He apparently continued in showbiz with his own troupe of minstrels and thespians, because *The Homer Republican* of January 30, 1913, reported his plans for performances to be held outdoors "under canvas" in Groton and "his home town, Homer."

Eva Tanguay was born in 1878 in Canada, but before she reached the age of six, her family moved to Holyoke, Massachusetts. While still a child, she developed an interest in the performing arts. She made her first appearance on stage at the age of eight at an amateur night in Holyoke. In her earliest days she was promoted through a small theater company operated by one Paul C. Winkelmann. Soon, she was touring professionally with a production of a stage adaptation of the popular Frances Hodgson Burnett novel *Little Lord Fauntleroy*.

She performed at least once in 1893 at the Opera House in Cortland. Three months before her appearance on the Homer stage, *The Holley Standard* (October 4, 1894), described her as "A great favorite and vivacious and captivating artiste . . . who is without exception the most successful Child Actress that has yet been seen. . . . She is a good singer, superb dancer, and was loudly encored." The paper went on to point out she had played to a packed house in Harrisburg, Pennsylvania. On November 17, 1894, *The New York Dramatic Mirror* noted she had played to "good houses" at the Olean Opera House.

Soon after the Homer performance and perhaps a Christmas break, she appeared nearby again. This time it was in McLean. According to the *Cortland Evening Standard* of Tuesday, January 8, 1895, "Eva Tanguay appeared in the comedy 'The Californian Detective,' last Saturday evening at the opera house. It was the best play ever presented in this place."

Tanguay eventually landed a spot in 1901in the Broadway musical *My Lady,* and it was the 1904 show *The Chaperons* that caused a rise in her popularity. By 1905, she was performing in vaudeville as a solo act, where she would spend much of the remainder of her career.

In truth she possessed only an average voice, but her energy, enthusiasm, and sense of abandon on stage while she performed her suggestive songs made her an audience favorite. She went on to have a long-lasting vaudeville career and eventually commanded one of the highest salaries of any performer of the day. In 1910, she was earning as much as $3,500 a week (about $90,000 in 2020 dollars), out earning the likes of contemporaries Enrico Caruso and Harry Houdini.

Eva Tanguay is best remembered for her brassy, self-confident songs that symbolized the emancipated woman. Those songs included "It's All Been Done Before but Not the Way I Do It," "I Want Someone to Go Wild with Me," "Go as Far as You Like," and "That's Why They Call Me Tabasco."

She was nicknamed the "I Don't Care Girl" after her most famous song, "I Don't Care," came out in 1905.

Tanguay was known to spend lavishly on publicity campaigns and costumes. Early in her career, a manager told her that money made money, and she never forgot the advice. She would buy huge ads at her own expense, and on one occasion, allegedly spent twice her salary on publicity.

One of her showbiz strengths was gaining free publicity with outrageous behavior off stage. In 1907, she stayed with married entertainment journalist and publicist C.F. Zittel in a Brooklyn hotel for nearly a week. Zittel's wife uncovered the affair by hiring detectives dressed as room-service bellhops to burst into the room. The event made headlines and only seemed to enhance Eva's reputation, popularity, and box-office success. She also got her name in the papers for allegedly being kidnapped, allegedly having her jewels stolen, and for being fined $50 in Louisville, Kentucky, for throwing a stagehand down a flight of stairs. Apparently, she firmly believed that bad publicity was better than no publicity at all. Consequently, she is considered the first performer to achieve national mass-media celebrity. Edward Bernays, "the father of public relations," described Tanguay as "our first symbol of emergence from the Victorian age."

Like Madonna and Lady Gaga of our era, Tanguay's costumes were as extravagant as her personality. In 1910, a year after the Lincoln penny was issued, Tanguay caused a sensation by appearing on stage in a coat entirely covered in the new coins. Did not Lady Gaga wear an infamous dress made of raw meat at the 2010 MTV Video Music Awards?

Tanguay was officially married twice. Her first marriage was to dancer John Ford in 1913, but they divorced after four years. Following her divorce, Tanguay was romantically linked, though never married, as was sometimes reported, to vaudeville dancer Roscoe Ails. In 1927, at the age of 49, Tanguay married her piano accompanist, 23-year-old Al Parado. Shortly after the marriage she had it annulled on the grounds of fraud. She claimed that Parado had at least two other names which he used so frequently that she was not sure which one was real. Actually, the marriage was another of her publicity ploys. She had it dissolved when it did not yield the intended promotional benefits.

Tanguay made only one known recording. In 1922 Nordskog Records marketed her signature song, "I Don't Care." She also starred in two film comedies. The first, *Energetic Eva,* made in 1916, and *The Wild Girl,* the next year, captured on the screen her lusty stage vitality.

With the Wall Street crash of 1929, Tanguay was said to have lost more than $2 million (about $30,000,000 in 2020 dollars). She retired from show business during the Depression. Cataracts caused her to lose her sight, but

Sophie Tucker, "The Last of the Red-Hot Mamas" and a friend from vaudeville days, paid for an operation that helped to restore some of her vision.

At the time of her death on January 11, 1947, in Hollywood, Tanguay was working on her autobiography, to be titled *Up and Down the Ladder*. She was interred in the Hollywood Memorial Park Cemetery, now called Hollywood Forever Cemetery. In 1953, Mitzi Gaynor portrayed Tanguay in a fictionalized version of her life in the film *The I Don't Care Girl*. Tanguay's signature song was also recorded by Judy Garland and Eydie Gorme among others.

If you want to read a page burner of a biography, I recommend Andrew L. Erdman's *Queen of Vaudeville: The Story of Eva Tanguay* (Ithaca, NY: Cornell University Press, 2012). It is a detailed account of an American celebrity who once graced the stage of Homer's opera house, embraced the "Roaring Twenties" with abandon, and died in relative obscurity in a bungalow in Hollywood.

December 31, 2020

THE SHAM BATTLE OF 1880

American Civil War reenactments are an effort to recreate the appearance of a particular battle or other event associated with the American Civil War by hobbyists known as Civil War reenactors, or "living historians." Civil War veterans recreated battles as a way to remember their fallen comrades and to teach others what the war was all about. The Great Reunion of 1913, celebrating the 50th anniversary of the Battle of Gettysburg, was attended by more than 50,000 Union and Confederate veterans, and included reenactments of elements of the battle, including Pickett's Charge.

Modern reenacting is thought to have begun during the 1961–1965 Civil War Centennial commemorations. In 1986, *Time* magazine estimated there were more than 50,000 reenactors in the U.S. In 1998, the 135th anniversary re-enactment of the Battle of Gettysburg took place near the original battlefield. There have been several estimates on the number of participants, but it is widely agreed that it was the largest re-enactment ever held anywhere in the world, with between 15,000 and 20,000 re-enactors participating and about 50,000 spectators watching.

Locally, the Homeville Museum component of the Central New York Living History Center has hosted a "Civil War Reenactment" in recent years. At this event, reenactors presented cavalry demonstrations, skirmishes, infantry and artillery drills, including formation movements, loading and firing. This was not something new for the area. One local reenactment occurred on

Image 10.7 Eva Tanguay, "the girl who made vaudeville famous." *Private collection, courtesy of Beth Touchton.*

Thursday, June 10, 1880, at the Cortland Fairgrounds. The *Cortland Standard* of June 17, 1880, "estimated that fully ten thousand people were in town and from seven to eight thousand were on the Fair Grounds to witness the Sham Battle." Wickwire Brothers' wireworks was closed for the day, along with the chair factory and Benton's planing-mill.

The Field Day and Sham Battle event was the fund-raising idea of Cortland's Excelsior Hook and Ladder Company. The newspaper reported that over $1,500 was taken in at the gate and approximately $125 in admissions to the grandstand, meaning a tidy profit of around $1,100 was made after expenses. $1,000 in 1880 is equivalent in purchasing power to about $25,482.16 in 2020.

As the sun rose that day, bringing perfect weather, a gun was fired signaling the opening of the day's activities. Soon, the roads leading from Homer and elsewhere to Cortland were clogged with carriages and people on foot "bound for a day of fun, sight-seeing and enjoyment." There was also going to be an opportunity to see purportedly one of the only four Gatling guns in the State—"one of the most terribly destructive weapons known to modern warfare," proclaimed the *Cortland Standard* of May 5, 1880. This gun belonged to the Binghamton City Guards. The same issue of the *Cortland Standard* had predicted

The day will be one long to be remembered, and will bring vividly to mind the scenes through which the boys in blue were called upon to pass in the late war. The companies are composed largely of veterans, and the interest of the occasion will be intense as the main incidents of a battle will be presented in the most realistic manner.

Scheduled to be the Officer of the Day was the commander of the 185th Regiment, Syracuse's General Gustavus Sniper (yes, that's his name, and his equestrian statue is near St. Joseph's Hospital in Syracuse). There were three Cortland County companies in the 185th Regiment, primarily from Cortlandville, Homer and Marathon. The Homer Company (E) was under Robert P. Bush, a Homer school teacher when he was mustered in as Captain of the Company.

Company B of the 51st Regiment of Syracuse was invited to participate as was the Binghamton City Guards and Battery L of Binghamton. Battery L was said to be "the best drilled Battery in the State" with a membership of 75 men. In addition, six or seven bands and several fire departments were to be part of a parade expected to be "one of the finest ever witnessed in this section" of the state. In short, a large number of visitors from out of town were to join in the day's events.

Sixty-four members of Binghamton's Battery L, under the command of Capt. L. L. Olmstead, arrived by train the night before and camped on the grounds near the depot. At 5:30 on the morning of June 10th, they assembled and, led by the Battery L Band, marched through the streets of Cortland to their breakfast at the Sperry House on East Court Street. In short order, Capt. A. Chryst and his Company B of the 51st Regiment arrived on the fairgrounds, followed by Capt. E. G. Judd and the Binghamton City Guards. The Guards were accompanied by the Whitney's Point Fire Department and Band. The Emerald Hose Company, the W. W. Engine Company, and the Cortland Wagon Company Band met the Cazenovia, Canastota, and DeRuyter Fire Departments and their bands and escorted them to the fairgrounds.

The first event of the day was a long-range target practice by Battery L. It was said that "some excellent shots were made at a sixteen-foot square plank target one-half mile distant" in full view of the grounds. The target most likely would have been on a rise of ground so the crowd could see it. It had to be away from people and roads. The area northwest of the fair buildings seems the likely site for the target. This event was followed by a rifle match between the Syracuse and Binghamton teams over a 200-yard range. The 51st Regiment team won.

The highlight of the day, the Sham Battle, was next on the program. For this, General Sniper commanded both "sides" with B. E. Miller, C. W. Wiles, John Sizelan of Cortland and Major Auer and J. D. Roney of Syracuse as aides. The "fort" was defended by Battery L and a detachment of the Binghamton City Guards. The rest of the City Guards and Company B of the 51st Regiment comprised the attacking party. The *Cortland Standard* of June 17th described the "battle":

> The opposing forces threw out skirmish lines, and these while 'lying low' discharged round after round of blank cartridges. The skirmishers of the attacking party finally became emboldened and advanced with the reserve following in the rear. A couple of guns from the Battery warned them that they were on dangerous ground and they beat a retreat. The attacking party again and again advanced, a continuous fire from the Battery driving them back, and they beat a precipitate retreat. A flank movement was made by a detachment from Co. B, under command of Lieut. Nearing, moving to the right through the crowd and coming up from the other direction, the main force keeping up an incessant firing to attract the attention of those in the fort until the proper time, when a grand charge was made and the fort captured and the white flag run up. It was said by veterans to be a very true representation of the manner in which two armies meet, and would compare favorably with sham battles held elsewhere which they had attended.

Next on the agenda was the parade led by General Sniper and his staff, trustees in carriages, and six bands scattered through units of local and visiting firefighters. Cortland's Excelsior Hook and Ladder Company brought up the rear. Cortland's Emerald Hose Company was sporting for the first-time new uniforms of gray. Trimmed with gold and green cord, the appearance they made was described as "superb." The "best-looking military organization ever in Cortland" was reported to be the City Guard of Binghamton. Led by their band and wearing white pantaloons and large bear-skin hats, the Guard "made a very striking appearance" as they gave a dress parade in front of the Sperry House. The parade through the city's principle streets, reported to be "the most imposing spectacle of the day," culminated with the military companies being entertained at Cortland's hotels.

Precautions were taken to maintain public safety during the day's events. No teams of horses were permitted to enter the fairgrounds, and it was noted that Battery L had over ten years of experience in the "sham battle business" and had "yet to record their first accident." The newspaper claimed the crowds were "the most orderly . . . zsever seen" in the city, and "with very few exceptions the day appeared to be one of genuine enjoyment." Those "exceptions" must have referred to the eight men apprehended for public intoxication and the swindler who managed to get out of town after selling small boxes of soap which he claimed also contained various sums of money up to $5. A later newspaper reported on the disappearance of some regimental flags used in the event, and the owner was asking for their return.

All in all, a unique educational opportunity filled with colorful military pageantry and music was afforded the residents of Homer and the other environs of Cortland on June 10, 1880. That was a mere fifteen years after the most decisive event in U. S. history came to an end. Now, 155 years later, the fratricidal conflict remains deeply embedded in the nation's psyche and identity. The public's fascination, as witnessed in the Sham Battle of 1880, has been ongoing and extends far beyond historical interest or scholarly attention. Today, many serious reenactors wish to have an "immersive" experience, trying to live, as much as possible, as someone of the 1860s might have. They spend much time and money on "authentic" wardrobes and equipment, eating seasonally and regionally appropriate food, and staying in character throughout an event. A "sham battle" with as much realism as possible allows one to get closer to an ancestor who may have fought in the war. But for that ancestor it was no "sham battle."

Thanks must go to Homer's Ed Raus for providing copies of the Cortland Standard *news articles about the Sham Battle of 1880. Sometimes, a historian comes across material that is not germane to the topic being researched, but the information is too interesting to discard. That is what has happened to Ed. Thus, he comes across "nuggets of gold" for this column and the municipal archives, and it is much appreciated.*

Chapter 11

Article at the start of 2021

January 14, 2021

PROPOSED ANNEXATION OF HOMER
BY THE CITY OF CORTLAND

The Village of Homer and the City of Cortland are adjacent to each other. Anyone traveling south on the Homer-Cortland Road can hardly tell where the Village of Homer ends and the City of Cortland begins. Did you know it was proposed at one time for the demarcation on the map to be erased and the Village annexed by the City? Such a proposal was recommended by an anonymous Homer resident. It came forth in a letter to the editor found in the January 5, 1905, edition of the *Homer Republican*. This is the proposal in its entirety:

WANTS TO ANNEX CORTLAND

A Correspondent Believes It Would Increase Values in Homer and Reduce the Tax Rate.

To the editor of the *Republican*:

SIR—Please allow me to thank you kindly for allowing your paper to be used in presenting to the people of this village things for consideration.

Having been a taxpayer here for very many years, I must admit that I have been grieved for a long time in seeing property gradually decreasing in value, especially in selling value. The latter statement is illustrated in the sale of the Schermerhorn property—seven acres of land finely located for $5,000, not one third the cost of the buildings. Again, the property lately purchased by the Briggs brothers for $3,000—not a third of what it would cost to build the house. And still another—that bought by M. A. Whiting—ten rods frontage and three acres of land for $2,500, not half it would cost to erect the buildings. Other similar cases might be cited.

It is conceded that our system of fire alarm is very faulty and has been for a long time. An argument raised by those who are opposed to an up-to-date system is to wait until a new town hall is built. I fear many buildings will be removed by the fire demon and some even crumble away before the people in this village will vote to increase the now excessively high tax rate for such a luxury.

In view of the situation I can see but one way to get a lower tax rate and the much-needed improvements—that is to open a way to interest capitalists to invest their money here, thereby giving more property to be taxed. This desirable state could doubtless be brought about by being annexed to the city of Cortland.

I am credibly informed that one of her wealthiest citizens lately remarked, that if Homer was annexed to Cortland he could clearly see a fine field to invest money there and that many others would see the same. Many years ago, when Syracuse was a small city she reached out to the north and annexed the village of Salina. A few years later from the northwest she took Geddes and more recently on the south Danforth was added and then Elmwood. Many citizens in these villages were opposed to becoming a part of Syracuse, but the far seeing in both city and village knew it was a wise move, as the magic-like increase in population and value of property with the many advantages and comforts brought to the people have proven. Three hundred and fifty-one buildings for various purposes were erected in Syracuse in 1904 at a cost of $3,745,630.

If the suggested relation should be brought about there would be a much lower tax rate as has been clearly shown by the figures recently published in your columns.

It is a fact that this high rate bears heavily upon the class who own or are trying to pay for their small homes. The question for them to solve is, will they continue to plod on under this burden or will they arouse and seek relief; will those more favored who can easily, if not willingly, meet the demand, awake, use their best judgment with no ill will to any and accept the relief at hand.

Homer would have two aldermen, more supervisors [legislators] than now in the county and soon many very desirable improvements. For one I am heartily in favor of having the village of Homer annexed to the city of Cortland.

Some of the people there may object, but the substantial, close thinking class cannot fail to see that the beautiful and many feet higher location of Homer would greatly increase the attractiveness of their city of which they may now be justly proud, but of which it might be said in a short time, to be the most desirable city for residence and business in central New York.

A SUBSCRIBER.

Since this proposal was made, there have been a few other suggestions that local municipalities ought to consolidate. None have proceeded any further than did the proposal of 1905. Part of the understandable resistance to such recommendations is the fear of a loss of identity. While Homer once contested Cortland for the designation of county seat, looking back on it, it appears to have worked out for the best. Cortland expanded as a city of commerce with an institution of higher learning, while the village of Homer remained a village and maintained its quaint architectural and historical charm. It can boast of a couple of Historic Sites and one Historic District. That District includes the iconic Little White Church on the Green dating to the 1830s and well over 200 other structures covering a range of architectural styles. It is a perfect laboratory for historical architectural studies and has a rich history of which the community can be proud. There is something to be said for the preservation and celebration of one's historic identity. It is that unique identity, rooted in the past, that binds us all together as a community today.

[2020 Note: It has been said that the Homer community sees itself as "different." Well, maybe, just maybe, we are "different," and it is our sense of connection to our unique past that makes us that way. It shows in our official Homer Village seal designed by Stephanie Urso Spina, Ph.D.]

****

Homer's public historian continues to put forth stories of Homer's past in *The Homer News*. There seems to be no shortage of events and people to write about. The heart of Central New York just oozes history.

Bibliography

Algeo, Matthew. 2015. *Abe & Fido: Lincoln's Love of Animals and the Touching Story of His Favorite Canine Companion.* Chicago: Chicago Review Press.
Bacon, Benjamin Wisner. 1913. *Theodore Thornton Munger: New England Minister.* New Haven: Yale University Press.
Best, Frank E. 1899. *John Keep of Longmeadow, Massachusetts and his Descendants.* Chicago, Illinois: Frank E. Best, 61–65. Copy in Homer Town archives, Main St., Homer, NY.
Bird, Ina Hurlbut. 1930s. Scrapbooks with photos and clippings of her news articles in the 1930s about ancestral life on the Scott Road. In Homer Town archives, Town Hall, Homer, NY. Blodgett, Bertha Eveleth. 1932. *Stories of Cortland County for Boys and Girls.* First published inthe *Cortland Standard*, then in book form. Cortland, NY: Cortland County Historical Society.
Brandt, Nat. 1990. *The Town That Started the Civil War.* Syracuse, NY: Syracuse University Press.
Burden, Howard W. 1973. *"History of the Homer Fire Department."* In a booklet prepared in observance of the centennial of the Homer Fire Department and the 80th Annual Central New York's Firemen's Convention held in Homer from July 18–21, 1973. Printed by the Cortland Press.
Carpenter, Francis Bicknell. Personal diary, version transcribed by Emerson Ives, grandson, along with letters from Daniel Carpenter and William Carpenter. Copy in Cortland County Historical Society, Cortland, NY. Not the same as Carpenter Diary entry transcriptions made as part of the Cowdrey notes in the same society.
———. 1866. *Six Months at the White House with Abraham Lincoln: The Story of a Picture.* New York: Hurd and Houghton.
Cohen, Robert, ed. 2007. *Dear Mrs. Roosevelt: Letters from Children of the Great Depression.* Chapel Hill: University of North Carolina Press.
Cowdrey, Mary Bartlett. Extensive research notes on Carpenter and transcriptions of selected entries from his diary at Cortland County Historical Society, Cortland, NY. Accessed February 2010.

Davies, M. 1982. *Woman's Place is at the Typewriter: Office Work and Office Workers 1870– 1930*. Philadelphia, PA: Temple University Press.

Dexter, Mary. 2002. Unpublished, meticulously researched, and compiled materials on the hamlet of Little York in the Town of Homer, NY. In possession of Larry and Sylvia Nye of Little York, NY.

Dillon, Schuyler "Bill." Undated post-World War II letter to another unnamed veteran. In the Town archives, Town Hall, Homer, NY.

Erdman, Andrew L. 2012. *Queen of Vaudeville: The Story of Eva Tanguay*. Ithaca, NY: Cornell University Press.

Files (photocopies) on mural painted in the Homer Post Office. National Archives & Records Administration, Still Picture Branch, NWCS, Room 5360, in College Park, Maryland. Ordered by Homer teacher Colleen Redenback in 2001; now owned by the Homer Post Office, Main Street, Homer, NY.

Fish, E. Belcher. Letters to Cousin Mary dated August 31, 1856 and June 1863. In the author's collection.

Fiske, Margaret. 2020. In-person interview of 99-year-old daughter of Homer's former local historian R. Curtis Harris. At Walden Place, Cortland, NY, February 5.

Florey, Kitty Burns. 2012. "A Picture of Language." In the Opinion Pages of *The New York Times* (March 26). Accessed online: https://opinionator.blogs.nytimes.com/2012/03/26/a-picture-of-language/.

Frail, Catherine. 2017. In-person interview regarding Nellie Randall. At Homer Town Hall, July 17.

Furgurson, Ernest B. "Moment of Truth: Scandal in the Election of 1884." Accessed online in 2020 at https://www.historynet.com/moment-of-truth-the-election-of-1884.htm.

Gazetteer and Business Directory of Cortland County, N. Y. for 1869. 1869. Compiled and published by Hamilton Child. Syracuse, NY.

Goodwin, Hermon Camp. 1855. *Pioneer History, or, Cortland County and the Border Wars of New York*. Published by Dixon & Case.

Green, Harvey. 2003. *The Light of the Home: An Intimate View of the Lives of Women in Victorian America*. University of Arkansas Press.

Hamilton, Harriet. 1964. "David Harum & David Hannum." In *Yesteryears*, a quarterly magazine for the appreciation and study of New York regional history. Vol. 8, No.29, Sept., Scipio Center, NY.

Harris, R. Curtis. c. 1950s. "Homer and the U. S. Mail." Typed six pages in a three-ring binder compiled by Harris, in the archives, Town Hall, Homer, NY.

———. 1995. "Sig Sautelle: A Circus and an Era." Reprinted in *The Crooked Lake Review* (October).

———. 1958. "The Bicycle." In *Cortland County Chronicles*, Volume 2, 237–239. Cortland, NY: Cortland County Historical Society.

Haskell, Jr., Albert J. Various dates. Personal scrapbooks containing news clippings, copies of letters, and "The Klan Episode" written by him in longhand. In possession of his descendants, Joseph Haskell and Colleen Stafford.

Howe, Herbert Barber. 1939. *Jedediah Barber, 1787–1876*. New York: Columbia University Press.

———. 1968. *Paris Lived in Homer.* Cortland, NY: Cortland County Historical Society.
———. Bound, typewritten documents on Rev. John Keep. Archives in the Homer Town Hall, Homer, NY.
Hughes, John P. 2008. "Homer's Sig Sautelle." In *Life in the Finger Lakes* (Summer).
Johnson, Curtis D. 1989. *Islands of Holiness: Rural Religion in Upstate New York, 1790–1860,* 11, 81–82, 120–123. Ithaca and London: Cornell University Press.
Keep, John. 1865. Letter of May 7 to Francis B. Carpenter. Cited in Mary Bartlett Cowdrey's extensive research notes on Carpenter and transcriptions of selected entries in his diary. Cortland, NY: Cortland County Historical Society.
Kunzog, John C. 1970. *Tan Bark and Tinsel.* Self-published.
Odyssey Yearbook. 1936–1951. Homer Central School, Homer, NY. In Homer Alumni Association collection in The History Center at Key Bank, Main Street, Homer, NY.
O'Shea, Jane C. 2014. *Westcott's Tale: Revisiting 19th Century Central New York.* CreateSpace Independent Publishing Platform.
Pierce and Bickford, architects in Elmira, NY. 1908. A cache of letters sent in the Spring of 1908 to individuals in Homer, NY, regarding the proposed building of a Town Hall. Xerox copies of carbon copies provided to the late Anna Hilton of Homer on July 20, 1977, by Tania Werbewsky from the Regional Archives collection of Olin Library at Cornell University; now in possession of Russ Darr, President of The Landmark Society of Cortland County.
Pitman, Robert (Chief of Police for the Village of Homer, NY). 2019. Material on the history of the Homer Police Department. Archives, Town Hall, Main Street, Homer, NY.
Raus, Jr., Edmund J. 2004. *Ministering Angel: The Reminiscences of Harriet A. Dada, a Union Army Nurse in the Civil War.* Gettysburg, Pennsylvania: Thomas Publications.
Russell, Rev. James H. 1963. "Anniversary Sermon" observing the 100th anniversary of the dedication of the Homer Congregational Church. Sunday, July 14. Copy in archives, Town Hall, Homer, NY.
Sampson, Isaac Marshall. 1900. *Poems.* Published in Homer, NY. Copy in archives, Town Hall, Homer, NY.
Smith, H. P., ed. 1885. *History of Cortland County.* Syracuse, NY: D. Mason & Co.
Stoddard, William Osborn. 1885. *Winter Fun.* New York: Charles Scribner' Sons.
Stoddard, Jr., William O., editor. 1955. *Lincoln's Third Secretary: The Memoirs of William O. Stoddard.* New York: Exposition Press.
Sweeney, Martin A. 2019. *A Brief History of Education in Homer: 1819–2019.* A bicentennial souvenir booklet available through The Landmark Society at the History Center at Key Bank in Homer, NY.
———. 2012. *Death In The Winter Solstice: A Narrative of a True Murder Mystery in Homer.* Cortland, NY: Cortland County Historical Society.
———. 2011. *Lincoln's Gift from Homer, New York: A Painter, an Editor and a Detective.* Jefferson, North Carolina and London: McFarland & Company, Inc.
Town of Homer Minutes. 1795 to Present. Archives in Town Hall, Main Street, Homer, NY.

Village of Homer Minutes. 1835 to Present. Archives in Town Hall, Main Street, Homer, NY.

White, Andrew D. 1905. *Autobiography of Andrew Dickson White,* Volume I. New York: The Century Company.

PERIODICALS USED

American Demographics: 1994
Chicago Daily Tribune: 1884
Cortland County Republican: 1860, 1861, 1876, 1879, 1880, 1882
Cortland County Sentinel: 1900
Cortland County Whig: 1851
Cortland Evening Standard: 1894, 1900, 1901, 1902
Cortland Observer: 1814
Cortland Standard: 1873, 1876, 1880, 1893, 1896, 1902, 1909, 1911, 1912, 1924, 1925, 1935,
1955, 1964, 1971, 1973, 1978, 2002
County Republican: 1876, 1877
Daily Journal: 1857
Evening Herald: 1901
Harper's: 1856
Homer Independent: 1960, 1961
Mc'Grawville Express: 1845, 1847, 1848
New-York Times: 1884
New York World: 1896
Owego Evening Blade: 1884
Republican & Eagle: 1830
Rumsey's Companion: 1856
Skaneateles Free Press: 1912
Syracuse Herald-American: 1965, 1987
The Cortland Democrat: 1892, 1897, 1898, 1901, 1907, 1913, 1924, 1929, 1959
The Cortland Republican: 1905, 1912
The Daily Argus: 1901
The Gazette and Farmer's Journal: 1904
The Holley Standard: 1894, 1914
The Home Magazine: 1899
The Homer Post: 1932, 1933, 1935
The Homer Republican: 1861, 1877, 1882, 1884, 1885, 1886, 1891, 1893, 1895, 1899, 1901,
1905, 1906, 1908, 1909, 1912, 1913, 1914, 1916, 1917, 1918, 1919
The New York Dramatic Mirror: 1894
The Port Chester Journal: 1901
The Post-Standard: 1938, 1942
The Poughkeepsie Eagle: 1902

The 7 Valley Villager: 1963
The Syracuse Herald Journal: 1945
The Waterville Times: 1912
The World: 1899
Time: 1925, 1938, 1986
Washington Post: 2014
Waterloo Observer: 1901

CONTRIBUTIONS

The historical archives of the Town and Village of Homer, NY, are full of accounts of past Homer individuals and events. Some of the accounts are contained in news clippings, brochures, notes, and other ephemera. Since 2008, such material came to the Historian through the mail, email, phone and in-person interviews at the Historian's office or elsewhere. Selected accounts found their way into the articles published in *The Homer News* and in this book. Those contributors have been named in the articles and prove that documenting local history is a community effort.

Index

Numbers in ***bold italics*** indicate pages with photographs.

5 Albany Street in Historic District (first brick house), 12, 49, ***52***, 60, 167, 229, 230, 257, 259
20 Clinton Street in Historic District (oldest residential structure), 217, 229
16 N. Main Street in Historic District, 327
18 N. Main Street in Historic District, 75
43 N. Main Street in Historic District, 13
81 S. Main Street in Historic District, ***53***
86 S. Main Street in Historic District, 51
87 S. Main Street in Historic District, 49, 229; Prof. George L. Burr and, 229, 230–31
90 S. Main Street in Historic District (also known as "The Hedges"), 51, ***53***, 229, 231, 359
2010 Census of Town of Homer, xi
2010 Census of Village of Homer, xi

Academy on the Green, 13, 16, 31, 57, 75, 97, 98–99, 110–11, 163, 168, 194, 284, 315, 325, 326, 329, 333, 340, 350, 357, 363, 371; annual student exhibition at, 157; attended by children of Sig Sautelle's circus employees, 302; centennial of, 26; 1819 Charter of, 50, 179, 320; 1893 bell and, 56; *Family Magazine* of 1837–38 describes Homer Village and, 179; fire of 1945 at, 31, 221–22, 300; Jedediah Barber and, 75, 184; railroad benefits, 358; teacher E. Belcher Fish's letters and, 98–102; twenty-seven districts centralize with, 222, 240–41
ads of Homer businesses 1876–1880, 374–77
Albany Post Road or Turnpike (Route 90), 12, 47, 231; historic sites in Homer and along, 48–59
Albert J. Durkee Memorial Park, 33
Albright, John, 197–98, 199
Alvords and "the Scott Road," 240
Andrews, O. B., 377
Armitage, Albert Wesley, 207
Armstrong, Frances, 22, 26
Atwater Cemetery (Homer), 193, 245, 326

Babcock, Willoughby and brothers, 63, 224

Ballard, Caleb, 231
Ballard, Horatio, 12
Ballard, John, 231
Ballard, Joshua, 51, 147–48, 149, 229
Baptist Church (now the Homer Center for the Arts), 179
Barber, Charles, 109
Barber, Donald, xv
Barber, George J. J., 185, 354, 355, 357
Barber, Jedediah (or "Uncle Jed"), 13, 16, 57, 75, 174, 354, 358, 359; Bank of, 57, 76; The Great Western (or Barber Block) and, 13, 16, 51, 57, 58, 75, 76, 174, 177–87, *180*, 185, 239, 244, 292, 358, 360, 366, 377; Herbert Barber Howe's biography of, 187, 354, 358; Homer merchants besides, 184; Miss Van Buskirk of Preble describes generosity of, 182; Mrs. C. E. Parmalee Butler describes personality of, 180; railroad bankruptcy and, 358
Barber, Lydia Jane, 109
Barber, Matilda, 186
Barber, May Buell, 186
Barber, Paris, 16, 17, 55, 58, 107–8, 109, 156–57, 185, 224, 231, 354, 357; Ralph Rural's poem by, 108
Barber, Samuel McClellan, 17, 169
Barber, Watts, 185, 287, 354, 357
Barker, Luther, 172, 173
Beardsley, Kathy, 62
Beebe, Joseph, 9, 39, 48, 58, 59, 245
Beebe, Rhoda, 9, 10, 39, 48, 58, 59, 245; Charles Kingsbury's account of, 247; marker recognizes heroism of, 245–47
Bellardini, Mary Alice, 238, 327
Berggren-Thomas, Priscilla, 345
bicycling fad in 1880s and 1890s, 360, 361–64; Cortland County Cycle Path Association and, 363, 364; Cortland Wagon Company and, 361; democratizing effect of, 363; Dr. H. S. Brauman during, 364; Homer Wheelmen Club and, 361; Susan B. Anthony's comment on, 362
Bigelow, Albert, Rev., 287–90; Cleveland for President opposed by, 287, 289; rallies for Civil War enlistees in Homer and, 287–88; Theodore Munger's opinion of, 288
Bird, Ina Hurlbut, 181, 182, 239; the Hurlbut family's life in 19th century town of Homer described by, 239–45
Blackwell, Elizabeth, Dr., 371
Blanden, Arthur, 69–70
Blay, Joshua, 360
Bloomer, Amelia Jenks, 13, 26, 73; childhood home of, 73–77; Homer visit in 1850 by, 77
Boies, Israel, 358
Bootleggers, 175–77; Brockway Big Six Speed Wagon used by, 176
Bradford, George W., Dr., 284, 321–22
Bradford, Simeon S., 4
Brewery Hill, 111–12
Bridges (rare lenticular truss) in Homer (National Historic Site), xii, 236–39; Water Street bridge, rarest of, 237–38; William Oscar Douglas designed, 236–37
A Brief History of Education in Homer:1819–2019 by Sweeney, xv, 220
Briggs, John, 281
Briggs Pool, 210–12; Charles Briggs and, 212; Gary Weatherby's poem about, 210–11
Brockway, George, 269–72, 279
Brown, Don "The Popcorn Man," 193–*95*, 197; Francis Carpenter recalled, 194–95; Ruth Scheetz locates gravestone of, 197
Brown, Josephine, 14, 35
Buckingham Place, 28
Bundy, Gail, 62, 158, 161, 195
Burgoyne, "Gentleman Johnny," General, 148
Burlingame, Michael, xii, 95

Butler, Arthur, 166–67
Buttre, John Chester, 172

Cadwallader, William, DVM and wife Jean, 344;
Homer Animal Clinic on West Road operated by, 342, 344–45
Carpenter, Augusta Prentiss (or "Gus"), 128, *129*, 168, 365
Carpenter, Clement DeWitt (or "Witt"), 170
Carpenter, Cora Anderson, 365
Carpenter, Elliott, 168
Carpenter, Florence, 168
Carpenter, Francis Bicknell, 4, 5, 13, 37, 39, 45, 50, 56, 127–28, *129*, 167–75, 183, 365, 366; Andrew D. White and, 173; *Arbitration Picture* of 1891 painted by, 350; birthplace on Route 11 of, 168; Charles Dickens and, 254; Glenwood Cemetery and, 128, 175; Harold Holzer's opinion of, 15, 50, 255; Henry and Nanette Orr and, 128; Homer's Henry Wheadon stands in for portrait of Willie Lincoln for, 172–73; *The Inner Life of Abraham Lincoln* by, 254; *The Lincoln Family* painted by, 172; Lincoln penny and five-dollar bill and, 252; Luther Barker, Homer photographer and, 79; Mathew Brady's Photographic Parlor and, 252; Paris Barber and, 16, 75, 169, 173–74, 254; portrait of Augusta Prentiss (fiancée) by, 128, *129*, 365; rare watercolor by, 365; reminiscences of Lincoln for the *Independent* penned in Homer by, 254; Sanford Thayer and, 173, 254; *Six Months at the White House with Abraham Lincoln: The Story of a Picture* by, 97, 173; subjects of portraits by, 50, 149, 168, 170, 173; "Trustee Paintings" rendered by, 50, 56, 222; visit to Homer in 2020 by descendant of, 365–66; William Sydney Mount and Charles Loring Elliott, artists and friends of, 365. *See also Emancipation Proclamation* painting
Carpenter, Herbert "Bertie" Sanford, 168, 365
Carpenter, William Wallace, 4, 15, 56, 169; Wesley Huffman of Preble and, 170
Carty, Helen, 7
Cashion's Diner on Main Street, Homer, NY, 201, 300
"A Celebration of Lincoln in Paint and Print," xii, 37, 59, 95, 259
Central New York Living History Center, 167, 238, 380; Ken Eaton's Homeville Museum collection at, 359
Christmas and New Year traditions of the past, 149–54
Churchill, Winston, 188, 189
Civil War "sham battle" and parade in Cortland in 1880, 380–84; Gen. Gustavus Sniper of Syracuse participated in, 382, 383
Clark, Stephen Watkins, 7–9; *A Practical Grammar* and other grammar books by, 7–8; method of diagraming sentences created by, 8, 100; outhouse prank pulled on, 221, 239
Cleveland, Grover, 43, 289–90, 328
Clinton, DeWitt (Governor), 178; Jedediah Barber names Village of Homer street after, 178
Cogswell, Wilbur, 43, 142–46
Coleman, Jr., Harry R., 154
Common (also the Green or park), 4, 13, 14, 16, 49, 55, 57, 107, 127, 154, 179, 198, 214–15, 220, 221, 231, 239, 250, *256*, 275, 284–85, 323, 335, 337, 361; case of the missing Christ Child from Nativity on, 154; ice skating area on, 107, *154*, 273; Village of Homer versus First Religious Society regarding, 286

Congregational Church (Homer), 3–5, 16, 48, 56, 154, 170, 179, 222, 231, 284, 326, 373; centennial anniversary of, 288; dedication in 1863 of, 4, 56, 287; "Town Clock" in steeple of, 284, 285
Congressional Medal of Honor, 16, 54
Conway, Pat "Patsy," 187, 217
Cornell University, 28, 51, 56, 75, 173, 174, 217, 228, 229, 238, 269, 344; replacement of Thurston Avenue bridge at, 214
coronavirus pandemic as of July 16, 2020, 338
Cortland (city), 385, 387
Cortland County, 9; centennial of, 20; controversy over storage of nuclear waste in, 35; establishment of, 12; sesquicentennial of, 33
Cortland County Historical Society (and Suggett House), 6, 65, 130, 149, 195, 373; Mindy Leisenring Riha, director of, 220
Cortland County Medical Society, 318; formation of, 318
Cortland County Traction Co., 18, 27; Homer-Cortland Streetcar of, *19*
Cortland Rotary Club, 346, 349
Crampton, Charles T. ("Uncle Top"), 191–93
Crampton, Edmund, 191–93
Crandall, Daniel, Captain, 197–99
Crandall, William G., 301, 325, 366
Cravath, Oren, 45
Crawford, Randy, 36
Creal, Harold L. "Cap," 28, 32
Crosley, Charles R. "Jug," 69–70

Dada, Harriet A., Civil War nurse, 370–74; buried in Oakwood Cemetery in Syracuse, NY, 373; children of Homer Congregational Church support, 373; "A Cortland County Nurse in Action" by Haller inspired by, 373; Daughters of Union Veterans of the Civil War in Cortland County and, 373; Doctor Caleb Green of Homer endorses, 371; Dorothea Lynde Dix and, 371
Darby's Mill, 75
David Harum Bowling Alley, 226
David Harum by Westcott, 17, 35, 54, 229, 248, 249; Homeville of, 54, 229, 248; *Westcott's Tale* by Jane O'Shea and, 229
David Harum Hotel, 70, 71
Dear Mrs. Roosevelt: Letters from Children of the Great Depression, edited by Cohen, 162
Death in the Winter Solstice: A Narrative of a True Murder Mystery in Homer by Sweeney, 6, 152–53
de Tocqueville, Alexis, 338
DeVoe, Eli, 5, 15, 37, 50, 167; Allan Pinkerton and, 95–96
Dickson, Andrew, 231, 354, 358
Dillon, Schuyler "Bill," 66–68
Dixon, J. R., 292
Dobbins, Dennis (also "Cabbage King"), 327–34; "the house that cabbage built" and, 327, *328*, 331–34
documenting local history as a community effort, 393; Catherine Frail, example of, 191; Colleen Redenback, example of, 132; Doris Phalen, example of, 191; Gail Bundy and Kathryn Bundy Locke, example of, 157–61; Jennifer Greenfield, example of, 161–62; Steve Malchak, example of, 165; Ward Dukelow, example of, 353
dog behavior, regulations, and care, 342–45
Doyle's Pub (later Dasher's and Dasher's Corner Pub), 377
Durkee, Florence Foster, 25

East Homer, xi, 14, 261
Economy Paving Company, 213; Homer's rare Pine Street bridge and,

238; Marion Hudson Withey recalls early history of, 213–14
Einstein, Isidore "Izzy," 70–73
Elizabeth Brewster House, 118, 224, 226
Emancipation Proclamation (document), 4–5, 15, 50, 151
Emancipation Proclamation (painting) or *The First Reading of the Emancipation Proclamation before the Cabinet* by Carpenter, 5, 15, 50, 169, 171, 350; Abraham Lincoln's opinion of, 171; Alexander Hay Ritchie's print of, 79–80, 172; Congress accepts gift of, 174; exhibition across the North and in Homer of, 76, 171; Homer men pose as "material assistance" for Ritchie print of, 79, 172; Mary Todd Lincoln's opinion of, 80; Noah Brooks opinion of Ritchie print of, 79, 172; Rev. John Keep's opinion of, 5, 80
Episcopal Church in Homer (now Little White Church Community Center), 13, 17, 31, 55–56, 179, 214–*20*, 323, 357; architect Hagerman's description of, 218–19; preservationist Sam Gruber, PhD, and his opinion of, 219
Erie Canal, 74, 178, 230, 358; bicentennial of construction of, 177–78

Factory Hill, 184, 292
Falter, Shawn, Private, 15
Ferris, Don, xiv, 6, 26
Fifth Great Western Turnpike, 58
Finkbeiner, Ed, xiii
Finkbeiner, Laura, xiii
fires discovered by boys on same day in 1900, 233–36
The First Religious Society of the Town of Homer, 55, 56, 154, 215, 286
Fitts, Lawrence E., 34

Forbes, Frederick J., Sr., 22
Fortnightly Club, 149
Fourth of July in the past in Homer, 16, 334–38, 358; community reading of the U. S. Declaration of Independence during, ***339***
Fragnoli, Roland "Frog," 180, 182

Garrison, William Lloyd, 3
Gettysburg (or Battle of), 4, 15, 16, 43, 56, 169, 170, 237, 287, 371, 380
girder from 9/11, 97
Glenwood Cemetery (National Historic Site), xii, 16, 58, 128, 170, 197, 216, 223–24, 246, 323, 326; four of "transcendent importance" buried at, 224; Rural Cemetery Movement and, 157, 223, 224; significant architecture at, 223–24
Grand Army of the Republic (G.A.R.), 157, 324, 325, 326, 337, 351
Grant, Ulysses S., 349–51, 353; *Alabama* arbitration (Treaty of Washington) and, 350, 352; Homer's affinity for, 351–53; Lincoln and, 353; Mark Twain and, 353; memoirs of, 353; Ron Chernow's biography of, 353
The Great War (WWI) and Homer, 25, 326
Gustafson, John, 32
Gutches, Earl, 28

Halpin, Frederick W., 174; Abraham Lincoln's opinion of his portrait by Carpenter for print by, 174; Village of Homer and print by, 174
Hannum, David H., 17, 54, 232, 248, 249; Cardiff Giant Hoax and, 17, 54, 232, 248; house in Historic District lived in by, 229, 232; signage kerfuffle of 2019 in Homer and, 247–50, 262, 266
Harpur, Robert, 10
Harris, Jaff, 205–6

400   Index

Harris, R. Curtis, 13, 114, 301, 344, 360, 364
Haskell, Albert, Jr., Cortland County D.A., 71, 165, 166, 176, 177; Ku Klux Klan prosecuted by, 85–94; Rotary prank perpetrated by, 346–49;
Haskell, Tom, 349
Haudenosaunee, 9, 48
Hayes, Dan, 55
Health Camp Road's origins, 65–66
Herr, Benjamin L., Rev., 324, 325
Hicok, William, 185
Hilton, Anna Morse, 19, 220, 267, 327
"Historic Homer: The Town that Lights Up the Night," 127
historic identity of a community, xv, xvi, 248–50, 353, 365, 387
History of Cortland County (1885) by Smith, 111, 146–49, 198, 247, 322
Holzer, Harold, xii, 15, 50, 95
Homer as "a new Lincoln mecca," 37, 95, 256
Homer Center for the Arts, 54–55, 127, 220
Homer Central School 222; bus drivers' responsibilities for, 317; centralization of, 222; School Resource Officer (SRO) program and, 294; school secretaries, past and present, of, 313–17; skeletons unearthed in elementary building of, 216; time capsules of, 2
Homer Coronet Band, 217, 337, 351
Homer Fair Grounds, 358
Homer Gulf Road built by prisoners, 366–70; local financing of, 366–68, 369
Homer Historic District (or Old Homer Village), xii, 37, 127, 215, 220, 233, 327
Homer History Center at Key Bank, xii, 168, 191, 219, 220, 229, 233, 267, 327
Homer Hospital and Training School for Nurses, 118–27; Marguerite E. Hakes and, 118, 119, 126, 127

Homer Leisure Hour Club, 158
Homer Men's and Boys' Store, 180; when a pool hall was above the present-day, *208*
Homer National Bank, 168, 23, 267–68; Shirley Clark's donated news article on early history of, 268
Homer Sennightly Literary Club, 158; Eleanor Roosevelt's visit with, 158, 161
Homer Town Hall, 9, 74, 365; Capitol Theater at, 17, 29–31, 32, 33, 153; centennial of, 9; Charles F. Colton, architect of, 20, 272; construction of, 18, 19, 20–22, 32, 272; dedication of, 23; entertainments at, 24, 25, 26, 33; fire at, 31; glass negatives showing construction of, 22; graffiti at, 26, 32; Pierce & Bickford, architects, express outrage over selection of architect for, 268–73; renovations at, 36–37; school uses of, 31, 34; senior citizens' center at, 34; Tender Loving Care Award to, 37
"houses of ill repute" in Homer, 284, 285
Howe, Alton, 163–66
Hurricane Hazel remembered, 212–13, 224, 226
Huttleston, Donald, 69–70

Jebbett, Anita (Town Clerk), 21, 28
Jermy, Charles W., Jr. ("Bud"), 334
Jermy, Charles W., Sr., 33
Jermy, Charles W. III ("Chip"), 334
Jones, Robert, 35

Keator Opera House in the Barber Block, 15, 21, 50, 57, 186, 338, 351, 378
Keep, John, Rev. (or "Father Keep"), 3–5, 56–57, 97; dedication of Congregational Church and, 4, 57; Munger's opinion of, 4, 57; Oberlin College and, 4, 57

Index

Kimberly, Mary, 360
Kingsbury, Sara, 185
Kneeland, A. Judson, 17
Knobel, J. Henry, 28
Knobel, Rona, 23
Knobel, Thomas, 23, 24, 28
Ku Klux Klan, 83–94, 349; Cortland Rotary hijinks of 1921 and, 346–49; Homer and activities of, 86

Lamberson, Matilda and "a house of ill-fame," 284
The Landmark Society (of Cortland County), xii–xiii, 19, 219, 220, 233, 327; Russ Darr, president of, 220, 268
Lawson, Donald, 207–8, 224, 301
Legg, Cora Carpenter, 365
Lincoln, Abraham, 14, 15, 39, 43, 49, 50, 51, 60, 77, 127, 128, 151, 155, 169, 173, 174, 183, 229, 230, 231, 249, 313, 349, 353; Fido and, 345; four reactions to assassination of, 77–79; revealed by Francis B. Carpenter in paint and print, 262–66; a review of Homer's significant historic connections to, 251–56
Lincoln, Robert Todd, 350
Lincoln Monument Project proposed by Frank Porcu, 97, 128, 175
Lincoln's Gift from Homer, New York by Sweeney, xv, 5, 50, 77, 128, 158, 175
Lincoln's Third Secretary edited by William O. Stoddard, Jr., 256–57, 259; first chapter of, 256–58
Little York, xi, 14, 32, 35, 37, 38–39, 58, 166, 168, 194, 336, 337, 364; Barb Dowd Gregg's reminiscences of, 209–10; early history of, 38–46; Larry and Sylvia Nye and, 38; Mary Dexter's research on history of, 38; swimming at lake at, 32, 46, 163
Little York Creamery, 46
Little York Ice Company, 46; Horse and wagon of, **46**

Litz, F. X., 330, 366
Locke, Kathryn "Kay" Bundy, 158, 161, 211

The Madness of Mary Lincoln by Emerson, 95
Mansion House hotel on Main Street, Homer, NY, 354
manufacturing of wagons and cutters in Homer, 130–31
Masterson, Jim, 225–26
McCabe, Darren "Hal," xiii
McGovern, George, xii, 95
Mechanics Hall, 54, 284
Memorial Days of the past in Homer, 62–65, 322–27
Meneely Bell Company of Troy, NY, 216
Merring, E. E., Rev., 324, 325
Methodist Church (Homer), 57, 179
Military-provided no-cost health care programs, 294
Military Tract of the State of New York, 10, 48, 197
Miller, John, Dr., 318–19, 357
Miller, Simon P., 292
Mineah, Elma, 28
Ministering Angel: The Reminiscences of Harriet A. Dada, a Union Army Nurse in the Civil War by Raus, 370
Moore, Asa, 15, 43–44
Munger, Theodore T., Rev., 168, 288, 350
Murder in the Winter Solstice by Sweeney, xv

National Hotel in Homer, 19, 77
National Register of Historic Places, xii, 1, 220, 236, 269
Newton, Katherine (Mrs. Jesse C. Newton), 134–37, 141, 158, 160–61
Newton Line Company, 153
New York Central College in McGrawville, 357; Sharon Stevans and Smithsonian regarding, 360

Index

Niederhofer, Tom, 76
Norton, Llewellyn P., 16, 54, 325

Olmstead, J. H., Rev., 326
Osborn, John, 12, 49, 54, 110–11, 230, 257–58
Ostrander, Harry Clarke, 60–62
Otis, Fessenden Nott, 168, 169, 170; Francis Carpenter and *A View of Homer* mural by, 168, 267
Owen, Lewis S., Dr., 318, 319–20

"paperless" communication, 2, 97
Pennfield Corporation controversy, 35
Phillips Free Library, 31, 256, 340, 345
Phoenix Hardware Company, 361
Pioneer History of Cortland County by Goodwin, 246–47
plank roads, 285, 357
Plummer's Turkey Farm Kitchen, 226; Lynn Swan describes, 226–28
poem about 19th century travel by rail, 359–60
postal service in Homer and environs, 113–18; Don VanSlyke and, 114, 118
Potter, Carleton, DVM, 344
Price, Richard, 184, 292
Prohibition, 175, 322

Quinlan, David P., 128, 250, 365
Quinlan, Patrick, 6, 152, 293, 294, 377
Quinton, Amelia Stone, 97

railroad service through Homer, 57, 354–59; Delaware, Lackawanna and Western Railroad provides, 359; grand opening of, 358; handyman Kendall at depot as part of, 358; origins of, 354, 355–58; passenger station in Homer as part of, *359*
Randall, Nellie Docherty, 187–91, 228; *Nellie's Cookbook* by, 190; notables in WWII D.C. fed by, 188; recipe for apricot marmalade by, 191
Raus, Edmund, Jr., 142, 220, 239, 291, 365, 370, 384; books by, 374

readings from *The Homer Republican* 1886–1919, 338–42
Reed, Edward C., 354
reminiscences of bygone Homer days and places, 199–201, 204–14
Riggs, Lewis, Dr., 320–21, 355
Robinson, William A., Rev., 16, 323
roller-skating venue in Homer, 26, 360; Jake Metzgar and, 360, 375; racers at, 361
Romanelli, Frank and Homer Post Office mural, 131–42
Rood, Jeanette, 211
Roosevelt, Eleanor, and Homer, 158–61, 188, 189
Roosevelt, Franklin D. (or FDR), 161, 188, 189, 190; Homer girls' letter to, 162
Route 90 Yard Sale, 47
Russell, James H., Rev., 288
Ryan, Barry and Pat, 327, 334

Samson, George Washington, 51, 102; *The Bumble Bee* and, 230
Samson, Isaac Marshall, 102; "Homer" (poem) by, 102–3; Poem about the bicycle rage by, 362
Satterly, George (also Satterlee and "Sig Sautelle"), 235–36, 301–8, *302*, 325; Circus Hall of Fame and, 308; "Circus House" in Homer built by, 302, *308*; "Homer's Sig Sautelle" by Hughes tells of ventriloquism of, 302; news accounts of trials and tribulations of, 303–8; "Sig Sautelle: A Circus and an Era" by Harris about, 308; *Tan Bark and Tinsel* by Kunzog and, 301
Schermerhorn, Anna, 15, 231
Schermerhorn, Jacob Maus, 15, 51, 229, 231, 359; Stoddard and the Lincolns receive, 231
Schermerhorn, Mary, 188, 189
Searl, Jesse, Dr., 320
Sennightly Literary Club, 158
Seward, William H. (Secretary of State), 15, 50, 151

Sherman, William, 75–76, 178, 357; "S" nails of, 75–76
Sherman Exchange (or Block) and Mansion, 75–76, 149, 178–79, 184, 284, 366, 375
Simmons, John Yale, 326
slavery (or slaves), 2–5, 57; John Keep's opinion of, 3; New York State's abolition of, 3; U. S. Grant and, 353
Smith, Moe, 70–73
Smith, Stephen, Dr., 97, 350
"Smitty" the junk man of Maple Avenue, 207
Sons of Veterans of the Civil War, 324, 325, 326
Spanish flu of 1918–19, 309–13; COVID-19 and, 309; Ralph McConnell family and, 312
Spina, Stephanie Urso, Ph.D., 239, 250, 387
Steger, Don, 221
Stephens, Henry, 355, 357, 358
Stimson, Enos, 18, 146, 231, 318
Stimson, Oren, 355
St. Margaret's Church in Homer, NY, 224, 333
St. Mary's Cemetery in Cortland, NY, 189, 329, 333
Stoddard, Eleanor H., 59–60; visits to Homer by, 59, 60, 259
Stoddard, William O., 5, 12, 15, 16, 37, 49, 59, 60, 155–58, 167; birthplace of, *52*, 167, 229, 230; cockfighting and, 112; Emancipation Proclamation and, 96, 229, 230, 258; excerpts from *Winter Fun* by, 80–83; Francis B. Carpenter and, 96, 174, 255; student pranks at Homer's Academy described by, 110; *The Volcano under the City* (NYC Draft Riots) by, 156
Stories of Cortland County for Boys and Girls by Blodgett, 152, 182, 228–33, 247
The Suffragette's Saga: A Murder Mystery (fiction) by Sweeney, 6

Sweeney, Paul, 214
Syracuse, Binghamton and New York Railroad, 359
Syracuse and Binghamton Railroad, 44, 96
Syracuse University, 132

Tanguay, Eva ("I Don't Care Girl"), 377–80, *381*; Homer's George W. Ripley, advance man for, 378; Keator Opera House and, 377–78; Performed at Cortland and Mclean Opera Houses, 378; *Queen of Vaudeville: The Story of Eva Tanguay* by Erdman about, 380
Team of Rivals by Goodwin cites Carpenter and Stoddard, 255–56
telephone service in Homer 1884–1959, 295–301; Deny Hartnett ("Mr. Telephone") and, 300–301; Homer exchange operators provided, 296–301, *298*; Margaret Harris Fiske interview about, 300–301
Tioughnioga River, xi, xii, 9–10, 37, 57, 74, 168, 181, 222, 236, 245
Tioughnioga River Trail, 239, 360, 364
Todd, Amos, 9, 39, 48, 58, 59, 246
Town of Homer, xii, 37, 128, 236, 238, 245, 266; "Baby Boom" effect on, 32; bicentennial of first settlement of, 35; bicentennial of nation and, 34; Civil War and, 14–15, 99–102; distilleries in, 111; earliest occupations in, 11, 12, 19, 58; earliest officers of, 10–11, 291; earliest settlers of, 9–10; early Board meetings in, 11, 12, 13, 49, 291–92; 1810 Census of, 12, 49; 1869 *Business Directory* for, 259–62; energy problems and, 37; establishment of school districts in, 12; first female born in, 11; first frame building in, 11; first grist mill in, 74–75, 238; first male born in, 11; first wheeled vehicle in, 11; Great Depression and, 27–28; Historic

Advisory Committee of, 128; history of newspapers in, xii, xiii, 1; locations in 1890s of Board meetings for, 17; municipal consolidation and, 34, 35; municipal historians for, 26; naming of, 10, 48; organization of, 10–11, 291; separation of Town of Cortlandville from, 13; voting machines used by, 18
Tubbs, Benajah, 111
Turnpike construction, 58, 178

Underground Railroad, 45, 49, 58, 258

"The Village Green" by Tompkins, 23
Village of Homer, 245, 385; behaviors prohibited by 1897 Ordinances of, 274–77; bridge building in 1866 in, 283; gas streetlamps in 283, 284; heritage tourism and, 94–98, 248; hotels in, 18–19; incorporation of, 14, 179, 292; James Street office of, 34; life in 1866–1871 in, 283–86; official seal of, 250, 387; Ordinances of 1849 in, 202–4; Ordinances of 1906 prohibiting winter diversions in, 273–74; proposed annexation in 1905 by city of Cortland of, 385
Village of Homer Police Department, 275, 291–95, 337; accountable to the mayor, 292; Charles Taylor, Sr. (also "Heavy Taylor") of, 225–26, 293; Chief Helms of, 293; Chief Mack and initial police bike patrol unit of, 294; Chief Robert Pitman of, 293–95, 323; Chief Samson of, 293; Chief Tom Davis of, 293, 344; George "the Cop" Vernum of, 28–29, 225, 293; Officer Bigsby of, 336–37; Officer Carson of, 293, 343; Officer Michael Howell of, 295; School Resource Officer (SRO) program and, 294–95
Village of Homer Recreation Department, 33

Volunteer Homer Fire Department of Village of Homer, 18, 277–81, 337, 351; Howard Burden's history of, 281, 286, 298; James Street Firehouse of, 281, *282*; steel girder from 9/11 tower near, 97

Washington, George, 10
Weatherby, Gary, 211
Webb, Adin, 57, 147–49
Wharton Brothers (also Wharton Moving Picture Company of Ithaca), 25, 308
Wheadon Hall on Main Street, Homer, NY, 172, 288
Wheelmen (bicyclists), 103. *See also* bicycling fad in 1880s and 1890s.
White, Andrew Dickson, 51, 75, 232, 238, 350; *Autobiography* of, 217; birthplace of, 51, *53*, 228, 229; Episcopal church in Homer and, 56, 217
White, Asa, 74, 217, 238
William G. Pomeroy Foundation, 224, 245
Williams, Frank J., xii, 95
Windsor Hotel on Main Street, Homer, NY, 339
Winter Fest, 273
Wisdom's Gate tavern (also "temperance tavern" and Braeside Tearoom), 51, *52*, 102, 188, 228, 229–30
Wolner, Louis J., 31, 221, 222, 316
"A woman's place" in 19th century, 105–7; *The Light of the Home* by Green describes, 107
Woodward, Ward A., 181
Woolworth, Calvin, 168, 350
Woolworth, Samuel Buell, 50, 357
Wright, William, 35
Wright's Tavern, 59

Young, Gerald, 28

About the Author

After close to forty years in a classroom bringing the past to life for students of United States history, **Martin A. Sweeney**, now retired, enjoys serving as the historian for the historic town and village of Homer, NY. As a public historian, he has a regular column on local history in Homer's newspaper. A life-long admirer of our Civil War president, Sweeney is the author of *Lincoln's Gift from Homer, New York: A Painter, an Editor and a Detective*. He has other published books and articles on Homer's history. He is a former Rotarian and former member of the Homer Board of Education. In 2004, he was the recipient of the New York State D.A.R. Outstanding History Teacher of the Year.

www.ingramcontent.com/pod-product-compliance
Lightning Source LLC
Chambersburg PA
CBHW030235240426
43663CB00037B/488